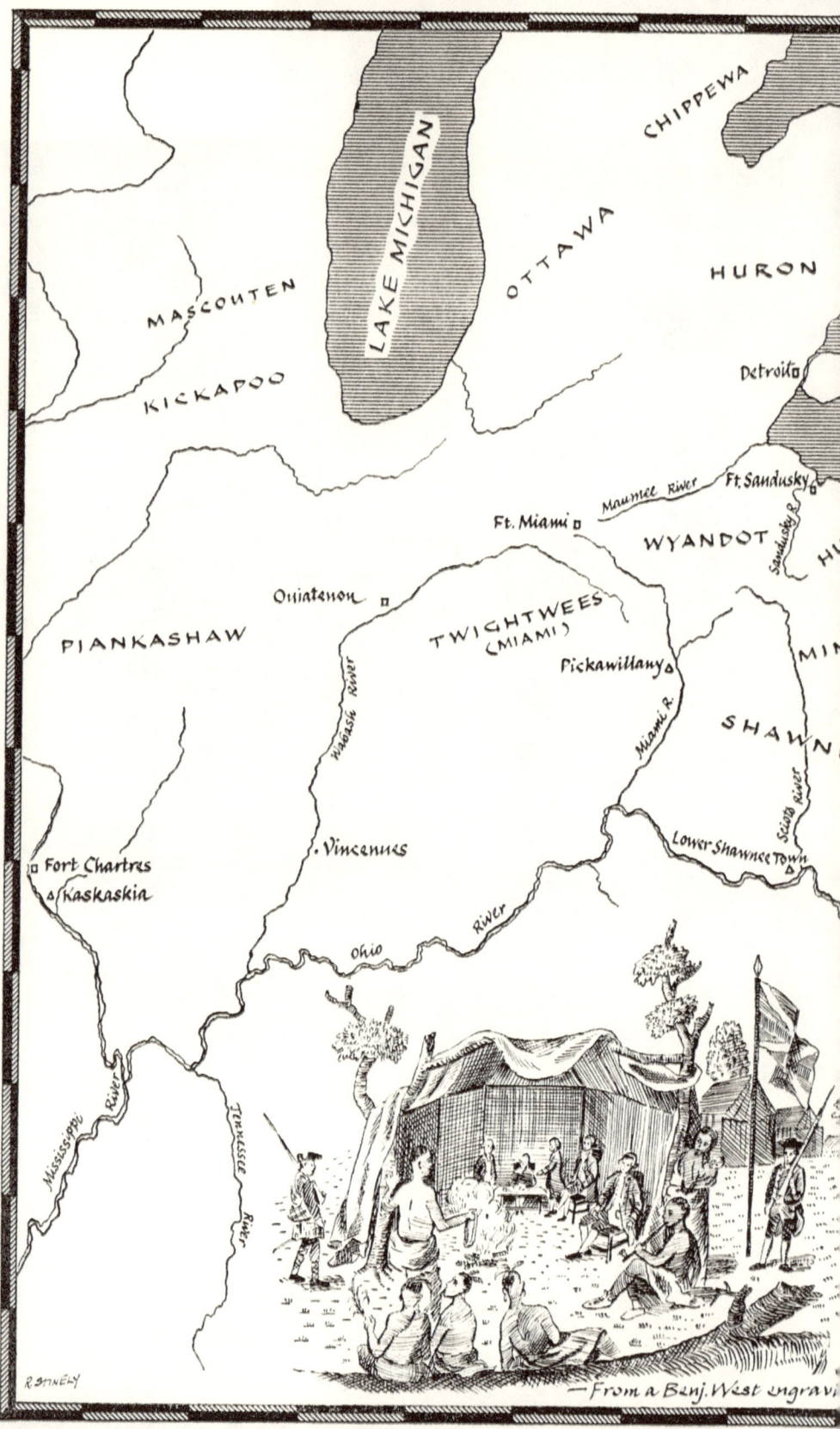
— From a Benj. West engrav[ing]

GEORGE CROGHAN
Wilderness Diplomat

The Institute of Early American History and Culture is sponsored jointly by the College of William and Mary and Colonial Williamsburg, Incorporated. Publication of this book has been assisted by a grant from the Lilly Endowment, Incorporated.

GEORGE CROGHAN
Wilderness Diplomat

By

Nicholas B. Wainwright

PUBLISHED FOR THE
Institute of Early American History and Culture
AT WILLIAMSBURG

BY

The University of North Carolina Press • Chapel Hill

COPYRIGHT, 1959, BY
THE UNIVERSITY OF NORTH CAROLINA PRESS

Manufactured in the United States of America

THIS BOOK WAS DIGITALLY PRINTED.

To
Lois V. Given
and
R. Norris Williams, 2nd

Preface

AMONG AMERICA's historic figures are many whose names are all but unknown, although men of lesser worth have become national heroes. George Croghan is one of these forgotten men. Thanks to Albert T. Volwiler's scholarly monograph, *George Croghan and the Westward Movement*, Croghan's rightful place in American history, carefully and sensitively assessed, is ably recorded. Nevertheless, his name is unfamiliar to the reading public.

During the more than thirty years which have elapsed since Dr. Volwiler's book was published, much new material relating to Croghan has been uncovered. The Amherst, Loudoun, Abercromby, and Gage papers are now available. In addition, painstaking editors have amassed rich sources in the publication of such impressive collections as the Sir William Johnson and the Colonel Henry Bouquet manuscripts. Dribbling erratically and unpredictably into our libraries have come many acquisitions, large and small, which contain data about Croghan.

Although this new material invites a reappraisal of Croghan's career, it is overshadowed by a single find—the discovery of Croghan's personal papers. In 1939, while examining the enormous archives of the John Cadwalader family of Philadelphia, I came upon the contents of a trunk of papers which had been in Croghan's possession at the time of his death in 1782 and which had been turned over by his executors to Thomas Cadwalader in 1804.

A few years after my survey of their manuscripts, the Cadwalader family generously presented to the Historical Society of Pennsylvania all the documents it had so carefully preserved for many generations. The Croghan papers constitute a small section of this voluminous accumulation, but it is a section large enough to fill four manuscript boxes with correspondence and diaries, and four with receipted bills representing thousands of Croghan's transactions. These papers make possible the telling of Croghan's life in a much more comprehensive and intimate way than heretofore.

When Dr. Volwiler wrote his *Croghan* there were not nearly as many special studies available on the major events in which Croghan became involved. Consequently, he found it necessary to devote much space to background material. Another source of interest for Dr. Volwiler lay in his subtitle, *The Westward Movement*. My endeavor has been to focus on Croghan the man, avoiding digressions into background material now available in other books, and not attempting to associate him with a great American theme. My sole aim has been to explore the life of a most unusual American.

Many people have helped me as I followed Croghan's trail and recorded his story. In particular, I wish to express my gratitude to the late Albert T. Volwiler and to Roy L. Butterfield, Milton W. Hamilton, William A. Hunter, John V. Miller, M.D., Howard H. Peckham, John E. Pomfret, and Frederick B. Tolles. Finally, I could not have completed this study had I not had full access to the main storehouse of Croghan documents, the Historical Society of Pennsylvania, the sympathetic approval of its director, R. Norris Williams, 2nd, and the encouragement and assistance of its associate editor, Lois V. Given.

I am grateful to the American Philosophical Society for a grant which facilitated my research.

NICHOLAS B. WAINWRIGHT
Philadelphia, Pa.
October, 1958

Contents

Preface	vii
1. Up the Ladder	3
2. Hockley, Trent, and Croghan	22
3. Collapse of the Indian Trade	47
4. Aughwick Indian Agency	69
5. Military Services	86
6. Deputy to Sir William Johnson	110
7. The Campaigns of 1758	135
8. Consolidating Western Conquests	156
9. Amherst's Indian Policy	184
10. Illinois Mirage	201
11. The Indian Boundary	239
12. Croghan's Forest	259
13. Pittsburgh Land Speculator	273
14. End of the Trail	300
Bibliographical Essay	311
Index	317

Maps

	PAGE
Western Pennsylvania in Croghan's time	11
Scene of Croghan's New York activities	263
Croghan's Indian land purchases near Pittsburgh	280
The proposed Vandalia and Indiana land grants in which Croghan held shares	280

GEORGE CROGHAN
Wilderness Diplomat

1

Up the Ladder

OUT OF A PAST so dim and forgotten that the year of his birth is lost and the names of his parents unrecorded, George Croghan fled his native Ireland during the potato famine of 1741. He came to Pennsylvania and settled on the western frontier.

For the next thirty-five years he dexterously juggled business failure and success. His name grew legendary as a speculator in western lands and as a projector of inland colonies. The foremost of Pennsylvania's Indian traders, Croghan was recognized as the leading negotiator with the western tribes during the colonial period.

No man led a more adventurous life in colonial America. No man witnessed as many historic moments in the conquest of the old frontier. Active in preliminary events which led to the French seizure of the Ohio Valley, fomenter of an Indian uprising, molder of Indian policy, he was with Washington on the Fort Necessity campaign. The next year he led Braddock's Indian scouts and, after the fateful battle, assisted the general from the field. He campaigned in the Blue Hills of Pennsylvania and along the Mohawk Valley during the war which followed. He witnessed the desperate charges of the Black Watch at Ticonderoga. He marched with Forbes to capture Fort Duquesne.

As Sir William Johnson's right-hand man for fifteen years in the Indian department, he conducted treaties with Teedyuscung and hundreds of other native chiefs. He soothed the French tribes at Detroit so that Robert Rogers, the ranger, could take over that fort without bloodshed. He negotiated with hostile Indians to permit the successful occupation of the Illinois country by British troops. It was he who pacified Pontiac. He was tomahawked, shipwrecked, alternately rich and poor, despised and praised, rejected and sought after. He walked with the great and humble of his day. He forcibly expressed the democratic spirit which was to be America.

Croghan took snuff, drank heavily, loved to dress richly, and to live on a grand scale. When he addressed himself to his contemporaries, his native background stood out like a beacon—orally, in his strong, Irish brogue, and, on paper, in a handwriting and spelling so unschooled as to approach illiteracy. A master of conviviality, his easy good nature made him an idol on the frontier. He was never dull. His openhanded generosity often surpassed his ability to pay, but that did not deter him, for his heart was large, his nature charitable.

His belief in the future of the West led him into disastrous speculations in land, and those who loaned him money lived to regret it. For Croghan did not keep his promises; he was not candid; he misrepresented; he lied. Because he seldom permitted himself to do anything in a straightforward way, and because he was dogged with bad luck, all too many of his ventures ended in misunderstandings and financial loss. But he was an astute diplomat, a born actor, a master of the poker face. Few could fathom him, but most agreed that self-interest was the sole guide of his life. With wit and charm, he knew how to raise money from the toughest merchants of his day and how to spend it graciously and lavishly—the time of reckoning could wait.

No portrait of Croghan is known to exist. In the thousands of letters and documents to and from him, or relating to him, no mention is found of his appearance. But if a likeness of Croghan's face were available, it would not supply a key to his character; it would be merely a disguise, a pleasing façade which aided him in his eighteenth-century confidence game. To understand Croghan, it is necessary to follow the twists and turns of his extraordinary career. A pattern of action at once heroic and regrettable can be discerned by accompanying him along the long road he traveled.

The road led westward over the Schuylkill on Philadelphia's High Street ferry. It was a rough, unfinished wagon trace most of the way to Lancaster, and something less than that to Peter Tostee's plantation near the Susquehanna. Such as it was, it was the "great road" which bound the metropolis to the colony's receding frontier.

The young Irishman viewed the countryside with a shrewd and appraising eye. As he journeyed on, the well-ordered farms of the Quakers in the Philadelphia area gave way to the rich Lancaster Valley holdings of thrifty Germans, and these ripe fields, in turn, were followed by the less prosperous settlements of the Scotch-Irish. When he reached the Susquehanna, Croghan could see the misty Blue Hills which formed the far flank of the Cumberland Valley. Beyond was Indian country.

Croghan had engaged to enter the Indian trade, as the exchange of European goods for the Indians' furs and deer hides was called. By 1740, Pennsylvania traders, financed by wealthy Philadelphia merchants like Edward Shippen, had penetrated far beyond the mountain wall of the Alleghenies and were operating along the Ohio and Allegheny rivers and south of the shores of Lake Erie.

Peter Tostee was one of the principal traders in these areas. An experienced man, he stood in good credit in Philadelphia. Edward Shippen supplied him with merchandise. The first reference to Croghan, June, 1742, notes that Shippen delivered goods to the Irishman to take out to Tostee.[1] Presumably, Croghan learned the Indian trade from this older man. Presumably, he accompanied one of Tostee's heavily loaded pack trains when it set out in the fall of the year to the Indian villages of the Ohio country. Following a winter of bartering powder, lead, fineries, and rum for peltries, these pack trains, loaded down with hides and furs, reappeared in the settlements. After refitting and receiving a fresh stock of goods, they were off once more to engage in the summer trade.

The general area in which the traders sought the Indians, the great valley of the Ohio, was a vast hunting preserve. Into it had recently come several villages of the Shawnees and Delawares, tribes nominally dependent on the Six Nations in northern New York, though their distant location on the Ohio lessened that tie.

1. Shippen Papers, XV, 33, and XXVII, 71, Hist. Soc. of Pa.

Another important group was the Mingoes, hunters of Iroquoian stock. To the west lay the Twightwee (Miami) nation and the Wyandot and Ottawa tribes which frequented the Lake Erie region. Concurrent with the establishment of an Indian population in the Ohio basin was the realization by the French that these natives must be held under French domination and that Pennsylvania traders could not be tolerated. Croghan thus entered the trading arena at a hazardous time.

Although he maintained an association with "my trusty & well beloved friend Peter Tostee" for many years to come, Croghan soon struck out for himself. He became a property owner in 1743 through the purchase of a plot of ground in Lancaster. The next year he was in business on his own as an accredited and licensed trader. The scope of his operations was surprisingly large, for existing bills record his purchase from Philadelphia merchants of more than £700-worth of goods in 1744.[2]

That autumn Croghan transported his trading stock to a distant Seneca village near the mouth of the Cuyahoga River on Lake Erie, the site of present-day Cleveland. Activity of English traders in this area had recently alarmed the French, whose western headquarters were at Detroit. La Rivière Blanche, as they called the Cuyahoga, had been incorporated into their trading empire in 1742 at the request of Iroquois hunters who had lately settled there. These Indians had promised to drive the English away if French traders would supply their needs. In response, Céloron de Blainville, the commandant at Detroit, had sent some of his habitants, who returned prior to June, 1743, with about two hundred packs of peltries. From this time on, the French were active traders on the river, and they were determined to discourage English intruders.[3]

2. Power of attorney, Croghan to Tostee, Aug. 15, 1747, Darlington Memorial Library, University of Pittsburgh; Record Book D, III, 599-600, Lancaster County Court House; *Pennsylvania Archives*, Second Series, II, 619; Croghan's bills for 1744, Cadwalader Collection, Hist. Soc. of Pa.
3. E. B. O'Callaghan, ed., *Documents Relative to the Colonial History of the State of New-York* (Albany, 1855), IX, 1099; Charles A. Hanna, *The Wilderness Trail* (New York, 1911), I, 315-18. For a further discussion identifying La Rivière Blanche with the Cuyahoga, see Lawrence Henry Gipson, *The British Empire before the American Revolution* (New York, 1939), IV, 169-71, n. 61.

To their irritation, the Indians continued to deal with the English. At the outset, the Canadians had noted that "it would be well to profit by the advantages it [the Cuyahoga River trading area] presents, especially to deprive the English of them." When they found that these advantages were not denied the Pennsylvania traders, they urged the Ottawa, Twightwee, and other French tribes to attack them.[4] Meanwhile, in March, 1744, England declared war on France.

Such was the situation when news reached Detroit early in the autumn of the arrival on the Cuyahoga of several Englishmen, who were described as a militant little group, well-supplied with ammunition and "resolved to annihilate the French traders who were going to that quarter." Against this party, which was probably Croghan's, the French sent a picked band of thirty-five Ottawas to plunder and kill them. Like similar schemes in later years, the Indian attack never materialized.[5]

The dangers of operating beyond the fringes of English influence did not intimidate Croghan while he traded that winter on the shores of Lake Erie. Aggressive and alert, already master of Indian tongues, he rapidly increased the number of his ventures. Although the village on the Cuyahoga remained his headquarters, cargoes of his goods were sold in other places. One of these he had entrusted to Peter Tostee for trade far down the Ohio; meanwhile he extended his interests westward to the Wyandot tribe near Detroit.[6]

Such activity was more than his foreign rivals could tolerate. In April, 1745, when Croghan was preparing to pack his winter peltry out of the wilderness, a Frenchman and a "French" Indian arrived at his village to claim the trespasser as their prisoner and to confiscate his property. Fortunately for Croghan, his Seneca friends refused to give him up.

Taking all the skins his horses could carry, the trader hurried east, and on his way was joined by Tostee, a bearer of bad news.

[4]. O'Callaghan, ed., *New-York Col. Doc.*, IX, 1100, 1105.
[5]. *Ibid.*, 1111.
[6]. Croghan later related how in his trading days he had gone by land from the forks of the Ohio nearly to Detroit. *Collections of the Massachusetts Historical Society*, Fourth Series, 9 (Boston, 1871), 343.

Only a few days earlier, Tostee, with another Pennsylvania trader and a number of employees, had been plundered by a large band of French-led Shawnee Indians. They had taken everything that the Pennsylvanians had, including a canoeload of furs belonging to Croghan.

The traders came down to Philadelphia where they made depositions before Edward Shippen, at that time mayor. Croghan claimed that he had lost forty-eight horseloads of deerskins, four hundred pounds of beaver, and six hundred pounds of raccoon skins, but, though Tostee petitioned the Assembly for relief, as he was "entirely ruined" and utterly incapable of paying his debts, Croghan's resources tided him over the disaster.[7]

To cope with the emergency created by the defection of the Shawnees, Croghan was entrusted with a small present from the government to give to those few members of the tribe who still remained friendly.[8] This Shawnee present, probably advocated by Croghan, foreshadowed the policy he was soon to promote so vigorously—the policy of alienating the Ohio Indians from the French by Pennsylvania treaties and support.

About this time, Croghan entered into partnership with William Trent. Trent was an ambitious young man, well-educated, and son of an established family with important Philadelphia connections. The failure and death of his father, the founder of Trenton, New Jersey, when the boy was only ten years of age, had early altered his prospects. Like Croghan, Trent found employment in the Indian trade, serving as an apprentice or clerk for Edward Shippen.[9] In this position, Trent had an unrivaled opportunity to learn the merchandising end of the business and to meet many men actively engaged in it. By 1745, Trent had moved from Philadelphia to Shippen's frontier depot, the little settlement west of the Susquehanna known as Shippensburg, a step which brought him closer to the heart of the trade. Croghan also took an interest

---

7. Peters Mss., II, 32, Hist. Soc. of Pa.; *Votes and Proceedings of the House of Representatives of the Province of Pennsylvania* (Philadelphia, 1774), IV, 13.

8. Penn Mss., Accounts, I, 66, Hist. Soc. of Pa.

9. Trent's earliest known signatures, 1740-44, all appear on papers relating to Shippen's business. That Trent kept Shippen's books is disclosed in Shippen's letter of Jan. 1, 1754, Shippen Letter Book, Amer. Philos. Soc. For a biography of Trent, see Sewell E. Slick, *William Trent and the West* (Harrisburg, 1947).

in Shippensburg and may have used it as the base for his activities. According to one of Shippen's employees, writing from there on January 25, 1746, "Mr. Croghan tells me he will have a squair of the street lead out & resolves to have another house made, & that there will be too more inhabitants hear soon."[10]

Shippensburg, however, was not to remain Croghan's home. As early as October, 1745, he and Trent had jointly purchased a 354-acre tract on the Conedogwinet Creek in Pennsborough Township, a few miles across the Susquehanna from Harris' Ferry (Harrisburg). In the following year, Croghan acquired an adjoining tract of 171 acres. These were valuable properties, and Croghan rose rapidly in the frontier social scale. In 1743, he had been described as a yeoman; by 1745, he was known as a merchant.

The Pennsborough plantation served as Croghan's home until September, 1751, and, during his brief ownership became a landmark prominent enough to be printed on the maps of the day— "Croghan's." It was a thriving, busy place on which he raised much of the food needed in his enterprises and where he pastured his horses and beef cattle. On the smaller of the two tracts he operated a tannery for the processing of deer hides and nearby ran a store at which Indian goods were sold. Somewhere along the steep bluffs of the creek stood his house with its extensive view of the hazy, blue Kittatinny Hills. Looking eastward he could see the big water gap in the range through which flowed the Susquehanna, while to the northwest he could pick out a smaller gap which was soon to bear his own name, the only wind gap in the mountains for many miles.

In the first years of his trading activities, Croghan may have used the old Allegheny Trail which wound through the pass now known as McAllister's Gap. From 1749, or thereabouts, he preferred the "new" path, which was actually not a new route at all but Frank Stephens' old trail to Stephens' Gap (the gap which took on Croghan's name), and from there west to Franks Town. Descending the banks of the Conedogwinet, Croghan's pack trains forded the creek, came to Stephens' Path, and headed northwest a few miles to the gap. With the North Mountain behind

---

10. Joseph Shippen to James Wood, May 18, 1745, Darlington Memorial Library; David Magaw to Shippen, Shippen Papers, I, 73, Hist. Soc. of Pa.

them, his traders then traveled west through Sherman's Valley and across Path Valley, where in 1747 Croghan had obtained permission from the Indians to build a large house and to keep his trading horses. Avoiding the hills as much as possible, they led their plodding animals in a meandering course, threading their way toward the Allegheny country. Their progress was difficult to follow for any distance, for the mountains and valleys were heavily wooded and much of the time the little convoys were lost in the gloom of primeval forests. In the solemn hush of the woods through which they journeyed, the creaking of horses' gear and the dull thud of hoof on stone or fallen tree did little to relieve the awesome stillness of their surroundings.[11]

The coming and going of these men constituted the chief excitement at Pennsborough. The appearance of two or three traders with their train of pack horses, heavily burdened with deer hides and furs, was a dramatic moment. Imagine the arrival of Thomas Burney, who had come all the way from Pickawillany in the distant Twightwee country with a valuable cargo; or of Michael Teaffe, "more bold than prudent,"[12] dismounting after a wearisome ride from Sandusky on Lake Erie; or of Croghan himself, anxious to catch a first view of his plantation as he completed the last few miles of his return from the Lower Shawnee Town, far down the Ohio.

Assisted by several of Croghan's indentured servants and by one or two of his Negro slaves, the travelers relieved the tired animals of their packs and turned them out to pasture. Inspection of the packs was begun immediately, and the necessary steps were taken to insure that all the hides and furs would be in good condition when loaded for Philadelphia. Even now, down the dusty country lane leading to the store came Croghan's wagon, with a fresh stock of English goods needed for trade in the Indian country—the same wagon which would return to Philadelphia with the newly arrived shipments of skins from the Allegheny and the Ohio.

11. Nathaniel Nelson survey, Land Office Book, Copied Surveys, C, 154, 263, and Jacob Pyatt's petition, undated, to Governor John Penn, Bureau of Land Records, Harrisburg.

12. Shippen to James Burd, Aug. 21, 1752, Shippen Letter Book, 1751-52, Hist. Soc. of Pa.

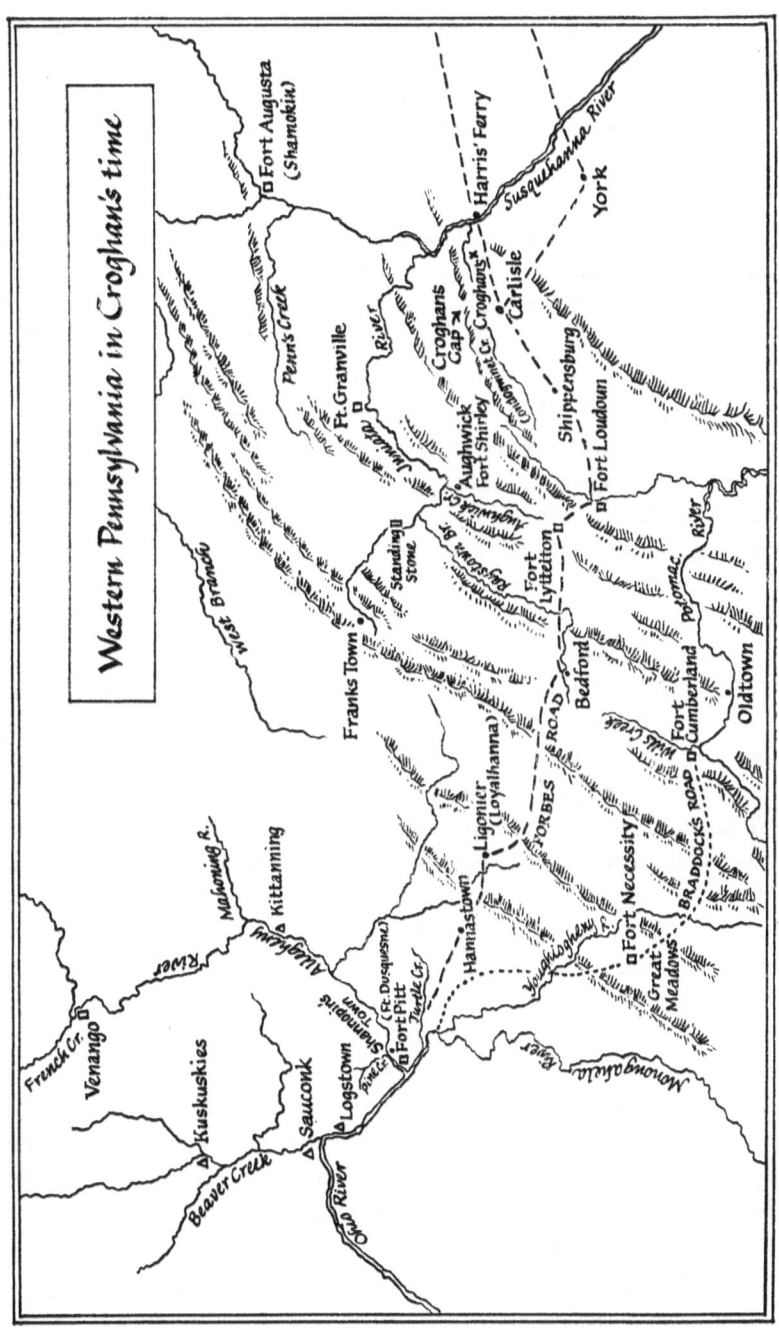

Those who lived and worked in the community which Croghan had created beside the Conedogwinet Creek are all but nameless now. Among them was Roger Walton, Croghan's Irish clerk and doubtless his storekeeper. There was also Thomas Smallman, a Dublin immigrant and cousin to Croghan. Smallman was a saddlemaker and may have worked in the tannery.[13] Since Edward Ward, Croghan's trusted half-brother, made his home with the trader, it may be that Croghan's mother had also joined him, perhaps as the wife of Thomas Ward, one of the trader's men for whose debts Croghan was frequently held responsible. Finally, Croghan's wife, that mysterious woman who has disappeared without leaving a trace of her identity—was she there too?

Croghan's plantation drew constant visitors who came to buy furs or to patronize the trading post and tannery. Its location on the Great Road from Harris' to the Potomac made it a natural stopping place for those who passed up and down that highway. On occasion, rising columns of dust marked the progress of cattle and horses purchased by Croghan from Major Andrew Campbell of Frederick County, Virginia.

Croghan's tenure of his Pennsborough lands provides an example of the way he obtained credit and multiplied his holdings. The large tract which he and Trent had acquired on October 7, 1745, was mortgaged in December for £200 to Abraham Mitchell, a Philadelphia hatter. Although this mortgage was satisfied in July, 1747, a new mortgage for £500 was taken out on it and the adjoining tract on December 3 with Jeremiah Warder, feltmaker and merchant of Philadelphia from whom Croghan purchased Indian goods. This loan was paid off on June 22, 1749, and five days later the properties, with several others, were mortgaged to Richard Peters, secretary of the Pennsylvania land office and of the governor's council, for £1,000.[14]

The Croghan and Trent partnership did not last long. In 1746, during King George's War, an expedition was planned against the French in Canada, and Pennsylvania's contribution to the campaign was set at four companies of soldiers. Trent sold

13. Walton's and Smallman's deed to Richard Hockley, Sept. 21, 1753, Cadwalader Coll., Hist. Soc. of Pa.
14. Peters Mss., II, 120, 186, Hist. Soc. of Pa.; Book B, 299, Lancaster County Court House.

out to Croghan and was commissioned as captain of one of the companies. An acquaintance later recalled that "before he engag'd in the Kings service he carried on the Indian trade successfully in partnership with George Croghan who is one of the most reputable & sensible traders, & Trent might by this time have made a fortune but ambition seiz'd him so violently that he broke up the partnership in hopes to be a man of figure in the conquest & settlement of Canada."[15]

Croghan continued in the Indian trade with increasing boldness and success, expanding his trading ventures throughout the Ohio country. The strategic fork where the Monongahela and Allegheny rivers met attracted his attention. Near this future site of Pittsburgh, he built a trading house. It was another prosperous year for him, one in which the Iroquois did him the honor of appointing him to their governing body, the Onondaga Council.[16]

During the winter of 1746-47, he once more resided among the Senecas near the mouth of the Cuyahoga. Business was extraordinarily good, for many Indians who in the past had dealt only with the French now brought their furs to him. This could by no means be attributed entirely to Croghan's bargaining talents but was largely the result of the inability of his rivals to send adequate trading stocks to the Indian country. The scarcity of supplies in the hands of Canadian merchants, a reflection of the efficiency of English naval activity, caused prices to soar. Many Canadians were forced to abandon the trade. Licenses, which had customarily been sold, were now given away to try to maintain some traders in business. To protect what remained of the Lake Erie trade, the Detroit commander was again ordered to send Indians to attack the English on the Cuyahoga.[17]

By 1747, efforts of that sort were futile, because the natives normally dependent upon the French were dissatisfied with the thin trickle of high-priced goods which came to them from Montreal. They were in a fit mood to listen to the blandishments of the English, and more and more of them turned to the Pennsyl-

15. Book B, 445-49, Lancaster County Court House; Peters to Penn, Nov. 24, 1748, Peters Letter Book, Hist. Soc. of Pa.
16. Wyoming Controversy, Penn Mss., 71, Hist. Soc. of Pa.
17. O'Callaghan, ed., *New-York Col. Doc.*, X, 2, 21, 38.

vania traders who circled the inland French empire in the Lake Erie region.

The most important Indian settlement between the Cuyahoga and Detroit, on or near Lake Erie, was at Sandusky. Here, a disgruntled Wyandot, Chief Nicolas, had brought his people from their village at Detroit. Nicolas warmly welcomed English traders, allowing them to build a blockhouse in his town. Under their influence and Nicolas' leadership, Sandusky became a center of intrigue against the French. Croghan's prominence in this movement can be surmised from the fact that he was known as "the trader to the Indians seated on Lake Erie." He is the only master trader recorded for that area.[18]

In the early spring, before Croghan left the Lake Erie country, five French traders from the Cuyahoga River, loaded down with furs, began their homeward trek to Detroit. Their route led past Sandusky, and, unaware of danger, they visited the town. That the British had inflamed the Sandusky natives now became apparent, for the natives fell on the unfortunate Frenchmen and murdered them. The Indians guilty of this massacre were not only the Sandusky Wyandots but Senecas from Croghan's village. From this bloody start developed the Indian conspiracy which ruffled the West in 1747, aimed at the destruction of the French posts. Detroit itself was threatened, while the fort on the Maumee River was partially burned. Although the French won out, they lost a number of their people at distant trading places before peace was restored.

According to an official French report, the English traders on the Cuyahoga had been responsible for the Indian outbreak. These men were accused of causing "all the ills and agitation of the upper country" and of instigating the natives to commit the Sandusky murders: "This conspiracy is fomented by the English, who, by force of presents and lies, excite the Indians against us, insinuating into their minds that we are not in a condition to furnish them with any supplies; that we have no goods, as they take all our ships, and that Quebec has been already captured."[19]

18. Alfred T. Goodman, *Journal of Captain William Trent from Logstown to Pickawillany* (Cincinnati, 1871), 15-16; *Pa. Archives*, I, 771.
19. *Collections of the State Historical Society of Wisconsin*, 17 (1906), 474-77; O'Callaghan, ed., *New-York Col. Doc.*, X, 84.

Croghan played a major role in stirring up the revolt. Indeed, the testimony of John Patten, an English trader captured by the French, puts the entire blame on the Irishman: "Croghan . . . had at all times persuaded the Indians to destroy the French and had so far prevailed on them, by the presents he had made them, that five French had been killed by said Indians, in the upper part of the country; that self-interest was his sole motive in every thing he did, that his views were to engross the whole trade, and to scare the French from dealing with the Indians."[20]

It was to Croghan that the Seneca warriors turned after the Sandusky massacre. On their behalf, he wrote a letter to the governor of Pennsylvania informing him of the uprising and confiding the Indians' hopes that they would soon seize Detroit. This letter, accompanied by the scalp of one of the murdered Frenchmen, brought the first news of the outbreak to Philadelphia. According to Croghan, "I am just returnd from the woods, and has brought a letter, a French scalp, & some wompom for the Governor from a part of the Six Nations Ingans that has there dwelling on the borders of Lake Arey. Those Ingans were always in the French intrest till now, butt this spring allmost all the Ingans in the woods have declared against the French."[21]

The natives, however, were unable to maintain their uprising and soon asked the French for forgiveness. But those tribes principally involved, the Sandusky Wyandots and the Twightwees, did not dare to renew their French alliance. In 1748, Chief Nicolas destroyed Sandusky and led his people eastward to Kuskuskies on the Mahoning River, while the Twightwees, under their militant leader Old Briton, settled at Pickawillany on the Great Miami. These moves of the two tribes were the chief result of the Indian war. They profoundly affected trading conditions in the Lake Erie and Ohio country. For Croghan, the uprising served as a springboard for his career: it led to his moving from the Cuyahoga to Pickawillany; and it brought him forward as a negotiator between the western Indians and the province of Pennsylvania.[22]

20. Neville B. Craig, *The Olden Time* (Cincinnati, 1876), II, 186.
21. Indians to Governor Thomas, May 16, 1747, and Croghan to Peters, May 26, 1747, *Pa. Archives*, I, 741-43.
22. *Coll. of the State Hist. Soc. of Wis.*, XVII, 474; O'Callaghan, ed., *New-York Col. Doc.*, X, 138, 162.

While the sporadic rebellion against the French was dying down, the Pennsylvania government, acting on Croghan's suggestion, voted £400 for a present to reward the western Indians. Conrad Weiser, the provincial interpreter and chief governmental adviser on Indian affairs, favored this action although it was not in line with traditional policy. Since the government had no facilities to transport goods to the Ohio country, Weiser recommended that the gift be entrusted to Croghan. "I always took him for an honest man, and have as yet no reason to think otherwys of him."[23]

But weeks passed, the present was not sent west, and Croghan grew uneasy. Reporting that the Indians were still "makeing warr very briskly against the French," he worried about what they would do if not encouraged. No doubt he feared that the Indians would accuse him of failing to support them after having involved them in a war. In deep concern, Croghan declared that if no present were provided, he would not dare send any of his traders to the Indian country.[24]

Impressed by this warning, the Pennsylvania Council requested him to deliver £200-worth of the present. Croghan's wagoner brought this gift to Harris' Ferry. But before arrangements to ship it out to the Indian country could be made, a party of fifteen Ohio natives arrived at Lancaster. Weiser, who was in Lancaster at the time, sent them on to Philadelphia, where they caught Franklin's eye for news. In his *Gazette* for November 12, 1747, Franklin wrote: "Last night came to town some *Indians* from *Ohio*, a branch of the *Mississippi*, all warriors, and among them one captain, on a visit to this government, about some particular affairs relating to the war betwixt the *English* and *French* in those parts." More precisely, the Indians had come to solicit Pennsylvania aid.[25]

In solemn council, colonial officials told the natives that they would be given a handsome present at Harris' Ferry and that in the spring Conrad Weiser would meet them at their council fire on

---

23. Weiser to Peters, July 20, 1747, *Pa. Archives*, I, 762; *Votes and Proceedings . . . of the Province of Pennsylvania*, IV, 62.

24. Croghan to Thomas Lawrence, Sept. 18, 1747, *Pa. Archives*, I, 770.

25. Peters Mss., II, 79, Hist. Soc. of Pa.; *Minutes of the Provincial Council of Pennsylvania* (*Colonial Records of Pennsylvania*), V, 119, 122, 139.

the Ohio to distribute an even larger gift. The part recently played by the Lake Indians was acknowledged with thanks, and mention was made of a small present of powder and lead which Croghan was sending to the Cuyahoga. In appreciation of such generosity, the Indians broke into weird shouts of approval and danced the war dance.[26]

Weiser escorted the natives to Harris' Ferry where, in Croghan's presence, he gave them the Pennsylvania goods, consisting mostly of powder, lead, and liquor. Croghan then set about providing men and horses to transport the present west. Before the Indians left, their leader told Weiser that "the French party is very strong among us, and if we had failed in our journey to Philadelphia, or our expectations wou'd not have been granted by our brethren in Philadelphia, the Indians would have gone over to the French to a man."[27]

This visit of the Ohio natives was an important one, for direct dealings with the western Indians had not been in line with accustomed procedure. Pennsylvania's traditional policy, as instituted by William Penn and zealously followed by his son Thomas Penn, had been to treat with the Iroquois confederacy on all important Indian matters. Pennsylvania recognized the Six Nations' lordship over all the tribes in the colony. The Delaware, Shawnee, and other local Indian groups could not independently sell lands or make war or peace—such important matters were the prerogative of the Onondaga Council. In the 1740's, however, a situation arose which threatened the ascendancy of the Six Nations. With the drifting of the Delaware and Shawnee tribes, as well as groups of the Iroquois themselves, to the Ohio country, a large Indian population was established far from the heart of the confederacy in New York. Though the Onondaga Council sent viceroys to rule over this shifting population, a wedge had been thrust into the control which the Six Nations had previously enjoyed.

During the winter of 1747-48, the present promised the Ohio Indians was assembled. Valued at £850, it consisted in part of eighteen barrels of gunpowder, a ton of bar lead, forty guns, fifty dozen knives, sixty-five hundred flints, and twenty dozen hatchets.

---

26. *Minutes of the Provincial Council of Pa.* (*Col. Rec. of Pa.*), V, 145-52.
27. Weiser to Peters, Nov. 28, 1747, *ibid.*, 167.

But when the time drew near for Weiser to deliver these goods, the interpreter grew uneasy and doubtful. Information he had received indicated that the Ohio Indians were not at war with the French and that no good purpose would be served in giving them a present.[28]

To decrepit old James Logan, Pennsylvania's senior statesman and expert on Indian matters, Weiser's veering point of view was distressing. The influential Logan put his foot down; Weiser was to deliver that present. However, as the interpreter could not go at the time originally appointed, the governor and Council accepted Logan's advice: "As G. Croghan has waited long wth his horses he ought not to be sent empty away, and I wod imagine he might have at least £300 with him and to have Conrad send a suitable lettr with him."[29]

Croghan's disappointment at the delays must have been intense. Though he sent out his trading cargoes in March, he remained behind at Pennsborough with a pack train of about twenty horses awaiting the government's present. It did not come. Instead, Croghan received word that Pennsylvania's goods were not yet ready to go and that he was simply to deliver a token present and notify the Indians of the reasons for the delay: "The Council is sensible you have been at an expense & that your detainment at home must be a considerable inconvenience to you, and therefore desire you will make a charge of everything, that you may be paid to your satisfaction."[30]

Early in April, Croghan journeyed to the Ohio to inform the natives that unforeseen business prevented Weiser from coming as early as had been expected but that he would be with them by the middle of the summer. On April 28 and succeeding days, Croghan treated with the Indians in council, presumably at Logstown, a trading village on the Ohio. With him he had twelve horseloads of gifts to distribute, containing barely half enough ammunition to supply the fifteen hundred natives whom he estimated were on hand. Acting with the independence which was so characteristic

---

28. Inventory of the present, and Weiser to Peters, Mar. 28, 1748, *ibid.*, 197, 212-13.

29. Logan to Weiser, Mar. or Apr., 1748, and Logan to [William Logan], no date, Logan Letter Book, 1748-50, Hist. Soc. of Pa.

30. Peters to Croghan, Mar. 31, 1748, *Col. Rec. of Pa.*, V, 214.

of him, Croghan doubled the size of the gift by including goods of his own for which he blithely billed the government.

In excellent humor and strong for the English, the Indians told Croghan that the Six Nations alone had 730 warriors settled on the Ohio, and "we have one thing to acquaint you with, that is there [is] a great nation of Indians come from the French to be your brothers as well as ours, who say they never tasted English rum yet, but would be very glad to taste it now." This was an introduction for deputies of the powerful Twightwee nation, which, having recently attacked the French, now sought an English alliance.[31]

Not until mid-June did Croghan return to Philadelphia to present his report and his expense account. It was evidently he who brought the letter from the Shawnee and Six Nations Indians at Logstown, announcing that they were coming to Lancaster to present the Twightwee deputies to the government of Pennsylvania. To meet the Twightwees, the governor's Council sent interpreter Andrew Montour, a half-breed recommended by Weiser. Weiser himself prepared to go to the Ohio to deliver the provincial present. According to his instructions, "Mr. George Croghan, the Indian trader, who is well acquainted with the Indian country and the best roads to Ohio, has undertaken the convoy of you & the goods with his own men & horses at the publick expence."[32]

The arrival of the Twightwees prevented Weiser from setting out. Croghan reported that the Indian visitors would be in Lancaster on July 15, and commissioners were immediately appointed to meet them. The government had wanted the treaty held in Philadelphia, but letters from both Weiser and Croghan confirmed the fact that the Indians were afraid of sickness in that city and insisted that the meeting be held at Lancaster.[33]

The Lancaster conference took place at the courthouse with Conrad Weiser and Andrew Montour serving as interpreters and many townspeople in attendance. Croghan was also there, caring

---

31. Minutes of treaty and expense account, *ibid.*, 287-89, 294-95.
32. Weiser's instructions from acting governor Anthony Palmer, June 23, 1748, *ibid.*, 289-93.
33. Thomas Cookson to Peters, July 14, 1748, and Weiser to Peters, July 14, 1748, *Pa. Archives*, II, 9-10; *Col. Rec. of Pa.*, V, 298, 300.

for the Indians and signing his name as a witness to the treaty which solemnly admitted the Twightwees to the English chain of friendship. This treaty-making took five days and made strong impressions on those present. Not only was it of importance as a military entente, but it promised wonders for the fur trade. The Twightwees controlled a fabulous hunting country which hitherto had not been readily accessible to the English. That country was now open to them and, in effect, denied to French competition.[34]

Croghan and the Indians returned to his Pennsborough plantation, where the natives rested a day or so before setting off extremely gratified with their reception in Pennsylvania. Croghan packed up the Indian present Weiser was to deliver and had it on the trail to the Ohio country, escorted by half a dozen of his "hands," before Weiser himself arrived.[35]

Weiser and his party followed Croghan down the trail, cutting through the mountains at McAllister's Gap. With Weiser was Benjamin Franklin's son William and William Trent, Croghan's former partner, now released from military service. From Croghan's they rode twenty miles to Robert Dunning's, and the following day, thirty miles to the Tuscarora Path. There they crossed the Tuscarora Hill and came to a sleeping place called the Black Log, a twenty-mile ride. The next day they went twenty-four miles to within a short distance of the Standing Stone on the Juniata, a property later owned by Croghan. A short day's ride of twelve miles was followed by one of twenty-six, which brought them to Franks Town, so-called, although there were no cabins. At this place they overtook the pack train and the provincial present, temporarily at a standstill because of the illness of four of Croghan's men. Leaving the train at Franks Town, Weiser's party crossed the Allegheny Hill to the Clear Fields, sixteen miles. The next day a thirty-four-mile journey brought them to the Shawnee Cabins, where some of Croghan's men with twenty pack horses were found preparing to return to the assistance of the party at Franks Town, and the following day a nearly equal distance was traveled to reach Ten Mile Lick. One more day's travel of twenty-six miles and the waters of the Allegheny came

34. Minutes of the treaty, *Col. Rec. of Pa.*, V, 307-18; Weiser to Peters, Aug. 4, 1748, *Pa. Archives*, II, 11.
35. Croghan to Peters, Aug. 8, 1748, *Pa. Archives*, II, 13.

in view at Chartier's Town. Leaving their tired mounts, Weiser and his friends canoed sixty miles down the river to Logstown, where they were greeted joyfully by the waiting Indians. Logstown was located about eighteen miles below the juncture of the Monongahela and the Allegheny, and was the place where the western Indians had recently kindled their council fire.[36]

At Logstown, Weiser, assisted by Montour, explained everything that had happened between the English and the Twightwees at Lancaster. Weiser informed the Indians that the war between the French and English was now over and that consequently Pennsylvania could not give them war supplies, but he had brought them a present. Thereupon, the Pennsylvania gift, including a valuable remembrance from James Logan, was turned over to the Indians. Virginia had also sent £200-worth of goods which Croghan had transported to the Ohio.[37]

If Croghan now allowed himself a breathing spell, after seven arduous American years, it was well merited. From a modest start, he had established his own business, conducting it on an increasingly large basis until, by 1748, he was the outstanding Indian trader in the province. In achieving this success, he had demonstrated an organizing ability of no mean order, for the conduct of his trade was complex. His qualities of leadership were enhanced by the apparent sincerity and guilelessness of his personality. Philadelphia merchants liked and trusted him. They staked him yearly to large credits in goods. Among his fellow traders he was tremendously popular.

Unquestionably, his outstanding achievements were his diplomatic successes with the natives. Croghan played a central role in the important change in the Twightwees' allegiance, which grew out of the uprising of 1747. His contribution to the development of Pennsylvania Indian policy was fundamental, and his responsibility for bringing the western Indians into the English interest was freely acknowledged in government circles.[38]

36. Weiser's journal, *Col. Rec. of Pa.*, V, 348-58; Penn to Peters, Feb. 20, 1749, Penn Letter Book, II, 255, Hist. Soc. of Pa.
37. Weiser's receipt to Croghan, Sept. 17, 1748, Cadwalader Coll., Hist. Soc. of Pa.
38. Peters to Penn, undated, Penn Mss., Official Correspondence, V, 199, Hist. Soc. of Pa.

2

Hockley, Trent, and Croghan

BRITISH DOMINATION of the fur trade and the promising Twightwee alliance encouraged William Trent to resume his partnership with Croghan. Trent had been demobilized after a disappointing military career. The intended Canadian expedition had never taken place, and, after some eighteen months of service, Trent was once more a civilian.

Both Trent and Croghan were optimists, persuasive and eloquent. As they discussed the fur trade they fairly glowed with confidence, and their enthusiasm was more than one of the shrewdest men in Pennsylvania could resist. Richard Peters, the provincial secretary, had accompanied the Indian commissioners from Philadelphia to Lancaster. There he had helped manage the treaty as best he could, wearied though he was by the heat and by restless nights spent in a flea-ridden bed. And there he had fallen under the spell of Trent and Croghan.

Peters' career had been a checkered one. A member of a respectable Liverpool family, he had attended Westminster School in London where, at the tender age of fourteen, he had been inveigled into marriage by a charwoman. Snatched from the shadow of the Abbey by his frantic father, Peters was hurried abroad to Leyden to resume his studies. Later he returned to London, read law at the Inner Temple, and then decided to prepare for the ministry in the Church of England. Shortly after he was ordained a priest, Peters learned of the death of his wife. Free at last, he married again, this time a most suitable bride, a ward of the tenth Earl of Derby. Just when the curate was eagerly awaiting the birth of his first child, all his splendid hopes were blasted by the appalling reappearance of the charwoman, still, alas, very much alive. Hastily leaving his wives, the young man came to Philadelphia to make a new start.

For a time, Peters preached at Christ Church where he became a controversial figure. Temporarily, he laid aside his priestly ambitions and accepted the secretaryship of the land office; in 1743 he was appointed to the additional posts of clerk and secretary to the provincial Council. Gaining the ear of Thomas Penn, he became the proprietor's confidential adviser and, as such, an important man in the government of Pennsylvania.

Peters' character was a complex of piety and worldliness; he was equally at home in saving souls and in making fortunes. His charming blandness of manner cloaked a talent for deception. Gregarious, politically intent on pleasing, blessed with a social ease unusual in one of snobbish temperament, Peters rose steadily in stature. Old James Logan found him "an ingenious man in all respects."[1]

It is not surprising that Secretary Peters of the land office became a speculator in real estate and soon acquired large holdings. So extensive were his dealings that he maintained he had "considerably expedited the settlemt of lands over Sasquahana where the bulk of my purchases are." In his search for gainful speculations, he pondered the recent rumor that Virginians were going to open a trade in the Ohio country and make settlements there. "This," wrote the secretary, "will undoubtedly rob this province of great advantages." Already, Lord Fairfax and his friends had sent Hugh Parker, a former apprentice of Edward Shippen's, to the Ohio with "a large quantity of English goods & are hurrying into the trade wth all the expedition possible."[2]

If Trent and Croghan were backed by sufficient capital, Peters believed their operations would entirely frustrate the Virginians' plans. He wrote Thomas Penn, suggesting that money be advanced the traders since "they two can do more with the Indians than all the other traders put together."[3] Meanwhile, Croghan

---

1. Hubertis Cummings, *Richard Peters, Provincial Secretary and Cleric, 1704-1776* (Philadelphia, 1944), 20.
2. Peters to Penn, Oct. 20, 1748, and Oct. 26, 1749, Peters Letter Book, Hist. Soc. of Pa.
3. Peters to Penn, July 28, 1748, *ibid.*

and Trent had matured plans for a new partnership and Trent had come to Philadelphia in November, 1748, to obtain the necessary backing. After persuading several merchants to invest in the venture, he planned to sail for England to purchase Indian trade goods. By establishing direct contacts in London, thus eliminating the Philadelphia middlemen, Trent and Croghan hoped to achieve an economical method of operation.

During his stay in Philadelphia, Trent asked Peters for a letter of introduction to Thomas Penn. Peters, whose business it was to know what others were up to, then learned the full scope of Trent's and Croghan's plans. A few months later, Peters was to castigate Philadelphia as a "vile levelling place" and to complain that the "mercantile low conversation will gradually corrupt the best manners." How far Peters himself had been corrupted may be seen in his instant and avid desire to share in the Indian traders' proposals.[4]

Peters urged Trent to delay his arrangements and hurried off to see Richard Hockley. Hockley was a protégé of Thomas Penn, to whom he owed his education and to whom he was to be indebted for many favors in Pennsylvania. Despite his loyalty to his patron's family, there was something futile about Hockley. Erratic and gossipy, close and mean in money matters, he was almost devoid of business sense. Indeed, a future governor of Pennsylvania was to characterize him as "the least calculated for business of any man I ever knew." In 1748, he was desultorily employed in operating a dry goods store on Market Street. The prospect of backing Croghan and Trent delighted Hockley, who was confident that Penn would readily advance money to bring him into such an advantageous partnership.[5]

Encouraged by Hockley, Peters proposed a partnership of Hockley, Peters, Trent, and Croghan toward which Hockley and Peters would advance £1,000. Trent demurred at the amount offered, suggesting that it be increased to £2,000, a sum to which Peters agreed in expectation of borrowing the extra thousand on his own account from Thomas Penn. The matter now hinged on

4. Peters to Penn, Nov. 24, 1748, and May 1, 1749, *ibid.*
5. Peters to Penn, Nov. 24, 1748, *ibid.*, and John Penn to Mrs. Thomas Penn, Dec. 5, 1774, Penn Mss., Private Correspondence, V, 219, Hist. Soc. of Pa.

Croghan, of whom Peters wrote, "I did not expect that considering Mr. Croghan was exceedingly well found in servants & horses & proper materials of all sorts & actually carried on a trade for above one thousand pounds a year this money that he wou'd accept the proposals." But Croghan, whose supply of ready cash was never great, approved the arrangement.

Because of the uncertainty that Penn would lend Peters the extra thousand, articles of agreement signed on November 24, 1748, included only Hockley, Trent, and Croghan. The articles stipulated that Hockley was to advance £1,000 sterling to be laid out by Trent for Indian goods in London. Each of the three partners was to put up £368 in Pennsylvania currency to enable Croghan to purchase goods and horses for an immediate start. As to the method of operation, Hockley was to attend to all business done in Philadelphia, while Croghan and Trent were to manage everything else. The partners agreed to limit their dealings in the Indian trade to their mutual concern. When Philadelphia merchants heard of this new firm, they were considerably worried, fearing that Croghan's company would monopolize the trade.[6]

Within a week of the signing of the contract, Trent sailed from Philadelphia for a three-months' visit to London. His meeting with Thomas Penn proved a disappointment, for, although Penn was pleased with Trent's "modest engaging behaviour," the conservative, hard-headed proprietor recoiled from the desire of Hockley and Peters to enter the trade at his expense. Penn was convinced that his friends had no idea how rash a speculation they were courting. To Peters he addressed himself severely: "Trade ought to be left to traders. Government & offices to governors & officers. . . . I must totally disapprove of your engaging in it." As for Hockley, who had not yet been favored with a governmental post, Penn noted that the partnership articles were "a very wild scheme" and then, relenting, "Notwithstanding what I have now wrote I am unwilling to disappoint your scheme, and let Capt. Trent who has merit go back disappointed." He

---

6. The partnership articles are dated Nov. 24, 1748, Cadwalader Coll., Hist. Soc. of Pa.; Shippen to Hamilton, July 7, 1761, Balch Papers, Shippen, I, 125, Hist. Soc. of Pa.

advanced £500 for Hockley, who subsequently obtained the balance of his £1,000 by mortgaging his property.[7]

At the time Croghan signed the partnership articles, he promised Peters to liquidate his outstanding debts. In Philadelphia alone, these amounted to more than £3,000. Unfortunately, a promise from Croghan and its execution were different matters. Instead of reducing his debts, he borrowed more. As for his promise to refrain from any transactions not included in the partnership, Croghan participated in many enterprises during 1749 in which Hockley did not share. It was soon apparent that when Trent and Croghan found that Peters was not to be one of their partners, they lost interest in Hockley.[8]

Nevertheless, Croghan launched the partnership with many an exciting promise to Hockley of large profits. But Croghan had too many irons in the fire to devote as much time as he should to the new firm. Part of his energy was diverted to negotiating with the Iroquois for a land purchase. News of the Virginians' contemplated grant of 500,000 acres in the Ohio country may have goaded him to this step. At all events, he secured from the Six Nations permission to take up a large tract at a place of his own selection. In return, Croghan assembled an expensive assortment of Indian goods for the natives. It was possibly to raise money for this present that he mortgaged his home and other tracts to Richard Peters for £1,000.[9]

No wonder Croghan was unable to discharge his debts. Money which should have gone to creditors was gambled on property which lay so far west that no one knew when, if ever, it would be settled. Willingness to gamble, faith in the future of the West, and knowledge of land values—he had selected the site which later became the Pittsburgh area—were characteristics of Croghan.

While the trader busied himself with such affairs, the governor of Canada, determined to regain the Indian groups south of Lake

---

7. Penn to Hockley, Feb. 19, 1748/49, Correspondence of the Penn Family, 1732-67, 58, and Penn to Peters, Feb. 20, 1748/49, Penn Letter Book, II, 257-58, Hist. Soc. of Pa.

8. Peters to Penn, Nov. 24, 1748, Peters Letter Book, and Hockley to Penn, Feb. 15, 1749/50, Penn Mss., Official Correspondence, IV, 185, Hist. Soc. of Pa.

9. Hockley to Penn, July 2, 1749, Penn Mss., Official Correspondence, IV, 215, and Croghan's and Peters' indenture of June 27, 1749, Peters Mss., II, 120, Hist. Soc. of Pa.

Erie and in the Ohio country, ordered out a strong expedition under Céloron de Blainville to frighten off the English traders and to reprove the Indians for their disaffection. Included among the several hundred men in Céloron's command was the renowned interpreter Philippe Thomas Joncaire. Word of what was afoot reached Pennsylvania's Governor James Hamilton late in June. Hamilton immediately requested Croghan to check on the rumor.[10]

An unfortunate incident just at this time called for his service as a justice of the peace for Lancaster County, a position to which he had been appointed in April. Four Indian warriors returning to Onondaga had passed the trader's home and stopped about one mile beyond at a "stillhouse." There they got drunk, and one of them was killed by a companion. Croghan investigated the murder but received little help from the Indians, the most suspected of whom ran away. In exasperation, he exclaimed, "I think all stillers & tavern keepers should be fined for making the Indians drunk & espesely warriers." The proclamation of 1748, which had sought to discourage the importation of rum into Indian territory, was clearly a failure. Croghan wrote Peters: "I wish with all my hart the government of this Province wo'ld take some method to regulate the Indian trade & to prevent many disorders which arises from the carring of sperits in the Indian countrys."[11]

By the time Croghan arrived at Logstown, Céloron had come and gone, and the place was seething with unrest over the Frenchman's arbitrary behavior. He had scolded the Indians for their faithlessness and had ordered the English traders to leave. During the course of his travels, Céloron buried lead plates stating French claims to La Belle Rivière, the Ohio; his expedition, however, was a failure, for it did not win back the Indians nor did it drive away the English traders. The Indians were particularly antagonized by the lead plates, which they suspected to be an effort to rob them of their lands. Croghan did not remain long at Logstown; he had arrived sometime after August 8, and on August

---

10. *Col. Rec. of Pa.*, V, 387; Croghan to [Peters], July 3, 1749, *Pa. Archives*, II, 31.

11. *Col. Rec. of Pa.*, V, 378, 408; Croghan to [Peters], endorsed July, 1749, *Pa. Archives*, II, 32.

25 he was back in Philadelphia. The favorable news he brought the governor was promptly printed by Franklin.[12]

During the time when Croghan was on the Ohio, a momentous event in his life took place. On August 2, 1749, the three most important Iroquois chiefs resident in that area, in return for an immense quantity of Indian goods, confirmed him in the title of 200,000 acres in the vicinity of the forks of the Ohio. Many years later, Croghan called the attention of the Board of Trade to this grant; the Six Nations in appreciation of his "constant attention to the preservation of peace and as a testimony of the sincerity with which they desired its continuance, of their own ffree will and without any application on the part of your memorialist in the year 1749 in a publick council at Onondago made a grant to your memorialist of a considerable quantity of land and the same having been since confirmed to your memorialist by the deputies of the public council at a meeting of the western Indians holden for that purpose at Logstown, your memorialist has been earnestly and affectionately pressed by all the said Indians to give them a further proof of his regard for them by accepting the favour they intended for him." Croghan accepted the grant "with a view of preserving the British interest among those Indians," and "at a very large expence made them several presents out of his own private ffortune in token of his gratitude and the sense he had of their regard."[13]

Although this version of the land grant is too ingenuous to be credited, the fact remains that the Onondaga Council actually did think enough of Croghan to gratify him with it; in 1768, the Council confirmed the transaction so that its validity is not to be doubted. The Ohio lands which the trader thus gained represent one of his outstanding personal triumphs among the Indians. No Pennsylvanian, excepting the proprietors, was ever granted so much for his own use.

Despite the time and attention required for personal affairs and for governmental missions, Croghan carried on the fur trade more vigorously than ever. According to the major outlines of the management of the Hockley company, Croghan's time was

---

12. *Pennsylvania Gazette*, Aug., 31, 1749.
13. Undated memorial, Cadwalader Coll., Hist. Soc. of Pa.

spent, as much as possible, in the trading country, where he supervised employees in the field. Trent, who lived at Croghan's Pennsborough plantation after his return from England, controlled the shipment of skins to Hockley in Philadelphia and trade goods to Croghan on the Ohio. Trent also kept the company's books.

Although the Hockley partnership was Croghan's primary trading interest, it was rivaled by the partnership of Trent, Croghan, Robert Callender, and Michael Teaffe. Through these associations and in his own right, Croghan controlled the activities of probably one hundred men—independent traders, employees, indentured servants, and Negro slaves. It is conceivable that of the three hundred persons in the Indian trade operating out of Pennsylvania, one third were in one way or another connected with George Croghan. His prominence earned him the title "king of the traders."[14]

Despite this expansion of his interests, 1749, the year of the locust plague, was not favorable. Trent, when he came to Philadelphia in October, admitted that the Hockley company was not yet operating in the black, since it had been "impossible to get a return of skins from the woods this fall of any consequence." There had been some hard luck—Trent had been severely ill of malaria all summer and unable to get about; Croghan had also suffered from the same complaint. They were deeper than ever in debt, as "we have been obliged to buy a great many goods in order to fit out our hands." No remittances to English creditors were made that season, but the future looked bright. According to Peters, "The Indian trade is in a most flourishing condition and I know of but one thing that can hurt it, that is the French governor at Canada."[15]

A disappointment at this time was not of dangerous consequence. Money was easy, and the merchants were eager to enter the Indian trade. Peters wrote Penn that "if the trade was to remain in its present state unmolested by the French the traders

---

14. Douglas Southall Freeman, *George Washington* (New York, 1948), I, 329, n. 15. The first comprehensive biography of Croghan is in Hanna's *Wilderness Trail*, II. Hanna entitled Croghan "king of the traders."

15. Trent to Elias Bland, Oct. 8, 1749, Cadwalader Coll., and Peters to Penn, Oct. 26, 1749, Penn Mss., Official Correspondence, IV, 245, Hist. Soc. of Pa.

wou'd in a very few years be rich men, and, indeed, supposing the worst, as Mr. Croghan is to be in the Indian country, they cannot fail of making very considerable gain."[16]

Pennsylvania continued to control the trade, despite the efforts of the Virginians to put their ambitious Ohio Company into operation. Virginia's acting governor, Thomas Lee, complained to Governor Hamilton that Pennsylvania traders had so prejudiced the Indians against the company that it was utterly thwarted. Croghan, however, placed the blame on the ineptness of the southern agents and the Indians' shrewd suspicion that the Virginians planned to settle their lands. But Croghan did not like attempts of outsiders to enter the field. From Pickawillany in November, 1749, he wrote Peters: "The Indians hear has received an invition from Coll. Crisep & Mr. Hugh Parker to go down to see the Govenor of Marryland which perhaps may be a determent to the tread of Pensilvanie as the[y] want to enter into the Indian tread. I can put a stop to thire going down if you think itt convenent."[17]

Although Pennsylvania's western fortune continued to flourish, the year ended on an ominous note. In November, the partnership of Trent, Croghan, Callender, and Teaffe had sent two employees with a cargo of goods packed on seven horses to deal with a party of Wyandots, who were hunting on the headwaters of the Scioto River. In that area the traders were intercepted by the French, their goods confiscated, and they themselves carried off to Detroit. This robbery cost the partners more than £300.[18]

Croghan spent the winter of 1749-50 at Pickawillany, "Pick's Town," on the Great Miami. Since the Twightwees had but lately entered the English alliance, that winter's trading season was probably the first in which the Pennsylvanians visited them in force. Although it was a time of nominal peace, under Croghan's leadership the traders erected a stockaded fort. So evident were Croghan's activities in the anti-French movement that the Detroit

16. Peters to Penn, July 5, 1749, Penn Mss., Official Correspondence, IV, 219, Hist. Soc. of Pa.
17. Thomas Lee to Hamilton, Nov. 22, 1749, *ibid.*, 257; Croghan to Peters, Nov. 25, 1749, Indiana Historical Society; Peters to Penn, July 12, 1750, Penn Mss., Official Correspondence, V, 33, Hist. Soc. of Pa.
18. Ohio Co. Papers, I, 7, Hist. Soc. of Pa.

commandant offered $1,000 for his scalp. He became known as the "grand-interprète Anglois pour les sauvages." Vastly exaggerated accounts of the Pennsylvanians' plans were passed on to French headquarters by the gullible commander of their outpost on the Maumee River.[19]

Pickawillany was dangerously exposed to attack. Céloron had recently spent a week there, departing on September 20 after failing to make a favorable impression on Old Briton, the chief. At a conference about two months later, the Indians listened to a message from the Detroit commandant directing them under threats of reprisal to order the English traders away. Croghan was present at this meeting and wrote Peters that the natives received the French mandate with contempt.[20]

During his first winter in the new territory, Croghan built up his trading interests at Pick's Town and exerted the charm of his personality on Old Briton. With the passing of Chief Nicolas, Old Briton had become the leader of pro-English sentiment among the formerly French-influenced Indians. On all this, Croghan capitalized. According to a French officer in the Illinois country, Old Briton placed himself at the head of a new conspiracy to destroy the French, at the instigation of "the English man."[21]

While Croghan promoted the company's business in the Far West, Trent came to Philadelphia in January, 1750, to arrange for a shipment of skins to London. Excusing both Croghan and himself for keeping their accounts open, Trent promised that as soon as the roads grew passable in the spring, more skins would be sent. Like Croghan, Trent had embarked on all sorts of Indian trade arrangements that did not concern the unsuspecting Hockley.

Hockley, although indebted as a result of his entry into the Indian trade for £1,000 sterling and £368 Pennsylvania currency, remained in ignorance of the true state of his affairs. Unaware of Croghan's actual operations, he wrote Penn that Croghan "was concern'd in the trade before he gave it up to serve

19. *Col. Rec. of Pa.*, V, 483. For reports of the French officer, see *Collections of the Illinois State Historical Library*, 29 (1940), 105-216 *passim;* Albert T. Volwiler, *George Croghan and the Westward Movement, 1741-1782* (Cleveland, 1926), 78.
20. Croghan to Peters, Nov. 25, 1749, Indiana Hist. Soc.
21. *Coll. of the State Hist. Soc. of Wis.*, 18 (1908), 58.

the company." The Philadelphian had complete confidence in the trader: "We don't only sell to the Indian traders and pick & choose the best of them but are really Indian traders ourselves which is a great advantage as Mr. Croghan has an eye over all he trusts, and so well esteemed by the Indians generally that if he has a sortable cargo not one trader in the woods at the Indian towns can sell anything till he has done." The return of the trader to Pennsborough on April 30, 1750, gave weight to Hockley's praise, for Croghan brought with him "the greatest quantity of skinns ever heard of." All the traders had enjoyed a season of extraordinary success.[22]

Once again, duties of a public nature awaited Croghan, this time as a justice of the peace for Cumberland County. With the formation of this county in 1750, formerly the western part of Lancaster County, both Croghan and Trent were appointed magistrates, and it was in that capacity that they were called on in May and June to assist Richard Peters in expelling squatters who had established themselves on lands not yet purchased from the Indians.[23]

Although warned to leave the previous summer, homesteaders had continued to settle in Indian territory beyond the Kittatinny Hills. Complaints of the natives about this illegal entry had to be satisfied. Less than a year earlier the important Onondaga chief, Canasatego, had called attention to the encroachments of white men in the Juniata area and had warned, "We must not be depriv'd of our hunting country."[24]

Notifying the justices that he would require their services in ousting the troublesome settlers, Peters arrived at Harris' Ferry in the middle of May, accompanied by Conrad Weiser. Awaiting him were Croghan and several other magistrates. Harris', however, was not a suitable place to plan their campaign since it was not private enough, and Peters was happy to accept Croghan's invitation to stay at his plantation. There the secretary learned from the trader the exact state of the situation "over the hills."

22. Hockley to Penn, Feb. 15, 1749/50, and Peters to Penn, May 5, 1750, Penn Mss., Official Correspondence, IV, 185, and V, 5, Hist. Soc. of Pa.; Weiser to Hamilton, May 4, 1750, *Pa. Archives*, II, 45.
23. *Col. Rec. of Pa.*, V, 436.
24. *Ibid.*, 394-95, 400-1.

There were, it appeared, several large settlements at great distances from one another and difficult to approach because of the various "flights" of mountains. Croghan assured Peters that the settlers would not move voluntarily, but must be compelled by force.

Force Peters had, for the magistrates, thirteen in all, volunteered to accompany him. Uncertain how to proceed, Peters relied on Croghan, who mapped out a plan of operations. Croghan also supplied two of his servants to assist the company and laid in rum, whisky, bread, and salt provisions for the journey.

By May 21, Croghan had completed the outfitting of the party and it moved off, winding over Croghan's Gap down to Sherman's Creek north of the Blue Hills. Since everything depended upon the element of surprise, and since the settlement on the Big Juniata was the principal bone of contention, the group rode as rapidly as possible to that sore point. Although it met a number of people at Sherman's Creek and had to spend the night, its mission was kept secret. The following morning, without a word to the local settlers, the magistrates took the shortest route to their objective, climbing the Tuscarora Hill at a place so steep that even the Indian traders said they had never met with such an obstacle. Thus, they descended on the Juniata settlement without warning and, before the trespassers could escape to the woods, "took them prisoners, burnt their houses & sent the chief mutineer to jayl." Following this success, the party divided into two groups: one, under Peters and Weiser, traveled twenty-five miles down the Juniata to a small settlement at its mouth; the other, under Croghan, returned to Sherman's Creek, burned some houses, and put all the squatters under bond for their removal.

Both parties then met at Croghan's to map out the remaining part of their mission—visits to settlements in the Path Valley, Aughwick, and the Big and Little Coves, where they burned more cabins to strike terror in the hearts of those "vile people" who had had the audacity to take up unpurchased lands. The vigor with which the secretary conducted his unpleasant task excited Thomas Penn's admiration. The proprietor applauded Peters for having executed it "with an hussar spirit, nothing less than which will do with these people" and commented further, "I should have desired you to give Mr. Croghan & the other gentlemen my thanks." It may be added, however, that the net result of the effort was total failure; cabins were rebuilt, crops were sown, and new settlers poured in. Within a few years, their pioneer spirit was to cost them dearly, because they were to be among the first attacked in the Indian war which followed Braddock's defeat.[25]

About this time, Croghan's only white child, Susannah, was born, a fact which furnishes presumable evidence that he had taken a wife. No record has survived of his marriage, nor has mention of his wife been found in contemporary sources. It is possible that the mother did not long survive her child's birth.[26]

Before the expedition against the squatters, Trent had visited Philadelphia to inform Hockley that orders should immediately be sent to London for goods to the amount of £500 sterling. It was unhappily true that sufficient skins had not yet been received to pay for the first cargo, but Trent, in his persuasive way, was able to prevail on Hockley to raise the additional sum. Hockley borrowed the money on Trent's repeated assurances that skins would soon be sent down to pay off the debts on the first stock and to discharge the new loan.[27]

Trent and Croghan continued through the year in optimistic vein, Trent indulging himself with the purchase of some expensive English furniture. But creditors were becoming uneasy. As one of them wrote, "Your returns are so slow that it disheartens me."[28] In July, 1750, Trent was once more in Philadelphia arranging for the shipment of skins to London. Earlier in the year, the Hockley firm had sent a consignment to John Samuel, and in April, 830 summer and 30 fall skins had gone off to Elias Bland. During Trent's summer stay in Philadelphia, the company shipped 1,371 fall skins to Hyam and Son and another consignment to Bland. In September, a third shipment was made to Bland con-

---

25. Penn to Hamilton, Aug. 27, 1750, Penn Letter Book, III, 20-21, and Peters to Penn, July 12, 1750, Penn Mss., Official Correspondence, V, 29, 31, Hist. Soc. of Pa.; *Col. Rec. of Pa.*, V, 431-49.

26. Susannah Croghan's tombstone at St. James Protestant Episcopal Church in Evansburg, Pa., records that she died "Dec. 24, 1790. Aged 40 Years."

27. Hockley's statement, undated, Cadwalader Coll., Hist. Soc. of Pa.

28. Bland to Trent, July 9, 1750, Cadwalader Coll., Hist. Soc. of Pa.

sisting of 2,360 fall skins. These last three lots were valued at £1,176 Pennsylvania currency.[29]

A new development in the company's affairs may have crystallized during Trent's July visit to Philadelphia—Hockley decided to go to England. Elias Bland, the London agent, had failed, a disturbing situation that Hockley wanted to investigate. Furthermore, he was anxious to see his patron Thomas Penn and to repair his digestion by taking the waters at Bath. He sailed in the fall, leaving to Richard Peters the management of his affairs.

In London, Thomas Penn fretted over Céloron's expedition down the Ohio. Previously, Penn had opposed governmental protection for Indian traders, but the French threat to his province changed his point of view. "I think . . . [something] should be done immediately, if it can be by consent of the Indians," he wrote Governor Hamilton; "it is of great import to the trade of the Province to have a settlement there [on the Ohio or Allegheny], and a house a little more secure than an Indian cabbin." Penn offered to contribute £400 to build a "house" of stone with small bastions and to give £100 a year for its upkeep. He urged that the Assembly be prevailed on to vote what other funds were necessary for this building, which would "in some measure protect the trade and be a mark of possession."[30]

The Quaker Assembly, however, would have nothing to do with forts, although it was willing to vote presents to maintain the good will of the Indians. It provided a gift for the Twightwees which Croghan took west in the fall of 1750, and in September, when Hamilton learned that Joncaire was setting up a French trading post on the headwaters of the Allegheny, the Assembly voted a large present for the other western Indians, which Croghan was to deliver the following spring.[31]

Croghan's importance grew with every step Pennsylvania took to guard its new alliance with the western tribes. He was continually called on for advice, and it was his facilities that were used to transport presents. No other trader equaled him in prestige.

29. Hockley, Trent, and Croghan folder for 1750, *ibid.*
30. Penn to Hamilton, Feb. 12, 1749/50, Penn Letter Book, II, 295, Hist. Soc. of Pa.
31. *Votes and Proceedings . . . of the Province of Pa.*, IV, 137, 146, 152, 156.

The Pennsylvania Council called Croghan "the most considerable Indian trader." According to Richard Hockley, "Conrad Weiser has frequently told me that Croghan's interest with the Indians is next to his own, and shoud he dropp Croghan is the fittest man to succeed him." Admired by the English, Croghan was hated by the French, a hatred recognized by William Johnson in the far-off Mohawk Valley. Johnson first mentioned the trader in September, 1750: "The French at De Troit and thereabouts have offered and given some Indians great presents to go and take or destroy one Mr. Croghan and Lowry, two of the chief men who trade from Pennsylvania, and have the most influence on all Indians living thereabouts of any that ever went among them, or in all likelihood ever may."[32]

Unfortunately, Croghan's prominence did not bring success to the Hockley trading firm. Croghan and Trent had been slow and irregular in sending skins to Philadelphia, and the company's debts had mounted. When long-promised skins failed to reach Philadelphia in October, 1750, Peters accused Trent of diverting them to other purposes. Trent's and Croghan's debt, wrote the worried cleric, had swollen to thousands of pounds despite the fact that

Mr. Croghan declared over and over to me that he woud not owe a groat of his old debts by Christmas Day, nor take up any more goods on his private account, nor trade separately any more, and engagd for you that you shoud do the same. Instead of that, I am told that Mr. Croghan and you have jointly gone into a larger trade than ever, and that both you for yourself and he for his self likewise takes up goods to trade on your own private accounts.... Now sir, let me ask you was you in Mr. Hockley's place, or in the place of any of his friends, is it possible if this be so, not to believe that Mr. Hockley is likely to come off loser, nay must do it? Are not all the horses used promiscuously? Are not many things which at an estimate of your own he paid his part for used in common? And will not all mankind say that the bad debts will be thrown upon the partnership account, nay is it possible to make up accounts? And if not who must suffer? Where lies

---

32. Minutes of Council, Sept. 19, 1750, and William Johnson to Governor George Clinton, Sept. 25, 1750, *Col. Rec. of Pa.*, V, 461, 481; Hockley to Penn, Feb. 15, 1749/50, Penn Mss., Official Correspondence, IV, 185, Hist. Soc. of Pa.

the risque? On you or Mr. Croghan? No. On Mr. Hockley entirely.[33]

Croghan spent the winter journeying through the Indian country. With him went Montour as an emissary to tell the natives of a conference to be held at Logstown in the spring when the big Pennsylvania present recently voted by the Assembly would be given to them. Croghan was intent on personal business, but he too had an official responsibility—the small present for the Twightwees which he was to deliver.[34]

Leaving Logstown about November 17, where he bade farewell to the resident "parcel of reprobate Indian traders"—an observer noticed that Croghan was an "idol among his countrymen the Irish traders"—Croghan rode to the Wyandot town of Muskingum, a settlement of about one hundred families. This was one of his main trading places.

Stories of French depredations, which he heard at this village, were so alarming that Croghan ordered all Englishmen to rendezvous there while the Indians also gathered in council. To dramatize his position, Croghan flew the English colors from his trading house, an example followed by the Muskingum chief. One of Croghan's partners, Michael Teaffe, arriving from Lake Erie, brought warning that the Ottawas were no longer safe to trade with. From Pickawillany came word that the Twightwees, at least, were still true—they had barely been dissuaded from killing some French deserters, whom they now held for Croghan to dispose of. Later in the winter, the French retaliated by capturing three traders, two of whom were in Croghan's service.[35]

During the weeks which Croghan spent at Muskingum, he was joined by Christopher Gist of Maryland. Gist was searching for lands suitable for settlement by the Ohio Company, a subject he did not dare mention to the Indians or the traders. He had come, he told Croghan, to inform the Indians of a Virginia present which was to be given them at Fredericksburg in the spring.

33. Peters to Trent, Nov. 13, 1750, Cadwalader Coll., Hist. Soc. of Pa.
34. Croghan's winter journey is based on William M. Darlington, ed., *Christopher Gist's Journals* (Pittsburgh, 1893), 31-66.
35. Penn to Hamilton, July 29, 1751, Penn Letter Book, III, 77, Hist. Soc. of Pa.

After a conference with the Wyandot king and his council, Croghan's party left Muskingum in the middle of January and rode to the mouth of the Scioto River, opposite the Lower Shawnee Town, where they were ferried across. This town was another important trading place, comprising about 140 huts, which housed 300 men. Croghan had a large storehouse there.

At a meeting held in the Indians' long, bark-covered council hall, Croghan reported that the French had offered a large reward for both Montour and himself, dead or alive. Confident of the natives high regard, Croghan had no fears for his safety. After a two-weeks' stay at the Shawnee town, the group rode on toward Pickawillany, averaging thirty or more miles a day in the six-day journey. The country they passed through was level and rich, well-watered and timbered, abounding in turkeys, deer, and buffalo.

On February 17, 1751, they came to the Great Miami, and after rafting their goods and saddles across, arrived at the outskirts of Pickawillany, a village of four hundred families. Observing the proper protocol, the visitors halted and fired their guns, a signal which brought forth a warrior whose pipe they all ceremoniously smoked before receiving his invitation to enter the town. Preceded by the English colors, Croghan and his friends were escorted to the king.

Croghan remained with the Twightwees only two weeks, but they were busy ones with repeated conferences in the long house where the Pennsylvania present was delivered. He supervised the repair of the Pick's Town stockade, which was strengthened by an inside lining of logs. During his stay, four Ottawas arrived and were welcomed though they carried a French flag. Their efforts to persuade the Twightwees to return to the French proved unavailing.

Just before the arrival of the Ottawas, some twenty Wea and Piankashaw Indians from the Wabash, members of the Twightwee family, petitioned Croghan to be taken into the English fold. Although without authority to make treaties, Croghan, on behalf of the governor of Pennsylvania, accepted these tribes as allies of the English nation, entitled to the "privilege and protection of the English laws." The indentures for the alliance were drawn up by Gist. No doubt, it would have been bad policy not to have encouraged the Weas and Piankashaws, although Croghan need not have gone as far as he did in formally ratifying an entente with them. For this independency of action, he was later reproved by the governor, and the Assembly voiced its displeasure at his entering into engagements unwarranted by his instructions.[36]

Shortly before the trader left Pick's Town, he visited the long house to see the warriors' feather dance, which was performed by three colorfully painted men who carried long sticks to which were fastened feathers woven into the shape of a bird's wing. In this guise, "they performed many antick tricks, waving their sticks and feathers about with great skill to imitate the flying and fluttering of birds, keeping exact time with their musick." From time to time, as they danced, a warrior would step up and strike a post, a signal for the music and dancing to cease while the brave gave an account of his achievements in war. Then the dancers would proceed as before.

During Croghan's absence, Pennsylvania's latest Indian present had remained at, or near, his plantation on the Conedogwinet. To transport it to the Ohio, Trent informed the government, would cost £245, a higher rate than the customary charge of 30 per cent and a cost which the authorities considered exorbitant. Trent, no doubt, wanted to fix as high a price as possible because the trading partnership was falling on evil days. The past winter on the Allegheny had been the hardest ever known, and the Indians had had an unprofitable hunting season. Many of the traders' horses had frozen to death. In Philadelphia, an ominous rumor was current that a merchant was about to sue Croghan for a debt of £3,500.[37]

The trader returned from the wilderness in late March or early April, 1751. With him, he brought Samuel Saunders, murderer of Simon Girty, an Indian trader. Girty, whose son was to win a terrible name as a renegade, was one of the squatters whom Croghan had evicted from Sherman's Creek the previous year. Delivering Saunders to the sheriff of Cumberland County, Croghan continued on to Philadelphia to meet the governor and

---

36. Isaac Norris to Hamilton, May 9, 1751, *Col. Rec. of Pa.*, V, 526.
37. *Votes and Proceedings . . . of the Province of Pa.*, IV, 186-87; *Col. Rec. of Pa.*, V, 490; Trent to Peters, Mar. 7, 1750/51, N. Y. Hist. Soc.; Peters to Trent, Mar. 11, 1750/51, Cadwalader Coll., Hist. Soc. of Pa.

to help plan the forthcoming Indian conference. This meeting was to have been managed by Weiser, but the interpreter, unable to undertake the task, had recommended that "George Croghon and Andrew Montour are able and every way qualified to do that business."[38]

Reluctantly, Croghan agreed to take Weiser's place. It was not convenient for him to go back to the Ohio, and he knew that the Assembly did not trust him. But, since the governor was insistent, Croghan visited Weiser to work out the agenda. Evidence of the Assembly's suspicion of Croghan may be seen in their laconic comment on learning that the trader, not Weiser, was to deliver the present; they hoped the present would have a good effect among the Indians, provided it was "properly distributed by the persons appointed."[39]

Croghan and Weiser differed sharply in their conception of the status of the Ohio Iroquois. Croghan was impressed by the Mingoes. He noted that in recent years their numbers had been greatly augmented and that they had their own council, similar, though inferior, to that at Onondaga. Furthermore, he could hardly disregard their injunction to Peters and himself in June, 1750, that they had become a great body and expected to be treated as such. On the other hand, the Onondaga Council had spoken very plainly to Weiser. According to the New York chiefs, the Ohio Indians were only hunters and not counsellors or chief men and had no right to receive presents except through the Six Nations chief responsible for them.[40]

As far as the authorities could tell, the Six Nations in New York were in a declining condition, while their off-shoots in the Ohio country were becoming ever stronger. The problem, as stated by Peters in 1753, was essentially the same two years earlier:

It becomes very difficult to judge rightly in Indian affairs, so many Indians have left their towns among the Six Nations and gone &

---

38. *Votes and Proceedings . . . of the Province of Pa.*, IV, 186, 189, 215; Weiser to Hamilton, Apr. 22, 1751, *Col. Rec. of Pa.*, V, 518; Penn to Peters, Feb. 24, 1750/51, Penn Letter Book, III, 42, Hist. Soc. of Pa.

39. Norris to Hamilton, May 9, 1751, *Col. Rec. of Pa.*, V, 526; Peters to Weiser, Apr. 13, 1751, Peters Mss., III, 35, Hist. Soc. of Pa.

40. *Col. Rec. of Pa.*, V, 439, 478-79.

settled to the westward of the branches of the Ohio that these wanderers with the Shawonese, Delawares, Owendaets, & Twightwees make a formidable body, not less than fifteen hundred. . . . They keep up in appearance a sort of dependence on the Council at Onondago, but they knowing their strength will pay no more regard to the old people there than may agree with their humor.[41]

The contradictory views which Croghan and Weiser held about giving gifts had led to their disagreement months before the trader visited Weiser in the early spring of 1751. Weiser feared to offend the Onondaga Council by treating their young men as an independent people. Croghan, however, believed that the Ohio Iroquois would be affronted to see all the other tribes receive gifts and get none themselves, and refused to become involved in the conference if it were to be handled in that way. "Upon this difference of opinion between two persons who are supposed to understand Indian affairs the best, I cannot satisfy my own mind," complained bewildered Governor Hamilton.[42]

Fortunately, Croghan and Weiser were able to work out a compromise whereby Croghan was authorized to use his own discretion in giving presents to the Mingoes. There remained the delicate question of the fort which Thomas Penn so much desired. During the past winter, Croghan had written the governor that the Indians had requested one on the Ohio. Hamilton had discussed this matter privately with some leaders of the Assembly, but they had refused to countenance the idea.[43]

Hamilton, therefore, had to move carefully in order to keep peace in his government. To obtain more specific information about the Indians' request, he instructed Croghan to sound them out in a private manner, "expressly forbidding him to make any publick mention of building a fort." Croghan believed that a fort on the Ohio was necessary to save the Indian trade. Although, during the past winter, he had reported the Indians' request for one, he had later admitted that he had no good authority for such a message, since it was merely

---

41. Peters to Penn, Sept. 28, 1750, and c. September, 1753, Penn Mss., Official Correspondence, V, 59, VI, 105, Hist. Soc. of Pa.

42. Hamilton to Penn, Nov. 18, 1750, *ibid.*, V, 89.

43. Hamilton to Weiser, Apr. 27, 1751, Peters Mss., III, 38, Hist. Soc. of Pa.; *Col. Rec. of Pa.*, V, 517-18, 520.

based on an informal conversation with a few natives "not very considerable for their influence." Again, in April, 1751, he had once more pressed for a fort, dwelling on the French menace and writing, "Since there seems to be a good disposition in all the Indians towards the English, it is my opinion, that it be immediately proposed to the Indians to erect for them a trader house or place of refuge this summer. If the Indians consent, as they probably will, this will secure them from the French."[44]

On May 18, Croghan and Montour reached Logstown with the Pennsylvania present. The impressive number of Indians who had gathered for the meeting greeted them joyfully, firing guns and flying English flags. Several days later, the redoubtable Joncaire came down the river with forty warriors. In council, the French leader warned the tribes that they must cease dealing with English traders. Unintimidated, an Iroquois chief angrily replied: "You are always threatning our brothers what you will do to them, and in particular that man," pointing to Croghan. "Now if you have anything to say to our brothers tell it to him if you be a man. . . . Our brothers are the people we will trade with, and not you."

Croghan's Indian conference was held on May 28 and 29 and was entirely successful. Well pleased with Governor Hamilton's messages and presents, the natives denied that the French had any right to their lands. However, the matter of greatest note which Croghan recorded was their spokesman's request for an English fort on the Ohio.[45]

Hamilton had certainly not expected to see anything in the treaty minutes about a fort, but the request seemed quite in order as it appeared to come directly from the Indians and not at the suggestion of Croghan. In his message to the Assembly, the governor did not stress the need of what he tactfully called a strong house. Nevertheless, in a private conference with the most influential assemblymen, he urged its expediency. The Friends did not argue the question; they merely referred to their religious tenets. Isaac Norris and Israel Pemberton suggested that the

---

44. *Col. Rec. of Pa.*, V, 522; Croghan to Hamilton, Apr. 11, 1751, and Hamilton to Penn, Apr. 30, 1751, Penn Mss., Official Correspondence, V, 133, 135, Hist. Soc. of Pa.

45. Croghan's journal and treaty minutes, *Col. Rec. of Pa.*, V, 530-39.

Indian traders build the fort with the assistance of Penn's offer of financial aid. Thomas Penn, of course, was delighted with the attitude of the Indians. He again recommended that the fort be built of stone and that "if anything is done it should be under the direction of George Croghan, and he be obliged to build it and keep . . . men constantly in it." Penn directed Hamilton and Peters to confer with Croghan if the Assembly refused to sanction the fort, in order that such a structure might somehow or other be erected.[46]

There the matter rested until August, when the Assembly met. Although Pennsylvania traders had controlled the Ohio country despite the increasingly hostile activity of the French, retention of the trade now depended upon adequate defense measures. Gloomily, the Assembly called in Andrew Montour to testify. Were Montour to back up Croghan's minutes of the Logstown meeting, the Assembly would very likely have to circumvent its scruples and to vote the necessary funds to erect an English bastion on the Ohio.

But Montour, the interpreter at Croghan's conference, did not support the trader. To the astonishment of the assemblymen, the half-breed contradicted Croghan's account and flatly denied that the Indians had asked for a fort. According to Montour, Croghan made the proposition, and the Indians agreed to take it under advisement, but Montour doubted that they would ever consent to a fort. This testimony ripped Croghan's reputation to shreds. In denying the necessity of a fort, the Assembly tartly noted that Croghan had misunderstood or misrepresented the information contained in the minutes. More in sorrow than in anger, Hamilton wrote Penn that "it should seem that Croghan had imposed upon me and the Province by a false representation, for which we have both great cause to be offended with him; and the Assembly who never thought well of him were really so."[47]

Although the trader immediately obtained a statement from Montour which substantiated the minutes of his Logstown treaty,

---

46. Hamilton to Penn, June 27, 1751, Penn Mss., Additional Misc. Letters, I, 70, and Penn to Peters, Sept. 28, 1751, Penn Letter Book, III, 105, Hist. Soc. of Pa.

47. Hamilton to Penn, Sept. 14, 1751, Penn Mss., Official Correspondence, V, 173, Hist. Soc. of Pa.; *Col. Rec. of Pa.*, V, 547.

no one was convinced by the interpreter's about-face, least of all Conrad Weiser, who noted that Montour had a guilty conscience and was avoiding him. Croghan demanded a hearing before the Assembly and offered to bring down the Indians and Indian traders present at the Logstown meeting. But his moment had passed.[48]

In rejecting the trader's aggressive Ohio policy, the Pennsylvania Assembly declared that fair dealings and occasional presents would hold the Indians as allies. By satisfying itself with this mistaken and totally ineffective policy in the face of an increasingly serious situation, the colony defaulted its leadership in the West to Virginia's Ohio Company.

The deflation of Pennsylvania's western aspirations did not essentially affect the firm of Hockley, Trent, and Croghan; that company was already insolvent. Shortly after the Assembly had disposed of Croghan and the fort, Richard Peters, as Hockley's attorney, wrote Trent to inquire whether any skins were to be shipped to London to pay off debts or to buy more goods.[49] Trent's reply was evidently of the same discouraging tenor that had prevailed for so long. Realizing that matters had reached a crisis, and aware that Croghan's creditors were becoming more and more restive, Peters foreclosed his mortgages on Croghan's plantations in Cumberland and Lancaster counties. This action marked public acceptance of the firm's failure.

During the summer of 1751, Croghan had tried unsuccessfully to readjust his outstanding debts. In September, when he realized that failure was imminent, he "sold" his tanyard to his half-brother Edward Ward and to his clerk Roger Walton. In an effort to save something from the impending wreck, he also included household furnishings, four Negro slaves, goods from his trading store, his cart, and all the cows, sheep, and horses on his plantation. Although Ward and Walton made it appear that they had purchased the property for £2,000, it was common knowledge that they could not possibly have commanded such a sum. Several months later,

---

48. Peters to Weiser, Sept. 19 and Sept. 25, 1751, Peters Mss., III, 47, 48, and Weiser to Peters, endorsed February, 1753, Correspondence of Conrad Weiser, I, 17, also Hamilton to Penn, June 19, 1752, Penn Mss., Official Correspondence, V, 245, Hist. Soc. of Pa. Croghan never did clear up this matter, nor was word ever received from the Indians according to their promise in Croghan's minutes.

49. Peters to Trent, Aug. 24, 1751, Cadwalader Coll., Hist. Soc. of Pa.

the property was reconveyed to Hockley, one of Croghan's largest creditors, since it was conceded that the earlier manipulation was not valid.[50]

Hockley, returning from London in October, was anxious to learn from his partners the exact state of affairs. Croghan, however, had gone out to the Ohio, "as he pretends to collect in skins," but Trent had been elected a member of the Assembly from Cumberland County and was expected in town for its opening on October 24. Though elected, Trent did not serve. Instead, he too slipped off to the Indian country. [51]

The local effect of Croghan's and Trent's failure was profound. Governor Hamilton, informing Penn of "this unfortunate affair," observed that the two traders

while they flourished, drew a great trade to that part of the country [the area around Carlisle], and made money circulate briskly, but so unexpected a bankruptcy in them who were the principal dealers, had made everybody desirous of withdrawing their effects from that precarious trade as soon as possible, which must necessarily occasion a great scarcity of money in those remote parts, and will, I fear, retard the progress of the town, as well as lessen the value of the lands for the present.[52]

The collapse of Croghan and Trent, who had fled, according to gossip, to escape their many debts, caused a widespread loss of confidence in the Indian trade. Even Edward Shippen, probably the outstanding merchant in the business, was soon soliciting a government office: "I shall have the more time to attend the business, as I have some thoughts of quitting the Indian trade."[53]

Various causes contributed to Croghan's failure. Both he and Trent had borrowed heavily to promote what turned out to be the overexpansion of their trading interests. While money was readily available in 1749, and still procurable in 1750, by 1751, their creditors had become alarmed at the unpaid balances. Moreover, the Philadelphia market was overstocked with English goods,

---

50. Conveyance dated Sept. 17, 1751, and Thomas Cookson and Enoch Flower to Trent and Croghan, Nov. 23, 1751, *ibid*.
51. Hockley to Penn, Oct. 10, 1751, Penn Mss., Official Correspondence, V, 183, Hist. Soc. of Pa.
52. Hamilton to Penn, June 19, 1752, *ibid.*, 245.
53. Shippen to Penn, Mar. 21, 1752, *ibid.*, 231.

and an unhealthy credit situation had developed. The year 1750 produced a bumper crop of skins, but, by the time they were sold in 1751, their value in London had fallen very low. Prices did not improve during the year, and those dealing in skins lost money. Croghan and Trent thus found themselves in an impossible position.

From the beginning of his connection with Hockley, Croghan had been in constant need of funds, and what he obtained had gone into expanding his business—no provision was made to meet his mounting debts. Speculation in land served only to circumscribe his ability to pay. Although out-and-out dishonesty need not be imputed to him in his partnership relations with Hockley, Croghan consistently duped the Philadelphian, whose investment was not kept separate from Croghan's other trading activities. During the entire period of the Hockley partnership, the Indian trade was marked by a rapid increase in the number of traders who engaged in cutthroat competition characterized by unsound ethics and dishonest trade practices. Increased rivalry resulted in underselling, which, as Richard Peters had prophesied in 1749, could only "make broken traders and broken merchants and ruin all."[54]

Actually, Croghan was far from ruined.[55] He had advanced goods to the Indians who owed him a return in furs and skins. Moreover, he still owned horses, gear of all sorts, and western trading houses. Nevertheless, his credit as a businessman was severely curtailed, for the demands of his creditors found his assets frozen. The valuable plantations at Pennsborough, symbols of promising prosperity, had been seized by the mortgage holder. His debts were heavy, his creditors numerous. Temporarily, only one course of action remained open—retirement into the Indian country. There he would be safe from the confining hand of the law, and there he might be able to salvage his trading interests.

54. Peters to Penn, July 5, 1749, Peters Letter Book, and Hamilton to Penn, Sept. 24, 1750, Penn Mss., Official Correspondence, V, 57, Hist. Soc. of Pa.
55. Croghan's and Trent's debts were estimated to be £10,000. Shippen to Penn, Nov. 25, 1754, Balch Papers, Shippen, I, 37, Hist. Soc. of Pa.

3

Collapse of the Indian Trade

THROUGHOUT THE WINTER, Croghan and Trent remained in eclipse in the wilds of the Ohio country, secure from their creditors. Little was known of their activities, except that they were following their trade. Despite the cloud which had descended upon Croghan, Governor Hamilton still believed him to be the most sensible of all the traders and the man best qualified to serve the province in everything relating to the western Indians. Nevertheless, he lamented that Croghan's heavy debts had worn down his usefulness: "I have observ'd him of late very much perplexd on that account." The governor reserved most of his strictures for Croghan's treatment of Hockley, who he feared had been "vilely used" in the partnership.[1]

Toward the close of the winter trading season, William Trent cautiously emerged from the woods and wrote to Edward Shippen to procure a letter of license. This was an instrument which, if signed by his creditors, would guarantee him freedom from arrest and so permit him to visit Philadelphia. Shippen succeeded in obtaining a letter good for four months. "It was with much difficulty I got the letter signed by so many," wrote Shippen.[2]

Protected by this immunity, Trent hurried to Philadelphia. The merchants, he found, were willing to advance Croghan and him more goods, but wanted to know the true status of their affairs. Hockley, in particular, was eager to learn what could be recovered

---

1. Hamilton to Penn, Nov. 29, 1751, Penn Mss., Official Correspondence, V, 193, Hist. Soc. of Pa.
2. William Harrison to [Edward Shippen], Mar. 1, 1752, Amer. Philos. Soc.; Shippen to Harrison, Mar. 9, 1752, and Shippen to Trent, Mar. 9, 1752, Shippen Letter Book, Hist. Soc. of Pa.

from the firm. Trent did all he could to placate him with promises of full restitution. Like Croghan, Trent was free and easy with promises—promises all too often unfulfilled. Everything, so Trent's confident manner seemed to indicate, was going to be all right. After a month in the East and many talks with creditors, Trent rode off to rejoin Croghan at Logstown. With him he brought for his partner's signature a document terminating the Hockley relationship. In monumental understatement, it read: "As we have found that our carrying on the said trade does not answer our expectations we do therefore hereby mutually agree to dissolve."[3]

The dissolution of the Hockley partnership, however, did not relieve Croghan's financial plight. During 1752, Croghan kept in touch with Edward Shippen, to whom he owed money. Occasional shipments of skins were sent to Shippen on behalf of the partnership of Croghan, Callender, and Teaffe, though none represented the debt of £702 said to be owed by the Hockley partnership. Croghan ingratiated himself with Shippen by assisting in transporting furs and skins owed the merchant by other traders, but his own skins seldom appeared. Peters, chagrined at the mess in which he had involved Hockley, did all he could to bring Croghan to the point. To talk things over, Peters urged the trader to appoint a rendezvous, "and let it be in Virginia if that will suit but not in Pensylvania for fear of arrest." Ugly rumors persisted that three or four hundred horseloads of skins had come down belonging to Croghan but disguised under the names of Callender and Teaffe so as to escape creditors. There was probably some truth in these rumors.[4]

Despite the undercurrent of resentment from Croghan's creditors, influential men in the province soon began to see the events of the past summer in clearer perspective, and the trader's reputation regained some lost ground. Veracity of the claim that the

---

3. Peters to Penn, Mar. 20 and June 20, 1752, Penn Mss., Official Correspondence, V, 229, 255, Shippen to [Mr. and Mrs. James Burd], May 1, 1752, Shippen Letter Book, statement dated May 20, 1752, Cadwalader Coll., Hist. Soc. of Pa.

4. Shippen to Croghan, Aug. 8, 1752, and Shippen to Burd, Dec. 12, 1752, Shippen Letter Book, and Peters to Croghan, Nov. 3, 1752, Cadwalader Coll., Hist. Soc. of Pa.

Collapse of the Indian Trade

Indians wanted a fort would turn on the outcome of a treaty to be held by the Virginians at Logstown in June, 1752. "If they ask & obtain leave to build a fort," wrote Peters, "it shoud seem that Croghan reported the truth, if not, that Montour's account given to the Assembly is the true one."[5]

The purpose of Virginia's Logstown treaty was closely allied with the Ohio Company's efforts to comply with the terms of its grant, which required the company to erect a fort and settle a hundred families on its original tract of 200,000 acres. When this was accomplished, the Company was to receive an additional grant of 300,000 acres. Although the lands the Virginians planned to settle were supposed to lie within the boundaries of their province, they could not be settled safely without permission of the natives.

Montour acted as interpreter between the Virginians and the Ohio Iroquois, Delawares, Shawnees, and Wyandots. A man of consummate impudence, only half-civilized, seemingly "unintelligible" to the discerning Peters, frequently and wildly drunk, and generally in debt, Andrew Montour was the connecting link between the colonial governments and the Ohio Indians during Croghan's eclipse.[6]

Although Pennsylvania played no official part in the conference, Croghan was there and exerted considerable influence, admonishing the Indians that Governor Hamilton wanted them to treat the Virginians kindly. The Indian speaker was the Half King, the Six Nations' viceroy of the Ohio Indians and one of the sachems who had confirmed Croghan in his land grant of 1749. Graciously, the Half King complimented Croghan in the presence of the Virginia commissioners.

Brethren, it is a great while since our brother, the Buck (meaning Mr. George Croghan) has been doing business between us, & our brother of Pensylvania, but we understood he does not intend to do any more, so I now inform you that he is approv'd of by our Council at Onondago, for we sent to them to let them know how

---

5. Peters to Penn, June 20, 1752, Penn Mss., Official Correspondence, V, 251, Hist. Soc. of Pa.

6. Weiser to Peters, endorsed February, 1753, Correspondence of Conrad Weiser, I, 17, and Peters to Penn, Dec. 14, 1752, Feb. 7, Sept. 11, and Nov. 6, 1753, Penn Mss., Official Correspondence, V, 313, and VI, 5, 105, 115, Hist. Soc. of Pa.

he has helped us in our councils here; and to let you & him know that he is one of our people and shall help us still & be one of our council, I deliver him this string of wampum.[7]

To the Half King, the Virginians delivered their speeches and presented their gifts, which he divided among the tribes present. After the usual expressions of good will, the Indians appointed Shingas as king of the Ohio Delawares, and they went far to vindicate Croghan by requesting the Virginians to build a fort at the forks of the Ohio. The Virginians also gained their coveted permission to settle west of the Alleghenies, and, under Christopher Gist's leadership, a settlement was soon made.

Since the Twightwees did not attend the meeting, the Virginia commissioners reserved a part of the present for them, but a disaster at this time radically changed the western situation. While its active men were away hunting, the French attacked Pickawillany in a brutal assault which abruptly terminated English influence in the Twightwee country. The massacre at Pick's Town, a place known far and wide as "the village where George Croghan generally trades," hurt the Pennsylvanian severely. Driven with heavy losses from his favorite trading country, he fell back on his plantation on Pine Creek four miles above the forks of the Ohio. There he had many improvements, including pastures to graze his horses and ten acres of fenced corn fields.[8]

The Pine Creek establishment and Croghan's over-all trading ventures had to be supported by an eastern terminus which would take the place of his Pennsborough plantation now owned by Peters. This substitute base he acquired in an irregular way by a direct purchase from the Six Nations of a tract of more than four thousand acres on the waters of Aughwick Creek about forty miles west of Carlisle.[9]

If 1752, with its Pickawillany disaster, had been a bad time for Croghan, the year 1753 was far worse, for it saw the virtual end of the Indian trade. Early in the spring, Duquesne opened his campaign to drive the English out of the Ohio Valley. Em-

[7]. "The Treaty of Logg's Town, 1752," *Va. Mag. of Hist. and Biog.*, 13 (1906), 165.
[8]. *Col. Rec. of Pa.*, V, 550; Ohio Co. Papers, I, 7, Hist. Soc. of Pa.
[9]. For the size of the Aughwick grant, see John Armstrong to David Kennedy, Aug. 1, 1793, Bureau of Land Records, Harrisburg.

ploying more than a thousand men, he began the construction of a string of forts, the first of which was erected on Lake Erie at Presque Isle. This fort soon became an important link in the line of communications which passed westward from Montreal through Niagara to Detroit and beyond and served primarily as the lake depot of a new line projected down the Ohio Valley to the Mississippi and New Orleans. The second link in this chain was Fort LeBoeuf, located on French Creek, Rivière aux Boeufs, and connected to Presque Isle by a rough road. Both forts were virtually completed by August, and plans were well matured for the building of a third at Venango, where French Creek flows into the Allegheny. A fourth outpost was planned for the Logstown area. Duquesne's forceful measures had their inevitable effect on the Indians, who were much impressed by his display of strength and purpose. The natives began to desert the English, notably the chastened Twightwees, most of whom went over to the French that summer.

The undeclared war so narrowed the areas in which English traders could safely operate that they were soon in full retreat. Early in 1753, Croghan and Callender were down the Ohio at the Lower Shawnee Town where Croghan and his men had traded for years. By February, however, Croghan abandoned the place because of the depredations by French-influenced Indians. The month before, a party of traders employed by Trent and Croghan had been captured by a marauding band of Ottawas "at a place called Kentucky," about 150 miles from the Lower Shawnee Town. Croghan and Trent lost five of their men and a valuable trading stock. Callender "had but bad success"; he was plundered of six hundred "bucks" worth of goods. From the Twightwee country came word that three of John Finley's hands had been killed "near the little Pick Town"; Finley himself was missing. Michael Teaffe's men were robbed near the lakes. Worst of all was the intelligence that three hundred Ottawas were daily expected at the Lower Shawnee Town. Croghan slipped off through the woods, convoying one hundred horseloads of skins to the comparative security of the Allegheny country. Trent was in Virginia when a letter from his partner reached him with news of the English withdrawal. "I intend leaving directly for Allegheny," Trent wrote

Governor Hamilton, "with provisions for our people that are coming through the woods and up the river."[10]

By early May, the traders had congregated at Croghan's place on Pine Creek. A score of miles below them on the Ohio the Logstown Indians, utterly demoralized by the times, sought refuge in drunkenness. The gloom of the white men, who saw their business ventures collapsing one by one, was little relieved by their escape from wandering bands of hostile Indians. The picture became ever blacker. On May 7, they learned that the French, who had been on the headwaters of the Allegheny since March, were preparing an invasion. The following day messengers from the Onondaga Council confirmed the news that the French would soon attack.

As there was no safety for Englishmen west of the Alleghenies, the traders retired toward the settlements, notifying the Pennsylvania and Virginia governments of the French advance. In response to the crisis, Pennsylvania voted £800 to preserve the friendship of the Indians, and the governor of Virginia gave arms and powder to Trent for distribution among the natives.[11]

Meanwhile, Croghan and his associates packed their peltry over the mountain wall to Raystown, a place noted for the public house of convivial Garrett Pendergrass. It was there that Edward Shippen found Croghan in May. Shippen was not only anxious to collect the money owed him but was under pressure from Peters to do something for Hockley. At Croghan's request, the merchant had obtained a letter of license signed by most of the principal creditors, but it did not cover debts which the trader owed to numerous persons in Cumberland and Lancaster counties; these "troublesome" country people had refused to sign the letter. Their debts, though many, were small in amount, and Croghan paid them off within the next two months. Although the letter of license permitted him considerable freedom, he did not dare visit Philadelphia.[12]

10. *Pennsylvania Journal*, May 3, 1753; Darlington, ed., *Gist's Journals*, 192.
11. *Executive Journals of the Council of Colonial Virginia* (Richmond, 1945), V, 412, 420, 422, 428-29; *Votes and Proceedings . . . of the Province of Pa.*, IV, 246-47.
12. Peters to Penn, May 3, 1753, Penn Mss., Official Correspondence, VI, 47, Hist. Soc. of Pa.; Shippen to Joseph Shippen, Aug. 28, 1753, Amer. Philos. Soc.

Shippen and Croghan discussed their business affairs in detail, with Croghan promising to pay all his debts. Impressed with Croghan's earnestness, Shippen wrote Peters that the trader would certainly make good "if there be faith in man." Shippen received from Croghan fifteen horseloads of skins on the account of Croghan, Callender, and Teaffe. He had taken pains to keep on Croghan's good side and obtaining these skins gave him much satisfaction, for, to the best of his knowledge, he was the only one of the trader's major creditors who had received any payment so far—the Philadelphia merchants had not yet seen so much as a groat.[13]

At Raystown, Croghan learned that Trent had been commissioned by Governor Dinwiddie of Virginia to transport the colony's Indian present to the Ohio. Since Trent was in need of pack horses for this purpose, Croghan loaned him forty. During the time that Croghan was at Wills Creek delivering the animals, a despairing message was received from the Ohio Indians, begging Governor Dinwiddie to send "a number of your people" to protect them from the French. Croghan, who had seen Dinwiddie's instructions to Trent to assure the Indians that troops would be sent whenever necessary, now believed that Dinwiddie would be forced to build the long-debated fort. So significant did the Indians' message seem that he took a copy of it and rode to Shippensburg, where he gave it to Edward Shippen for transmittal to Governor Hamilton.[14]

Trent, meanwhile, returned to Logstown, where in August the Indians accepted Virginia's war supplies and agreed to oppose the French. They showed their loyalty by appointing the Half King to warn the invaders to move off. Despite the brave words he heard at the treaty, Trent could see that French influence was spreading. Even while they talked, the enemy descended on Venango, where they captured several English traders.[15]

[13]. Peters to Penn, July 5, 1753, Penn Mss., Official Correspondence, VI, 73, Hist. Soc. of Pa.

[14]. *Col. Rec. of Pa.*, V, 635; Ohio Co. Papers, I, 1, and Ohio Co. folder, Cadwalader Coll., Hist. Soc. of Pa.; Shippen to Hamilton, July 1, 1753, Amer. Philos. Soc.

[15]. *Col. Rec. of Pa.*, V, 659; Mary Carson Darlington, *History of Colonel Henry Bouquet* (n.p., 1920), 17-40.

At Winchester, in September, 1753, the Virginians, having enticed a group of prominent Ohio Indians to attend, conducted another futile conference. Croghan rode down from Aughwick and heard Scarouady, who spoke for the Indians, reverse their previous request for a fort. At a later session, however, doubtless after some private meetings with Croghan, Scarouady consented to the erection of a stronghouse to store Virginia's present of ammunition. From Winchester, the Indians, one hundred strong, journeyed to Carlisle to meet their Brother Onas, Pennsylvania. The desirability of such a conference had been urged on them by Croghan and Montour, but despite Croghan's persuasion they refused to go to Philadelphia or even to Lancaster, as they were in a hurry to return home. Carlisle, a new, crude village of some sixty-five log cabins, was as far as they would come.[16]

Croghan rode express from Winchester to Shippensburg, where he arrived September 18 with a letter for Governor Hamilton from William Fairfax, who had conducted the Virginia conference. Fairfax announced that the Indians were on their way to Carlisle and that "for particulars I take leave to refer to Mr. Croghan, who has kindly assisted me." When Hamilton received this message from Shippen, he immediately appointed three commissioners, Isaac Norris and Benjamin Franklin of the Assembly and Richard Peters, to meet the Indians and to give them the entire present of £800, which the Assembly had voted in May.[17]

Arriving at Carlisle, the commissioners called on Croghan to find out what the Indians wanted. The trader described the Winchester meeting and, supported by Weiser, stressed so strongly the importance of pleasing the natives that the commissioners decided to purchase additional goods to add to the present of ammunition and arms at that moment en route from Philadelphia.[18]

Before its arrival—and Scarouady refused to open the conference until the goods were in hand—Croghan's partners, Callen-

---

16. Shippen to Hamilton, Sept. 9, 1753, Amer. Philos. Soc.; Lois Mulkearn, ed., *George Mercer Papers Relating to the Ohio Company of Virginia* (Pittsburgh, 1954), 80; Peters to Penn, July 5, 1753, Penn Mss., Official Correspondence, VI, 73, Hist. Soc. of Pa.

17. Fairfax to Hamilton, Sept. 14, 1753, *Col. Rec. of Pa.*, V, 657; Shippen to Hamilton, Sept. 18, 1753, Burd-Shippen Papers, I, 7, Amer. Philos. Soc.

18. *Col. Rec. of Pa.*, V, 665, 668-69.

der and Teaffe, sent in word that the Half King's mission to the French had failed. Not only had the French refused to pay any attention to his demands that they depart, they had insulted him, treating him with contempt and calling him an old woman. On his return to Logstown in late September, the Half King, shedding tears of mortification, urged the few remaining English traders not to venture their persons or goods west of the Ohio, as the French would certainly seize them.[19]

The Carlisle conference began on October 1 with the customary protocol of condolences. Scarouady, speaking for the representatives of the tribes present, the Six Nations, Shingas and his Delawares, the Shawnees, Twightwees, and Wyandots, repeated much that he had recently told the Virginians, advising against English settlements beyond the Alleghenies and urging Indian trade reforms. Indicative of Croghan's influence was Scarouady's announcement that he desired to keep up a correspondence with his Brother Onas and that Croghan would represent the Indians in carrying on their side of the exchange. Should any presents be sent them, Scarouady continued, Croghan's house at Aughwick would be the proper place to deliver them.[20]

Since the commissioners' power was limited to disposing of the Indian present, they could do no more than make professions of friendship, a performance which did not impress unsteady chiefs like Shingas. Because of the threatening situation on the Ohio, they decided against sending out the entire gift with the natives. Instead, they entrusted the bulk of it to Croghan to hold at his place until he received further orders from the governor. The conference then terminated, and, as the Indians hurried homeward, Croghan returned to Aughwick entrusted by both Indians and whites with helping to keep alive an ancient tradition of friendship.

The Carlisle treaty did much to reinstate Croghan in the good graces of the government. Once more he had become the link between the western Indians and Pennsylvania. His most notable accomplishment was winning Isaac Norris' confidence. Norris, speaker of the Assembly and powerful Quaker politician, had not been kindly disposed toward Croghan, but at Carlisle he succumbed to the magnetism of the man's personality. According to Peters,

19. *Ibid.*, 669.   20. *Ibid.*, 675.

"Isaac Norris has a mighty opinion of him, and will heartily recommend him to the Assembly to be employed for the government in Indian affairs." Peters himself had a good word for the trader, praising his helpfulness at the meeting and noting that he "appeard to have the absolute confidence and management of the Indians."[21]

While it is certain that the government of Pennsylvania had not wanted to depend upon Croghan again, it found itself once more obliged to accept him as its intermediary with the western Indians. The lack of any other suitable man for the job, the Indians' announcement that Croghan was their appointee to carry on their correspondence, and the strategic location of the trader's home at Aughwick all combined to re-establish him in the unofficial position he had held before his debacle in 1751. Croghan's star was no longer in eclipse; although widely distrusted, he had regained a position of vital importance at a momentous time.

Not long after Croghan returned to Aughwick, he was stricken with an illness which nearly proved fatal. Dr. Robert Thompson of Lancaster came to attend him and held out little hope for his recovery. Shippen, who had been so carefully coaxing the trader to make payments on his debts, was stunned at this news. Hurrying to Aughwick, he found that Croghan "could not speak to me or he would not do it." Home again in Lancaster by mid-November, Shippen suggested to James Burd, his son-in-law, "If you should goe to Mr. Croghan and find him well disposed to me & Mr. Lawrence, maybe he will give us a bill of sale for his horses, skins and debts." Burd, visiting Aughwick about November 20, found Croghan recovering. "Let him take care of relapses," nervously warned Shippen; "I am very uneasy when I consider how I stand circumstanced to him." The trader had thirteen horseloads of skins at Aughwick which Shippen hoped to obtain. Despite Croghan's repeated promises throughout the year to reduce his debts, the merchant had received nothing more than the fifteen horseloads in May, but he continued to keep up hope, "for to quarrel with him would ruin all."[22]

21. Peters to Penn, Nov. 6, 1753, and Dec. 7, 1753, Penn Mss., Official Correspondence, VI, 113, 145, Hist. Soc. of Pa.
22. Peters to Penn, Nov. 26, 1753, Penn Mss., Official Correspondence, VI, 133, and Dr. Thompson's receipted bill for £10 dated Apr. 9, 1754, Cadwalader

At the time Croghan fell ill, events in the Ohio drama were reaching a climax. Although Virginia had obtained permission to build a fort, Dinwiddie continued to await instructions from England. At long last, in October, 1753, the Virginia governor received authorization to erect forts on the Ohio and orders to attack the French if they invaded British territory and refused to retire. He was not, however, to carry the war beyond "the undoubted limits of His Majestie's dominions." On October 27, Dinwiddie announced to his Council that George Washington had volunteered to find out from the French forces by what authority they encroached on the Ohio.[23]

Like the Virginia governor, Hamilton also wanted to learn whether the French were trespassing on British territory. The arrival of two Shawnee braves from South Carolina provided him a favorable opportunity to investigate the western situation. The Shawnees, suspected of committing crimes on the frontier, had been captured in the southern province months before and confined in the Charleston jail. Their arrest was a flaming grievance to the Ohio natives.

By returning the Shawnees to the Ohio, Hamilton could kill two birds with one stone, because he would be able to heal an open sore in Indian relations and at the same time have an excuse to send a confidential agent with them as their escort. For this intelligence mission, Hamilton selected John Patten, a former Indian trader who had a reputation as a map maker. Included in Patten's instructions was the order that he "take a particular account of the road from Carlisle, so as to know how far westward Shanoppin is from thence." Shannopin's Town was near the forks of the Ohio, in a key location for control of the western country, and soon to be the approximate site of Fort Duquesne and still later of Pittsburgh. Patten was ordered to engage Montour as interpreter for the governor's message concerning the return of the two prisoners and to consult with Croghan about how the message should be delivered.[24] Early in December, Patten and

---

Coll., Hist. Soc. of Pa.; Shippen to [William Allen], Aug. 16, 1755, and to the Burds, Nov. 17, Nov. 22, Nov. 26, and Dec. 31, 1753, Shippen Letter Book, Amer. Philos. Soc.

23. *Executive Journals of . . . Colonial Virginia*, V, 442-44.
24. *Col. Rec. of Pa.*, V, 699-700, 707-8.

his charges left Philadelphia, arriving at Aughwick after Croghan's departure for the Ohio country. Anxious to arm the Indians with Pennsylvania's warlike present, the Irishman had headed for the disputed juncture of the Monongahela and Allegheny rivers shortly after Christmas.[25]

Croghan's return to the Allegheny was undoubtedly spurred on by the activities of William Trent. Trent, appointed factor of the Ohio Company in 1752, had become increasingly involved in Virginia affairs. In July, 1753, he and two others were designated by the company's stockholders to build their fort on the Ohio River and to construct a wagon road from the company's store at Wills Creek to the mouth of Redstone Creek on the Monongahela, about thirty-seven miles above its juncture with the Allegheny River. At Redstone Creek, Trent was to build a fortified storehouse for supplies which could be carried later by water to the mouth of the Monongahela, where Fort St. George was to be erected.[26]

When Croghan arrived on January 12, 1754, at John Fraser's trading post on Turtle Creek about eight miles from the Ohio River, Trent may already have been busy constructing the Redstone depot, although Croghan did not say so in his official report. Instead, the trader dwelt in detail on information Fraser gave him about Washington's mission. On his return to Virginia, Washington had stopped at Fraser's and confirmed what the traders had surmised: the French were determined to drive the English out of the Ohio country that spring.

Croghan rested at Fraser's overnight, completing his journey the next day to Shannopin's Town where he met Montour and Patten. Together the three men and their respective parties went on to Logstown to find the Indians in an ugly frame of mind and drunk. Croghan's mission was complicated by the arrival of a French reconnaissance party and by the natives themselves, who remained drunk for ten days. At length, the Pennsylvanians were able to hold their conference, release the Shawnee

25. *Ibid.*, 703; Shippen to the Burds, Dec. 31, 1753, Shippen Letter Book, Amer. Philos. Soc.
26. Another source gives the fort's name as Fort Prince George, *Collections of the Virginia Historical Society*, New Series, 3 (Richmond, 1883), 343; Mulkearn, ed., *Mercer Papers*, 68. Thomas Cresap to [   ], May 20, 1767, Hist. Soc. of Pa.

prisoners, and present the goods entrusted to Croghan by the commissioners at Carlisle. The Half King and the other chiefs of the region, among them Scarouady, Shingas, and Delaware George, begged the English to build and man a trading house immediately, "as our enemies are just at hand, and we do not know what day they may come upon us." The natives promised to fight the French as soon as the English came to their assistance.[27]

Too few and too late, some English were on their way—Virginia had taken action. After Washington's return to Williamsburg in January, 1754, Dinwiddie took emergency steps. To furnish a guard for the fort builders, Trent was commissioned a captain and authorized to raise one hundred men "to keep possession of His Majesty's lands on the Ohio." As reinforcements for this body, which was to be recruited from the Indian traders, a company of one hundred militia was called up under George Washington.[28]

When Trent received his commission and orders from Dinwiddie, he enlisted about thirty men, constructed rafts, and floated supplies down the river to the fort site. Croghan was preparing to leave Logstown early in February when Trent detained him. To Governor Hamilton, Croghan wrote:

I would aweated on your honour in company with Mr. Mountour and Mr. Patten, butt that Mr. Trent is just come outt with the Verginia goods, and has brought a quantity of toules and workmen to begin a fort, and as he can't talk the Indian languidge, I am obligd to stay and assist him in delivering them goods, which is Mr. Montour's advice, butt I hope to be att my house at Aughick by the 20th.

With the assistance of Gist, hurried plans were made before Trent left to recruit more men and supplies and to send a hasty appeal to Washington for help. Trent had learned from Croghan that four hundred French were on their way.[29]

Although Croghan was unable to return to Philadelphia

27. *Col. Rec. of Pa.*, V, 731-35; *Pa. Archives*, II, 118.
28. *Executive Journals of . . . Colonial Virginia*, V, 460; *Coll. of the Va. Hist. Soc.*, New Series, 3 (1883), 55-57.
29. Croghan to Hamilton, Feb. 3, 1754, *Pa. Archives*, II, 119; Penn Mss., Indian Affairs, I, 51, and Ohio Co. Papers, I, 10, Hist. Soc. of Pa.; *Maryland Gazette*, Mar. 14, 1754.

with Montour and Patten, he gave them the journal of his mission, as well as letters to the governor and secretary. Noting that the Indians were eager to defend themselves, he once more stressed the importance of a fort to protect the country and the Indian traders. At such a fort, the traders could find security, and it would be possible to regulate their trade practices. The Indians, wrote Croghan, looked to Pennsylvania in the French crisis: "I ashure you they expect a treading house & to be suply'd with necessarys to cary on the war." Hamilton accepted Croghan's opinions, but the Assembly, refusing to be swayed, dextrously sidestepped the issue.[30]

Despite much discouragement, Croghan continued to do his best as an Indian agent. Intelligence of threats made by La Force, a brilliant French officer, had to be sent on to Philadelphia. According to a contemporary account, "When La Force had made his speech to the Indians, they sent a string of wampum to Mr. Croghan, to desire him to hurry the English to come, for that they expected soon to be attacked, and pressed him hard to come and join them, for they wanted necessaries and assistance, and then would strike." Not only did the natives need powder, lead, and arms to repel the invader, they needed food. So disrupted was their life that they were no longer able to care for themselves. Croghan purchased large quantities of country produce, hopefully anticipating that the government would support the Indians in their hour of trial.[31]

The trader feared that his colony's backwardness when contrasted with Virginia's aggressiveness would lead the natives to believe that the only reason for Virginia's solicitude was her aim to settle the Ohio country, and, consequently, that there was little to choose between the French and the southerners. Andrew Montour shared Croghan's views and warned that unless Pennsylvania or New York furnished military aid the Indians would not oppose the enemy: "They don't look upon their late

30. Croghan to Peters, Feb. 3, 1754, *Pa. Archives*, II, 118.
31. Croghan to Hamilton, Mar. 23, 1754, *Col. Rec. of Pa.*, VI, 21; *French Policy Defeated, Being, An Account of all the hostile Proceedings of the French Against the Inhabitants of the British Colonies in North America, For the last Seven Years* (London, 1755), 60; bills for Croghan's provisions dated Mar. 21 and Apr. 15, 1754, are in Cadwalader Coll., Hist. Soc. of Pa.

Collapse of the Indian Trade

friendship with Virginia as sufficient to engage them in a war with the French."[32]

Once again, Croghan hammered at the traditional policy of deferring to the Onondaga Council: "The government may have what opinion they will of the Ohio Indians, and think they are oblig'd to do what the Onondago Counsel will bid them, butt I ashure your honour they will actt for themselves att this time without consulting the Onondago Councel."[33]

The lack of cooperation among the colonies made the French seizure of the forks of the Ohio a simple matter. While Croghan's half-brother Ensign Edward Ward labored on the Virginia fort with only forty men and in the absence of his captain, who was at Wills Creek to get provisions, the enemy arrived on April 17. Ward had no recourse but to capitulate to an army which he estimated to total a thousand men. His capitulation marked the collapse of the English trans-Appalachian movement and brought on the second phase of the rivalry for the Ohio basin, opposition of force by force.

News of the French seizure sounded through the frontier country like a thunderclap, but in Philadelphia its echo evoked no action. Croghan and Montour impatiently awaited instructions in the new crisis. None came. Pennsylvania's government was deadlocked between the governor's wish to meet the situation realistically and the Assembly's deadening passivity. Units of the newly formed Virginia regiment, soon to be reinforced by several companies from other colonies, represented the only organized opposition to the invaders. By May 24, this forlorn hope, under the command of Washington, had advanced to the Great Meadows, west of the main ridge of the Alleghenies, where a fortification—Fort Necessity—was thrown up.

Although Croghan had received little, if any, official encouragement, he prepared to assist the Indians and, in the first part of May, sent a supply of provisions to the Ohio worth about £200. This shipment was to await his coming with an additional supply worth £300. If he did not hear from Hamilton, he planned to

---

32. Croghan to Peters, Mar. 23, 1754, *Pa. Archives*, II, 132; Montour to Peters, May 16, 1754, *Col. Rec. of Pa.*, VI, 46.
33. Croghan to Hamilton, May 14, 1754, *Pa. Archives*, II, 144.

sell his bacon and flour to Washington, instead of distributing it among the Indians as a Pennsylvania gift.

A few days before his departure, Croghan received a message from the Half King bidding him to come immediately. It was this message, coupled with word of the Indians' desperate plight, which hurried Croghan westward. Before leaving, he wrote Governor Hamilton, "I asshure your honour Andrew Montour & my self has a very different part to act att present, from the several mesidges we have delivered the Indians to ashure them of the asistance of the English governments."[34]

Little is known of Croghan's visit to the Indians in the latter part of May, 1754. It is probable that, mounted on his new brown gelding, Woolabarger, a natural pacer, he visited the Half King near the place where the French were industriously erecting Fort Duquesne. While he was still in the wilderness, his express rider apparently returned to him with instructions from Governor Hamilton to purchase flour for the natives. Croghan went to Winchester for this purpose. Governor Dinwiddie, who met him there on May 29, was disappointed to learn that his purchases were not intended for the Virginia forces, yet the presence of Croghan and Montour was opportune. If Croghan was able to buy and transport flour for Pennsylvania, could he not do the same for Virginia and supply Washington's expedition?[35]

When Dinwiddie put this question to the trader, Croghan bluffly assured him that ten thousand pounds of flour would be immediately delivered to Washington. Croghan entered into an agreement with Major John Carlyle, the Virginia commissary, to deliver fifty thousand pounds of flour at his own risk to Washington's camp within fifteen days from the date of the contract, May 31, and blandly informed Dinwiddie that he already had forty thousand pounds at hand. The trader also agreed to furnish two hundred horses for the supply needs of the expedition.[36]

To buy the flour he had promised, Croghan set his half-brother

---

34. *Ibid.*

35. Croghan bought the horse on Mar. 2, 1754, for £20, Calwalader Coll., Hist. Soc. of Pa.; *Coll. of the Va. Hist. Soc.*, New Series, 3 (1883), 215.

36. *Coll. of the Va. Hist. Soc.*, New Series, 3 (1883), 189, 321; Stanislaus Murray Hamilton, ed., *Letters to Washington and Accompanying Papers* (Boston, 1898), I, 5, 8.

Edward Ward to work. Judging from results, Ward's efforts were a total failure. By June 17, Major Carlyle was writing Washington about Croghan: "As he is with you pray oblige him to perform his agreement, I understand he's not a man of truth, & therefor not to be depended on, the Governour see into him, before he left Winchester, & was sorry he put him into any trust but as he's to act by your directions, doubt not but you'l take care of him." But Washington had no success with Croghan. Small wonder that Dinwiddie exclaimed, when he learned that Washington had been six days in want of flour, "Croghan has deceived us."[37]

The arrival of Edward Shippen at this moment could scarcely have been welcome to the trader. According to the merchant, who tried to raise some money from Trent and Croghan, he found to his astonishment that they were "intirely destitute of either skins or goods. They complain that the French had blockt up the Indian trade & therefore that they could not venture to go to Allegheny to collect in their outstanding debts which were very large. They informed me that their horses were employed in the service of Major Washington carrying provisions & ammunition to the camp at Fort Necessity and Great Meadows."[38]

Dinwiddie had not relied on Croghan for supply services alone. On June 1, he assigned Croghan as interpreter to assist Washington in delivering Indian presents and to advise the Virginian in Indian matters. Croghan, wrote Dinwiddie, was "a gent. well acquainted with Ind'n affairs." The governor requested Washington to "shew him a proper regard." Impressed, Washington replied that he would be "particularly careful in consulting Mr. Croghan and Mr. Montour, by whom I shall be advised in all Indian affairs agreeably to your directions."[39]

Croghan was with Washington at Fort Necessity on June 12 when Washington learned that reinforcements had probably ar-

37. Hamilton, ed., *Letters to Washington,* I, 5, 26; *Coll. of Va. Hist. Soc.,* New Series, 3 (1883), 220; Washington to Dinwiddie, June 12, 1754, John C. Fitzpatrick, ed., *The Writings of George Washington* (Washington, 1931), I, 76-77.
38. Shippen to Penn, Nov. 25, 1754, Balch Papers, Shippen, I, 37, Hist. Soc. of Pa.
39. Dinwiddie to Washington, June 1, 1754, *Coll. of the Va. Hist. Soc.,* New Series, 3 (1883), 186-87, 229; Washington to Dinwiddie, June 10, 1754, Fitzpatrick, ed., *Writings of Washington,* I, 75.

rived at the new French fort and that the Delawares and Shawnees had taken up the hatchet against the English. Despite this news and the virtual failure of his supply system, Washington resolved to push on to Redstone Creek. Co-operating with this decision, the Half King sent messengers to Indian towns to summon their warriors to meet the English on the Monongahela. Croghan and Montour also sent runners to invite the Delawares and the Shawnees to be present.[40]

On June 18, when Washington's small force had arrived at or near Christopher Gist's settlement, barely a day's march from the Redstone, his advance was halted by Ohio Indians who had come from Logstown, evidently acting as spies for the French. In the three-day conference which ensued, Croghan had his part to play. Washington warned the forty Indians present to choose between the French and English and invited them to send their families to the safety of the settlements while their warriors fought at his side. The meeting proved a severe disappointment. At its conclusion, the Shawnees simply disappeared into the forest, evidently returning to the French, while the Delawares under the leadership of Shingas also refused to join Washington, so that they too remained under the shadow of the invaders. Worse yet, immediately after the conference, the Half King and all the remaining Indians, despite every entreaty, returned to the Great Meadows, thereby depriving Washington of their services when most wanted.[41]

To bring them back, the Virginian sent Croghan to remind them of their promises to fight at his side. The trader located the Half King and his party near Wills Creek, where he found that they had received a message enjoining them not to participate in an offensive war on either side but to remain neutral, which they intended to do. Nevertheless, Croghan persuaded three warriors to return.[42]

Despite every kind of hardship and disappointment, Washington was resolved to move forward to the mouth of Redstone Creek, there to build and hold a fort until sufficiently reinforced to advance to the Ohio. News received from Scarouady soon altered

40. Fitzpatrick, ed., *Writings of Washington*, I, 76-77; John C. Fitzpatrick, ed., *The Diaries of George Washington* (Boston, 1925), I, 92-93.
41. Fitzpatrick, ed., *Diaries of Washington*, I, 93-100.
42. Joseph Turner to Peters, July 18, 1754, Hist. Soc. of Pa.

this bold plan, for the Virginian learned that the French were preparing to attack him in overwhelming strength. Instead of advancing, Washington ordered a retreat.[43]

At the time of this withdrawal, Trent and Croghan had a pack train and a supply of trading goods at Fort Necessity. When they heard of the retreat of the Virginia forces, they tried to remove their property, but their horses were pressed to bring the cannon and stores from Gist's to the Great Meadows and were not returned in time. On July 1, Washington regrouped his forces at his improvised fort in the meadows. His men by now were so few in numbers and so feeble from overwork and scanty rations that the friendly Indians again deserted. Three days later, the French arrived and, after an unequal battle, forced the capitulation of the English. According to Edward Ward, Trent and Croghan supplied Washington with the powder and lead without which his forces "wou'd not have had ammunition to make the least defense that day the French defeated them."[44]

In the recriminations which followed the unfortunate campaign, no one was more criticized than Croghan, that "vile" man, as the authorities described him. Washington's strictures sum up the official attitude. Of the total failure of Indian support, he wrote that "notwithstanding the expresses, that the Indians sent to one another, and all the pains that Montour and Croghan (who, by vainly boasting of their interest with the Indians, involved the country in great calamity, by causing dependance to be placed where there was none), could take, [they] never could induce above 30 fighting men to join us, and not more than one half of those serviceable upon any occasion." As for supplies, the disappointed officer continued, "The promises of those traders, who offer to contract for large quantities of flour, are not to be depended upon; a most flagrant instance of which we experienced in Croghan, who was under obligation to Maj. Carlyle for the delivery of this article in a certain time, and who was an eyewitness to our wants; yet had the assurance, during our sufferings, to tantalize us, and boast of the quantity he could furnish, as he did of the number of horses he cou'd command; notwithstanding, we were equally disappointed of

43. Freeman, *George Washington*, I, 395-99.
44. *Ibid.*, 401-5; Ohio Co. Papers, I, 7, 10, Hist. Soc. of Pa.

these also; for out of 200 head he had contracted for, we never had above 25 employed in bringing the flour that was engaged for the camp and even this, small as the quantity was, did not arrive within a month of the time it was to have been delivered."[45]

The role which Croghan played in the Fort Necessity drama thus appears to have been far from distinguished. The trader's customary over-optimism, his penchant for taking on more than he could handle and for making promises without a proper evaluation of logistics, had trapped him into this situation. Dinwiddie would have done well to have assigned Croghan responsibilities either in supply or in Indian management, but not in both. Ordered to Washington's camp, Croghan had to entrust the procurement of flour to his half-brother and so could not give it his personal attention. The French seizure of many of his pack animals may partially explain his inability to meet the horse contract. As always, Croghan's self-interest stood in the way of the ideal performance of his job, for, in partnership with Trent, he never lost sight of trading opportunities, even in the darkest days.[46]

His lack of success in influencing the natives is more understandable. The Indians, a calculating, logical people, saw no future in assisting an undermanned, tragically ill-supplied expedition. Washington had few presents to give them, which was unfortunate, and the natives resented his vigorous efforts to get the most out of them. Furthermore, they were not comfortable in their new-found Virginia friendship. If Croghan failed to supply Washington with Indian allies, Dinwiddie was equally unsuccessful in persuading the southern Indians to enlist in the campaign. Despite his ineffectiveness, there is no reason to believe that Croghan had not tried to do as much or more than any other man to save the situation. For years he had urged that the Ohio country be fortified, constantly pointing out the all-important effect this would have on the natives. When, at last, a weak, hurried effort was made, he could scarcely be blamed for his inability to persuade the Indians to support a lost cause.

The French seizure of the forks of the Ohio and their defeat

---

45. Washington to William Fairfax, Aug. 11, 1754, Fitzpatrick, ed., *Writings of Washington*, I, 92, 95.

46. Croghan stated that the French seized ninety-one of his horses. Ohio Co. Papers, I, 8, Hist. Soc. of Pa.

of Washington ended the Pennsylvania Indian trade. In common with most of the other traders, Croghan's financial losses were heavy, in fact, the largest losses suffered by a single trader. He later estimated them at £16,000 and also calculated that fifty-two of his employees had been captured or killed by the French.[47]

Croghan, whose hold on his ambitious trading interests had been badly shaken in 1751, thus saw in 1754 the loss of all that he had labored to build up. Although he may have been their ideal, Croghan was not the exact prototype of the Pennsylvania trader, who was considered the lowest and most depraved of men. A merchant who knew the traders well characterized them as "a sett of the most debased banditti that ever infested a government, the greater part goal gleanings and the refuse of Ireland."[48] The major complaint against them was their evil influence among the natives, whom they cheated at will after making them drunk. This practice brought chaos to the Indian trade and ruin to honest traders. That Croghan followed honest trading methods did not necessarily connote an innate streak of nobility in his character. If for no other reasons, he preferred legitimate trading because it would not have paid him to indulge in sharp practices. Sly tricks were practical for men operating in a small way; for Croghan, whose business was relatively vast and who was seeking to build a permanent organization, they would have been ruinous. Because of his fair dealings, he was popular with the Indians, and it was doubtless this sound approach which enabled him to pyramid his activities into the largest trading venture in the West.

Illicit procedures by competing traders not only hurt Croghan's business but endangered English relations with the Indians. Croghan's letters to Governor Hamilton repeatedly emphasized the necessity of stringent control of the trade and the importance of banning rum from the Indian country. At the Carlisle conference of 1753, he won over Isaac Norris and Benjamin Franklin to the desirability of such reforms, but their interest was awakened too late to be effective. All in all, it is reasonable to conclude that

47. Croghan to Amherst, Sept. 26, 1763, Amherst Papers, W. O. 34/39, fol. 413, Public Record Office, London.
48. Baynton and Wharton to Richard Neave, July 1, 1760, Baynton and Wharton Letter Book (1758-60), 403, Hist. Soc. of Pa.

Croghan represented a positive, worthwhile influence in the Indian trade.

The capture of Fort Necessity concluded his services with Virginia. His efforts to recoup his fortunes through the southern colony had been unsuccessful; he owed money to the Ohio Company with which he had recently been trading, he had lost a supply of goods to the French at Fort Necessity, and he was deeper in debt than ever. For his most recent operations in partnership with Trent, he had little more to show than £127 owed by Washington.[49] True, he had certain charges he intended to make against the Virginia government, but they would be disallowed when presented.

From the collapse of English power in the western country, Croghan rode home to Aughwick. A fugitive from his Pennsylvania creditors, he fully realized that he must brave the danger of hostile Indians in the unprotected backcountry or risk arrest. Croghan must have wondered what the future held for him. As the welcome sight of his Aughwick plantation with its broad acres of young corn met his eyes, a way of life receded, never to be fully reclaimed. His days as an active Indian trader were over.

49. Ohio Co. folder, Cadwalader Coll., Hist. Soc. of Pa.

4

Aughwick Indian Agency

THE SUMMER EVENTS OF 1754 were heatedly discussed in Philadelphia's new coffee house. While British pride was affronted by French victory at the Great Meadows, deep-rooted feelings of suspicion lingered over Virginia's responsibility for the debacle. Many believed that the ambitious schemes of the Ohio Company had brought on the invasion. Shortly before Washington's defeat, Isaac Norris commented on the prevailing opinion that "the Ohio Company are endeavouring to engage all the colonies under the sanction of the King's commands to defend their lands upon that river." Torn by jealousies, the colonies found it difficult to unite on common measures of defense.[1]

Meanwhile, petitions poured in on Governor James Hamilton from the backcountry where the frontiersmen quaked in fear of an Indian war. From many scattered settlements came their prayers for arms and ammunition. Once again, the governor turned to the Assembly for money for defense purposes, and, once again, that body refused to grant succor except on terms which violated Hamilton's instructions against taxing the Penn estates. With mounting impatience, the frustrated governor awaited his successor in office.

Penn had been unsympathetic to Hamilton's pleas to resign. With the French menacing the Ohio country, the proprietor wrote of Hamilton's resignation, "It will look like throwing up a commission in the day of battle." But Hamilton was adamant, and, in

---

1. Isaac Norris to Robert Charles, Apr. 19, 1754, Norris Letter Book (1719-56), 49-50, Hist. Soc. of Pa.

1754, Penn appointed Robert Hunter Morris, former chief justice of New Jersey, to succeed him.[2]

The appointment of a colonial from a neighboring province added a new topic to the coffee house discussions, in which the proprietor's purchase in July of Indian lands west of the Susquehanna was the latest gossip. The news that Morris, an unbending supporter of the royal prerogative, was soon to become governor was most unfavorably received. Angry Philadelphians bitterly commented that Penn might just as well have sent the Devil, for Morris was a tyrant: "He shall sitt in hott water if he shews his Jersey airs."[3]

Echoes of provincial politics must have had an unreal sound to those on the fringe of the English settlements. The French were so close, and their menace was so real. From "Powtomack," Virginia, on July 7, 1754, William Trent wrote, "You may expect to hear of nothing but continual murders committed by the French Indians, who may be immediately expected down upon the back inhabitants. The French sent me word they intended to come & see me soon. They make no doubt of being masters of all America."[4]

To the exasperation of the Virginia authorities, the friendly Indians refused to accept that colony's protection. Instead, the Half King and Scarouady, with a group of Mingoes from the Ohio, settled at Aughwick, where, according to Andrew Montour, "As there is a large body of them and no ground there to hunt to support their families, they expect their brothers the Pennsylvanians will provide for their families as their men will be engaged in the war."[5]

The Virginians blamed Croghan for enticing these Indians from their control. Croghan, however, had not urged the Indians to come to him: "The government of Virginia imagines if itt was nott for me, that all the Indians wold a staid there, in which they really rong me." The presence of the Indians at his home was a

---

2. Penn to Peters, Jan. 9 and Feb. 1, 1754, Penn Letter Book, III, 193, 296, Hist. Soc. of Pa.

3. Hockley to Penn, Aug. 4, 1754, Correspondence of the Penn Family, 1732-67, 73, Hist. Soc. of Pa.

4. Trent to Burd, July 7, 1754, Shippen Papers, XV, 119, Hist. Soc. of Pa.

5. Montour to Hamilton, July 21, 1754, Col. Rec. of Pa., VI, 130.

serious nuisance: "Had I been at Wills' Creek when they sat off I should have endeavored to have made them stay in Virginia at the camp before I would have drawn such an expense on the province or such a trouble on myself."[6] So high was Croghan's prestige with the friendly western natives that they would take no important step without his advice. In August, a Philadelphia newspaper reported: "There are ten Indians come to Aughwick, from the Lower Shawney Town; what they are after none can tell, nor will they impart their errand to any, not even to their Half-King, untill they see George Croaghan who is now in Virginia."[7]

Croghan, who may have visited Wills Creek to see William Trent or the commander of the Virginia troops, Colonel James Innes, soon returned to Aughwick and found awaiting him not only the deputation of the Shawnees, headed by their young king, but his old friend Delaware George and several other Delawares just in from Fort Duquesne. Delaware George brought a letter addressed to the commanding officer in Virginia from Captain Robert Stobo, one of Washington's officers taken hostage at the Great Meadows. Indiscreetly, Croghan opened the letter—"the Indians would have the letter broke open"—and made a copy of it for the governor of Pennsylvania. "Haste to strike," wrote Stobo, who pointed out the weak condition of the fort. Croghan was later severely censured for opening the document, since his action endangered the secret that Stobo had sent intelligence and, thereby, imperiled the brave hostage's life. Governor Sharpe of Maryland was so aroused that he suspected treason. Sharpe wrote to the governor of Pennsylvania urging him, unless he was satisfied as to the falsity of prevailing rumors about Croghan, "to have him a little observed, it has been asserted that he is a Roman Catholick, & that one Campbell, a person of the same persuasion [Campbell was suspected of having visited the French fort], generally resides at his house."[8]

6. Croghan to Hamilton, Aug. 30, 1754, *ibid.*, 160-61; Croghan to Peters, Dec. 2, 1754, *Pa. Archives*, II, 212.
7. *Pennsylvania Journal*, Aug. 22, 1754.
8. Croghan to Hamilton, Aug. 16, 1754, and Stobo's letter of July 29, 1754, *Col. Rec. of Pa.*, VI, 140-43; Horatio Sharpe to Robert Hunter Morris, Dec. 27, 1754, *Archives of Maryland* (Baltimore, 1888), VI, 153.

In several speeches to the Half King and Croghan, the Shawnees and the Delawares confirmed Stobo's report that the French could be defeated easily, for only a small part of their army remained at Fort Duquesne. The Indians, uneasy at the backwardness of the English to take advantage of their opportunity, had come to Aughwick to learn if any preparations were afoot to attack the fort that fall. "They all seem to think if the English does nothing this fall, when they have it in their power, that the Ohio lands will belong to the French."

The Half King, seemingly realizing that the fealty of the western Indians had now reached its ultimate test, sent messengers summoning Shingas, the Delaware king, as well as the rest of the Delawares and Shawnees, and requested Croghan to ask Governor Hamilton (Robert Hunter Morris had not yet arrived) to meet them at Aughwick or to send a representative. When forwarding the Indian messages, Croghan wrote, "It is my opinion this meeting will determine the Ohio Indians either in favour of the English or French." Croghan also sent Hamilton an account of the expense he had been put to since the Indians had quartered themselves on his plantation: "I hope the Assembly will allow this account, that I may be able to pay the people whom I had the flour and meat from, or else I shall be obliged to discharge the Indians and send them home for I am not able to bear the expense myself."[9]

Hamilton appointed Weiser to meet with the Indians at Aughwick and gave him £300 to provide for their support. "A prudent behaviour," the governor wrote Croghan, "in the management of such an important concern as is now committed to your care will recommend you to the favour of the Government." But Croghan found his position very awkward. Realizing full well the government's reluctance to trust him with money, he hoped that an agent would be appointed to purchase food for the natives, "by which means the government might be full satisfied of the prices of provisions and the quantity that would serve."[10]

9. Croghan to Hamilton, Aug. 16, 1754, *Col. Rec. of Pa.*, VI, 140-41.
10. Hamilton to Croghan, Aug. 23, 1754, Cadwalader Coll., Hist. Soc. of Pa.; Croghan to Hamilton, Aug. 30, 1754, *Col. Rec. of Pa.*, VI, 160-61.

Weiser, who arrived at Aughwick on September 3, had the following to say about Croghan's situation:

> I counted above twenty cabbins about his house, and in them at least two hundred Indians, men, women and children, and a great many more are scattered thereabouts, some two or three miles off, and frequently come to fetch meal at Mr. Croghan's. He has between twenty-five and thirty acres of the best Indian corn that ever I saw. He sends his servants every day to fetch four or five bags full of roasting ears for them, but there is not an hour in the day but what some steal into it and fetch more, and upon the whole it is my opinion they will destroy one-half of it before it can be gathered in, to say nothing of the butter, milk, squashes, pumpkins they daily fetch, for all which if he be not allowed he must be a great loser. I advised him to charge for it what was reasonable, and to get two or three creditable men (as often come there from the inhabited parts) to value the corn that the Indians took away, and certify it. I cannot see what can be done else. Mr. Croghan must either be trusted to buy and distribute provision or the government must keep a man there in whom they can confide to receive the provision from Mr. Croghan or those that bring it and so distribute it according to the Governor's instructions; however, I believe the Indians will scatter before the winter comes, at least some of them. The bloody flux got among some of them, and Lewis Montour, Andrew's brother, disturbs them often by bringing strong liquor to them. They cannot help buying and drinking it when it is so near, and Lewis sells it very dear to them, and pretends that his wife, which is an ugly Indian squa, does it. He sends Indians to the inhabitants to fetch it for him, and Mr. Croghan can by no means prevent it because they keep it in the woods about or within a mile from his house, and there the Indians will go (after having Notice) and drink their cloathing and so come back to George Croghan's drunk and naked.[11]

In conference with the Indians, Weiser delivered Hamilton's explanation that the colony's backward military state was "entirely owing to an unfortunate disagreement between me and the Assembly about the mode of raising the money," and he united with the Half King and Scarouady in requesting their followers to remain

11. Weiser to Hamilton, Sept. 13, 1754, *Col. Rec. of Pa.*, VI, 148-50.

at Aughwick until the new governor arrived, when, presumably, an aggressive military policy would be adopted. Weiser settled Croghan's accounts, amounting to about £170 and entrusted most of the remainder of the £300 to Croghan, who "might (if he intended it) purloin a great deal of it, but I have the opinion of him that he will do justice."[12]

On September 8, after pleading with a very drunken Andrew Montour to accompany him, Weiser left Aughwick. When Montour—"on one legg he had a stocking and no shoe on the other a shoe and no stocking"—saw Weiser mount his horse, "he swore terrible." Montour, whose friendship with the older man had been resumed only the previous March, had been at his worst since he joined Weiser at Harris' Ferry, where he promptly got drunk. The two quarts of rum which Weiser bought for the trip were nearly all consumed by Montour the first day. In his cups, the half-breed turned ugly, "corsed & swore," and abused the Indian agent, always apologizing, however, when sober.[13]

Croghan's letter to Colonel Innes about Weiser's Indian conference has not been preserved, but its contents may be surmised from Dinwiddie's reaction, for Innes sent the letter to the governor. Touching on his connection with Major Carlyle earlier in the year, which had led to "differences" between himself and the quartermaster, Croghan suggested that Virginia send presents to the Indians at Aughwick, at the same time pointing out that he was not going to act as agent for Virginia. Dinwiddie tartly observed that Croghan's unwillingness to serve was no loss "for I am convinced he does nothing without private views of int[eres]t."[14]

After Weiser's departure, time passed uneasily at Aughwick, where the Indians awaited word of Pennsylvania's plans for repelling the enemy. No word came, and the Indians' concern for their future grew pressing. Croghan's situation was an anxious one, and the murder of trader Joseph Campbell in September gave warning of smoldering danger. In his magisterial capacity, Croghan, accompanied by several chiefs, went immediately to the

12. *Ibid.*, 149, and Weiser's journal, *ibid.*, 150-60.
13. Paul A. W. Wallace, *Conrad Weiser* (Philadelphia, 1945), 371-72.
14. Dinwiddie to Innes, Sept. 18, 1754, *Coll. of the Va. Hist. Soc.*, New Series, 3 (1883), 320-22.

scene of the crime to take depositions. The murderer, a Six Nations Indian, had escaped.[15]

Dangerous as its location was, far beyond the settled parts of the colony, Aughwick, nevertheless, was the goal of many travelers. From Shippensburg, in September, came Edward Shippen's son-in-law James Burd to obtain the original contract of the Hockley, Trent, and Croghan partnership—"Its' a great many sheets, very long." Dispossessed and drifting Indian traders wandered in and out of Croghan's settlement. The principal visitors, however, were the Indians who came and went between the British settlements and the French forts as spies for both sides. Croghan was diligent in forwarding to Philadelphia the intelligence they brought and served as the colony's main source for western information.[16] Expecting that the French would send Indian war parties against the back settlements, he warned that "if the French prosecute this schame I dont know what will become of the back parts of Cumberland County which lays quite nacked, the back parts of Virginia and Mareyland is coverd by the English camp, so that most of the inhabitance there are safe." Croghan's own safety at Aughwick was in jeopardy; he had received word that the French were going to do everything in their power to kill him, a fate they also held in store for Andrew Montour, the Half King, and Scarouady.

On September 27, 1754, he wrote Hamilton: "I hope as soon as his honour, Governor Morris, is a rived I shall hear what is to be don with those Indians, for I a shure yr honour itt will nott be in my power to keep them together much longar." Unless the English soon took some action of military consequence, their "slow moshens" would result in the desertion of all the natives. Only a few days later, the colony lost its most important Indian friend when the Half King died of alcoholism.[17]

Far away, in Philadelphia, boomed the guns of His Majesty's sloop *Baltimore* and of the Association Battery saluting the arrival on October 3 of Robert Hunter Morris. Two weeks later in his first message to the Assembly, the new governor dwelt on the state

15. Croghan to Hamilton, Sept. 27, 1754, *Pa. Archives*, II, 173.
16. Burd to Shippen, Sept. 25, 1754, Shippen Papers, I, 159, Hist. Soc. of Pa.
17. Croghan to Hamilton, Sept. 27, 1754, *Pa. Archives*, II, 173-74, 178; Weiser to Peters, Oct. 12, 1754, Correspondence of Conrad Weiser, I, 47, Hist. Soc. of Pa.

of the frontiers and urged the assemblymen to exert themselves in defense of their country. He laid before them letters received since August from Croghan and Weiser. But the Assembly refused to do anything more than pay for the Indian expenses at Aughwick.[18] This halfway measure scarcely represented vigorous policy, but the Assembly was satisfied, stating that if any matters of importance should come to the governor's attention, "we shall chearfully attend the Governor's call." Matters of importance to Croghan at his isolated outpost did not excite the legislators safely ensconced in Philadelphia.

By every Indian that came from the Ohio, Croghan learned of French preparations to attack the back settlements, measures evidently designed to prevent an English expedition that fall, of which Croghan dryly remarked, "I think they need not dread." To Richard Peters, Croghan wrote on October 16: "Colonel Innes has built a fortification at the mouth of Wills' Creek opposite to the new store called Fort Mount Pleasant. He has invited the Indians that is here to go to see him and receive a present from the government of Virginia which he will deliver them. They set off to-morrow but leaves their women and children here behind till they return, which they expect will be in ten days." Belatedly, Governor Morris urged Croghan to keep him fully informed on the Indian situation: "Mr. Peters has mentioned you to me in a very favourable manner, & I am glad the Province has a man at this critical time among the Indians that they so much depend upon."[19]

By this time, the Aughwick Indians, 180 strong, had settled themselves for the winter, and their leader, Scarouady, was on his way to the Onondaga country to gain support for an Indian war on the French. Unfortunately, the burden of caring for the natives had become increasingly unbearable for Croghan. Announcing his determination to leave Aughwick and forsake his charges, he bitterly commented, "I am very scencable the government has very little publick feath." Had not Weiser, on behalf of the province, assured Croghan that he would be sent more money to support the Indians? And was it not true that nothing

---

18. *Votes and Proceedings . . . of the Province of Pa.*, IV, 328-34.
19. Croghan to [Peters], Oct. 16, 1754, *Col. Rec. of Pa.*, VI, 180; Morris to Croghan, Nov. 25, 1754, *Pa. Archives*, II, 203.

more had come out of Philadelphia? Despite the fact that the Indians were continually teasing him about the government's promises to maintain them, he had refrained from applying for more support; it might look "as if I wanted to make a hand for my self out of the publick money." As a result, he had been forced to advance £150 of his own funds for the Indians, "and the winter coming on, and no provision made for them, made me determin to leave the plase to them selves."[20]

Croghan complained to Governor Morris that the Indians always expected him to fulfill the government's promises: "They imagin I have received orders from yr honour to suply them with such things as they want, and begins to think I intend to cheet them outt of their rites." On the other hand, Croghan knew that government officials did not trust him with money. "To acquitt my self from reflections on boath sides, I should be glad some other person wold be appointed to provide for them who phaps may do itt beter than I can."

It was simply his desire to avoid censure that made him want to retire from the care of the Indians and not the lack of pay for his services: "I ashure yr honour I neaver received a farthing for my own time & truble spent on those ocations in my life from the government. Itt is true they allways paid me for the services of my horses, butt neaver considered me one farthing for my truble, tho' I remember last winter when John Paten was sent out to Ohio with a letter, the government alowed him £50. I was sent outt at the same time, and was outt three months but neaver had the least acknolidgement made me."[21]

Although the Assembly, to which Croghan's letters were referred, was willing to contemplate his retirement, Governor Morris was not. He knew that Hamilton had promised the trader compensation and realized that he had been engaged more or less constantly in Indian affairs throughout 1754. As a token of salary, Morris sent £50 and asked Croghan to set his own wages, "that there may be no further misunderstanding in this line." "It is expected," wrote Morris, "whilst the Indians shall be main-

---

20. Croghan to Morris, Nov. 23, 1754, *Col. Rec. of Pa.*, VI, 181; Croghan to Peters, Dec. 2, 1754, *Pa. Archives*, II, 212.
21. Croghan to Morris, Dec. 2, 1754, *Pa. Archives*, II, 209.

tained by this governmt that you will act for it in their troublesome affairs." The governor also paid a bill of £65 which Croghan had submitted, forwarded £100 to be laid out for the Indians, requested Croghan to set his own charge for the destruction of his corn, and told him that whenever he needed money for his public services he was to draw on the treasurer or on Peters. All this was highly satisfactory, as was Peters' letter informing him that he was "considered by his Honour and the House as the agent for the Province." Mollified by this support, Croghan remained at Aughwick.[22]

Pennsylvania's failure to defend its western lands had already resulted in the defection of the Shawnees. They had come to Aughwick to learn their "Brother Onas's" plans to repel the French, but, discouraged by the colony's inactivity, had departed despite all that Croghan could do to persuade them to stay. Although fearful of exceeding his authority, Croghan gave them £42-worth of goods to retain their good will. "I realy don itt for the good of the government," he somewhat apprehensively explained to Peters, "as every body is sencable I can have no vews of tread." Even after Morris had straightened out Croghan's Indian expenses, the instructions he gave him did not allow for such generosity in dealing with the Indians. Later in December, Croghan was in a dilemma for goods to give to Indians who were in need: "Hear is the Half King's famely in a pour condition and Alequeapy the old quine is dead and left several children, and Scarrady's wife & seven children should be given something in his abstance." The Indian agent did all he could to keep expenses down, supplying the Indians chiefly with corn, and once a month giving them a keg of liquor for a frolic. It was necessary to entertain them occasionally, but even more necessary to keep whisky traders away. Croghan advertised in Cumberland County, warning the inhabitants not to sell liquor to the natives.[23]

The epic year 1755 dawned with Croghan holding together the only Indian band in Pennsylvania that might be used to fight the

22. *Col. Rec. of Pa.*, VI, 189; Morris to Croghan, Dec. 7, 1754, Public Records Division, Harrisburg.

23. Croghan to Peters, Dec. 5 and Dec. 23, 1754, and Croghan to Morris, Dec. 23, 1754, *Pa. Archives*, II, 212-13, 218, 219; Morris to Croghan, Dec. 10, 1754, Public Records Division, Harrisburg.

French. Its warriors were soon to have their day, whichever side they ultimately espoused, because the French and Indian War was about to come on in all its fury.

When the English finally realized the seriousness of French encroachments, the ministry ordered the colonies to repel force with force. Efforts to follow this directive had resulted in the capitulations of Croghan's half-brother Ensign Edward Ward on the Ohio and of George Washington at Fort Necessity. Since the colonies lacked the capability of protecting themselves, the Duke of Cumberland, captain general of the British army and a son of George II, persuaded the king to send troops to America commanded by a general officer. A grand plan was set forth to roll back the enemy from Forts Duquesne, Niagara, Crown Point, and Beauséjour in Nova Scotia.

Two British regiments were designated for the service, and, in addition, two colonial regiments were ordered raised by Governor William Shirley of Massachusetts and wealthy Sir William Pepperrell of Kittery, a hero of the previous war with France. The command of the North American forces was given to Major General Edward Braddock, who was ordered to proceed to Virginia and concentrate his troops at Wills Creek for an attack on Fort Duquesne. During the ensuing military activity, the camp at Wills Creek took on the name of Fort Cumberland in honor of the royal duke. Preceded by his deputy quartermaster general, Sir John St. Clair, Braddock arrived at Williamsburg on February 23, 1755, for a conference with Dinwiddie; his two regiments of regulars sailed into Hampton Roads during the first part of March.

Croghan, meanwhile, remained with the Indians at Aughwick. In sending Speaker Isaac Norris his account of expenses, in March, 1755, he wrote: "Expenses runs very high you will see by my acount butt I ashure you itt was nott in my power to mentain them less—they dont seme to incline to go from hear till they see how this warr will end." Croghan hoped that the balance would be paid his messenger so he could reimburse his suppliers and that the government would send him instructions "how to manidge fer the future."²⁴ But the Assembly was by no means ready to settle Croghan's accounts. The sums charged for wheat and flour seemed exorbitant, a calculation disclosing that each Indian must have had five pounds of flour a day, "which we think a very high charge." Virtually terminating their support of the Aughwick Indian agency, the Assembly allowed Croghan £50 on account and referred his charges to one of their Cumberland County members, Joseph Armstrong, "a very grave serious man."²⁵

Although the Assembly thus displayed its customary suspicion of Croghan, the government was about to call on him for additional services. In the middle of February, Sir John St. Clair had written Governor Morris on the necessity of preparing a wagon road westward through Pennsylvania toward Fort Duquesne. This communication would facilitate troop movements and serve as a supply route. On March 10, Morris and his council decided to comply with St. Clair's request. The first step was to survey the road, which was to pass through Raystown to a terminus located at the three forks of the Youghiogheny River, the "Turkey Foot." A road was also to be surveyed from Raystown to Wills Creek. Accordingly, a commission was drawn on March 12, directing five residents of Cumberland County—George Croghan, John Armstrong, James Burd, William Buchanan, and Adam Hoops—to make the surveys.²⁶

Instructions were sent to John Armstrong at Carlisle to convene the road commissioners and to caution them that their work required prudence, secrecy, and the utmost expedition: "If the Indians enquire leave it to Mr. Croghan to give them an answer, vizt that the inhabitants want to find out roads to carry their flower or any thing else that he pleases." The commissioners held an initial meeting at Francis Campbell's store in Shippensburg, where, oddly enough for a man who was supposedly out of funds, Croghan paid the bill for their entertainment.²⁷

24. Croghan to Morris, Mar. 25, 1755, Etting Coll., Misc. Mss., I, 82, Hist. Soc. of Pa.
25. *Votes and Proceedings . . . of the Province of Pa.*, IV, 393, 395, 396; Peters to Penn, June 20, 1752, Penn Mss., Official Correspondence, V, 251, Hist. Soc. of Pa.
26. *Col. Rec. of Pa.*, VI, 300, 317-18.
27. Peters to Armstrong, Mar. 15, 1755, *ibid.*, 323-24; Isaac Norris Mss., Road Cutters Accounts, Hist. Soc. of Pa.

On March 29, Croghan and his associates set out from Carlisle. Each man rode his own mount, and four pack horses (three of them provided by Croghan) carried the necessary supplies, which included rum, whisky, bacon, cheese, butter, flour, sugar, powder, and lead. In addition to the five commissioners, the party included two chain carriers for the survey, two men to tend the horses, two or three men to blaze trees, and a number of Indians. From time to time, the expedition was augmented by guides known as "pilots." Croghan could seldom divorce personal acquisitiveness from public service, and it was no doubt he who suggested that the commissioners take up five tracts of land, not to exceed four or five hundred acres each, provided such tracts were discovered along the course of their survey. The tracts were discovered and were balloted for, each commissioner receiving one.

According to their subsequent report, headed by Croghan's signature, the road commissioners proceeded "with the greatest industry" and reached the waters of the Youghiogheny on April 11. At that point, they were obliged to turn back because of intelligence from Wills Creek that a large party of French and Indians lay just ahead, hunting and scouting. So great was the fear of the Aughwick Indians who accompanied Croghan that all but one had already deserted. Although the commissioners were unable to reach their terminus, Croghan promised that there would be no difficulty in locating an excellent road to the Turkey Foot, and that he would be available when the time came to pilot the road makers from the place where the commissioners ceased blazing.[28]

Croghan and his friends rode down to Fort Cumberland, where the quartermaster general accorded them an interview on April 16. Furious with Pennsylvania's lack of support for Braddock's expedition, Sir John St. Clair stormed "like a lyon rampant," arrogantly refused to look at the drafts of the road, and swore that the road should have been begun long ago, that Pennsylvania's dilatoriness would delay the campaign and perhaps cost many lives because the French had just that much more time to rein-

28. Isaac Norris Mss., Road Cutters Accounts, Hist. Soc. of Pa.; *Col. Rec. of Pa.*, VI, 484-85; Burd to Peters, Sept. 22, 1755, Public Records Division, Harrisburg.

force Fort Duquesne. In nine days' time, St. Clair thundered at Croghan and his astonished friends, instead of marching to the Ohio, he would bring his army into Cumberland County, kill the cattle, carry away the horses, burn the houses, and later, if defeated by the French, he would pass through the province with drawn sword, treating its inhabitants as traitors should be treated. In fact, declared Sir John, he would not hesitate to impress the Pennsylvania Assembly.[29]

Returning to Aughwick after twenty-five days of road surveying, Croghan received orders from Governor Morris to muster all the Indians he could and to join Braddock's expedition immediately. He was also to send messages to all the distant tribes inviting them to reinforce the British army. From Richard Peters came a warning to lay aside all other business, for Braddock was severe when his orders were not punctually obeyed. "It is my opinion that notwithstanding all the expence of this Province upon the Indians they will not assist the army at all," wrote Peters. The provincial secretary was certain the Indians were "absolutely debauched" and would not fight, but he hoped that they might prove useful as spies or scouts.[30]

Governor Morris' letter arrived at Aughwick on the evening of April 30, and, the following day, Croghan sent messengers to summon the western Indians to join Braddock, while Scarouady's Aughwick Indians prepared to set off for Wills Creek. An unaccustomed quiet descended on Aughwick on May 2 when Croghan and his faithful band moved southward on the trail. Even Croghan's horses were no more to be seen, for they had been hired out for the expedition. Of Croghan's family, only Edward Ward remained to care for the establishment and its several Negro slaves.[31]

Peters had given Croghan reason to believe that faithful public service might be rewarded by an act of Assembly relieving

---

29. Croghan and road commissioners to Morris, Apr. 16, 1755, *Col. Rec. of Pa.*, VI, 368-69.

30. *Ibid.*, 371, 372; Peters to Croghan, Apr. 23, 1755, Public Records Division, Harrisburg.

31. *Col. Rec. of Pa.*, VI, 374-75, 398-99. In March, 1755, Burd estimated that Croghan could furnish fifty horses for Braddock by the middle of April. Shippen Papers, I, 173, Hist. Soc. of Pa.

him of his debts. Despite this hope, his chaotic personal affairs were complicated by his frequent government missions. After his arrival at Fort Cumberland, he wrote Governor Morris that he did not want to continue buying provisions for the Aughwick agency, "as I find it very difficult to settle my accounts, as I can't go to Philadelphia myself to see them settled." In May, the Assembly grudgingly paid some of Croghan's bills on the recommendation of Joseph Armstrong.[32]

More important to Croghan than the liquidation of these liabilities was a new letter of license which he and Trent procured from most of their creditors for the generous period of six years. The terms of the agreement have not been preserved, but evidently Croghan promised to pay to those creditors who signed the document the value of his horses and the money he was to earn from the army. Edward Shippen, one of two major creditors who refused to sign, was alarmed to see Croghan's assets compromised in favor of others. To James Burd, who had undertaken to collect the debt for him, Shippen wrote, "Act as wise as a serpent, & as harmless as a dove, for Mr. Croghan may possible be led but can not be drove."[33]

By this time, Burd was occupied in building the provincial military road he had helped survey. His favorite daydream was collecting from Croghan on Shippen's behalf. Earlier he had expected Croghan to meet him at Adam Hoops's, after Croghan had convoyed the Indians to Wills Creek. At Hoops's, Burd was to present all the necessary papers and settle his father-in-law's accounts. "Dont be uneasy that this affair is not settled before now," Burd encouraged Shippen, "as it is entirely owing to severall things occurring that has prevented it, but rest assured if I live it shall be done upon Mr. Croghan's return." But Croghan did not return around May 6 as promised. By the time Burd heard that the Indian agent would meet him on the road later in the month, his optimism had lessened: "It will give me a great deall of un-

---

32. Croghan to Peters, Dec. 2, 1754, *Pa. Archives*, II, 211; Croghan to Morris, May 20, 1755, *Col. Rec. of Pa.*, VI, 398-99; *Votes and Proceedings . . . of the Province of Pa.*, IV, 398, 401.

33. Shippen to [Mr. & Mrs. James Burd], date illegible, but 1755, Shippen Papers, III, 137, Hist. Soc. of Pa. Joseph Simon, the Jewish merchant of Lancaster, negotiated the letter of license for Croghan.

easiness if I should be disappointed & baffled in this affair." Still later, on May 31, Burd wrote, "I expect G. C. at our camp every day." But Croghan never came.[34]

Although Croghan's speculations in land held out some hope for reducing his debts, his deals usually became so involved that little cash came to hand. His home at Aughwick was part of the large tract he had acquired directly from Indian owners before the sale of the Six Nations' lands to Pennsylvania in 1754. Penn was much upset at Croghan's transaction and at first refused to recognize it, stating that if the natives were to be allowed to grant lands to individuals, "we shall have Indians practic'd upon for the private advantage of every worthless fellow that goes among them." Croghan's subsequent offer to locate a good tract of land for the proprietor found Thomas Penn more mellow.[35]

But soon Penn was amazed to receive an offer from Croghan to sell him his improvements. Penn considered this an extraordinary idea: "I would not give him one shilling for the whole of it. I think the location of twelve tracts of good land of more value than all these improvements, which tracts I suppose he proposes for Mr. Hockley's benefit, that is the location of them." Croghan did indeed plan to locate valuable lands as a service to Hockley, but like many of Croghan's real estate ventures, this one ended unhappily. According to surveyor John Armstrong, in 1755 "at the joint instance of Messrs. Hockley & Croghan I made twelve surveys in the new purchase, the bargain betwixt these gentn broke up, and neither of them paid me one shilg of fees. After some years Geo: Croghan by vertue of his Indian deed was granted the lands on the whole of Ochwick p an order sent to me to survey them."[36]

Penn's change in attitude which permitted Croghan to retain the Aughwick lands—only a few months before Penn had sworn he would never grant him an acre—was conditioned by at least one practical factor. Croghan had sold quite a few pieces of his tract,

---

34. Burd to Shippen, Apr. 27, Apr. 29, May 15, May 31, 1755, *ibid.*, I, 179, 183, 191.

35. Penn to Peters, Feb. 21 and May 29, 1755, Penn Letter Book, IV, 38, 89-90, Hist. Soc. of Pa.

36. Penn to Peters, July 3, 1755, *ibid.*, 118; Armstrong to James Tilghman, Mar. 5, 1773, Bureau of Land Records, Harrisburg.

and, if his title was to be invalidated, others would also suffer. Indeed, some Aughwick purchasers were quick to realize the weakness of their titles. On October 9, 1755, four of them united in a warning published in the *Pennsylvania Gazette* that they would not honor their notes given to Croghan for his lands. Penn found it wise to permit Peters to let the first appliers have the land in the new purchase, "and in particular to George Croghan which as you will observe takes off the dispute from us to private people."[37]

Business difficulties had harassed the Indian agent during the past four years and were to continue to harass him until his death. He found relief from such worries when engaged in government service, and an episode of high adventure was now at hand. Early in May, 1755, Croghan and his Indians straggled out from the woods to find themselves before a large crude fortress. While the Indians set up a shelter camp, Braddock's troops were marching up from the south, and Fort Cumberland, where Croghan awaited the next spin of the wheel, took on a dramatic significance in the struggle for empire.

[37]. Penn to Peters, Aug. 14, 1755, Penn Letter Book, IV, 140-41, Hist. Soc. of Pa.

5

Military Services

ON MAY 10, 1755, the Indians listened with delight to a seventeen-gun salute from Fort Cumberland's four-pounders, heralding the arrival of the commander in chief, Major General Edward Braddock. With astonishment, they observed the well-disciplined marching order and cadenced tread of his foot soldiers. A veteran of the Coldstream Guards, about sixty years old, short and stout, imperious and hot-tempered, a little uncouth, undeniably brave, Braddock was a thoroughly professional soldier and a thoroughly angry one. He had been deceived and tricked by colonials on all sides, but by none to the extent that Governor Dinwiddie had imposed upon him. Where were the hundreds of southern Indian warriors that Dinwiddie had promised him? He fired that question at Croghan. Where was the Virginia governor's transportation, the wagons and horses needed to move the army over the mountains? Where were the provisions?[1]

Croghan was only too happy to turn his attention from Braddock's ill humor to a letter from Colonel William Johnson. "Tho unacquainted (wh I am sorry for)," wrote the New Yorker, "I must beg leave to take the liberty of desiring you to speak to Scarooyady or Half King in my name." The purpose of the message was to inform Scarouady of Johnson's appointment as Indian superintendent, and of his wish that the chief do all he could to help Braddock.[2]

---

1. Winthrop Sargent, *The History of an Expedition against Fort Du Quesne in 1755* (Philadelphia, 1856), 112, 115, 132, 373-74, 407; Freeman, *George Washington*, II, 15.

2. Johnson to Croghan, Apr. 23, 1755, James Sullivan, Alexander C. Flick, and Milton W. Hamilton, eds., *The Papers of Sir William Johnson* (Albany, 1921-57), I, 475-76, hereafter cited as *Johnson Papers*.

Croghan replied to Johnson as to a kindred spirit: "I should be glad to keep up a corrispondance with you and shall by every oppertunity let you know what is doing in these parts." Having heard that Johnson had been inquiring about his Indian trade losses, Croghan described how French aggression had cost him thousands of pounds. It was difficult for the former trader to forget his losses, particularly in the presence of Richard Peters, who, accompanied by Richard Hockley, arrived at the fort on May 22. The purpose of Peters' visit that hot, droughty month was to expedite James Burd's work on the new road and to confer with Braddock on what was wanted for the army. Knowing he would meet Croghan and Trent, he brought Hockley with him.[3]

Hockley's most pressing embarrassments were suits threatened by Edward Shippen and his partner Thomas Lawrence to recover £702 and by John Carson of Paxtang to recover £900. Both of these sums were said to be debts owed by the partnership. Trent and Croghan willingly signed statements that the goods which these amounts represented had not been purchased by the Hockley partnership but by Trent and Croghan for their other enterprises. Moreover, Croghan promised a power of attorney to Hockley to collect his losses to the French if the government should refund them to him. Croghan had high hopes of such a settlement because he had presented his case to Braddock, and the general had not only promised to help him obtain restitution in England but had given him assurances of success. According to Hockley, "Croghan is in great repute with the General, has ten shillings sterling a day allow'd him as conductor to about 40 Indians of the Six Nations who have taken up the hatchett against the French and are to be as out scouts to the army."[4]

Braddock had indeed taken both Croghan and Montour into service, and the Indians, after receiving a present from the general and an exhortation to take up the hatchet, had demonstrated their enthusiasm by making "a most horrible noise, dancing all night." The next day, the day that Captain Horatio Gates of later

---

3. Croghan to Johnson, May 15, 1755, *ibid.*, 496-97; *Col. Rec. of Pa.*, VI, 383-84.

4. Document signed by Trent and Croghan, May 24, 1755, and Hockley to Penn, June 23, 1755, Penn Mss., Official Correspondence, VII, 43, 65, Hist. Soc. of Pa.

Revolutionary renown arrived with his independent company of New York, the Indians chanted their war song and swore that the French were their perpetual enemies.

On this token of fealty, Braddock called for a warlike celebration and a show of power. Arrayed in martial order in the artillery park were the howitzers, twelve-pounders, and coehorns which Lieutenant Colonel Thomas Gage had just brought up to Fort Cumberland. While the gunners bent to their work, drums and fifes accompanied the cannonade to the intense wonder and pleasure of the Indians. Afterward, the natives retired to their camp, ate a bullock, and prepared their own celebration.[5]

It was a fine night for the war dance. The twinkling stars looked down on a large plot of grass marked out for the ceremony, around which stood the officers and soldiers, as at a cricket match in England. In the center of the grass two fires illuminated the scene, and near the fires sat a group of men and women beating on parchment-like deerskins stretched over brass kettles. The time they kept was good, but their tunes were terrible and savage. Their singing was much the same, creating sensations of fear and passion. Weird as their playing was, it was surpassed when, with a frightful shout, a band of dreadful figures rushed from the blackness of the forest into the ring. With a nimbleness hardly conceivable, they struck the ground in exact time to the music. The dancers were Croghan's warriors sparsely dressed in furs, some with their hair decorated with feathers, others with the heads of beasts. Their bodies, painted and oiled, glistened against the light. Their waists were girdled with bear or deerskins; from many of the skins hung the tails of animals.

In single file, the dancers postured and bounded around the fires, while the kettledrums beat out the rhythm. Soon, boys appeared carrying blazing sticks of lightwood for the dancers, and the frolic was cast into a noonday glare. After dancing for awhile, the warriors divided into two parties and set up a horrible song: "the sound would strike terror into the stoutest heart." Then the two groups ran at each other, acting out a fight. This mock conflict ended when, at the signal of a dismal cry, the dancers rushed from the ring leaving behind one warrior, who was supposed to

---

5. Sargent, *Expedition against Fort Du Quesne*, 378, 379.

have mastered an enemy. Striking the ground with his tomahawk, he went through the motions of scalping, and, holding up a real scalp which had hung among his ornaments, he sang of his nation's achievements against the French, naming the Indian warriors and how many Frenchmen each had killed. Thus the dance ended.[6]

Encouraged by the demonstration, Braddock asked Croghan to send another messenger to the Ohio to bring in the leaders of the Delawares and Shawnees. Croghan complied, and eight days later his messenger returned with three Delaware chiefs. In return for Braddock's kind treatment and presents, the Delawares promised to join him with many warriors. Croghan seems to have believed them. An officer who was a member of the expedition was more discerning, though a neophyte in Indian affairs. "These people are villains, and always side with the strongest," he wrote.[7]

Not only were the Delawares not to be counted on, but even Croghan's Aughwick Indians were ready to desert. A few days after their great dance, Peters found Scarouady and his companions extremely dissatisfied with not being consulted by the general. Moreover, the Indians were embroiled in frequent quarrels, "their squas bringing them money in plenty which they got from the officers, who were scandalously fond of them." On Peters' recommendation, the general at last prevailed upon the warriors to send their dependents home. Most of the men accompanied the women and children to Aughwick. Although expected to return, they never did. They had danced their war dance. Under the circumstances, that was enough.

Indian affairs had been badly handled by Colonel Innes before Braddock's arrival. William Johnson gave this as one of the reasons why he was unable to persuade the New York Indians to join Braddock. Unfortunately, when Braddock took over, conditions did not improve. Despite all that Croghan could do, the Indians slipped away; when they were really needed, only eight remained.[8]

6. *The Expedition of Major General Braddock to Virginia . . . Being Extracts of Letters from an Officer* . . . (London, 1755), 18-21.
7. Sargent, *Expedition against Fort Du Quesne*, 314, 380.
8. *Col. Rec. of Pa.*, VI, 397; Shirley to Peters, May 21, 1755, *Pa. Archives*, II, 321; Johnson to Thomas Pownall, July 31, 1755, *Johnson Papers*, I, 804; Croghan to Morris, May 20, 1755, *Col. Rec. of Pa.*, VI, 398-99.

On May 30, the advance guard of the army began its march to the Little Meadows, twenty-two miles away. There a supply base was to be established. "Thus we marched out," wrote one of the officers, "the Knight swearing in the van, the Genl cursing & bullying in the center & their whores bringing up the rear."[9]

Just a few days before he left Fort Cumberland, Braddock wrote Secretary of State Sir Thomas Robinson that he had gathered a group of Six Nations Indians from Pennsylvania's frontiers: "The number already with me is about fifty and I have some hopes of more." However, when Edward Shippen's son Joseph visited the forces at the Little Meadows, there were only eight Indians present. "Josey" asked Croghan what had become of the rest, and was told that they had accompanied their families to Aughwick but would rejoin the army before it reached the Great Meadows. Croghan also said that he was certain "40 or 50 more from the back woods would join him between the Great Meadows and the ffrench ffort which they would have done at ffort Cumberland were it not for fear of the ffrench coming to their cabbins to destroy their families." It was evident that up to the last minute both Braddock and Croghan hoped for the support of a large number of natives.[10]

Alarmed by the fact that his army was advancing at the rate of but two miles a day, Braddock held a council of war and decided to lead a picked force of about thirteen hundred men on a rapid march to Fort Duquesne. To prepare the way for this flying column, St. Clair moved out on June 18 to cut a road to the Little Crossing of the Youghiogheny. With him went Croghan and the Indians. The following day, Braddock marched with the

9. John Rutherford to Peters, endorsed as received on Aug. 13, 1755, Peters Mss., IV, 41, Hist. Soc. of Pa. Croghan's activities at this time are confused by a fictitious letter supposedly written by him from non-existent Fort Louther about Captain Jack, a mythical frontiersman. This letter and other spurious documents published by Samuel Hazard in *The Register of Pennsylvania* (Philadelphia, 1829), IV, 416, have been accepted as genuine by several historians.

10. Braddock to Robinson, June 5, 1755, W. O. 34/73, foll. 35-37, Public Record Office, London; Shippen to William Allen, July 4, 1755, Shippen Papers, I, 207, Hist. Soc. of Pa.

main body, leaving Colonel Dunbar in command of the rear echelon, which was to push forward as speedily as possible.[11]

Hostile Indians skulked around the flanks of the British column as it inched its laborious way over rough ground. On June 25, three men who went beyond the sentry line were shot and scalped. By this time, the army had forded the Great Crossing of the Youghiogheny, about sixteen miles from the Little Meadows. Near the Great Crossing, Croghan and his Indian scouts had discovered a large party of enemy Indians which St. Clair drove off.[12]

With the army nearing its goal, Braddock ordered Croghan on July 3 to send some Indians to Fort Duquesne for intelligence. The general had often urged the natives to make this scout, but he had been unable to induce them to leave the column after they had passed Washington's fort at the Great Meadows. With considerable difficulty, Croghan at last persuaded two of them to go on this mission. Christopher Gist, the general's guide, also slipped off on a reconnaissance. All three scouts returned on July 6 with word that the way was clear. The Indians had crept within half a mile of Fort Duquesne and had scalped a French officer.[13]

Most of July 7 was spent in reconnoitering for the best approach to the fort. St. Clair, assisted by the Indians and guides, was in charge of this work and selected a route which crossed the shallow Monongahela twice, in order to avoid a dangerous place called the Narrows. On July 8, the army moved forward and camped that night twelve miles from the French fort.

Long before dawn on the fateful July 9, the day the army expected to win its prize, Braddock's forces were in motion. In the van, as usual, was Lieutenant Colonel Gage with a strong detachment. Next came St. Clair with 250 men, opening a road for the wagons. Braddock followed with the main body. Croghan was at his customary post at the head of Gage's troops. The march continued unchallenged; both crossings of the Monongahela were

---

11. Freeman, *George Washington*, II, 53; Sargent, *Expedition against Fort Du Quesne*, 336.
12. *Col. Rec. of Pa.*, VI, 460.
13. Sargent, *Expedition against Fort Du Quesne*, 209, 349.

successfully accomplished, and a joyful feeling prevailed that the French would not fight. At two in the afternoon, Gage, who had taken a defensive position after making the second crossing, was ordered to continue the advance.

Preceded at about two hundred yards by guides acting as scouts, Gage's troops marched forward in columns of four, protected by flankers. The underbrush was thick at first, but, about a quarter of a mile beyond the Monongahela, the soldiers found themselves in an open wood through which carriages could have driven with ease. Gage had not proceeded far when there was a commotion at the front, and the guides came running in with word that they had encountered a large body of French and Indians. Engineer Harry Gordon and George Croghan were both at the very head of Gage's men and saw the enemy charging down on them. Gordon and Croghan had a full look at the attackers, before they divided to flank the British under cover of the forest, and were in agreement with the guides that there were only three hundred of them. Actually, there were nearly eight hundred French and Indians in the engagement.[14]

According to Croghan, the French wore shirts and the Indians were naked. Leading the war party, Croghan saw Captains Beaujeu, Dumas, and DeLignery, who signaled with their hats to open the attack. While Gage's flanking parties ran in to join the advance detachment, the French and Indians scurried through the woods and ravines and virtually enveloped the vanguard. Enemy bullets came from all directions, taking a terrible toll. The most disconcerting feature of the battle was that the British could not see their assailants, so cleverly did the enemy take advantage of available cover. Gage later stated that he would be willing to swear under oath that he did not see more than one Frenchman or one Indian during the entire action. It is not surprising that Gage's men were soon driven back in confusion on Braddock's main body. There, they broke through the ranks, creating a tactical situation that could not be corrected.[15]

---

14. Gipson, *The British Empire*, VI, 91-92; Stanley McCrory Pargellis, *Military Affairs in North America, 1748-1765* (New York, 1936), 62.

15. Pargellis, *Military Affairs in North America*, 103, 117; Charles Swaine to Peters, Aug. 5, 1755, Peters Mss., IV, 38, and Norris to Robert Charles, Nov. 27, 1755, Norris Letter Book (1719-56), 91, Hist. Soc. of Pa.

Death fed gluttonously on the bewildered British army in the terrifying scene that followed. Braddock did his best to rally his men, but all in vain, and in the end he too was struck down, fatally wounded. The efforts of his troops to drive off the enemy proved altogether futile. Croghan later said that "many of our people fired twenty four rounds & never saw the enemy." Defeat became retreat, and retreat, a rout.

Only a few followers were interested in rescuing their fallen commander. His aide-de-camp, George Washington, helped bring Braddock off the field. Croghan, too, remained with the dying leader and assisted Washington in lifting the general into a wagon to convey him out of danger. One of the survivors of the day maintained that Croghan had asked to have the command and to allow the men to spread out. Such stories gained wide acceptance. Another anecdote was circulated that Braddock in his despair, and wanting to die on the field, attempted to seize Croghan's pistols. When questioned about this tale, Croghan vouched for its truth.[16]

After the guns were laid down, the pens were taken up, and blame was liberally distributed. The popular censensus placed the fault on the highest and the lowest levels—Braddock's leadership and the cowardly behavior of the enlisted men. In defending their own records, the principals involved had to besmirch the records of others. Croghan was no exception. He felt sensitive over his inability to influence more than eight Indians to serve on the expedition. Actually, he had no cause for embarrassment. Neither Dinwiddie nor Johnson had been able to persuade a single warrior to help Braddock.

Two years after the disaster, Croghan placed the blame on Colonel Innes. Innes, wrote Croghan, had informed the general that ten Indians would be enough to accompany the army, more would be troublesome. Accordingly, Braddock ordered Croghan, who had fifty warriors with him, to send all but eight or ten back to Aughwick. Croghan concluded his apologia by stating, "I am yet of opinion that had we fifty Indians instead of eight, that we

---

16. Norris to Charles, Nov. 27, 1755, Norris Letter Book (1719-56), 91, Hist. Soc. of Pa.; John Campbell to John Smith, July 17, 1755, Penn Mss., Official Correspondence, VII, 85, Hist. Soc. of Pa.; Goldsbrow Banyar to Johnson, July 26, 1755, *Johnson Papers*, I, 772; Sargent, *Expedition against Fort Du Quesne*, 386-87.

might in a great measure have prevented the surprise, that day of our unhappy defeat."[17]

This explanation for the disappointing performance of the Aughwick Indians cannot be credited. Scarouady gave a truer account; "He was a bad man," said the chief of Braddock. "He looked upon us as dogs; and would never hear any thing what was said to him ... he never appeared pleased with us, & that was the reason that a great many of our warriors left him & would not be under his command." If Braddock had told Croghan to retain only eight Indians and to send the rest home, the chief would not have taken pains to account for their departure as he did. When Croghan left Colonel Innes, who remained on as post commander at Wills Creek, it is clear that he expected to be joined by all the Aughwick Indians, to say nothing of fifty more Indians from the Ohio. Were not all this true, it would be difficult to believe that Braddock had been influenced by Innes, a man of notoriously bad reputation for Indian management. Braddock had placed a high value on the service of Indian auxiliaries. He had been bitterly disappointed when Dinwiddie's promised hundreds of southern warriors did not join him. It is unlikely that he would voluntarily have reduced his available Indian support from company size to a corporal's guard. Colonel William Johnson had warned Braddock that the Iroquois were "a begging & insatiable set of people & expect to be denied nothing. ... a delicate conduct is necessary till they have heartily entered into hostilities against the French." Braddock lacked the necessary delicacy.[18]

His defeat threw the western counties into a panic. When first reported, the event was scarcely credited. Then, on July 17, Governor Morris received confirmation from William Trent. Bad news poured in on the governor. Already the Indians had invaded the back parts of Virginia, scalping and burning. They had attacked Burd's road cutters, who fled to the settlements. Moreover, Morris learned that Delaware George, a loyal Indian, had

17. Sargent, *Expedition against Fort Du Quesne*, 407-8.
18. Colonel Thomas Dunbar, third in command to Braddock, explained the dearth of Indians by saying, "General Braddock cou'd not get above eight or nine to attend him." *Col. Rec. of Pa.*, VI, 593, and also see 589; Johnson to Braddock, May 17, 1755, *Johnson Papers*, I, 513-14.

come in haste from the Ohio to warn that the French and Indians would soon descend on Pennsylvania's frontier.[19]

The governor did what he could to hearten the people of Cumberland County. He encouraged them to form companies of volunteers and issued commissions to the officers. He laid out an area in the center of Carlisle for the construction of a log fort and ordered a similar defense to be built at Shippensburg. All this he did without money and without a militia law, for the Assembly had provided neither. Morris' defense measures, however, could not stem the rising hysteria.[20]

During the confusion following Braddock's death, the Indian manager and his charges left the army. Croghan, unpaid for his services, returned home. He well knew what the English repulse would bring on, and, gathering an armed band of between thirty and forty men, "a volunteer company on my own expence," he prepared to fortify Aughwick by building a stockade around his house.[21] Officials, military and civil, temporarily forgot the once indispensable man. Governor Morris was disappointed in Croghan because his messages to rally the western Indians to Braddock's standard had not even been answered. Convinced that Croghan had little influence, the governor turned to reliable Conrad Weiser for advice on Indian affairs.

Even the natives so long resident at Aughwick turned their backs on Croghan and moved to safer places of refuge at Harris' Ferry and in the Shamokin area up the Susquehanna. As late as November, Scarouady did not know where the Indian agent was living. When told that Croghan was still at Aughwick, the chief urged that he be warned to move at once or he would certainly be killed.[22]

"In distress for a little money," Croghan visited Shippensburg in October. There the consuming topic of conversation was the

19. Trent to Morris, July 17, 1755, C. O. 5/46, Part III, fol. 394, Public Record Office, London; Morris to Peters, July 17, 1755, Peters Mss., IV, 23, Hist. Soc. of Pa.; Peters to James De Lancey, July 19, 1755, *Johnson Papers*, I, 751.
20. Morris to Sharpe, July 20, 1755, *Pa. Archives*, II, 382; Morris to Penn, July 31, 1755, *Col. Rec. of Pa.*, VI, 517.
21. Croghan to Johnson, Sept. 10, 1755, *Johnson Papers*, II, 30.
22. William Buchanan to Croghan, Nov. 2, 1755, Shippen Papers, II, 7, Hist. Soc. of Pa.; John Armstrong to Morris, Nov. 2, 1755, *Pa. Archives*, II, 452.

ravages committed by the Indians along the Virginia border. Communications with Fort Cumberland were cut off and its commanding officer had written, "The smoke of the burning plantations darken the day, and hide the neighboring mountains from our sight." The enemy were slaughtering or carrying away all the whites they could find. They fell on the southwestern settlement of Patterson's Creek, killing more than forty settlers.[23]

At the terrible news of this raid, Charles Swaine, the government's commissary at Shippensburg, urged Croghan to send him Indian intelligence. Croghan complied with a warning that the removal of the Susquehanna natives to the French-dominated Ohio would signal a general attack. The French, Croghan learned from an Indian sent to him by his friends on the Ohio, were determined to destroy all the back settlements that winter. According to the native courier, only by withdrawing from the woods could Croghan save his scalp, which would be "no small prize to the French." The Irishman had long expected a large-scale attack along the frontiers. "Indeed," he wrote Swaine, "it is only what I thought the Indians always aimed at, and what I feared they would accomplish, for I see all our great directors of Indian affairs are very short sighted, and glad I am that I have no hand in Indian affairs at this critical time, where no fault can be thrown on my shoulders."[24]

A week later, on October 16, the storm broke, snapping the traditional chain of friendship between the Delaware nation and Pennsylvania. A band of Indians, principally from the Allegheny town of Kittanning, massacred more than a score of German settlers along Penn's Creek, a stream which emptied into the Susquehanna.

News of Indian attacks produced a frenzy of activity. The governor convened the Assembly; James Hamilton rushed to Lancaster in an effort to bring order out of chaos and to distribute military commissions among the unpaid volunteers. The terrifying reports from the frontiers became ever worse, and excitement ran higher with each new account of Indian massacres. Conrad Weiser, colonel of the Berks County militia, heard that "the people at

23. Norris Mss., Road Cutters Accounts, Hist. Soc. of Pa.; Hamilton, ed., *Letters to Washington*, I, 103.
24. Croghan to Swaine, Oct. 9, 1755, *Col. Rec. of Pa.*, VI, 642.

Auchwick & Juniata are cut off, and among others George Croghan." All over the province men armed and marched to the defense of the western frontier.[25]

Savage blows leveled the Cumberland County settlement in the Great Cove on October 31, when more than half its pioneers were slaughtered. Shingas, the Delaware king, led this raid and was supported by the Shawnees. Fresh disasters were hourly expected. Carlisle was considered to be in serious danger, and Montour expressed his opinion that Lancaster would be taken before Christmas. In this unparalleled emergency, Morris called on the Assembly to grant money for defense and to prepare a militia bill.[26]

The Assembly promptly drew up the same sort of money bill that Morris had rejected in the past, the stumbling block being the provision that the proprietors' estates would be taxed along with all others to raise the money. The Assembly also posed an interesting, if untimely, question. What, they inquired of the governor, had alienated the Delawares and Shawnees? Morris, whose temper had reached the breaking point, was in no mood to deal tactfully with such a question.

Croghan could have answered the query realistically. He had seen how, step by step, the prestige of the English had been broken in the West. He had done what he could to prevent that breakdown, but he could neither stem the flood of French power nor animate the inert government of Pennsylvania. Under the circumstances, the alienation of the Indians by the crafty, able, hardworking French was inevitable. Opposed to the autocratic centralized government of the Canadians were the disorganized semi-democratic governments of the colonies, and in the midsection of the invaded area lay Pennsylvania, a pacifistic state. Its Quaker-dominated Assembly would not or could not comprehend that military action was necessary. The Indians saw how the wind blew. How could they oppose the French if the English themselves were unable to do so successfully? There was no room for neutrality; the Indians had to declare one way or the other, and they chose what appeared to be the stronger side.

Other explanations for the alienation of the western Indians are

25. *Ibid.*, 667, 670.
26. Armstrong to Morris, Nov. 2, 1755, *Pa. Archives*, II, 452.

secondary. True, those Indians resented the huge Albany purchase of 1754 in which the Six Nations of New York sold western lands to Pennsylvania. Their resentment, however, stemmed not so much from the fact of the sale as from the fact that they did not receive any of the purchase money. Of course, the Indians could also complain of land frauds, of the Ohio Company's settlement, of whisky traders who cheated them, and of other inequities, but all such complaints were minor. The alienation of the Delawares and Shawnees was the result of successful French power policies opposed to utterly inadequate countermoves by the colonies.

If the Assembly was backward, the spirit of the people was not. About a thousand armed men marched to Harris' Ferry to meet a rumored attack. By this time, virtually all the settlers on the far side of North Mountain had abandoned their homes or had been killed. Fears were expressed for Croghan's safety, and an expedition under James Burd and Adam Hoops was organized to go to Aughwick for his relief.[27]

While the Pennsylvania volunteers rushed from one threatened area to another, many of the back settlers sought safety in York or Chester counties, in Maryland, and in Philadelphia. The roads leading east were crowded with refugees. "Almost all the women & children over Sasquehannah have left their habitations," Peters wrote Penn on November 8, "& the roads are full of starved, naked, indigent multitudes.... Not one twentieth man has arms." The situation had not improved by November 25 when Peters again wrote: "The pannick is inconceivable in every part of the country.... The number of [enemy] Indians will most assuredly encrease, & if Croghan or Montour or Scarroyady are worthy of credit, the French have engaged most of the nations of Indians over the Ohio in their interest."[28]

It is significant that Croghan's opinions were once more being quoted in official circles. The former Indian trader had extricated himself from oblivion by a letter to James Hamilton. At Swaine's request, Croghan had written on October 9 about Indian affairs,

27. Adam Hoops to Morris, Nov. 3, 1755, *ibid.*, 462-63, 472; see Croghan's warning of Indian danger, Burd-Shippen Papers, I, 19, Amer. Philos. Soc.
28. Peters to Penn, Nov. 8 and Nov. 25, 1755, Peters Letter Book, Hist. Soc. of Pa.

but Governor Morris, to whom his letter was sent, ignored it. On November 12, Croghan visited Shippensburg and may again have been solicited by Swaine to write to the governor. If such was the case, Croghan compromised by sending his Indian intelligence to Hamilton, with the comment that "itt was my duty to have wrote to the present governor, butt as he has nott thought proper to desire me to give him any accounts of Indian affairs, since the defate of Gineral Braddock, I did nott now how his honour wold take it from me, or what creadett he wold give to such an account, as I have nott the lest acquaintance of his honour."

In sending Hamilton his information, Croghan referred to his misfortunes in trade which obliged him to live so far away that he could not forward intelligence promptly. However, if what he had to say was deemed worthy of notice, he would be glad to send it to the government. Croghan believed that the Indians from whom the officials were drawing information "are only amuseing the government, while they are privey, if not asisting to the merders done." As for his present circumstances, the Irishman informed Hamilton that he had built a stockade fort at Aughwick which he occupied with about forty men, "butt how long I shall be able to keep itt, I realy can't tell."[29]

Croghan's letter made a profound impression on Hamilton, who had just returned from Lancaster County and realized the desperation of the situation better than anyone in Philadelphia. He had long known Croghan and had always believed him to be a valuable man. It was ridiculous that in the present acute emergency the province should be denied the services of such a man, simply because he owed money and could be jailed if he appeared in Philadelphia. Hamilton moved to rectify the situation.

With an extraordinary unanimity of purpose, factions long at war united to relieve Croghan of his embarrassments. Most of Croghan's (and Trent's) principal creditors were assembled, someone must have read them the riot act, and fifteen of them signed a petition to the Assembly. Although the petition was on behalf of both Croghan and Trent, Trent was included only because he was Croghan's partner. Reciting the traders' impoverishment through

29. Croghan to Hamilton, Nov. 12, 1755, *Pa. Archives*, II, 483-84.

losses to the French and Indians, the creditors pointed out that "the said George Croghan has been for some time, and is now, at Aughwick, in the most melancholy and deplorable circumstances, in a condition very defenseless, destitute of all kinds of provisions, but what is procured at the hazard of his life, and daily liable to the invasion and massacre of our barbarian enemies." The only reason Croghan remained at Aughwick, the petition continued, was his fear of arrest for debt. Unfortunately, it was next to impossible, so numerous were his creditors, to have them all sign a general letter of license on his behalf. The petitioners were certain that keeping Croghan at Aughwick would serve no good end, and, "taking into their consideration the great knowledge of the said George Croghan in Indian affairs, his extensive influence among them, and the service and public utility he may be of to this province in these respects," they prayed the Assembly to pass an act relieving Croghan and Trent from arrest for debt for a period of ten years.[30]

This petition was received by the Assembly on November 26, when the petitioners were instructed to bring in their request in the form of a bill. Indicative of how the most powerful figures in the government were lining up in Croghan's favor is a letter written by Speaker Isaac Norris on November 27: "George Croghan behaved extreamly well under Genl Braddock, he was in the van and saw the enemy before they devided to flank the Army.... It is said Genl Braddock would have been scalped by the Indians had it not been for the timely assistance of Croghan who helped him into a waggon & conveyd him out of danger when his own soldiers had fled and left their General." Stories such as this enlisted sympathy for Braddock's Indian manager.[31] On December 2, Morris ceremoniously signed the bill into law. Concurrently, orders were sent Croghan to come to Philadelphia. Considering the extreme difficulty which Morris and the Assembly experienced in agreeing on legislation, the speedy passage of this most unusual act was truly extraordinary.[32]

30. *Votes and Proceedings . . . of the Province of Pa.*, IV, 524-25.
31. Norris to Robert Charles, Nov. 27, 1755, Norris Letter Book (1719-56), 91, Hist. Soc. of Pa.
32. According to Morris, the relief act was passed so that "the Province might have the benefit of his [Croghan's] knowledge of the woods and his

The amicable legislative process which benefited Croghan and Trent contrasts with the incredible stress and strain between the Assembly and governor over two important defense bills. No longer able to withstand the overwhelming popular demand, the Assembly passed a militia act on November 25. It is not surprising, however, that its maiden effort at organizing a militia was fantastically coy and unrealistic. After providing for the raising of armed forces, the act stipulated that the officers were to be elected by the vote of the enlisted men, and it provided that the forces could not be marched more than three days beyond the inhabited parts of the province, nor detained longer than three weeks in any garrison without voluntary agreement by every man in the command. Morris signed the bill, *faute de mieux*.[33]

Two days later, on November 27, he signed an act granting £60,000 for the king's use to support Pennsylvania's war effort. Fortunately, Thomas Penn had offered a gift of £5,000, and the Assembly, taking this into consideration, waived the tax on the Penn estates. However, the Assembly did not give Governor Morris, who was cordially disliked, control of the fund. The expenditure of the £60,000 was delegated to a commission made up mostly of assemblymen, including Franklin, but also including the respected James Hamilton of the governor's council.

The commissioners believed that the best way to safeguard the frontier was to wage an offensive war against the aggressors, but they wanted advice and sent for Croghan, representing Cumberland County, Conrad Weiser of Berks County, and James Galbreath of Lancaster County, in order to obtain their opinions. Of the commissioners' interview with these men, Hamilton wrote, "I cannot say we have received much satisfaction from them." Nevertheless, the commissioners accepted their advice to build a chain of forts to secure the frontier before offensive action was considered. The policy of building forts from the Potomac to the Susquehanna, and, indeed, from the Susquehanna to the Delaware, had been ad-

---

influence among the Indians." Morris to Charles Hardy, July 5, 1756, *Pa. Archives*, II, 689-90.

33. *The Statutes at Large of Pennsylvania from 1682 to 1801* (Harrisburg, 1898), V, 197-201. This act was disallowed by George II on July 7, 1756.

vanced by many and had, in part, been recently urged on the Assembly by a petition from Cumberland County.[34]

The plan called for four forts to be located at strategic points west of the Susquehanna, as well as a number of forts between that river and the Delaware. Croghan's interest lay in the four western forts. The most important of the four was to be Fort Lyttelton, located about twenty miles from the settlements on Burd's unfinished road. Twenty miles north of Fort Lyttelton was Croghan's stockade, soon to be christened Fort Shirley. It stood near the path used by the Indians and Indian traders to and from the Ohio, and it was consequently on the Indians' easiest route into the settlements. Some fifteen miles northeast of Aughwick, near the mouth of a branch of the Juniata called Kishacoquillas, a third fort to be named Fort Granville was projected. That fort would command a narrow pass where the Juniata flowed through the mountains and would protect the Juniata settlements. The final fort, Pomfret Castle, was to be placed approximately midway between Fort Granville and the Susquehanna for the further protection of the Juniata settlements.[35]

The commissioners made Croghan a captain and ordered him to return to Cumberland County, build the new fortresses, and recruit their garrisons. "I knew not whom else to employ," Hamilton wrote Morris, "and upon supposition that he is honest [there was always that doubt], no body is fitter for that service." Thus, despite all the ignominy that had been heaped on his head over the past years and despite his failure and enforced exile, Croghan was still considered the most effective Pennsylvanian west of the Susquehanna.[36]

Amply provided with credit, Croghan hurried off on his important assignment. At Joseph Simon's store in Lancaster, he paused on December 22 to purchase "silver truck" worth £50 for Indian gifts and other stores for the government. A little later,

---

34. *Col. Rec. of Pa.*, VII, 153; William Shirley to Morris, Nov. 15, 1755, and Shippen to William Allen, Dec. 16, 1755, Penn Mss., Official Correspondence, VII, 153, 185, Hist. Soc. of Pa.; Hamilton to Morris, Dec. 18, 1755, *Pa. Archives*, II, 537-38; *Votes and Proceedings . . . of the Province of Pa.*, IV, 504.
35. Morris to Shirley, Feb. 9, 1756, *Pa. Archives*, II, 569.
36. Croghan's orders, and Hamilton to Morris, Dec. 18, 1755, *ibid.*, 536, 538.

he ordered 250 tin canteens from Simon. Pressing on toward the frontier, Croghan recruited the western forces. On December 27, he paid a tavern keeper £8 "for soulgers expenses for dayet and loging 3 dayes." Since the bill should not have been much more than a shilling a day per man, this charge could have cared for about fifty men. Before the first of the year, Croghan with 180 recruits left the settlements and crossed the mountains. According to Governor Morris, Croghan went about the business entrusted to him "in a very expeditious manner," though, as might have been anticipated, "not as frugally as the commissioners for disposing of the publick money thought he might have done." But Croghan had scarcely time for bargaining while recruiting, supplying, laying out forts, and persuading Indians to act as messengers and scouts.[37]

He had received some military supplies in Philadelphia and provided other necessary stores from his own resources, including a hundred tomahawks, a swivel gun, and twenty-nine firearms. The service of supply was far from perfected, and many of Croghan's men were armed with rifles which actually belonged to their captain. These rifles were far superior to the government's smoothbore guns, for, although a man might take a full minute to clean, load, and discharge a rifle, during which time a smoothbore gun could be fired three times, the rifle was much more accurate.[38]

Early in January, Croghan received orders from Governor Morris to bring as many Indians as he could to a peace meeting at Carlisle. These instructions were difficult to comply with promptly, and Morris and the other members of his party, including Weiser, Peters, and Shippen, were kept in a state of exasperated impatience awaiting the Irishman's arrival. Moreover, the number of Iroquois Croghan finally sent in from Aughwick was so small that the conference was doomed to be inconsequential. Nevertheless, the talks went on for three days, ending with the usual expressions of friendship and the customary donation of presents.[39]

37. Simon's and James Long's bills in Cadwalader Coll., Hist. Soc. of Pa.; *Pennsylvania Journal*, Jan. 1, 1756; *Pa. Archives*, II, 690; Hamilton, ed., *Letters to Washington*, I, 190-92.
38. *Pa. Archives*, Second Series, II, 695; *Pa. Archives*, III, 25, and II, 633, 643.
39. *Col. Rec. of Pa.*, VI, 779; Richard Peters Diary, Dec. 8, 1755-Jan. 8, 1756, Hist. Soc. of Pa.; William Logan to John Smith, Jan. 16, 1756, Smith Papers, Lib. Co. of Phila.

The proper disposition of military matters at Carlisle was far more important than the Indian treaty. Croghan reported that he had raised the three hundred men required to garrison the four forts and had partially built Fort Lyttelton. Morris, with the approval of the commissioners, divided Croghan's men into companies of seventy-five enlisted men, officered by a captain (salary 7s.6d. a day), lieutenant, and ensign, and issued commissions to the officers. James Burd was appointed captain of Fort Granville with Edward Ward as his lieutenant. Croghan's second in command at Fort Shirley was a Scottish physician, Hugh Mercer, who was destined to rise to the rank of general during the Revolution and die at the Battle of Princeton. Indian trader Hugh Crawford served as Croghan's ensign, and Thomas Smallman, Croghan's cousin, acted as commissary of the fort. The four western companies were the cream of Pennsylvania's military force, because, unlike the men raised under the new militia act, their soldiers were all regularly enlisted in the king's service for a period of ninety days, and the officers were selected by the government and not by vote of the enlisted men.[40]

The next two months at Croghan's fort were filled with excitement, for the enemy was ceaseless in his forays against Pennsylvania's back settlements. Although it had been expected that the captains would keep detachments scouting between the forts, this proved impossible because of the difficult supply situation. Instead of scouting when not guarding the garrison, the men were used to protect supply convoys, since contractors would no longer venture out to the forts. Consequently, the Indians were hardly impeded in their murderous attacks.

Fort Shirley was too strong for the natives to assault; the best they could do was to lurk about it, picking off stragglers. Late in January, nineteen-year-old John Baker, an indentured servant of Croghan's, went out of the fort to the nearby garden where he was captured and taken to the Ohio Indian village of Kittanning, home of the two most feared Indian leaders, Shingas and Captain

---

40. William West to [   ], Jan. 12, 1756, Morris to the Council, Jan. 21, 1756, Peters to Penn, Feb. 17, 1756, Penn Mss., Official Correspondence, VIII, 13, 21, Hist. Soc. of Pa.; Morris' orders to Burd, Jan. 17, 1756, and Hugh Mercer to Burd, Feb. 17, 1756, Shippen Papers, II, 21, 27, Hist. Soc. of Pa.

Jacobs. The place was thronged with young English prisoners. Baker made his escape in March and returned to Fort Shirley.[41]

A few days after Baker was kidnapped, two Delaware warriors were hospitably received at the fort, where they were given presents and, in turn, promised to bring in a large number of warriors to help the English cause. On their departure, they persuaded one of Croghan's men to come with them to take a drink of whisky, and, when a little way from the fort, tried to murder him. A friendly native gave the alarm, and a rescue party soon terminated the two Delawares' earthly rambles.[42]

Shingas and his band remained on the war path. On February 11, 1756, some of his warriors captured John Craig near John McDowell's mill. Shingas asked Craig questions about Croghan: Why had Croghan gone on Braddock's expedition? Why had Croghan been returned to favor with the government of Pennsylvania? Shingas also described the campaign which would bring the Delawares victoriously to Philadelphia that summer "and particularly threatned that if they could catch George Croghan, Monocatootha [Scarouady] and Andrew Montour they would burn them." In hopes of capturing Croghan, Shingas kept fourteen Indians scouting about Fort Shirley. On February 29, the chieftain and his Delawares raided McDowell's mill. Ensign Hugh Crawford, with a sergeant and thirteen of Croghan's men, were drawing provisions there when the Indians attacked. Two soldiers were killed in the inconclusive skirmish.[43]

As the winter wore on, conditions in the little forts grew more and more desperate. Provisions were scanty; there was little ammunition (not three rounds per man at Fort Granville); and less than half the men had been issued guns. To make matters worse, the men had not yet been paid, and their terms were due to run out at the end of the month. It was clear that many of them would refuse to re-enlist.[44]

41. Examination of John Baker, Penn Mss., Official Correspondence, VIII, 63, Hist. Soc. of Pa.
42. *Pa. Archives*, II, 571; *Pennsylvania Gazette*, Feb. 19, 1756.
43. *Pennsylvania Gazette*, Mar. 18, 1756; Benjamin Blett to Burd, Mar. 5, 1756, Shippen Papers, II, 33, and deposition of John Craig, Penn Mss., Indian Affairs, II, 77½, Hist. Soc. of Pa.
44. *Pa. Archives*, II, 611, 613, 623.

Early in March, Croghan was called to Philadelphia for a conference with the commissioners, who were so horrified at his expenditures that they censured him and also expressed their disapproval of his friendly relationship with his enlisted men. His temper worn thin by difficult services over the past months, Croghan angrily resigned his commission. Richard Peters' reaction to the resignation of a man who had received special protection by an act of Assembly just so he could serve the colony sums up local sentiment. To the outraged Peters, Croghan was "that vile knave."[45]

As if Croghan was not in enough trouble, the highest authorities in England suspected him of treason. The cause of the furor was two letters addressed to the former French ambassador to Great Britain, the Duke de Mirepoix, by a man who signed himself Filius Gallicae. Intercepted in Ireland, these letters were evidently written in Philadelphia in January, 1756, and were of a highly treasonable nature. Two more letters, written in March to the Duke by the same anonymous person, were also intercepted.[46]

In brief, the author of the letters confided that he had been commissioned to organize a large army in Pennsylvania to capture Fort Duquesne. Because his sympathies were French, and because he was secretly a Roman Catholic, he wanted to betray his trust and use his forces against the English. This would not be difficult to do since many of his soldiers would be selected from the Irish and German Roman Catholics of the province. These men would prefer to fight for Louis XV than for George II. The writer asked the Duke for letters signifying French approval of this action and for money to make it possible.

Lord Halifax, president of the Board of Trade and Plantations, was obliged to treat the matter seriously because almost every fact mentioned in the first letter was true, or appeared to be true. The ministers of state all agreed with Halifax that here was treason of the deepest dye. The guilty man must be discovered. But who was he? Washington and Governor Shirley were mentioned as

45. Shippen to Burd, Mar. 24, 1756, Shippen Papers, II, 35, and Peters to Penn, Apr. 25, June 26, Dec. 26, 1756, Penn Mss., Official Correspondence, VIII, 73-75, 125, 213, Hist. Soc. of Pa.
46. *Annual Report of the American Historical Association for the Year 1896* (Washington, 1897), I, 690.

possibilities. Halifax, however, believed that the letter writer was an Irishman, and George Croghan became the principal suspect. The military leaders on their way to America to take over the North American command were ordered to inquire about him and arrest him if guilty. In commenting on the letters in a secret communication to the Duke of Devonshire, Secretary of State Henry Fox wrote, "One Capt George Croghan, an intriguing, disaffected person, and Indian trader in Pensylvania was very much suspected."[47]

In the description which Filius Gallicae gave of himself, there was much that actually fitted Croghan and much that could have fitted him. To begin with, the writer complained that he had been ill-used by the English governors in America. What was Croghan's record on this score? Morris of Pennsylvania had ignored him for months after Braddock's defeat; Dinwiddie of Virginia had refused to settle his accounts; Sharpe of Maryland suspected him of treasonable activities.

Writing on January 6, 1756, the mystery man stated that "within these 15 days" he had been asked to head an army to be raised in Pennsylvania for service against Fort Duquesne. Croghan was ordered to raise the western forces of Pennsylvania on December 17, 1755.

Moreover, the writer described himself as well known to the English, who considered him a faithful subject of King George. He understood French and most of the Indian languages. With the exception of his knowledge of French, this was all true of Croghan and virtually limited the identity of the author to that of an Indian trader or an Indian agent. Who else knew the Indian tongues? The writer went on to add that he was single, nearly thirty-eight years old, had been bred a soldier and had passed most of his life in the service of the English. Nothing is known of Croghan's life before he came to America, nor is the year of his birth known. He could have soldiered in Ireland, he may have been about thirty-eight, was almost certainly single, and he had devoted much time to public service.

The writer also stated that he had sent intelligence to Contrecoeur at Fort Duquesne when Braddock was on the march and

47. *Ibid.*, 688-93.

had later received a letter of thanks from Captain Dumas, who gave him a large share of credit for the French victory. Dumas' letter was brought to the informer by an Indian friendly to the English. Croghan was one of the few men capable of fitting into this sinister picture.

If the above description applied or could apply to Croghan, there were other matters which did not apply to him, nor could they apply to anyone, for the author was of a mendacious turn, leavening truths with lies. The outstanding falsehood in his account was the statement that he had levied ten thousand men out of the complement of fifteen thousand he was to raise in Pennsylvania.

The author of these letters must have been a well-informed Philadelphian whose imagination was caught by the commission given Croghan to raise a force in mid-December. He seems to have put himself in Croghan's position and then to have described it in exaggerated terms. Since he interlarded valuable data with palpable untruths, a logical conclusion would be that the letters were not treasonably motivated; perhaps they were a hoax, although they might have been written to entice money from the French or to damage Croghan. There were many who did not like Croghan, many who had lost money by him. In December, 1755, these people saw him receive the unprecedented protection of the ten-year relief act and also learned that he was placed in a position of important military trust. These letters may well have been a deliberate attempt to discredit him, an attempt which may have been related to an anonymous attack upon him published in England only a few months earlier.

The most serious feature of the Filius Gallicae letters was the information that Pennsylvania abounded with Irish and German Roman Catholics who would be happy to overthrow the British in favor of their co-religionists. For all the English authorities knew, this frightening statement could be true; Roman Catholics were not trusted by the English in pre-Revolutionary days. Although Croghan was not a Roman Catholic, he had recently been branded as one. In a violently partisan document, *An Answer to an Invidious Pamphlet, entituled, A Brief State of the Province of Pensylvania*, published in London in 1755 to counter an anti-

Assembly pamphlet, Croghan was bitterly attacked by an anonymous author. The pamphleteer wrote, "One George Craghan, an Irish papist, as an Indian trader was frequently employed by the government of Pennsylvania to carry presents to the Indians living on or about the Ohio, and to bring their answers back." The trader's "vile attempt to impose upon the Assembly" in 1751 was exposed when Croghan as Governor Hamilton's "tool ... fell a sacrifice to the Assembly's resentment." Croghan's subsequent career was disclosed in an inglorious light. "He has never since dared to come within 100 miles of Philadelphia. Having quitted Pensylvania, he went and offered his service to the Ohio Company in Virginia: but they rejected it: upon which he crossed over the mountains, and now lives at Logstown or at Aughwik, doing all the mischief he can in revenge, by influencing the Indians and French against the English."

When General Daniel Webb arrived in New York in June, 1756, he brought several of the intercepted letters. When these were compared with letters of Croghan's sent to New York by Governor Morris, it was obvious that Croghan could not have written the treasonable communications. Nevertheless, the authorities remained wary for a time, but it is unlikely that Croghan ever knew of the Filius Gallicae episode.[48]

48. *Ibid.*, 698; *Pa. Archives*, II, 689-90, 694.

6

Deputy to Sir William Johnson

SHORTLY AFTER Croghan's resignation from Pennsylvania's military force in March, 1756, his friends Scarouady and Montour arrived in Philadelphia from a visit to New York, where they had decided to gather the Indians who had fought with Braddock and move to the Mohawk Valley. Their plans may well have influenced Croghan, who realized that Pennsylvania no longer had any use for him but who hoped that in New York the situation would be different. New York was the seat of the war, and there he could seek employment either with the army or with Johnson's Indian service.[1]

It took Croghan two months to turn over his Aughwick command to Hugh Mercer—Croghan's cousin Thomas Smallman remained with Mercer as ensign of his company—and to care for his personal affairs. On March 15, 1756, the disgruntled commissioners paid him £213 for goods and food supplied the four companies he had raised, but it was not until June 1 that they paid him £200 for building Fort Shirley.[2]

The recovery of the trade losses he had suffered from the French and Indians before 1755 was his most pressing personal problem. The original schedule of Trent's and Croghan's losses had disappeared with Braddock's baggage. In making up their new lists, the partners scoured the countryside to find their fellow traders and to collect from them certified statements of the amounts they, too, had lost to the enemy. In April, May, and June, they

---

1. *Col. Rec. of Pa.*, VII, 64.
2. *Pa. Archives*, II, 632-33; *Votes and Proceedings . . . of the Province of Pa.*, IV, 618, 620.

secured depositions from fifteen traders. This group, headed by Croghan and represented by William Trent as attorney, was to become known as the "suffering traders" of 1754. They prepared a memorial to the Crown praying for reparations and arranged to have their demands presented through another memorial from the Philadelphia merchants who had been concerned in the Indian trade.[3]

Leaving the final arrangements of these matters in Trent's hands, Croghan hastened to Albany, a quaint Dutch village which was then the hub of English military activity in North America. An important trading place, it lay at the intersection of two invasion routes by which the French could descend on New York. One of these routes was supplied by Lake Champlain, Lake George, and a portage to the Hudson. The French part of this water system was protected by forts at Crown Point and Ticonderoga, while the British end was covered by two forts at the portage, Fort Edward on the Hudson and Fort William Henry on Lake George. The other invasion route led from the fortified English post of Oswego on Lake Ontario, up the Oswego and Oneida rivers, across Oneida Lake, up Wood Creek to the carrying place to the Mohawk River, and then down the Mohawk to Schenectady and Albany.

At Albany, Croghan, aided by a letter of introduction from Governor Morris, waited on Governor Shirley to solicit his pay earned under Braddock. Shirley exercised powers as commander in chief while awaiting the arrival of a new general. The defensibility of Oswego, whose garrison of one thousand men was in imminent peril of being cut off, was his chief worry, but his principal interest was in an attack he had planned on Ticonderoga and Crown Point. For this drive Shirley had accumulated a provincial army of seven thousand men.[4]

Croghan did not linger in Albany. Closely pursued by Levy Andrew Levy, whom Joseph Simon had sent all the way from Lancaster to collect money owed by Croghan, the Irishman was soon on his way over the twenty miles of road which led to Schenectady, where the waters of the Mohawk came in view.

3. Ohio Co. Papers, I, 5-33½, Hist. Soc. of Pa.
4. Gipson, *The British Empire*, VI, 192.

Twenty miles up the Mohawk, after passing only a score of houses, he dismounted at Fort Johnson. Truly, Fort Johnson was a suitable mansion for a man as rich and powerful as its owner. Moreover, this large stone building was surrounded by barracks, a mill, barns and stables, as well as all sorts of other improvements, including a large Indian council chamber.[5]

The place was thronged with colorful groups of natives, Indian agents, and soldiers, most of whom were preparing to leave for Onondaga where an important treaty was to be held. The present had already been poled up the Mohawk on bateaux. Croghan recognized several old friends—Scarouady, Montour, and the Aughwick Indians—but most of the faces he saw were new to him, including that of the man whose fame and position had sped him "express" from Philadelphia.

William Johnson had come to America in 1738 at the age of twenty-three. Tall and rugged and of commanding presence, he was soon the outstanding Indian trader in the Mohawk Valley, attaining remarkable influence among the Iroquois, who called him Warraghiyagey—"he who does much business." This prominence won him the post of superintendent of Indian affairs in 1755, and in that year, serving as a major general, he commanded an army of colonial troops in a campaign against Crown Point. Johnson did not attain his objective, but he did vanquish a strong French force at Lake George and captured Baron Dieskau, the enemy leader.

Retaining the colonelcy of the Albany County militia, Johnson retired from his army command. Honors poured in on him; he was created a baronet and awarded £5,000, and on February 17, 1756, his commission from Braddock was superseded by a royal instrument appointing him "Colonel of Our Faithfull Subjects, and Allies, the Six United Nations of Indians & their Confederates, in the Northern Parts of North America." For this service he was granted a salary of £600 a year and was placed under the orders of the commanding general. Fortunately for Johnson, Shirley, with whom he was not on cordial terms, had been repudiated by the

---

5. Arthur Pound, *Johnson of the Mohawks* (New York, 1930), 124, 474; Croghan paid Levy at Fort Johnson on June 3, 1756, Cadwalader Coll., Hist. Soc. of Pa.

ministry, and the Earl of Loudoun, vested with viceregal powers and the support of many regiments of British regulars, was on his way to America.

To Croghan, Johnson represented success in the many endeavors in which the Pennsylvanian had failed—success as an Indian trader and as an Indian agent, success as a land speculator, and, above all, an overwhelming success with the highest authorities in the Empire. The background of the two men had much in common. Both were Irish immigrants of about the same age and of the Anglican religion, and both were men of wide ambition. Johnson's reaction to Croghan was immediate and warming. He appointed the Pennsylvanian at a salary of £200 to act as his deputy, empowering him to hold conferences, send messages, and treat with the Indians. From this auspicious start, a strong friendship developed, and Croghan found himself embarked on a fifteen-year career as Johnson's senior agent.[6]

All was bustle at Fort Johnson on June 3 when Sir William, Croghan, and a strong party set out for Onondaga to attend the ancient council fire of the Iroquois Confederacy. With the party went a Mohawk chief and some of his tribesmen and a delegation of thirty prosperous-looking river Indians. In addition to these natives and his personal followers, Johnson was escorted by the grenadier company of the Fiftieth Regiment.

With French Indians lurking in the woods and cutting the supply line to Oswego, Johnson's journey was dangerous, yet he felt compelled to make it. The Delawares and Shawnees had been called to the Onondaga council fire to make peace, which was reason enough to take Johnson there. Even more important, his visit gave him an opportunity to defeat French influence among the upper nations of the Iroquois, and to enlist all the nations in a concerted effort against the French.

Johnson arrived at Onondaga on June 18, when he made a ceremonial entrance. To the accompaniment of songs of condolence honoring the sachem Red Head, who had lately died, Sir William marched at the head of his party to within sight of the Onondaga Castle. There, the way was blocked by the chiefs, sitting in a semi-circle across the road. The mournful singing con-

6. *Johnson Papers*, IX, 470-71, 538.

tinued for another hour before Johnson led the Indians into the castle, where songs of sorrow gave way to thunderous salutes of celebration.[7]

Johnson did not stay in the castle but pitched his tent five miles away on Onondaga Lake, to be near his present-laden bateaux. This was the place he selected for his conference. Croghan's presence at the ensuing meetings was noted in the minutes by the secretary, who placed the deputy's name at the head of the otherwise unnamed "Gentlemen who attended Sir William." As Johnson had feared, the Iroquois had been dangerously infected by the French, but by skill and forceful persuasion he brought them back into the British camp. The chiefs vowed their fealty and promised to send their warriors to fight the enemy. Unfortunately, little could be done about the Delawares and Shawnees, who did not attend the meeting in adequate numbers. Subsequently, some of them came to Fort Johnson, but despite their expressions of good will their visit proved little.

Shortly after these treaties, Johnson went to Albany to attend a council of war. At this council, it was decided that Oswego should be strengthened and that several companies of rangers should be raised to act with the friendly Indians in harassing the French. Little action followed, however, until Lord Loudoun, a sprightly, affable little Scottish nobleman, arrived. Johnson conferred with Loudoun about Indian department matters, requesting that a salary be fixed for a deputy agent to assist him and nominating George Croghan for the post. When Loudoun told him the story of the intercepted letters, Sir William disclaimed intimate knowledge of Croghan but held to his recommendation: "I believe him an honest man, but a little indiscreet." There was no question in Johnson's mind about Croghan's qualifications as an Indian agent, for he was "a person very acceptable to them & well acquainted with their customs and manners."[8]

With Loudoun at the helm, the British war machine went into action. A week or more after Johnson's interview with Loudoun, Croghan watched General Webb and the Forty-fourth Regiment

---

7. Treaty minutes, O'Callaghan, ed., *New-York Col. Doc.*, VII, 130-61.
8. Stanley McCrory Pargellis, *Lord Loudoun in North America* (New Haven, 1933), 90; *Johnson Papers*, II, 515, and IX, 483-87, 511-12, 538; Loudoun Papers, #1396, Huntington Library.

pass by Fort Johnson in bateaux on a leisurely ascent of the Mohawk to reinforce Oswego. At the German Flats, an upriver Palatine settlement, Webb received word of a long-feared catastrophe. The French under Montcalm had invested Oswego. The general hurried his force forward to the carrying place between Wood Creek and the Mohawk, where two of Johnson's officers, Captains Thomas Butler and Jelles Fonda, also encamped with a party of rangers and Indians.

From Albany, Loudoun canceled the provincial army's advance on Crown Point and ordered Johnson to call out a thousand of his militia and march them to the German Flats to reinforce Webb. Johnson acted vigorously, although the militia, worn out by similar calls earlier in the year, responded slowly to the crisis. A large number of Indians, however, including a band of more than fifty led by Scarouady and Montour, gathered at the Flats to support him. When Sir William arrived with one of his militia battalions on August 23, he found the Indians "vastly dejected," and for a very good reason—Oswego, the portal to the Iroquois country, had fallen.[9]

Exhausted by his efforts, and so weakened by dysentery that he was unable to sit up, Johnson ordered the warriors to accompany Croghan to the carrying place to assist General Webb. Croghan and his Indians, 150 strong, arrived at the portage just in time turn around and come back with Webb, who unfortunately had decided to withdraw. With the fall of Oswego and Webb's retreat, the heart of the Iroquois Confederacy lay open to the French, and the entire Indian picture altered disastrously. From then on, only the Mohawks could be counted as unquestionably true.[10]

This rapid change for the worse may have discouraged Croghan with the Indian service. Learning that ranger companies were wanted, Croghan visited Albany in the middle of September to solicit the command of one of them. Self-assured as ever, he told Lord Loudoun that he could raise two hundred recruits from among his friends in Pennsylvania and the southern frontiers, "the greatest part of them good woods men lately imployed by my self and other Indian treaders." Loudoun questioned Croghan in

9. *Johnson Papers*, II, 548, 549, and IX, 506, 508.
10. *Ibid.*, IX, 511-12; Loudoun Papers, #1704, Huntington Library.

a circuitous way concerning the intercepted letters and, fearful of trusting him with an armed command, decided that it would be better for the Irishman to remain an assistant to Johnson.[11]

While the agent was in Albany, his chief wrote Loudoun that Indian intelligence pointed to a full-scale French advance on Fort William Henry. Johnson feared that the provincial troops at that fort, and at Fort Edward only eighteen miles away, could not withstand an attack. By this time, it seemed clear that the French were not going to exploit their Oswego success and that the Mohawk Valley was secure. Loudoun withdrew the Forty-fourth Regiment from the Mohawk, concentrating all available troops to support the provincial garrisons, and ordered Johnson to bring up the Indians.[12]

The superintendent sent a war party to Fort Edward, but it took time to assemble the Indians in strength. The next group, some sixty-nine warriors, he assigned to Croghan, who was assisted by Captain Jelles Fonda and five rangers. Croghan's party took the road to Schenectady on September 29 and then cut across country through the woods to Fort Edward. Johnson followed on October 17 with sixty-three more natives.[13]

At Fort Edward, Croghan found himself in proximity to the two regiments which had served with Braddock, but he had little time for visiting. According to Loudoun, the Indians who had come up with the first war party had mostly deserted. To prevent his own charges from slipping away, Croghan stayed with them. Despite his vigilance, some of the provincial troops made off with the Indians' rations of venison after getting the natives drunk.[14]

Johnson's intelligence that the French would not attack from the direction of Oswego was correct, but it was in error in forecasting an advance from Crown Point. The major campaigns for

11. Croghan to Loudoun, Sept. 14, 1756, Loudoun Papers, Huntington Library; Loudoun to Johnson, Sept. 19, 1756, *Johnson Papers*, II, 562; Deposition of George Croghan at Albany, Sept. 20, 1756, Gifts and Deposits, Chatham Papers, 95, Public Record Office, London.
12. Johnson to Loudoun, Sept. 15, 1756, and Loudoun to Johnson, Sept. 16, 1756, *Johnson Papers*, IX, 528-29, II, 560-61.
13. *Ibid.*, IX, 549-51; *Pennsylvania Gazette*, Oct. 21, 1756; O'Callaghan, ed., *New-York Col. Doc.*, VII, 229-30.
14. *Johnson Papers*, IX, 553.

the year were, in fact, over. In November, Loudoun's army went into winter quarters.

Croghan returned to Fort Johnson, where he met Edmund Atkin, the superintendent for the southern Indians, who had recently arrived from England. While Johnson, Atkin, and Croghan talked, new plans for Croghan were formulating. Johnson and Loudoun were worried about Pennsylvania. Croghan, no doubt, knew the outlines of what had happened there since his departure. In July, Fort Granville had been destroyed by the enemy, and its small garrison carried off. While terrified frontiersmen implored the governor for the protection of regular troops, a provincial expedition countered with a successful raid on an Ohio Indian village. From Fort Shirley, still known not only to the Indians but to the French as "Croghan's fort," John Armstrong led four companies, one of which was commanded by Croghan's half-brother, to Kittanning, the principal home of the hostile Delawares. With fire and sword, the Pennsylvanians fell on this settlement, burned it to the ground, liberated prisoners, and killed the war chief Jacobs. After this victory, Fort Shirley was evacuated because Armstrong did not consider it defensible.[15]

Armstrong's victory did not end the Indian war, and the situation became even more involved because the Quakers, accustomed to arbitrating their own problems, now stepped in and tried to arbitrate the problems which had brought on the war. Moreover, although positively forbidden by Lord Loudoun to treat with the Indians, the Pennsylvania government had held a treaty with Teedyuscung at Easton in November. On November 22, Johnson, mindful of Quaker activities, urged Loudoun to issue a proclamation prohibiting any group of people from interfering in the management of Indian affairs. But more than this was necessary if Johnson was to fulfill his role as sole superintendent of the northern Indians. Unable to leave the Iroquois country and personally supervise the tangled state of affairs in Pennsylvania, he had only one alternative.[16]

15. Pargellis, *Lord Loudoun*, 92–93; Vaudreuil to Machault, Sept. 19, 1756, New France X, Canada, 1756-58, 343, Parkman 18, Mass. Hist. Soc.; *Col. Rec. of Pa.*, VII, 261, 278; Hamilton to Morris, Dec. 22, 1755, Penn Mss., Official Correspondence, VII, 197, Hist. Soc. of Pa.

16. Johnson to Loudoun, Nov. 22, 1756, *Johnson Papers*, IX, 559; Loudoun

On November 24, Johnson ordered Croghan to go to Philadelphia as soon as possible. As Johnson's deputy, Croghan was to investigate the Indian situation and to convince the natives that it was profitable for them to continue friendly relations with the English and the Six Nations and to cooperate with the army in the 1757 campaigns. He also was to inquire into the causes of the defection of the Delawares and Shawnees and to promise them justice.[17]

Returning to Philadelphia in December, 1756, after an absence of nearly six months, Croghan found that William Denny, the new governor, was as much at odds with the Assembly as Governor Morris had been. The struggle between the proprietary party and the anti-proprietary party, whose strength lay in the Society of Friends, had, however, taken a new turn.

Throughout the year, the Quakers had smarted under the lash of criticism. They had been accused of bringing on the Indian war by keeping the colony in a defenseless condition. Their halfhearted efforts at meeting wartime conditions, as embodied in the supply and militia acts of November, 1755, were termed unrealistic. The supply bill appropriated money for various purposes and "for the King's use." Its failure to mention military service drew the scorn of the Board of Trade, which excoriated the Assembly's "system of inaction, and neglect of the public safety." As for the militia act, authorities in England found it "in every respect the most improper and inadequate to the service which could have been framed and passed, and is rather calculated to exempt persons from military services, than to encourage and promote them." Delving down to basic principles, the Board stated that the legislature of every country was in duty bound to support and defend its government and its subjects, and that "the Assembly of Pennsylvania is in no degree exempted from this general law of nature and society."[18]

Largely through the genius of their leader, Israel Pemberton, the Quakers sought to regain prestige and save their colony from

---

to Denny, Sept. 22, 1756, *Col. Rec. of Pa.*, VII, 270; Julian P. Boyd, *Indian Treaties Printed by Benjamin Franklin, 1732-1762* (Philadelphia, 1938), lxxix-lxxx.

17. Johnson to Croghan, Nov. 24, 1756, *Johnson Papers*, II, 657-58.
18. *Votes and Proceedings . . . of the Province of Pa.*, IV, 628-29.

the sin of war. They organized the Friendly Association in 1756, which provided large funds to promote peace and good will with the Indians. They crowded into the governor's council chamber to assist him in Indian affairs. They attended the Easton treaty in November in large numbers, and it was no coincidence that at that treaty charges of fraud were thrown at the proprietors by Teedyuscung, the Delaware spokesman. The Walking Purchase of 1737 was based on a fraudulent deed, proclaimed the Indian king, and, although this injustice had not brought on the war, it had made the Indians strike harder. Despite the fact that the Walking Purchase had been made under the immediate supervision of such highly respected Quakers as James Logan and James Steel, the Friends called for a full investigation. If Thomas Penn's reputation was to suffer, so much the better, for it would enable the Quakers to shift the war guilt charge to the shoulders of the proprietors.

There can be little doubt that the Friends inspired Teedyuscung to accuse the proprietors of injustice in the 1737 walk. Nine months before the treaty at Easton, and long before the Quakers had conferred with Teedyuscung, Thomas Penn had learned of charges the Friends had prepared for the Delawares concerning the Walking Purchase. Thus, the intent to discredit the Penns by this stratagem dated back to the beginning of the Delaware war.[19]

In December, 1756, therefore, the Quakers, disregarding the bloody scalping knife, were ardently pressing for justice for the Indians. If the alleged twenty-year-old fraud could be adjusted, they claimed, peace would be restored. Peters and his fellow proprietary agents stood at bay. Obviously, the key man in the colony during the coming months would be the investigator of Teedyuscung's accusation. At this psychological moment, Croghan rode into Philadelphia.

Both factions were stunned to learn that Croghan had been fully empowered by Johnson to investigate the Indian situation.

19. "Dr. Fothergill has an account of another charge Friends has made up for the Delawares that they have been cheated, you know that was submitted to the Six Nations and if such a story is propagated let that part of the Treaty of 1742 be printed." Penn to Peters, Feb. 14, 1756, Penn Letter Book, IV, 232, Hist. Soc. of Pa.

"I fear the worst," lamented Richard Peters concerning Croghan; "how can I give credit to a man, who has told so many lies in Mr. Hockleys & other affairs to such a degree that I question whether he minds a word he says."[20]

Despite personal feelings, political leaders realized Croghan's importance and made advances to him. Croghan attempted to preserve a strict neutrality through his usual method of trying to please everyone. He promised Isaac Norris and other Quakers that he would see to it that the Indians' land claims would be carefully examined, and he convinced the Friends of his impartiality. It was noted that he appeared to be on the closest terms with Norris. To Peters, Croghan expressed great friendship, as well as a high regard for the proprietors, and promised the secretary that he would take no step without telling him about it. Croghan pointed out to Peters' dismay that all the lands west of the Alleghenies purchased by the Penns at Albany in 1754 (but not yet paid for) would have to be released to the Indians, as that purchase was a source of serious dissatisfaction both to the Ohio Delawares and to the Iroquois.

The government must settle its differences with Teedyuscung as soon as possible, Croghan informed Governor Denny, and every effort should be made to persuade the Ohio Indians to attend a meeting with the Delaware leader. Denny laid Croghan's advice before his council on December 14: "The Council knowing Mr. Croghan's circumstances was not a little surprized at the appointment, and desired to see his credentials."[21]

Croghan quickly dispelled the council's suspicions; indeed, all of his initial efforts were successful. Governor, council, commissioners, Assembly, Friendly Association—all agreed on the Indian meeting and on Croghan's proposals to send messengers to the native villages announcing the event. Money to pay the messengers was advanced him by the Assembly and the Friendly Association. Providing himself with the necessary belts of wampum, Croghan left for Harris' Ferry. Before long, couriers he had recruited from among the friendly Conestoga Indians were on their

20. Peters to Penn, Dec. 11, 1756, Penn Mss., Official Correspondence, VIII, 207, Hist. Soc. of Pa.
21. *Col. Rec. of Pa.*, VII, 354-55.

way to Teedyuscung at Tioga and to the Ohio country, carrying his invitations to a treaty.[22]

After a month spent at Lancaster and Harris' Ferry, Croghan returned to Philadelphia around the middle of February to meet Lord Loudoun, who was to hold a council there with the southern governors. The Indian agent and his servant took lodgings at the Indian King in Market Street, John Biddle's eminently respectable Quaker house, and awaited his lordship's arrival. As usual, Lord Loudoun was royally late. During this delay, the Indians, despite the severity of the winter, began to come down to the settlements in response to Croghan's messages.[23]

At last, on March 14, Lord Loudoun arrived in Philadelphia, where the governors of Pennsylvania, Maryland, Virginia, and North Carolina awaited him. Among other notables were Edmund Atkin, Colonel George Washington, and the senior officers of the Pennsylvania forces. Since the objective of the 1757 campaign was to be an expedition against the French fortress of Louisburg, after which Quebec might be attempted, Loudoun had come to concert a defense plan for the southern provinces.

Croghan had prepared a journal of Indian affairs from 1748 to 1755, which helped Loudoun understand the background of the present Indian troubles and which gave him a basis on which to advise Croghan about the coming treaty. The treaty presented a new feature, for, although Pennsylvania had to pay its costs, Croghan, not the governor of Pennsylvania, was to conduct the meeting. This situation relegated Pennsylvania's Indian negotiators, Richard Peters and Conrad Weiser, to a secondary role. Irritated, Peters wrote to Weiser, sarcastically referring to

22. *Ibid.*, 382-85, 391, 403-4; Peters to Penn, Jan. 10, 1757, Peters Letter Book (1755-57), Hist. Soc. of Pa.; *Votes and Proceedings . . . of the Province of Pa.*, IV, 672-73; Samuel Parrish, *Some Chapters in the History of the Friendly Association* (Philadelphia, 1877), 54-55; Shippen to Joseph Shippen, Jan. 12, 1757, and Charles Garroway to Burd, Jan. 23, 1757, Shippen Papers, II, 17, 101, Hist. Soc. of Pa.; Charles Thomson, *An Enquiry into the Causes of the Alienation of the Delaware and Shawanese Indians* (London, 1759), 103-4.

23. Croghan to Burd, Feb. 14, 1757, Shippen Papers, II, 111, and John Biddle's bill dated Mar. 26, 1757, Cadwalader Coll., Hist. Soc. of Pa.; Pargellis, *Lord Loudoun*, 218; *Votes and Proceedings . . . of the Province of Pa.*, IV, 702; Croghan to Johnson, Mar. 14, 1757, O'Callaghan, ed., *New-York Col. Doc.*, VII, 266.

Croghan as "a great man." Denny, however, felt no jealousy and willingly accepted Croghan's primacy in Indian affairs.[24]

As soon as he could take his leave of Loudoun, Croghan hastened to Harris' Ferry, where Scarouady and about 160 Indians, mostly Iroquois, were awaiting him. At Croghan's request, Johnson had sent these Indians to the treaty to help reconcile the Delawares. Fearful of smallpox, the natives refused Croghan's urgings to go to Philadelphia, but they consented to move their council fire to Lancaster. On April 7, Croghan encamped his party of Iroquois near that town and awaited the coming of Teedyuscung. He sent William Trent to Fort Allen to meet the Delaware king, but Teedyuscung did not come. For a complex of reasons, the bombastic Delaware feared the Six Nations and did not dare face the group that awaited him in Lancaster.[25]

The Indians who had come from New York to hear Teedyuscung's complaints and to urge him to make peace grew impatient as week after week passed. Hostile war parties struck the western frontier, and Croghan sent some of the Iroquois against them. The smallpox came with fatal consequences. Faithful old Scarouady fell ill with the dreaded disease and died. As their planting time approached, the Indians grew restive. At last, Little Abraham, a Mohawk sachem, told Croghan that a treaty must be held as soon as possible. This ultimatum was placed before Governor Denny, who, with the greatest reluctance, at last consented to come to Lancaster to represent Onas.[26]

Denny was the most extraordinary character ever appointed governor by the Penns. In his search for a military man for the office, Thomas Penn had applied to the Duke of Cumberland, who recommended Captain William Denny. Whatever his reputation in England may have been, Philadelphians found Denny peevish,

---

24. Croghan to Loudoun, Mar. 14, 1757, Loudoun Papers, Huntington Library; Peters to Weiser, Mar. 19, 1757, Correspondence of Conrad Weiser, II, 45, and Penn to Peters, Aug. 13, 1757, Penn Letter Book, V, 177, Hist. Soc. of Pa.

25. Shippen to "Dear Son," Mar. 28, 1757, Shippen Papers, II, 143, Hist. Soc. of Pa.; Croghan to Johnson, May 7, 1757, *Johnson Papers*, IX, 719; Boyd, *Indian Treaties*, 172; Anthony F. C. Wallace, *King of the Delawares: Teedyuscung, 1700-1763* (Philadelphia, 1949), 153.

26. *Col. Rec. of Pa.*, VII, 498-510; Norris to Robert Charles, February, 1758, Isaac Norris Letter Book (1756-66), 88, Hist. Soc. of Pa.

slow and averse to business, mean in money matters, unsteady in his opinions, disloyal to his employers, physically weak and timid, and so pathologically antisocial that he spent most of his time locked up with his books. "He likes nobody," complained Peters; "he seems to have no affections, his polite taste for men and books cannot suffer him to find any satisfaction in his station." A contemporary described Denny as "haughty without spirit, polite without manners, and learned without knowledge. With respect to business, always at home, yet never to be spoken with. In the morning for the proprietaries, at noon of no party, and at night, plump for the Assembly."[27]

Despite Denny's peculiarities, Croghan believed that he had a good understanding with him about the necessity for a candid inquiry into Teedyuscung's charges. But Croghan also noted that the governor was pretty much under Peters' influence. "Every one seems fond of an inquiry being made into the complaints of the Indians," Croghan wrote Johnson, "except some of the proprietary agents, who dont seem to like it. As to their dislike I take no notice of it, being determined to enter into no dispute with them on that head." Unlike Peters, the Quakers were eager to enlist Croghan's sympathies. The Friendly Association appointed Jeremiah Warder and Israel Pemberton to confer with him "on occasions and when they find it necessary."[28]

As May approached, Croghan lost confidence in Denny's integrity and became resentful of Peters' stiff attitude. In a confidential burn-this-letter note to one of the Quaker leaders, Croghan apologized (despite having sent at least three letters to the Friendly Association) for not having written to Norris or Pemberton. He had hesitated to do so for fear his letters might fall into other hands. "I see clearly the S[ecretar]y and C[ounci]l is doing all they can to make a differance between his honour and me however I am determind to act up to my instruc-

---

27. Penn to Morris, Jan. 10, 1756, Penn Letter Book, IV, 199, and Peters to Penn, Jan. 29, 1757, Peters Letter Book (1755-57), Hist. Soc. of Pa.; *The Port Folio*, Third Series (New York, 1813), I, 46-47; Nicholas B. Wainwright, "Governor William Denny in Pennsylvania," *Pa. Mag. of Hist. and Biog.*, 81 (1957), 170-98.

28. Croghan to Johnson, Mar. 14, 1757, O'Callaghan, ed., *New-York Col. Doc.*, VII, 266; Parrish, *History of the Friendly Association*, 60.

tions and lave them no room to find the least hole in my coat." The Indian agent solicited funds from the Friendly Association for the maintenance of the Indians and warned of the difficulty he would have in investigating the Indians' complaints, dismally informing the Quakers that the governor was going to do all he could to impede him.[29]

Denny, attended by members of his council, a large military escort (without which he would not move), representatives of the Assembly, and the provincial commissioners, who controlled the colony's funds, arrived in Lancaster on May 9. Israel Pemberton and more than a hundred Quakers also gathered there. Three days later, the conference convened at the courthouse. Except for the Senecas, the Six Nations were well represented. In his opening speech, the carefully prompted Denny expressed regret that Teedyuscung had not come and asked the Six Nations for advice in promoting peace between Pennsylvania and the Delawares. Little Abraham replied by suggesting that the Delawares would act in concert with the Senecas, the only nation they now recognized as their "uncles," and urged that messengers be sent to the Senecas inviting them, the Delawares, and Shawnees to a meeting where all differences could be settled.[30]

Denny was reluctant to issue an invitation for another treaty, and it was only with the greatest difficulty that Croghan persuaded him of its necessity. With Weiser's help, Croghan prepared the governor's speech accepting the Mohawk's advice. He also delivered a speech of his own, "warm & animated" according to a Quaker witness, beseeching the Six Nations to tell him about the frauds complained of by Teedyuscung and of any other injustices. Little Abraham answered that they knew nothing about Teedyuscung's charges. The trouble with the Delawares, Little Abraham concluded, was mainly caused by the whites settling their lands and driving them back into the arms of the French.[31]

29. Parrish, *History of the Friendly Association*, 61-62; Croghan to William West, Apr. 28, 1757, Norris Mss., Loan Office Accounts, Indian Charges, 27, Hist. Soc. of Pa.
30. Boyd, *Indian Treaties*, 176-77.
31. *Col. Rec. of Pa.*, VII, 527; letter dated May 18, 1757, John Baynton folder, Gratz Coll., Hist. Soc. of Pa.; Boyd, *Indian Treaties*, 181-82.

The Lancaster conference ended cheerfully with the distribution of a handsome present. The Iroquois departed well pleased, and messengers were sent to summon Teedyuscung and the Senecas. Although robbed of its main purpose, which was to conciliate Teedyuscung, the conference had, nevertheless, been quite satisfactory. Of course, it was disappointing that the Ohio Delawares had not attended, but Custaloga, the hostile Delaware chief at Venango, had responded in friendly spirit to Croghan's messages. He knew Croghan well and would have come to the meeting, so he said, if Croghan had sent him the proper belt—one which showed the figure of Croghan holding hands with Indians. Despite this obvious stall, it was now evident that the Ohio natives were no longer strongly sympathetic to the French.[32]

Croghan evidently managed the meeting in an able manner, for neither political faction found fault with him. The Pennsylvania government was pleased with the outcome, and Thomas Penn confessed that he thought the treaty a good one and that Croghan, in the face of Quaker keenness to find causes of complaint among the Indians, had behaved "tolerably well." The Quakers, anxious to see that the complaints of the Indians were not glossed over, were satisfied. Isaac Norris commented favorable on Croghan's prudent behavior. Weiser, not Croghan, had been the Quaker's enemy and had foiled Pemberton's efforts to keep the land grievances to the fore.[33]

At the conclusion of the Lancaster conference, Croghan would have returned to Sir William had it not been for a new development. Early in 1757, Dinwiddie, after long negotiations and much expense, had succeeded in bringing to Virginia nearly four hundred southern warriors to combat their foes the Shawnees, the tribe which had been primarily responsible for the ravages on the Virginia frontier. On May 1, a strong party of Cherokees pursued a band of enemy Indians into Pennsylvania, where they killed

32. Boyd, *Indian Treaties*, 174; Pemberton Papers, XII, 18, Hist. Soc. of Pa.
33. Penn to Peters, Aug. 13, 1757, Penn Letter Book, V, 177, and Norris to Charles Norris, May 17, 1757, George W. Norris Papers, and Israel Pemberton to "Dear Friend," May 30, 1757, Etting Coll., Pemberton Papers, II, 23, and Israel Pemberton to Samuel Fothergill, July 4, 1757, Pemberton Papers, XXXIV, 57, Hist. Soc. of Pa.; Wallace, *Conrad Weiser*, 469.

four of them. On Croghan's advice, Denny succeeded in obtaining a present for the Cherokees, which Croghan agreed to deliver.

From Carlisle, where he made his arrangements for this task, Croghan directed the Cherokees to come to Fort Loudoun, a new Pennsylvania fort on the southwestern frontier, to receive their gift. Croghan's messenger found the Cherokees treating with Edmund Atkin at Winchester. The southern braves were delighted with the news of the Pennsylvania present, but Atkin was horrified. Atkin, who had not received much support in his official position and had few presents to give, insisted that all gifts to southern Indians should pass through his hands. To Croghan, he frantically wrote, "The giving presents is so essential a part of my office that without that power in my hands it is impossible for me to do his Majesty any service at all, & any interfereing with me therein, as well as in talking, is striking directly at the root of my commission." Atkin ordered Croghan to send the Cherokees back and to report to him at Winchester, "for I think every thing is at stake in this district."[34]

Atkin's message reached Croghan as the Irishman, escorted by eighty soldiers, neared Fort Loudoun. Enemy Indians were active in the neighborhood; on June 10, the very day that Croghan received Atkin's letter, hostile natives routed a platoon of Captain Mercer's company in the Great Cove, killing its lieutenant and six men. Leaving the provincial present at Fort Loudoun, Croghan hurried to Winchester to adjust matters. Although sympathetic to Atkin's difficulties, Croghan saw nothing wrong in rewarding southern Indians who strayed into the northern district and performed meritorious services.[35] At Winchester, however, the northern deputy deferred completely to the southern superintendent. Some of Atkin's proposals were far from practical, but Croghan, perceiving how tenacious the southerner was, agreed to everything. Thanks to Croghan's help, Atkin was able to give the Cherokee band at Winchester a £100 present, and those Indians went home satisfied.

34. Croghan's journal, May 24-July 24, 1757, Penn Mss., Indian Affairs, 1757-72, 11-13, Hist. Soc. of Pa.; Edmund Atkin to Croghan, June 8, 1757, *Pa. Archives*, III, 175-81; John Richard Alden, *John Stuart and the Southern Colonial Frontier* (Ann Arbor, 1944), 71-72.

35. Armstrong to Denny, June 19, 1757, *Pa. Archives*, III, 187.

Late at night on June 15, an express reached Winchester with word that a strong force of French and Indians with wagons and artillery had left Fort Duquesne and was marching on Fort Cumberland. This false alarm created a tremendous stir and gave Croghan a favorable opportunity to gain control of a large Cherokee war party which came in with a captured French officer. Atkin gave a small present to the victorious Cherokees, "very trifling," according to Croghan, but, indeed, all Atkin had to give. The warriors, who had been four months in Virginia's service, were much displeased and prepared to go home in a huff. Capitalizing on this situation and the recent border alarm, Croghan prevailed on Atkin to let him take the Indians to Fort Loudoun, give them the Pennsylvania present, and then turn them over to Colonel John Stanwix, the district military commander. Atkin agreed to this plan, binding Croghan with all sorts of instructions which carefully guarded the southerner's position. As soon as Croghan brought the Cherokees to Fort Loudoun, however, he disregarded all that he had promised Atkin. "I am not ignorant how much Mr. Croghan had it really at heart to get those Indians to himself in Pensylvani," Atkin later complained, "nor of the arts employed to accomplish it."[36]

Croghan's tour of duty in western Pennsylvania was now over. He had received notice from Denny that Teedyuscung had accepted the invitation to a meeting and would soon be at Easton, and the governor had requested Croghan to "order your matters, so as to be here time enough to attend the treaty, which I will not open unless you be present." Croghan hurried back to Philadelphia, took up quarters at John Biddle's, and called on Denny.[37]

Teedyuscung, Denny informed Croghan, had arrived at Fort Allen and would soon come on to Easton. "And there," the unhappy governor continued, "it seems, I must meet him and hold the treaty." Croghan stayed in Philadelphia for ten days. At Stanwix's order, he purchased another handsome present for the Cherokees and sent it to Fort Loudoun. He inspected and approved the list of goods intended for the Easton present. He ran up small bills with the blacksmith, tailor, shoemaker, saddler,

36. Atkin to Denny, Sept. 15, 1757, *ibid.*, 268-73.
37. Denny to Croghan, June 23, 1757, *Col. Rec. of Pa.*, VII, 605.

and laundress. He purchased paper, quills, and wampum and, thus supplied and refurbished, rode off for Easton on July 17.[38]

The purposes of the Easton treaty were to make peace with the Susquehanna Delawares through Teedyuscung and to conduct an inquiry into his charges of fraud. Croghan hoped to play an impartial role. Again, as manager of the treaty, he was in the key position, with two bitterly divergent factions struggling for his support. On one side of the fence was the proprietary party led by Peters and Benjamin Chew, although nominally headed by the unstable Denny. This party had the support of Conrad Weiser, present as interpreter for the province. Resentful of Quaker interference in the running of the treaty—a direct infringement on the prerogative of the executive—and angry at Quaker efforts to discredit the Penn family, the proprietary agents presented a stony front to the inquiry.

Opposed to Peters and his adherents were the Quakers and the Assembly, represented by the Friendly Association, by Isaac Norris, and by the provincial commissioners. Although Denny had absolutely forbidden the Quakers to attend the treaty, they had come anyway. Insisting on their right to participate in Indian affairs, this unofficial group believed that only the Friends were capable of seeing that the Indians obtained justice. With respect to the governor's efforts to keep them away, Isaac Norris naively complained, "It seems almost treason for any others to interfere." Although the Friendly Association represented a noble effort of the Quakers, their attempt to restore peace with the Indians became too entangled with their belief that the Penns must be branded for wrongs done to the natives. Overzealous leadership by Pemberton and Joseph Galloway blunted the Association's finer purposes and gave it a dogmatic political cast. From first to last at Easton, the Friends championed the Indians against their own government, whispered words of warning in their ears, and animated Teedyuscung to press home his charges of fraud. Caustically, a distinguished Friend branded these activities as deceitful, for they were predicated on humanitarian designs "which appeared

38. Denny to Croghan, July 7, 1757, *ibid.*, 634; *Maryland Archives*, XXXI, 224; *Pa. Archives*, III, 270-71; Croghan's bill with John Biddle, July 16, 1757, Cadwalader Coll., and Penn Mss., Indian Affairs, 1757-72, 12, Hist. Soc. of Pa.; *Votes and Proceedings . . . of the Province of Pa.*, IV, 809.

no longer than some of them could obtain accusations against the proprietors from the Indians." On one occasion, the Friends so excited the natives against the white authorities that a massacre was narrowly averted. The Quakers, who had previously hindered Pennsylvania's war effort, now unwittingly hindered the province's efforts to make peace.[39]

Croghan arrived at Easton on July 18 and found Teedyuscung and some two hundred Delawares in town. Just after his arrival, the Senecas, more than one hundred, came in. Croghan told the Indians that he had come to hear their complaints, that he had brought a clerk to take down the minutes (William Trent, who had served as Croghan's secretary at Lancaster), and that if their charges were well grounded Johnson would give them justice. Teedyuscung, an impressive, tall, raw-boned man with a reputation as a hard drinker, signified his satisfaction. According to Weiser, Teedyuscung had come to make peace and was not going to prosecute his charge of land frauds. At least, that was what Teedyuscung said before the Quakers got to him.[40]

Denny, reassured by the information that a hundred of Weiser's soldiers were in Easton, arrived with his suite on July 20 and, in a friendly meeting with Teedyuscung on the following day, learned that the chief wanted a clerk of his own to take the minutes of the treaty. After conferring with Croghan, Denny denied the request. Teedyuscung raised no objections—he appeared indifferent—but that night Pemberton sought him out.[41]

The next day, four of the provincial commissioners accompanied Teedyuscung to the governor, and, in Croghan's presence, Joseph Galloway read a remonstrance. If Teedyuscung was not permitted to have a clerk, they warned, he would not attend the treaty. Denny again appealed to Croghan, and Croghan talked with Teedyuscung. The Indian gave Croghan no choice—no clerk, no

---

39. Norris to Robert Charles, Dec. 4, 1757, Isaac Norris Letter Book (1756-66), 84, Hist. Soc. of Pa.; William Logan to John Smith, Nov. 26, 1759, Lib. Co. of Phila.

40. O'Callaghan, ed., *New-York Col. Doc.*, VII, 322; Wallace, *Conrad Weiser*, 481.

41. Weiser to Denny, July 18, 1757, *Pa. Archives*, III, 221; O'Callaghan, ed., *New-York Col. Doc.*, VII, 289; Wallace, *Conrad Weiser*, 479; Wallace, *Teedyuscung*, 157; Theodore Thayer, *Israel Pemberton, King of the Quakers* (Philadelphia, 1943), 141; *Col. Rec. of Pa.*, VII, 657-58.

treaty—and laughingly refused to tell him how the idea of having his own secretary had come to him. Croghan, perforce, recommended that the demand be allowed. The Indian agent was convinced that the Quakers had told Teedyuscung that he could not place any confidence in Croghan's minutes. "As to his having a clerk or not having one," Croghan later wrote, "I think it a matter of little consequence but the having a clerk was not the thing. Those people [the Quakers], by his having a clerk, they had a counsellor for themselves, to put Teedyuscung in mind what they wanted him to say, and it appeared very clearly one day when he had got his speech drawn up in writing, and desired his clerk to read it off as a lawyer would put in a plea at the bar."[42]

The preliminaries of the treaty clearly indicated trouble ahead. Deeply worried, Croghan called on Isaac Norris and Joseph Galloway to express concern at the differences existing between the governor and the Quakers, which bade fair to ruin the treaty. After listening to Norris' arguments, he indicated that he would follow the Quaker line of reasoning and sent Trent to the speaker's lodgings to make a copy of the Quakers' case against the proprietors. His subsequent action was a saddening experience for Isaac Norris, who endorsed his retained copy of the charges, "G. C. had not spirit enough to do his duty."[43]

In an atmosphere of mutual distrust and tension, the Easton treaty, nominally a negotiation between Teedyuscung representing ten Indian nations and George Croghan representing Sir William Johnson, opened on July 25. Denny and six members of his council, Speaker Norris, and six provincial commissioners were present, as well as Quakers, soldiers, and Indians in profusion. Croghan's staff consisted of Thomas McKee, interpreter for the Crown, William Trent, secretary, and Jacob Duché of Philadelphia, assistant secretary. Teedyuscung had his own interpreter, John Pumpshire, and, unprecedented for an Indian treaty, his own clerk, Charles Thomson, a Philadelphia schoolmaster. Thomson, a thorough partisan, later wrote a book entitled *An Enquiry into the Causes of the Alienation of the Delaware and Shawanese Indians*.

42. O'Callaghan, ed., *New-York Col. Doc.*, VII, 322-23; *Col. Rec. of Pa.*, VII, 656-57, 660-61; Penn Mss., Indian Affairs, 1757-72, 13, Hist. Soc. of Pa.
43. Penn Mss., Indian Affairs, 1757-72, 13, Hist. Soc. of Pa.; *Col. Rec. of Pa.*, VII, 655; Papers of Dr. Franklin, 49, Part II, 40, Amer. Philos. Soc.

After several days of sparring, Teedyuscung privately informed Croghan that he intended to press his claims for lands which he believed had been sold to the Penns by Indians who did not own them and for lands which the Penns had acquired in the Walking Purchase. Teedyuscung demanded the deeds recording these purchases so that his claims might be properly judged and also asked for an Indian reservation at Wyoming, Pennsylvania, to belong to the Indians forever.

Weiser and Croghan both believed that the Quakers had dictated Teedyuscung's demands for him. Certainly, the indefatigable Charles Thomson had written them down for the chief and had prepared a rough map of the two million acres Teedyuscung wanted at Wyoming. Teedyuscung's attitude concerning the land purchases was a startling one. Acknowledging that the Penns had doubtless made fair purchases from the Six Nations, he threatened to disallow such purchases, since, he alleged, the Six Nations were not the rightful owners. Croghan and Weiser agreed that if Teedyuscung aired this view, it would strike at the heart of Pennsylvania's traditional recognition of the Iroquois league and would create a breach with the Six Nations of possibly fatal consequence. They, therefore, decided to quash the land inquiry for the present.[44]

Accordingly, on July 31, Denny attempted to divert attention from the land claims by urging an immediate confirmation of peace. After all, he pointed out, the land had not been the chief cause of the war and was but a trifling matter compared to the great goal of re-establishing harmony. Moreover, Denny informed the Indians, Croghan had no power to settle the land claims, which must be submitted to Johnson. As for the lands at Wyoming, the Indians were entitled to them and could have them.

Teedyuscung, prevented by Croghan from having a set answer read for him by Thomson, replied that he did not want to go to Johnson with his complaints. All he wanted was to see the deeds and the correspondence of the proprietors directing Johnson to conduct the inquiry. Copies of these papers could then be placed on the minutes and sent to Johnson. Despite Peters' objections, Denny accepted Croghan's advice that the deeds and correspondence must be produced.[45]

44. *Col. Rec. of Pa.*, VII, 683.   45. *Ibid.*, 691.

On the following day, the conference was called off because Teedyuscung was drunk. Even John Pumpshire, the king's interpreter, acknowledged that his chief was too far gone to attend to business. Charles Thomson, suspicious that the delay represented an effort to postpone showing the deeds, angrily maintained that Teedyuscung was no more drunk than usual.[46] All along, the Friends had warned the natives not to trust the treaty officials, and Thomson's protest over the postponement of the treaty now produced a crisis. As a result of the Quakers' disastrous technique, the Indians prepared to go on the war path. Equally capable of blowing hot or cold, the Quakers rushed in to calm the furious braves.

The day after the fracas, Denny laid the deeds on the table, saying, "And now let all future debates and altercations concerning lands rest here, till they shall be fully examined and looked into by Sir William Johnson." Again, Denny pleaded for a declaration of peace. Teedyuscung balked, referring to Denny's speech as a "rumbling over the earth"; plainly his interest still centered, as did the Quakers', on the question of the land frauds.[47]

If Teedyuscung was dissatisfied, so were his Indian followers, but for a different reason. While Croghan tried to reason with the chief, an angry murmur arose from the Indians. They had come to make peace and had long been away from home. So far, all they had heard was talk of land. Lapachpeton, one of the chief men, broke in on Teedyuscung, exclaiming violently, "Why did you bring us down, we thought we came down to make peace with our brethren the English, but you continue to quarrel about the land affair which is dirt." Sounds of approbation greeted Lapachpeton's words, and Teedyuscung realized that, in following Quaker advice, he was in danger of losing his influence with his own people. Melodramatically, he rose to the occasion and, without further ado, abruptly confirmed the peace, a stunning climax to a scene of utter confusion.[48]

That the charges against the proprietors had not been brought to a full boil was a grievous disappointment to the Quakers. They

46. Thayer, *Israel Pemberton*, 144.
47. *Col. Rec. of Pa.*, VII, 698-99.
48. *Ibid.*, 700; Penn Mss., Indian Affairs, 1757-72, 23, Hist. Soc. of Pa.

held Croghan in abhorrence, accusing him of keeping Teedyuscung drunk so that he would cut a poor figure in the minutes of the treaty. Because the Friends did not have their own way, Croghan became, in Pemberton's eyes, "as vile a wretch as could be pick'd up," one who "used every artifice in his power to prevent a settlemt of a peace."[49] A furious Isaac Norris wrote to Benjamin Franklin:

Circumstances which could not be made a part of the minutes were carried on without the necessary disguise, in which Geo: Croghan condescended to become a necessary tool. The law of this Province, not yet confirmed in England [protecting Croghan from his creditors]; the meanness of his former course of life, & his present involved situation, all probably, contributed to induce him to conduct himself as he did on this occasion, in opposition to his former repeated promises to me, before it came to a trial. The treaty laid before the House, is in the name of Geo: Croghan, who is there supposed to be making his report to Sr Wm Johnson, but what share he had in those minutes, besides, what they were compelled to make & collate at the publick conferences, you who are acquainted with our minute makers, need not be informed.[50]

Peters, the most powerful influence at Easton, had held the line for the proprietors and defeated Quaker efforts at investigation. He was in part motivated by a stubborn refusal to allow any controversy involving the Penns to be made public, and in part by a defense of the supremacy of the Six Nations, the basic tenet in Pennsylvania Indian policy then under attack by the Quakers. The Quakers, inexperienced in Indian affairs, had attempted to open a veritable Pandora's box of Indian troubles and spill its contents across a war-torn land. No amateurs in Indian affairs, Peters, Weiser, and Croghan were appalled at the probable consequences of Quaker success and, to the fury of the Friends, held the lid down.

Although Croghan had supported the supremacy of the Six Nations, Peters realized that he could not count on Croghan's support of the Penn interests. Peters' letter to Thomas Penn caused

49. Thomson to Samuel Rhoads, July 28, 1757, and Israel Pemberton to John Fothergill, Aug. 3, 1757, Etting Coll., Pemberton Papers, II, 27, Hist. Soc. of Pa.
50. Norris to Franklin, Oct. 17, 1757, Isaac Norris Letter Book (1756-66), 80, Hist. Soc. of Pa.

the proprietor to reply, "Your account of G— C—'s behaviour being such as had deceived all sides is very disagreable, as we know not what to depend on, to what purpose can he court Mr. Norris?" In leaving both sides with the opinion that he had double-crossed them, Croghan demonstrated that, as the Crown's representative, he had favored neither but had actually played the impartial role required by his position.[51]

Croghan had no illusions about the Easton treaty. He realized that it had merely produced a truce with the Delawares, rather than a peace: "I shall not wonder if I hear of their committing fresh hostilities." By showing how divided the English were, the treaty would lower Anglo-Saxon prestige and would not succeed in bringing the Ohio Indians into an alliance. Although he criticized both parties in Pennsylvania for neglecting the public good for their own selfish ends, he believed that Quaker interference had ruined the treaty: "The whole conduct of the Quakers seemed to me as if they wanted to make themselves popular with the Indians, and carry the management of Indian affairs out of the channel His Majesty had ordered them to go in, indeed they took every step in their power to distinguish themselves as a separate body of people from all His Majesty subjects."[52]

As the Indian agent journeyed back to Fort Johnson, his thoughts were frequently on the Quakers and their determined efforts to set up land claims for the Indians against the whites. Should the English lose the war to the French, would not the Indians under such incitement demand back all the land in the colony? As a speculator who was interested in acquiring land from the Indians, not in giving it back to them, Croghan could only shake his head and sigh, "Shure those people must be mad."[53]

51. Penn to Peters, Nov. 14, 1757, Peters Mss., IV, 122, Hist. Soc. of Pa.
52. O'Callaghan, ed., *New-York Col. Doc.*, VII, 323.
53. Croghan to Peters, Aug. 18, 1757, Penn Mss., Official Correspondence, VIII, 271, Hist. Soc. of Pa.; Croghan to [Peters], Dec. 18, 1757, Public Records Division, Harrisburg.

7

The Campaigns of 1758

THE CONVERSATIONS of Croghan and Johnson about the Easton treaty would not have been relished by either Thomas Penn or the Quakers. Johnson accepted his deputy's opinion that the treaty, hindered by the Friends, had resulted in merely a conditional truce and reported adversely on the Quakers to the Board of Trade. But Johnson was also irritated at the proprietors for challenging his statement, in an earlier report, that the Penn land purchase at Albany in 1754 was partially to blame for Pennsylvania's Indian troubles.[1]

In righteous indignation, Thomas Penn had demanded to know when his Indian policy had ever given dissatisfaction to the Six Nations. The basic tenet of that policy, so stoutly maintained by Peters and Weiser, was the recognition of the Six Nations as supreme in all Indian land purchases. The Albany purchase of 1754 was in line with that policy and had been fairly and openly made by Conrad Weiser. Yet, Johnson had criticized it. Despite all that Penn and Weiser might say in its defense, the 1754 purchase had proved an unwise one, for, in vulgar terms, Pennsylvania had bitten off more than it could chew.

Croghan criticized the 1754 purchase severely, and Johnson incorporated Croghan's thoughts into another letter to the Board of Trade: "The Indians are disgusted and dissatisfied with the extensive purchases of land, and do think themselves injured thereby. . . . This is one main cause of their defection

---

1. *Journal of the Commissioners for Trade and Plantations from January 1754 to December 1758. Preserved in the Public Record Office* (London, 1933), 347; Johnson to Loudoun, Sept. 3, 1757, and Johnson to Thomas Pownall, July 8, 1757, *Johnson Papers*, IX, 827 and II, 738.

from the British interest." Penn was soon to reply to Peters: "You write of George Croghan who, whichever side he may be now of is a bad man." Penn could see only two sides to the Indian question—his own and the Quakers'—but Croghan was not on either side. As an agent of the Crown, his views were independent of provincial party spirit and representative of an awakening imperial concept.[2]

Returning from a diplomatic visit to the Oneidas and Tuscaroras in October, Croghan found Sir William suffering from "a pleurisy & violent stitches," the beginning of a severe illness which totally incapacitated the superintendent for seven weeks. Indeed, Sir William's pain was so severe during this period that he was confined motionless in his bed.[3]

Such was Johnson's helpless condition when a detachment of three hundred French and Indians attacked the German Flats on November 12, wreaking a harvest of death, burning houses, barns, and the water mill, destroying or carrying off the livestock, and taking more than a hundred prisoners. Word that this attack would take place was sent to Johnson on November 11 by Captain Philip Townsend, who commanded a force of two hundred regulars at Fort Herkimer, just across the Mohawk from the threatened settlement. Townsend's message, received by Croghan early on November 12, was immediately forwarded to Loudoun in Albany. To the rescue of the Mohawk country, Loudoun dispatched a young brigadier, one of the army's white hopes, George Augustus Viscount Howe.[4]

By dint of hard riding, Lord Howe arrived at Fort Johnson on the night of November 12 and, on the following morning, was joined by four hundred soldiers from the Schenectady garrison. In addition to these regulars and two hundred more to follow from

2. Johnson to Lords of Trade, Sept. 22, 1757, O'Callaghan, ed., *New-York Col. Doc.*, VII, 276; letter dated Sept. 22, 1757, Richard E. Day, ed., *Calendar of the Sir William Johnson Manuscripts in the New York State Library* (Albany, 1909), 90; Penn to Peters, May 13, 1758, Penn Letter Book, V, 306, Hist. Soc. of Pa.

3. Johnson to James Abercromby, Oct. 21, 1757, and Johnson to Loudoun, Dec. 10, 1757, *Johnson Papers*, II, 748, 761-62.

4. E. B. O'Callaghan, ed., *The Documentary History of the State of New-York* (Albany, 1849), I, 515-18; for Townsend's letter see Loudoun Papers, Huntington Library.

Schenectady, Howe had the command of the four hundred regulars garrisoning Forts Herkimer, Hendrick, and Hunter, as well as some New York provincial troops and the militia. To reinforce Howe, Loudoun threw five companies of Highlanders into Schenectady.[5]

Rumors to the contrary, the enemy's objective had been attained in its raid on the German Flats. The invaders quickly withdrew, and, although Howe advanced to the Flats, there was little that the British could do except draw up reports on the disaster. Within a few days, Howe had returned to Albany, and his hastily improvised command had been released to garrison duty.

During the time that Howe was in the field, Croghan cooperated with him in seeking intelligence of the enemy and performed Sir William's duties, corresponding directly with Loudoun and General Abercromby. He had also gone to Fort Herkimer, surveyed the wreckage at the Flats, and sent out a reconnoitering party of Mohawks.[6] As soon as danger of enemy activity had subsided, Loudoun called on Croghan for a full report. His lordship was particularly concerned about the surprise feature of the raid.

Croghan answered Loudoun's letter from Fort Johnson and then set off again for the German Flats, where he interviewed an Oneida chief about the attack. In the presence of some of the German settlers, the Oneida indignantly refuted the charge that the Indians had not given ample warning of the raid. Fifteen days before the attack, the Oneidas had sent word and six days later had confirmed their message with additional information. The Oneida chief himself had come to the Flats and implored the Germans to go into the fort, but he was laughed at for his pains. Even after his final notice the night before the attack, when Captain Townsend belatedly awoke to the danger, and even after Townsend had fired his alarm gun, the settlers had remained in their homes. All this was true, acknowledged the surviving Germans. Clearly, it was not the fault of the Indians that the Palatines, jaded by false alarms, had not sought sanctuary. After

---

5. Howe to Loudoun, Nov. 12, 1757, and Loudoun to Delancey, Nov. 13, 1757, Loudoun Papers, Huntington Library.
6. Croghan to Loudoun, Nov. 20, 1757, *Johnson Papers*, IX, 855-58.

sending out another party of Mohawks to reconnoiter toward Oswego, Croghan returned to Fort Johnson.[7]

The Irishman shared Johnson's bitterness toward the army for not adequately protecting the German Flats. "All our garrisons is left two weak, and no regard paid to Indian intilagance," Croghan angrily wrote Peters. That the Six Nations refused to fight Lord Loudoun's defensive battles seemed understandable enough to Croghan, who resented the blame laid on the Indians by army officers. Were the army to attempt an offensive, the Irishman was confident that the Six Nations would rally to the colors. Alas, an offensive could not take place for many months, because, as Croghan wrote, "British offisers are to delicatt to undertake a winter expedition."[8]

The Indian agent found a variety of matters to engage his attention as 1757 drew to its close. He corresponded with a doctor about Johnson's condition and rejoiced to note the gradual recovery of the superintendent's health. Having a fondness for handsome dress, he purchased numerous garments in Schenectady. Decked out in crimson velvet, white jeans, knee garters, silver buttons, silk handkerchiefs, silk stockings, English shoes, and a beaver hat, Croghan must have cut an elegant figure. On December 17, he purchased twelve yards of ribbon, possibly as a gift for the daughter of Nickus of nearby Canajoharie, a sachem who, in social prestige, stood in the very first rank in the Mohawk nation. Sir William's amours with legendary numbers of Indian squaws were the talk of his contemporaries. The mistress of his house was an Indian, Molly Brant. Croghan needed no urging to follow his leader's example. Nickus' daughter became his mistress or wife—the alliance seems somewhat informal. Before long the couple had a daughter, Catherine.[9]

Still included among Croghan's correspondents was the backbiting but tenacious Richard Peters. Ever interested in what was

---

7. Croghan to Johnson, Dec. 3, 1757, *ibid.*, 859-63; Abercromby to Croghan, Dec. 2, 1757, Gratz Coll., Hist. Soc. of Pa.
8. Croghan to [Peters], Dec. 18, 1757, *Pa. Archives*, III, 319-20.
9. Campbell and Andrews Account Book, I, see dates of Sept. 18, Oct. 22, Dec. 6 and 17, 1757, New York State Library, Albany. On July 13, 1758, Croghan purchased an expensive sidesaddle from this firm. Thomson, *Alienation of the Delaware and Shawanese Indians*, 178.

going on in Pennsylvania, Croghan learned from Peters that the Indians had resumed their scalping. He also learned that Teedyuscung, closely chaperoned by the Quakers, had visited Philadelphia, where the chief had told Denny that Croghan was a rogue and that he would have nothing to do with Sir William Johnson. "In short he was very rude."[10]

Another Indian, one of greater stature than Teedyuscung, now placed his name for the first time on the recorded pages of history. At Fort Duquesne, Pontiac, an Ottawa chief, reported to the French Croghan's efforts to influence the Indians by a false story of the fall of Quebec. Proudly, Pontiac boasted of his superior attainments, which kept him above the power of evil suggestions.[11]

The powers of evil may well have had a hand in a speech purportedly sent by the Pennsylvania Quakers to the Six Nations and duly delivered, late in January, 1758, to Sir William Johnson. This alleged Quaker speech was an offer to supply the Indians with weapons to kill the English. It pointed out, however, that the Indians were to kill only the soldiers and not the Quakers. As Thomas Penn quite correctly remarked, the Quakers "do not understand the necessary subordination in government very well." Insubordinate though the Quakers were, it is unbelievable that they could have advised the Indians, "If you incline to carry on a war against any nation, we have every thing fitt to kill men with in plenty, such as guns, swords, hatchets, powder, lead, cloathing, and provisions, which we are ready to furnish you with." The episode remains murky and tends to cast discredit on the not overly scrupulous Johnson and Croghan, who solemnly testified to the speech and sent it to Loudoun.[12]

A few days later, Sir William ordered Croghan to the German Flats, the most advanced British post on the Mohawk River. There he was to supervise the fur trade and to see that the Indians received fair treatment. He was also to send Johnson all

---

10. *Col. Rec. of Pa.*, VII, 730-31; Denny to Johnson, Nov. 10, 1757, *Johnson Papers*, II, 751-56.
11. Day, ed., *Calendar of Johnson Manuscripts*, 92; Howard H. Peckham, *Pontiac and the Indian Uprising* (Princeton, 1947), 47-48.
12. *Johnson Papers*, II, 776-77; Penn to William Peters, May 25, 1758, Penn Letter Book, V, 317, Hist. Soc. of Pa. Croghan later claimed that the speech was written by John Hughes, one of Pennsylvania's provincial commissioners. Entry for Oct. 24, 1758, Richard Peters Diary, Hist. Soc. of Pa.

the Indian intelligence he could obtain. Accordingly, the deputy moved to Fort Herkimer, a large three-story stone house surrounded by a ditch and palisades.[13]

Presumably, Croghan brought his squaw with him, for he set up housekeeping. An alarming amount of liquor—Jamaica rum and that aristocrat of colonial wines, Madeira—was shipped to him from Schenectady, and a flood of other items followed—a rug, a blanket, dozens of knives, forks, teacups, teapots, a canister of good bohea tea, a creamer, a snuffbox, a compass, silver arm bands, and yards of yellow ribbon to deck out his paramour.[14]

Croghan had not been long at the Flats before the enemy struck again. At 3 A.M. on February 19, hostile Indians fired a house and barn just across the Mohawk from Fort Herkimer. Croghan, who was in the fort at the time, rushed out to find friendly native scouts and at 5 A.M. wrote a warning to Sir William. Johnson quickly concentrated eight hundred regulars, rangers, militia, and Indians at the Flats, while other troops moved up from Schenectady and Albany. As usual, there was nothing the soldiers could do. The enemy war party had vanished after scalping four men and a woman.[15]

To prevent future surprises, Croghan kept out a succession of scouting parties, which moved on snowshoes over the heavily snowed-in countryside. This was expensive, but at least he could write Johnson, "I think the enemy can nott stale upon us in the night."[16]

When the snows melted and spring freshened the land, orders arrived outlining the grand strategy for the campaigns of 1758. Loudoun, discredited by failures, was replaced by Abercromby, who was directed to invade Canada by way of Ticonderoga and Crown Point. Brigadier General John Forbes replaced Stanwix in Pennsylvania and was given the command of a force designed to capture Fort Duquesne. Stanwix, promoted to brigadier, re-

13. Johnson to Croghan, Jan. 30, 1758, *Johnson Papers*, II, 778; *Proceedings of the New York State Historical Association*, 14 (1915), 84.
14. Campbell and Andrews Account Book, I, see dates of Feb. 15, Feb. 27, Mar. 2, Mar. 11, Apr. 3, Apr. 28, 1758, New York State Library, Albany.
15. Abercromby to Loudoun, Feb. 19, 1758 (postscript Feb. 21), and Feb. 25, 1758, Loudoun Papers, Huntington Library; Croghan to Johnson, Feb. 19, 1758, *Johnson Papers*, IX, 876.
16. Croghan to Johnson, Mar. 12, 1758, *Johnson Papers*, II, 779-80.

turned to New York, where he was to construct Fort Stanwix at the Oneida Carrying Place to protect the Mohawk Valley. Amherst was charged with the command of another amphibious operation aimed at Louisburg, the Cape Breton fortress which guarded the entrance to the Gulf of St. Lawrence and the waterway into Canada.

On April 4, Abercromby informed Johnson of the year's military operations, told him that a large number of Indians would be needed to support his Canadian expedition, and conveyed Forbes's request that Croghan be sent to Pennsylvania to handle the colony's Indian situation. Although at first Johnson instructed Croghan to go to Forbes's assistance, he soon changed his mind. Branding Quaker activities as "flagrantly illegal" and sure to confound governmental action, Johnson wrote Abercromby, "Whilst Indian affairs are thus subjected to party views and opposition ... I can see little advantage which would arise from my sending Mr. Croghan or any other person thither. ... I am not jealous, sir, of incroachments upon my department. ... Let Pensilvania go on & negotiate peace with the Delawares."[17]

The superintendent rallied the natives to join Abercromby's expedition, sending his agents through the Indian country and directing Croghan to visit Oghquago, an Iroquois village on the Susquehanna. "I expect to be on my march from hence in 3 weeks from this day," Johnson told Croghan on May 29. "You will endeavour by every prudent measure to prevail on as many as have arms to bring them along for which a consideration shall be given them & to prevent women & children from coming with them." Despite a continuing flow of entreaties from General Forbes for his services, Croghan, accompanied by Andrew Montour, rode off on other duties.[18]

The Indian agents took the road to Canajoharie, where they met a scouting party just in from Oswego. The scouts had not seen the enemy, but they did bring back a piece of the cross which

---

17. Abercromby to Johnson, Apr. 4, 1758, *Johnson Papers*, IX, 891-94; Day, ed., *Calendar of Johnson Manuscripts*, 94; Johnson to Abercromby, Apr. 28, 1758, *Johnson Papers*, II, 825-33.

18. John Forbes to Johnson, May 4, 1758, and Johnson to Croghan, May 29, 1758, *Johnson Papers*, IX, 897-98, 908-12; Abercromby to Forbes, June 4, 1758, W. O., 34/44, foll. 217-18, Public Record Office, London.

the French had set up at Oswego after they had captured that place. Croghan sent this souvenir to Johnson and, turning south from the Mohawk River, rode down a trail which skirted the east side of Lake Otsego to the outlet at its southern end, where the Susquehanna River flowed narrowly away. The Irishman feasted his eyes on the beautiful scene, sublimely framed by mountain walls. The gentle sound of the water, flowing out of the lake on its twisty way to Pennsylvania, enhanced the ancient majesty of virgin timber. One day, Croghan would build his home there and name it "Croghan's Forest," and later it would be called Cooperstown. But June of 1758 was not a time for dreaming. Croghan hurried on, descending the Susquehanna to the Indian settlement at Oghquago, the location of present-day Windsor, New York.[19]

Impatiently, Johnson awaited Croghan's return. Impatiently, Abercromby called on Johnson to join him. Ill-humored letters passed back and forth. At length, having left a hundred Oghquago Indians on the trail, Croghan hastened in to Fort Johnson on June 27, just as the Onondaga, Oneida, and Tuscarora war parties arrived.[20]

During the next two days, the Mohawks, the Mohicans, and the Schoharie Indians appeared, and, on June 29, Johnson and two hundred warriors—as many as he could get sober enough to march ("liquor was a plenty among them as ditch water")—moved off for Lake George. Croghan remained behind to receive the Oghquago Indians, who trooped in on the following day. On the night of July 4, Johnson, with Croghan a day's march in the rear, encamped in the woods within ten miles of Fort Edward. To Abercromby at Lake George, Sir William sent a dispatch telling him that he hoped to join him with Croghan and his entire party on July 6.[21]

As it happened, this was just one day late. On July 5, Abercromby and sixteen thousand troops set off up the lake in an immense number of whaleboats, bateaux, and rafts. The army landed at a cove within a few miles of Ticonderoga early on the

19. *Johnson Papers*, IX, 914-15, and XI, 86n.
20. *Ibid.*, II, 842, 843, 850, 853-55, and IX, 936-37.
21. *Ibid.*, II, 871, 885-86, and IX, 939-40.

sixth. So far, all had gone well, but no sooner did the British seek to push forward than Lord Howe fell dead in a chance encounter with the enemy. The loss of their leader, who was the soul of the expedition, changed the entire spirit of the army. On July 7, the soldiers moved up to within a mile and a half of the fort, where they were joined the following morning by Johnson, his assistants, and 395 Indians.

It was then that Abercromby made his fatal decision. Fearful that enemy reinforcements would soon arrive, and underestimating the strength of the fort, he ordered an assault without waiting for his artillery to come up. Near the fort was a height from which the artillery could have blasted the French to pieces. Abercromby sent Johnson and the Indians to hold this strategic position, thereby providing Croghan an excellent view of the battle.[22]

From a little after noon until 7 P.M. on July 8, Montcalm and his French soldiers withstood a British force nearly five times superior in strength. Murderous fire cut down one desperate charge after another. Not even the unbelievable gallantry of the Black Watch could breach the French fortifications. The day of slaughter ended with a British retreat and an army and a general too demoralized to renew hostilities. The Ticonderoga fiasco terminated the Canadian invasion and broke off one of the prongs of the triple attack with which the brilliant William Pitt had hoped to overwhelm New France.

Abercromby dismissed his Indian auxiliaries and again ordered Johnson to send Croghan to Pennsylvania. News from that colony that the Cherokees were nearly out of hand for want of proper management and that an Indian treaty was to take place, the outcome of which would bear heavily on the success of Forbes's campaign, called for Croghan's services.[23]

General Forbes, beset with a bewildering variety of painful maladies, was a sick man when, in March, 1758, he received orders to command the expedition against Fort Duquesne. His troops were mostly provincial levies, his only regulars being a regiment of Highlanders and four companies of the Sixtieth Regiment, the

22. Gipson, *The British Empire*, VIII, 228.
23. Abercromby to Forbes, July 18, 1758, Huntington Library; Abercromby to Johnson, July 23, 1758, W. O., 34/38, fol. 44, Public Record Office, London.

Royal Americans. Pennsylvania had responded well in raising three battalions commanded by Colonels John Armstrong and James Burd—Croghan's fellow road commissioners of 1755—and Hugh Mercer, onetime lieutenant in Croghan's company at Fort Shirley. Virginia furnished two regiments under George Washington and William Byrd. Smaller units were sent by Delaware, Maryland, and North Carolina. As auxiliaries for these forces, some nine hundred Cherokee and Catawba Indians rendezvoused at Winchester. Unfortunately, they arrived too early and, after being clothed and armed by Forbes, nearly all went home before they could be used. Outraged at their behavior, the general complained that he had "no mortall that understands Indian affairs."[24]

Despite objections raised by Virginians, the plan of campaign matured into a march across Pennsylvania rather than up Braddock's Road from Fort Cumberland. This advance required the building of a wagon road through mountainous country and the creation of fortified supply depots, notably at Raystown and Loyalhanna. The tempo of the expedition was deliberate and painstaking to ensure against a surprise such as had overwhelmed Braddock.

Poor Forbes, frequently prostrated by his disorders, moved slowly west in the wake of his army. As usual, the service of supply under Sir John St. Clair had gone awry. St. Clair could be a very disagreeable man, and he was at his worst on this campaign. As the crippled Forbes swayed precariously in a litter slung between two horses, he bitterly blamed St. Clair for holding up the expedition for lack of supplies, "Sir John having served me as he did Gen Braddock promising every thing and doing no one individual thing in the world, except confusing what he undertakes." For one thing Forbes was thankful—it looked as if the French would have little Indian support. On August 18, the general wrote his second in command, Colonel Henry Bouquet: "After many intreigues with the Quakers, the commissioners, the Governour etc, and with the Governour and government of New Jersey and by the downright bullying of Sir William Johnson etc,

24. Forbes to Abercromby, June 7, 1758, Alfred Procter James, ed., *Writings of General John Forbes Relating to his Service in North America* (Menasha, Wis., 1938), 110.

I hope I have now brought a convention with the Indians of whatever denomination or tribe, pretty near to a crissis."[25]

Although Sir William realized the forthcoming "convention" at Easton would be an important one, he believed that his presence in the Mohawk country was even more important. Consequently, it became Croghan's responsibility to represent the Indian department. After a visit with Denny in Philadelphia, during which Denny had to rescue him from imprisonment for debt, the Irishman established himself at Easton and prepared to receive the Indians.[26]

Relieved to learn of Croghan's arrival, Forbes was also pleased to receive Croghan's promise to join the army with at least fifty Delawares as soon as the treaty ended. "His presence," Forbes wrote Denny, "would be a real satisfaction to me, as he is both acquainted with the country, & inhabitants."[27]

By September 21, there were at least three hundred Indians at Easton, but the Senecas and Cayugas had not yet arrived. Croghan noted that the natives were divided and suspicious of each other and that most of them despised Teedyuscung. Fearing that the Quakers would support the Delaware's claims to be a great man and king over many nations—claims which would antagonize the Six Nations—Croghan wrote Sir William, "I have a bad opinion of this treaty." Although delighted to learn that Amherst had conquered Louisburg, he was downcast over Forbes's prospect of success. The general's progress had been so slow and his supply situation was so bad that Croghan anticipated the failure of the expedition. Moreover, he feared for the army's vanguard, which he learned was close to Fort Duquesne: "I dread every day to hear that the enemy has given them a thrashing." Actually, a week before he expressed his concern, the enemy had crushed Forbes's advance party.[28]

Despite the fact that Montour was very industrious, "and dose nott drink att all," and despite Weiser's presence, the Indian agents

25. Forbes to Abercromby, July 3, 1758, and Forbes to Henry Bouquet, Aug. 18, 1758, *ibid.*, 168, 180-81.
26. *Johnson Papers*, II, 890, 896, and X, 2, 4.
27. Forbes to Bouquet, Sept. 2, 1758, and Forbes to Abercromby, Sept. 4, 1758, James, ed., *Writings of General John Forbes*, 195, 200; Forbes to Denny, Aug. 26, 1758, *Johnson Papers*, IX, 970.
28. Croghan to Johnson, Sept. 21, 1758, *Johnson Papers*, III, 3-5.

could do nothing with the natives, for they were continually drunk with liquor supplied by the provincial commissioners. Teedyuscung's behavior was so bad that Richard Peters came to Easton to try to keep him and his followers in order. Just as Peters was preparing to leave Philadelphia, Croghan was writing him, "I have this minitt 20 drunken Indians about me, I shall be ruin'd if the taps are nott stopt."[29]

Peters arrived at Easton on September 28 and called at Croghan's house, where the deputy agent, Weiser, Montour, and Nickus were interviewing messengers from the main body of the Six Nations, then on its way to Fort Allen. Teedyuscung, although drunk, paid his respects to Peters. The following day, about one hundred natives gathered in the treaty shed to petition Peters for clothes and guns. Teedyuscung, so inflated with his own importance that he now called himself king of eighteen Indian nations and, oddly enough, king of the Quakers, appeared and abused them, saying they were fools to do as the white men told them, that he knew better and would never make peace. He ranted on, turning his drunken spleen on the Six Nations. When Peters sent the sheriff to insist on his keeping sober, the "king" replied that he would pay no attention to Peters' orders. Nevertheless, the provincial secretary did succeed in cutting down on the consumption of rum.[30]

On October 2, Montour and Nickus left for Fort Allen to guide the big Seneca delegation to Easton. As Croghan pointed out, the Senecas had sent their young men to join the warring Delawares and had protected that errant tribe. The Seneca chief, Tagashata, was said to be Teedyuscung's adviser. It was vital, therefore, that the Senecas make peace with the English.

Richard Peters recognized that the success of the treaty depended largely on Tagashata's attitude and the conduct of Croghan and Montour. About Croghan, Peters was in despair: "Croghan is not to be found out. He declares himself disposed to promote a peace & reconcile the Indians to one another. No man more fair

---

29. Croghan to Peters, Sept. 26, 1758, *Pa. Archives*, III, 544-45; *Col. Rec. of Pa.*, VIII, 172.

30. Unless otherwise noted, the description of the Easton treaty is drawn from the Richard Peters Diary, Hist. Soc. of Pa., and the Benjamin Chew Diary and the treaty minutes, all in Boyd's *Indian Treaties*.

nor open than he pretends to be but Mr. Weiser thinks he has something in reserve." As usual, Croghan promised the Quakers that he would investigate the Delawares' charges of fraud, but, as both sides suspected, Croghan was playing his own game. Despite anything the Irishman might say to the leaders of the proprietary and anti-proprietary parties, he was resolved not to become involved in party politics. Unable to place confidence in Croghan, Peters observed, "If Mr. Montour does not instruct & inform us right we shall be at a great loss."[31]

With the arrival of the Senecas and Cayugas on October 5, as well as of Pisquetomen and other chiefs of the Ohio Delawares, the Indians were assembled for the treaty. Croghan prepared speeches to sound out Tagashata and set Mrs. Montour to making the necessary belts and strings of council wampum. On October 7, Denny and his council came to town.

Croghan's presence at the treaty was in an advisory capacity; Denny was nominally the English leader, though Peters was the power behind the throne. Denny arrived in Easton in a very bad humor and, by and large, continued in that frame of mind throughout the treaty. Little things upset him, making him unreasonable and "indecent in his expressions." He insulted his advisers and the Indians alike. Denny, who hated Indian treaties, was in a fury about his wife, who had temporarily escaped his clutches. This poor woman had been brought to Philadelphia by her husband a year earlier and had been required to bring with her a Mrs. Drage, who was acknowledged to be Denny's mistress. The governor's treatment of his wife scandalized Philadelphia.[32]

At Easton, Denny had his usual set of councilors and the protection of provincial troops. A redoubtable, eagle-eyed committee of the Assembly was present—Norris, Fox, Galloway, and Hughes. Israel Pemberton and others represented the Friendly Association. The principal Indians among the five hundred in attendance were Nickus, Tagashata, Thomas King of the Oneidas, and Teedyuscung.

Since the Quakers thought that the treaty was strictly between

31. Peters to William Logan, Aug. 2, 1758, Logan Papers, XI, 52, and Pemberton Papers, XIII, 21, Hist. Soc. of Pa.; *Johnson Papers*, III, 3-5.
32. Penn to Peters, Mar. 23, 1758, Peters Mss., V, 30, Hist. Soc. of Pa.

the province and the Six Nations, with Teedyuscung on the sidelines because he had already confirmed peace, they were not at first as active as usual. They did not insist on a clerk, and the minutes were taken by Peters and Benjamin Chew. The proprietary agents, in their turn, were so anxious to avoid trouble that they submitted to the Assembly committee for approval the speeches which were to be made to the Indians. But the more partisan of the Quakers were suspicious of the private conferences which Croghan was conducting with the chiefs of the Six Nations at his house. They feared that he was endeavoring to persuade the Six Nations to force Teedyuscung to withdraw his charges of fraud.[33]

These fears may have been groundless, but Croghan no doubt did encourage the northern Indians to reassert their ascendancy over the Delawares. The strategy adopted was for Tagashata to force the Delawares to acknowledge their error in taking up the hatchet and to promise to be good friends to the English. The Six Nations would then intercede for them to right whatever wrongs they had suffered. Realizing that this step was in the wind, the Quakers became increasingly uneasy. Joseph Fox complained that Croghan had the whole management of the treaty and that Denny let him do as he pleased.

At a public conference on October 11, Tagashata, scheduled to speak first, had neatly laid out his belts and strings in the proper order upon a table. Teedyuscung, however, claimed the floor and, ignoring Croghan's question about the propriety of his action, informed the company that he had nothing to do with the treaty as he had already made his peace. Disconcerted by this turn of events, which upset his plans, Tagashata adjourned the meeting until the following day, when he declared peace on behalf of Teedyuscung and all the other Delaware groups, including those who lived on the Ohio. The solemnity of this occasion was marred by Teedyuscung coming in drunk. Bolstered with courage found in the bottle of rum he carried, and furious with the Six Nations for demonstrating their superiority by speaking for the Delawares, Teedyuscung heckled the Iroquois speakers. He was the king of all the nations and of all the world, and the Six Nations were fools.

33. Thomson, *Alienation of the Delawares and Shawanese*, 172-73.

Speaking alternately in English and in his own language, he maintained that it made no difference what the Iroquois said; only he, Teedyuscung, could make peace or war. The way to gain good treatment from the English, he generously confided, was to make war on them and cut their throats. That was what he had done, and he would continue to do it as long as he lived. So spoke the man the Quakers championed.

The next session of the treaty opened quietly enough. Pisquetomen delivered messages of friendship from the Ohio chiefs and their request that they be informed when peace was declared. Then Nickus arose and, speaking with furious vehemence and pointing frequently at Teedyuscung, delivered so fiery a denunciation that Conrad Weiser did not dare translate a word of it. That evening, over Richard Peters' teapot, Denny and Croghan grumbled with irritation at Weiser for glossing over a situation which might have enabled them then and there to deflate the Delaware king.

The Quakers took immediate steps to support Teedyuscung's authority against the pretensions of the Six Nations. Israel Pemberton called the Indians together and told them to disregard what Nickus had said. Galloway fatuously maintained that Teedyuscung had the power he claimed and strongly opposed Croghan's supposed scheme to degrade him. From the anti-proprietary point of view, Croghan was a scoundrel. The commissioners were so incensed with him that they refused Peters' request for wampum, needed by the Indians for their speeches, on learning that the request had come through Croghan.

At a meeting on October 15, the conferences were once more resumed. Nickus struck at the core of Teedyuscung's pretensions. Who, he inquired, had made Teedyuscung the great man he claimed to be? He denied Teedyuscung's authority, and spokesmen for the other Six Nations, one after another, arose to repeat Nickus' words.

To the anguish of the Quakers, who relied on the Delawares for the charges of fraud brought against the proprietors, Teedyuscung was about to have his wings clipped. Beside himself with rage, Pemberton told Chew that Croghan, a rascal and a villain, was playing tricks with the Indians and was supported by the proprietary agents in everything he did. Heatedly Chew replied that this was entirely untrue; no one knew what Croghan was about. Although the provincial commissioners agreed with Pemberton that the Six Nations' attack on Teedyuscung was a contrivance of Croghan's, William Logan, an eminent Quaker, was convinced that the Iroquois were simply responding to Teedyuscung's public insults.[34]

The Delaware chief followed Pemberton's line as long as he could. He blamed his grievances on the 1737 purchase and claimed that his people owned lands as far as the headwaters of the Delaware, country known to belong to the Six Nations. His speech was ill received; in fact, Nickus, Tagashata, and other Iroquois chiefs walked out while he was talking. Teedyuscung soon reversed his extravagant statement. He also agreed to the fairness of the 1749 purchase, which he had previously branded a fraud. By so doing, he pared down his grievances to the purchase of 1737 and tacitly acknowledged the superiority of the Six Nations.

Thus, all the major Indian grievances in Pennsylvania, except the purchase of 1737 which was referred to the Crown, were settled, and the Indians all declared peace. Also, at this treaty, lands west of the Alleghenies purchased by the Penns in 1754 were deeded back to the Six Nations, thereby removing a cause of Indian discontent.

Despite its ludicrous features, the Easton treaty of 1758 was the most important Indian conference ever held in Pennsylvania. Denny attributed Forbes's subsequent victory to the effects of this treaty, an opinion of his on which even the Assembly agreed. Croghan's role in bringing the treaty to this happy end was fully acknowledged by Denny: "Mr. Croghan has exerted himself on all occasions for the good of His Majesty's service, and it required his peculiar address to manage the Indians, and counteract the designs of a wretched and restless faction." Peters, who well recognized Croghan's powers of charm and persuasiveness, but who also perceived other aspects of his character—"What a sad wretch it is"—believed that the Irishman had behaved well, "every thing

---

34. William Logan to John Smith, Oct. 17, 1758, Correspondence of John Smith, Hist. Soc. of Pa.

considered." This qualified praise of a provincial officer for an imperial agent, whom Peters entirely distrusted, does not do justice to Croghan's role at Easton.[35]

The Pennsylvania treaties of 1756 and 1757, held chiefly with Teedyuscung, had not ended the Indian war. During those years, the Six Nations exercised virtually no control over the Delawares. At Easton in 1758, however, the Six Nations had resoundingly reasserted their traditional dominance. Without their mediation, Croghan told Johnson, the treaty might have been a failure.[36] The main problem at Easton was not the coddling of Teedyuscung, so typical of previous treaties, but the proper handling of the Iroquois chiefs.

No one was more closely associated with the Iroquois at Easton than Croghan. Not only did he represent their friend, Sir William Johnson, but he was married to one of their people and even gave out, on this basis, that he was an Indian himself. The Six Nations habitually met at his house, and, among their chiefs, none was more influential than Nickus, the Irishman's father-in-law. These factors assisted the agent in molding Iroquois thinking, a process in which he was not bothered by any nice regard for ethics or scruples. Indeed, he was exposed in an effort to discredit a Quaker leader by fabricating a shameful story about him.[37] Although Croghan tried to cloak his antipathy for the Quakers and Teedyuscung, whom he privately called an infamous villain, it is noteworthy that the Quakers blamed him, not Weiser or Peters, for the Six Nations' treatment of the Delaware leader.[38]

Before Peters left Easton, Croghan obtained £150 from him to outfit the fifty warriors he had promised Forbes. It appears, however, that he was able to recruit only fifteen. With these natives, Croghan joined Forbes on November 20 at his camp, some

35. *Pa. Archives*, Eighth Series, VI, 4907, 4913; Denny to Johnson, Oct. 24, 1758, *Johnson Papers*, III, 10-11; Peters to Weiser, Nov. 10, 1758, Peters Mss., V, 59, and Peters to Weiser, Dec. 22, 1758, Correspondence of Conrad Weiser, II, 143, Hist. Soc. of Pa.
36. Johnson to Abercromby, Nov. 10, 1758, *Johnson Papers*, X, 54.
37. In an effort to discredit the Quakers, Croghan had told Teedyuscung that Isaac Norris was a member of the Connecticut company which planned to settle Indian lands at Wyoming. Challenged by the provincial commissioners, Croghan denied the story, but in such a way that he appeared plainly guilty.
38. Thomson, *Alienation of the Delaware and Shawanese*, 173; Croghan to Peters, Sept. 26, 1758, *Pa. Archives*, III, 544.

thirty miles east of Fort Duquesne. For the final phase of his campaign, Forbes had selected twenty-five hundred of his best soldiers and, leaving the army's baggage at Loyalhanna, was pressing in for the kill. Croghan went forward to the head of the column and employed his Indians as scouts.[39] It may have been some of Croghan's natives who discovered that the French, deserted by their Indian allies and unable to resist Forbes's relentless advance, had abandoned and burned Fort Duquesne on November 24. The next day, the British army occupied the forks of the Ohio. Included in the army's general orders for November 26 was the following paragraph:

Mr. Croghan is to encamp with the northern & Delaware Indians in a separate camp from the rest of the Line; and none of the troops are upon any account whatever to have any communication with them or speak to them; and who disobeys this order will be severely punished.[40]

The beauty of the setting formed by the wild hills, the forests, and the rushing waters of the Monongahela and the Allegheny was beyond Colonel Bouquet's cultivated powers to describe. But Bouquet's elation was surpassed by Croghan's. The very land the army camped on belonged to the Irishman, for it was part of the purchase he had made in 1749. Now, after four and a half years under the French flag, he had regained possession.

Having captured the site of the French fortress, the task which Forbes next faced was holding the ground he had won. Snow was in the air, and his army slept unprotected on the cold ground. The supply situation could not support a large body of troops at Pittsburgh, as the place was named by the British. Moreover, the term of service for many of the provincials was virtually over. Forbes, therefore, decided to leave Colonel Hugh Mercer at the forks with two hundred men to construct a small temporary fort. The rest of the army prepared to withdraw, and plans were made for protecting the communication to Pittsburgh by stationing gar-

39. Peters to Weiser, Dec. 22, 1758, Correspondence of Conrad Weiser, II, 143, Hist. Soc. of Pa.; Croghan's vouchers for 1758, Cadwalader Coll., Hist. Soc. of Pa.; Sylvester K. Stevens, Donald H. Kent, and Autumn L. Leonard, eds., *The Papers of Henry Bouquet: The Forbes Expedition* (Harrisburg, 1951), II, 610-11; James, ed., *Writings of General John Forbes*, 259-60, 262.
40. Joseph Shippen orderly book, Amer. Philos. Soc.

The Campaigns of 1758 153

risons at Loyalhanna (now named Fort Ligonier), Raystown (now called Fort Bedford), and the provincial Forts Lyttelton and Loudoun, as well as posts at Shippensburg and Carlisle.

Mercer's position was to be an extremely hazardous one. The French menaced him from Venango, LeBoeuf, and Presque Isle. There was also the Indian problem. Could the Ohio natives be trusted? When they discovered that his fort was poorly manned, would they unite again with the French? It was vitally necessary to come to terms with the natives before the might of the army melted away.

Some Ohio Delawares had approached Forbes after his victory, but most of them were terrified of his vengeance and had sought safety in flight. Forbes assigned Croghan and Montour the dangerous task of seeking out the Delawares and bringing them in to a conference. "As a private person I have no reason to say any thing in favour of Mr. C——," wrote the Irishman's creditor, Edward Shippen, "but this I am pretty sure of that if he could not bring them [the Indians] in, no man on the continent could do it, I dont except Sir William Johnston himself you see."[41]

Croghan sent runners to Kuskuskies, calling on the Delawares there to meet him at Sauconk, one of their villages located on the Ohio River, one mile below the mouth of Big Beaver Creek. On November 28, Croghan and Montour, escorted by six Delawares, set off on foot down the banks of the river. They passed through deserted Logstown, where Croghan noted that the French had built forty houses for the Indians. When he arrived at Sauconk, only a few natives were there to greet him. Most had fled from their fine French-built homes, but they trickled back during the night, their numbers increased by the arrival of the Indians from Kuskuskies. Croghan, assisted by Thomas King, the Oneida chief, presented a belt of wampum in the general's name, telling the natives that he had come to take them by the hand and lead them to Forbes. Among the two score Delawares who agreed to accompany him as soon as Custaloga arrived were the Beaver, Shingas, Delaware George, and Pisquetomen.[42]

41. Stevens, Kent, Leonard, eds., *Bouquet: The Forbes Expedition*, 613; *Archives of Maryland*, IX, 312-13; Shippen to William Allen, Dec. 18, 1758, Shippen Papers, III, 223, Hist. Soc. of Pa.
42. Croghan's journal of this mission is published in error under the name

Croghan and his party reached the forks of the Ohio on December 3, just in time to see Forbes, who could wait no longer, march off. It snowed that night, and Croghan, like the rest, had only the protection his blanket afforded. During the next two days, the Irishman assisted Henry Bouquet, the senior officer remaining. The English had not come to settle their lands, the colonel told the Delawares, but to open an extensive trade. Since they could not send traders to their towns to be plundered by the French as in the past, two hundred soldiers were to be left at Pittsburgh to protect the trade. Bouquet called on the natives to notify the western nations of the Easton treaty, and he invited their deputies to come to confirm the peace. According to Croghan's minutes, the Beaver agreed to all this on behalf of the assembled chiefs. Custaloga's report to the French tends to corroborate these minutes.[43] On the other hand, a Moravian missionary who was present wrote that the Beaver was firmly opposed to the English remaining, and he claimed that neither Croghan nor Montour had properly interpreted the Indians' words. Shingas, too, accused the Indian agents of dishonest conduct. There is certainly ample evidence that the Indians did not want an English fort west of the Alleghenies. When challenged on this point, Croghan angrily denounced the report as a "d—d lie." Whatever the attitude of the Indians, the white men had come to stay.

By December 8, Croghan had traveled the fifty-six snowy miles to Fort Ligonier. Forbes was there but too sick to see anyone, so Croghan continued on another fifty miles to Fort Bedford, where he spent the last two weeks of the year. The only advantage of staying at Bedford was the opportunity of celebrating with old friends, such as John Fraser, who were there. Living conditions at the fort were crude and cramped that bitterly cold winter. As the year wore out, men crowded together in huts for protection against snow, sleet, and rain. Morale was low, there were no fresh provisions, and the soldiers sickened fast. A lawless atmosphere permeated the place; horses were stolen nightly, and the king's

---

of C. F. Post in *Pa. Archives*, III, 560-65. Post's journal is in Reuben Gold Thwaites, *Early Western Journals, 1748-1765* (Cleveland, 1904), 234-91.

43. Stevens, Kent, Leonard, eds., *Bouquet: The Forbes Expedition*, 624-26.

stores plundered virtually at will. The women present added little refinement to the rough man's world that was Fort Bedford. That Croghan's time passed convivially is indicated by a bill which shows that within fifteen days he purchased seven quarts and nineteen bottles of wine, and two gallons, one quart, and a half pint of rum. Carousing was in order. Croghan drank to Amherst, who had replaced Abercromby as commander in chief, and gloried in his own remarkable, perhaps unique, achievement of participating in two of the three major campaigns of the year. It had been an active time. He had seen the ravages of the German Flats, the slaughter at Ticonderoga, the sly manipulations at Easton, and, lastly, the establishment of a British beachhead on the Ohio. Croghan enjoyed luxury, but he was not dependent on it. Ensconced in an atmosphere of disease, dirt, and cold, of alcoholic haze and smutty conversation, the Indian agent settled back with the ease of an old campaigner and drank the old year out.[44]

44. *Ibid.*, 637-38; Thwaites, *Western Journals*, 289, 290; Croghan's vouchers for 1758, Cadwalader Coll., Hist. Soc. of Pa.

8

Consolidating Western Conquests

AFTER THE VICTORY at Fort Duquesne, Croghan remained under Forbes's orders and, lacking other instructions, accompanied the general east. It is possible that Croghan and the Iroquois who had stayed with him formed part of the general's suite when Forbes arrived in Philadelphia on January 17. The welcoming din of the town's bells and the salutes from the battery paid tribute to the conquering hero. Forbes, his health ruined beyond repair, went into seclusion. Too far gone to attend to business, the dying soldier wrote repeatedly to Amherst, warning him that Indian affairs were "at sixes and sevens" and required the commander in chief's personal attention. He was too sick to see a delegation of Ohio Iroquois which came from Pittsburgh, escorted by Captain Edward Ward, to find out what the English were planning for the coming campaign. Restively, the natives awaited Amherst.[1]

Ominous French activity made the situation at Pittsburgh extremely precarious. Forbes increased the fort's strength to 450 men, who were squeezed into barracks built for a garrison of 200. Colonel Hugh Mercer had a frantic time. Indians came in to trade their furs, but despite the promises made at Easton, and more recently by Bouquet, there was not an adequate trading stock to supply them. On January 8, Mercer wrote Bouquet, "If George Croghan or any other interpreter is with the General, I should be glad he was returned." Croghan offered to go, but Forbes would pay no attention to him.[2]

---

1. *Pennsylvania Gazette,* Jan. 18, 1759; Croghan to Johnson, Jan. 30, 1759, *Johnson Papers,* X, 90–92; Forbes to Amherst, Jan. 6, 1759, James, ed., *Writings of General John Forbes,* 275.

2. Forbes to Amherst, Jan. 26, 1759, James, ed., *Writings of General John Forbes,* 285; Mercer to Bouquet, Jan. 8, 1759, Sylvester K. Stevens and Donald

Forbes was in ill humor with Croghan and Sir William. "I have all along thought," he wrote Amherst, "that the publick measures and the private interested views of Sir William Johnstone and his myrmidons have never once coincided in my time. Nor can I at present conceive why I am honoured with one of Sir Willm Johnstones people at this place, when during the summer, when there were nine hundred Indians at one time to be taken care off, I could not get a single person to look after them from Sir William."[3]

Since Forbes would not direct Croghan, Johnson appealed to Amherst, who placed Croghan under the orders of Colonel Bouquet.[4] Forbes lingered miserably until March 11, a shocking spectacle, emaciated to a skeleton. His successor in command of the Southern Department, General John Stanwix, was soon on his way to Philadelphia.

With the authorities awaiting orders from Whitehall for the campaigns of 1759, British military activity remained in the doldrums. Amherst, for want of more serious employment, spent his time dancing and giving parties in New York. Croghan, for his part, pacified the impatient Ohio Indian delegation, advised Denny on Indian affairs, and wrote Sir William that despite favorable trading opportunities—"the people of this province are all running wild after the Indian trade"—the government must spend a great deal of money to gain the Indians to the British interest. During his stay in Philadelphia, Croghan enjoyed the company of his mother, his half-brother Edward Ward, William Trent, and other old friends. He attended the sale of furs and hides in the auction area under the courthouse in Market Street and shopped for clothes far more lavish than those he had purchased in Schenectady. He acquired a collection of wigs, including a grey bagwig and a brown Spencer wig. But his pleasant Philadelphia visit was all too short. On April 3, Stanwix ordered

H. Kent, eds., *The Papers of Colonel Henry Bouquet* (Harrisburg, 1940-43), nineteen mimeographed volumes, British Museum Series, 21634-21655), Series 21655, 33, hereafter cited as *Bouquet Papers;* Denny to Mercer, Jan. 8, 1759, *Col. Rec. of Pa.,* VIII, 292.

3. Forbes to Amherst, Feb. 7, 1759, James, ed., *Writings of General John Forbes,* 289.

4. *Johnson Papers,* X, 103, 108.

him to go to Pittsburgh where he was to transact business with the western Indians.[5]

Croghan's stand-by orders were in minute accord with Pitt's grand scheme of operations which had reached Amherst in March. Once again, Pitt hoped to reduce New France by multiple attacks. Twelve thousand regulars under General Wolfe were to sail down the St. Lawrence and capture Quebec. Amherst was to direct a land invasion of Canada, destroying Ticonderoga and Crown Point along the route to the major objectives of Montreal and Quebec. A military post was to be re-established at Oswego. If practicable, Niagara was to be taken. In Stanwix's Southern Department, diversionary attacks were ordered to tie down the enemy and to safeguard the frontiers. In addition, Pitt ordered the construction of a strong fort at the forks of the Ohio.[6]

The French, too, had their plans for the Ohio country. DeLignery, former commander at Fort Duquesne, was ordered to remain at Venango and keep the Indians loyal. He was to "annoy" the English, force them to a diversion, protect Lake Erie, and, through his forays, disrupt the supply line to Pittsburgh. Strong reinforcements from Detroit and the Illinois country were sent to support him. If Niagara was not threatened, DeLignery was to employ his men against the British troops on the Ohio.

In the spring of 1759, French power in the West was very real. Early in March, Denny warned Amherst that the French and Indians would probably attack Pittsburgh as soon as the river was clear of ice. "We are infatuated," Peters wrote Weiser, "for want of a reinforcement the French fort will be retaken this month." The Ohio Indians were plainly disaffected, and Bouquet feared they would harass the Forbes Road. Because his temporary

---

5. Huck to Loudoun, Feb. 20, 1759, Loudoun Papers, Huntington Library; *Col. Rec. of Pa.*, VIII, 301; Croghan to Johnson, Jan. 30, 1759, *Johnson Papers*, X, 90-92; bills of Dr. Richard Farmar, William Henry, David Barnes, and Samuel McCresy in Croghan's vouchers for 1759, Cadwalader Coll., Hist. Soc. of Pa.; Nicholas B. Wainwright, ed., "George Croghan's Journal, 1759-1763," *Pa. Mag. of Hist. and Biog.*, 71 (1947), 313, hereafter cited as "Croghan's Journal."

6. O'Callaghan, ed., *New-York Col. Doc.*, VII, 355-60; Pitt to Amherst, Jan. 23, 1759, Gertrude Selwyn Kimball, ed., *Correspondence of William Pitt* (New York, 1906), II, 12-13.

fort was untenable against artillery, Mercer had orders to destroy it in case of an attack.[7]

Steps to make the Ohio beachhead impregnable date from Amherst's visit to Philadelphia in April, 1759—a visit reminiscent of Loudoun's two years earlier. On both occasions, governors of neighboring colonies attended, quotas of provincial troops necessary for the western operations were established, and Croghan advised the commander in chief on Indian affairs. Amherst met the Ohio Indian deputies on April 10 and, in a speech written by Croghan, satisfied them that English military operations were going to be on a large scale and that the natives could safely support Stanwix without fear of French retaliation. Two days later, the Ohio delegation, "after being gentely cloathed," set off on its return west, guided by Ward, to whom Croghan had given £10 for expenses. It is probable that Croghan had impressed on Amherst, as Sir William had already done in a warning against "ill-timed parsimony," that considerable money must be spent on the Indian department. At any rate, the deputy agent was ordered to purchase a substantial Indian present and was authorized to employ two assistants.[8]

Bouquet, still second in command in the Southern Department, wrote Colonel Mercer that "Mr. Croghan with your direction and assistance will I hope be able to support our interest with the Indians, till we can raise the troops and inforce your arguments by the weight of an army." It would require rare diplomacy to win over the natives who were already infesting the road to Pittsburgh. On his way to Lancaster, the Indian agent met an express rider from Fort Ligonier who told him that the French and Indians had recently killed more than thirty people in that vicinity, of whom eleven were invalids cruelly murdered and scalped on their way east to Fort Bedford. French ability to disrupt the supply line was all too apparent.[9]

7. Denny to Amherst, Mar. 3, 1759, *Col. Rec. of Pa.*, VIII, 284; Peters to Weiser, Mar. 2, 1759, Correspondence of Conrad Weiser, II, 149, Hist. Soc. of Pa.; *Bouquet Papers*, 21634, 10-11.

8. Speech dated April 3 and delivered April 10, 1759, Division of Records, Harrisburg; "Croghan's Journal," *Pa. Mag. of Hist. and Biog.*, 71 (1947), 313; Ward's receipt dated April 12, 1759, Croghan's vouchers for 1759, Cadwalader Coll., Hist. Soc. of Pa.; Johnson to Amherst, Feb. 22, 1759, *Johnson Papers*, X, 103.

9. Bouquet to Mercer, May 8, 1759, *Bouquet Papers*, 21652, 160; "Croghan's Journal," *Pa. Mag. of Hist. and Biog.*, 71 (1947), 314.

Croghan was happy to leave Philadelphia, for word had recently arrived that the king in Council had disallowed his relief act of 1755 and that he was no longer free of his debts. Only several long-time creditors in Lancaster, however, dared molest the Crown agent on his westward journey, and these he paid off in money and promises. The Irishman took the Indian present, which he had bought at Stanwix's orders, by wagon to Carlisle, where he loaded it on twenty-eight pack horses. Unsuccessful in his application for a military escort, Croghan led his party out of Carlisle on May 12. Besides the Indians who had wintered with him, his Negro slave, and the pack-horse men, Croghan was accompanied by his interpreter Andrew Montour and by his assistants William Trent and Thomas McKee. Well-mounted on his bay horse, two pistols in his saddle holsters, Croghan rode the familiar way to Shippensburg, Fort Loudoun, Fort Lyttelton—posts so thinly garrisoned that they could not mount adequate guards—and on to the important supply depot of Fort Bedford.[10]

Anxious to rush the Crown's Indian present to Pittsburgh, Croghan asked Lieutenant Colonel Adam Stephen of the Virginia regiment for an escort, but Stephen, who had arrived from Winchester on May 2 with three hundred provincials, had only twenty men left; the rest were escorting provision convoys. At this anxious moment, the enemy utterly routed a detachment of 110 soldiers, futilely attempting to protect a provision train within three miles of Fort Ligonier, and thereby served notice that escorts would have to march in greater strength than ever.[11]

Since no escort appeared imminent, Croghan sent Montour through the woods to Mercer's fort, where Montour collected all the natives he could to meet Croghan and sent messengers to call others to a meeting at Pittsburgh. Through these actions, the wily Indian agent hoped to weaken the French by enticing hostile warriors away from their control. Pittsburgh's supplies were so

10. "Croghan's Journal," *Pa. Mag. of Hist. and Biog.*, 71 (1947), 314; Croghan's vouchers for 1759, Cadwalader Coll., Hist. Soc. of Pa.; *Col. Rec. of Pa.*, VIII, 320.
11. Adam Stephen to Bouquet, May 2, 1759, *Bouquet Papers*, 21644, Part I, 120; Diary of James Kenny, May 21, 1759, Hist. Soc. of Pa. The published version of this diary—*Pa. Mag. of Hist. and Biog.*, 37 (1913)—should not be used in preference to the manuscript, as it is badly edited.

low that the garrison was on the verge of eating horses and dogs; both Croghan and Colonel Stephen agreed that if the enemy destroyed the next provision convoy, Pittsburgh and Fort Ligonier would have to be abandoned.[12]

At last, on June 8, Croghan's pack horses and the vital supply train, protected by a guard of three hundred soldiers, moved slowly away from Fort Bedford and wended their tortuous path toward the dreaded slopes of the Alleghenies. Pittsburgh's fate hung on the safety of this heavily freighted convoy with its large herd of beef cattle. Fortunately, Colonel Stephen's escort proved too powerful for the marauding bands of Indians. Augmented near Fort Ligonier by Montour and thirty natives, the supply train arrived at Pittsburgh on June 18. The famished garrison welcomed it by butchering forty cattle, which they ate almost raw, guts and all.[13]

Indians of various tribes, 164 in number, gathered to welcome the deputy agent, but their leaders were not present. The natives told Croghan that "our chiefs could not be certain that you were coming as they have been so often deceived this spring and winter by being told from time to time that you was on the road, for which reason they sent us to know the trueth." Croghan encouraged them to send for their chiefs so that peace could be confirmed and gave each Indian a suit of clothes.[14]

Treating with the Indians and giving them handsome presents to alienate them from the French was an important aspect of Croghan's work. Another aspect was the employment of Indian spies to scout the enemy at Venango, the base from which their war parties went out to attack the supply convoys. He was also assiduous in sending messages urging hostile tribes to withdraw from the French, and in writing intelligence reports to Stanwix. A fourth and extremely important part of his duties was the regulation of the Pittsburgh Indian trade.

Sir William Johnson and Croghan were both convinced that, while it was all important that the Indians not be crowded off their hunting lands by settlers, and that in time of need they be

---

12. Croghan to Horatio Gates, May 25, 1759, and Stephen to Bouquet, May 27, 1759, *Bouquet Papers*, 21644, Part I, 154-55, 157.
13. Joseph Smith to John Smith, Aug. 15, 1759, Lib. Co. of Phila.
14. "Croghan's Journal," *Pa. Mag. of Hist. and Biog.*, 71 (1947), 316-17.

supported by presents, a well-conducted trade with the natives was the best means of preserving their good will. To the Board of Trade, Johnson wrote: "An equitable an open & a well regulated trade with the Indians, is, and ever will be, the most natural & the most efficacious means to improve & extend His Majestys Indian interest."[15] It was up to Croghan to establish such a trade.

Pennsylvania had never succeeded in regulating its Indian trade, despite a law and proclamations which sought to license traders and penalize abuses. In 1758, the Assembly passed a stronger Indian trade act, naming commissioners to supervise the trade, banning the sale of liquor to the Indians, and creating a monopoly for the province of all trade west of the mountains. Three stores were set up by the commissioners, one at Fort Augusta, another at Fort Allen, and a third at Pittsburgh. Goods were sold to the Indians at established rates, and the furs and hides taken in exchange were auctioned in Philadelphia. From the very start, however, the Indian trade commissioners ran into difficulties. The sum of £4,000 which they were permitted to borrow to finance their stores was too small. Even when it was increased to £10,000, the capital proved inadequate. The commissioners had personnel problems as well. The £800-worth of Indian goods sent to Pittsburgh with Robert Tuckness in December, 1758, bogged down at Fort Loudoun, and Tuckness resigned. Not until June was his successor able to move the trading stock to Pittsburgh. During the many months before the province's store opened, Colonel Mercer had to allow an illicit trade between peddlers and the Indians. Israel Pemberton, by special permission of General Forbes and with the grudging acquiescence of the unhappy commissioners, opened his own store there. As a working principle, it soon became obvious that the Indian trade commissioners were not to exercise their monopoly privilege. Their disappointments were intensified when Croghan took over his duties.[16]

15. Johnson to the Board of Trade, May 17, 1759, O'Callaghan, ed., *Doc. Hist. of N. Y.*, II, 783.
16. *The Statutes at Large of Pennsylvania from 1682-1801*, 5 (1898), 320-30, 396-400; James, ed., *Writings of John Forbes*, 277; *Col. Rec. of Pa.*, VIII, 286; *Bouquet Papers*, 21652, 154, 160-61, and 21644, Part I, 100. Between December, 1758, and April, 1760, the commissioners sent £7,797-worth of goods to Pittsburgh. Indian Commissioners Papers, Gratz Coll., Hist. Soc. of Pa.

Croghan completely disregarded Pennsylvania's law, taking it upon himself not only to license Indian traders but to set prices. It mattered not to him that the commissioners had set their own prices; he called on their agent to adopt his schedule, which gave the Indians better trading values. Entirely opposed to a government monopoly and a bitter enemy of the store, Croghan claimed Stanwix had given him the right to open the trade to all. Actually, the inability of the commissioners to send enough goods to Pittsburgh doomed their expectation of engrossing the Indian trade.[17]

The commissioners and Pemberton both objected strenuously to General Stanwix about Croghan. Stanwix promised an investigation, which, in the end, proved favorable to the Indian agent. Disgusted and bitter, the commissioners then reported to the Assembly that the trade at Pittsburgh had been opened to the public in violation of the law, "the General being advised (as there is the strongest reason to believe) in this matter of public concern and moment, by a person remarkable in this province for his mismanagement of every private trust." They claimed that the people whom Croghan had licensed were trading liquor to the Indians, thereby obtaining the choicest furs and perpetrating the old abuses. It is certain that such idealism as had gone into the framing of Pennsylvania's "Act for Preventing Abuses in the Indian Trade" was doomed to failure because of its unrealistic features and Croghan's opposition. Again, ideally, Croghan's point of view in regulating the trade for the good of the Indians should have been disinterested and objective. Such characteristics, however, did not typify the Irishman. It was soon reported that Croghan was surreptitiously engaged in the Indian trade himself.[18]

While the enemy continued their depredations, scalping unwary victims, and even attacking Fort Ligonier in force, Croghan held a major conference from July 4 to July 11 with the chiefs of eight nations and the Wyandots, who represented eight more tribes. Five hundred Indians attended the meetings, which were held in a council shed several hundred yards up the Allegheny from

17. Diary of James Kenny, June 28, 1759, Hist. Soc. of Pa.; "Croghan's Journal," *Pa. Mag. of Hist. and Biog.*, 71 (1947), 319, n. 27; George Allen to William West, July 2, 1759, Gratz Coll., Hist. Soc. of Pa.
18. *Pa. Archives*, Eighth Series, VI, 5093-94; Diary of James Kenny, Aug. 19, 1759, Hist. Soc. of Pa.

Mercer's fort. The largest group present were the Delawares, led by their king the Beaver, a steady, quiet, middle-aged man of cheerful disposition and short stature.[19] Shingas, whom the Beaver had replaced, also attended.

The purpose of the meeting was to confirm peace. Croghan and Mercer had hoped that the chiefs would go to Philadelphia for this object, or at least await the coming of General Stanwix to solemnize the occasion, but the natives insisted on making peace then and there. Accordingly, Croghan, in his quiet but dramatic voice, opened the conference. He told the Indians of the Easton peace and of the boundary line agreed on there—the Allegheny Mountains beyond which settlers would not come. He called on the Indians to return their white prisoners and repeated that the British military forces would quit Pittsburgh as soon as the French were defeated and trade was safe.[20]

Croghan's conference appeared to be successful, although it was attended by difficulties. The Indians nearly ate Mercer out of house and home, and he was reduced to slaughtering the garrison's milk cows. Trade goods and presents ran out. Croghan had asked Pennsylvania to help supply Indian presents, but the commissioners characteristically refused his request. Worse yet, Croghan's spies came in with the unexpected news that the French had collected an overwhelming force and were preparing to move cannon down the river. The Indians, who saw that Pittsburgh was undermanned and on short rations, were not steadied in their new allegiance by these tidings.[21]

Mercer anxiously awaited the arrival of the next supply convoy, which was escorted by a detachment of the Royal American Regiment. This reinforcement would bring Pittsburgh's garrison up to one thousand men. He organized the traders and other civilians into a militia and tore down their houses near the fort, lest they shelter the enemy in an attack. Everyone moved into the fort. Croghan's Indians continued to bring in alarming intelligence of the powerful artillery-supported force which would assault Pittsburgh in a few days. Should the enemy simply intercept the

19. Diary of James Kenny, July 10, 1759, Hist. Soc. of Pa.
20. Treaty minutes, *Col. Rec. of Pa.*, VIII, 382-90.
21. Diary of James Kenny, July 14, 1759, Hist. Soc. of Pa.; Commissioners to Denny, July 25, 1759, *Pa. Archives*, III, 675.

supply convoy, "no less than a miracle can save our lives," wrote James Kenny, Pemberton's agent, on July 14. That very evening Pittsburgh learned of its salvation.[22]

The welcome news was brought by two of Croghan's Iroquois scouts just returned from Venango. There, on July 11, the French had concentrated 700 troops and about 950 Indians. On July 12, the French commander, while haranguing the Indians about the departure of the entire expedition for Pittsburgh, received orders to march directly to the support of Niagara, which was threatened by a powerful army and by Sir William Johnson and the Six Nations. Nearly all the French troops rushed off to Niagara, and their Indians dispersed, though enough remained to constitute a formidable hazard on Forbes Road. The arrival of the Royal Americans with supplies, on July 18, closed a frantic week of fear.

Croghan continued to court hostile Indians, who now began to desert the French. He gave presents to their chief men and, during his first month at Pittsburgh, handed out nearly twelve hundred suits of clothes to visiting natives. Supplies of presents sent forward by Stanwix flowed so rapidly through the Irishman's hands that he wrote the general, "The success I have met with in drawing the Indians from the enemy, and preventing others joining them, with the advantage gained by our intelligence will I hope make your Honour think the expence not ill bestowed."[23] This open-handed policy of friendship and largesse drew in many bands of natives with whom Croghan held ceremonial talks. His largest midsummer conference took place on August 7, when three hundred Indians agreed to bury the hatchet. The Beaver was a key figure at this and other meetings and exerted a helpful influence.

Not all the Indians who treated with Croghan were sincere in their pretensions. Some, after receiving their presents, skulked around Pittsburgh taking an occasional scalp or prisoner. This treachery aroused Amherst's fury and contempt: "Tis just like the scoundrells!" Horse stealing by the supposedly friendly Dela-

---

22. Mercer to Bouquet, July 11, 1759, *Bouquet Papers*, 21655, 41; *Pennsylvania Gazette*, July 26, 1759; Diary of James Kenny, July 14, 1759, Hist. Soc. of Pa.; "Croghan's Journal," *Pa. Mag. of Hist. and Biog.*, 71 (1947), 327.

23. Mercer to Stanwix, July 28, 1759, and Croghan to Stanwix, July 31, 1759, *Bouquet Papers*, 21655, 56-58.

wares constituted another problem to which Croghan was hard put for a solution. But at least the seige of Forbes Road was coming to an end. The last serious attack the Indians made on this supply line occurred on August 5, when a large convoy on its way to Fort Ligonier was heavily engaged.[24]

August 13 brought the anxiously awaited news that Sir William Johnson had captured Niagara. As Croghan had prophesied, this victory was followed by the withdrawal of the French, who destroyed their forts at Venango, LeBoeuf, and Presque Isle. Their Ohio River line was now untenable, and the best they could do in the West was to rebuild with feverish haste their tottering fort at Detroit. The Pittsburgh garrison joyfully cheered Johnson's success and word that Ticonderoga was, at long last, also in British hands. But the Indians, apprehensive of losing their bargaining position if the French were to collapse, looked grave and refrained from celebrating.

Of the French withdrawal, Colonel Mercer wrote, "No laurels are to be reaped upon the Ohio this campaign." But the objective of the Southern Department in 1759 was not the pursuit of laurels; rather it was the drab business of building a fort. Before construction could begin, stores ample enough to subsist the number of men necessary for the project had to be accumulated. Stanwix and Bouquet were hard pressed to find supplies and transportation.

Earlier in 1759, when Bouquet tried to provision Pittsburgh, the Indians had destroyed some of the food en route. Later, after the natives had declared peace with the British, they encamped at Pittsburgh and devoured the provisions as quickly as Bouquet could send them. "The King's orders are to build a fort," wrote the exasperated Swiss colonel, "which cannot be effected without a large body of men, and it is not possible to send them as long as the provisions forwarded are daily consumed by that idle people." Croghan was drawing four to five hundred rations a day for the Indians and could not comply with the order to "put an end to that useless consumption; which is our evident ruin." The Irishman tried to prevail on the Indians to go home, but his familiarity with them did not always work to his advantage. Having warned

---

24. Amherst to Pitt, Oct. 22, 1759, Kimball, ed., *Correspondence of William Pitt*, II, 192; *Pennsylvania Gazette*, Aug. 16, 1759.

Stanwix that Keekyuscung, Croghan's favorite messenger, "will drink," Croghan himself got drunk and fought with the old chief, receiving a black eye for his indiscretion.[25]

To the sound of saws merrily rasping away in chief engineer Harry Gordon's sawyer's pit, John Stanwix, accompanied by his personal train and his "set of musick," rode into Pittsburgh on August 29. James Kenny noted that the general "was very plain dressed & seems not proud." Stanwix, nearly seventy years of age, was doubtless one of the oldest English officers serving in North America. His career had been a distinguished one. He had been an equerry to the Prince of Wales and for many years a member of Parliament. Pennsylvanians respected him so highly that in 1756, during his first tour of duty in the Southern Department, they had elected him as assemblyman from Cumberland County. In June, 1759, Stanwix was promoted to major general. Nevertheless, he was a disappointed man, his pride bruised by Amherst's appointment as commander in chief. Stanwix had entered the army in 1706, exactly a quarter of a century before Amherst tried on his first uniform. He was now gamely resolved to erect the fort at Pittsburgh and then to retire to England, rather than serve longer under his former junior.[26]

Within a few days of the general's arrival, Captain Gordon began to build the new fort, a pentagon of substantial earth embankments protected by a deep ditch from the Monongahela to the Allegheny. With the garrison increased to thirteen hundred men, work went on briskly. Hostile natives kept their distance, and tranquility reigned.[27]

Croghan and Stanwix held two important Indian conferences in September and October with the Ottawas, Twightwees, Wyandots, and other nations. The professions of friendship and the promise to return white captives, on the one hand, and the explanations about the Easton peace, the boundary line of the Alleghenies, and the promises of a fair trade at Pittsburgh, on the

25. Croghan to Stanwix, July 21, 1759, Bouquet to Croghan, Aug. 10, 1759, and Bouquet to Pemberton, Sept. 1, 1759, *Bouquet Papers*, 21655, 49, 75-76, and 21652, 235.
26. Diary of James Kenny, Aug. 29, 1759, Hist. Soc. of Pa.
27. Shippen Papers, IV, 173, Hist. Soc. of Pa.; *Bouquet Papers*, 21644, Part II, 71, and 21654, 50; *Pa. Archives*, III, 685.

other hand, formed the basis of both discussions. The welcome given the Indians did not entirely lull the fears of a Wyandot leader, who tactfully warned Croghan: "You are appointed by the King to transact business with us, the Indians; you have hitherto done it to our satisfaction; we hope the King's general will act on the same principles."[28]

Croghan's principle was generosity to the Indians, a policy which many army officers no longer deemed necessary, for Wolfe had captured Quebec, and the war was nearly over. Stanwix, however, attributed his success in Indian affairs more to presents than to diplomatic oratory. To Pitt, he wrote that, with Croghan's assistance, he had brought the various Indian nations into alliance with the British. Stanwix approved past expenses, heavy though they were, but "nothing in comparison with the advantage of the furr trade re-establish'd here, and the sure and immediate protection of the three great provinces Virginia, Maryland & Pennsylvania." The gouty old general respected Croghan, insisting that the Indian agent remain with him at Pittsburgh and not return to Sir William Johnson as Croghan wanted to do.[29]

The general's complimentary attitude did little to soothe Croghan, who was discouraged with the army's control of the Indian department. Through his spies he knew that the French at Detroit were brewing fresh trouble for the British; he also knew that the Indian nations did not like the strong fort which Stanwix was building. Clearly, it was still necessary to give large presents to retain their friendship. In December, Croghan wrote Johnson that the British were not as indulgent with the Indians as the French were, for the army leaders now believed that the Indians had no recourse other than to ally themselves with the victorious power. "It is true we may say we have beat the French, but we have nothing to boast from the war with the natives," added Croghan, "yet it is thought every penny thrown away that is given them, which obliges me to think the service very disagreeable, tho'

---

28. Treaty minutes, Oct. 25, 1759, *Col. Rec. of Pa.*, VIII, 432.
29. Stanwix to Pitt, Nov. 20, 1759, Kimball, ed., *Correspondence of William Pitt*, II, 211-12; Charles Brodhead to Colonel Shippen, Dec. 15, 1759, Burd-Shippen Papers, I, 81, Amer. Philos. Soc.; Croghan to Johnson, Jan. 25, 1760, *Johnson Papers*, X, 134-35.

I will by no means resign without your consent and approbation."[30]

Johnson hastened to mollify his deputy: "I am extreamly pleased with your whole management this last campaign, & doubt not but as you always have, you will continue to exert yourself in your station." "I am of your opinion," continued the Indian superintendent, "that the French fm. Detroit with a few ill-disposed Indians may interrupt the convoys wth provisions to your post, & thereby distress that garrison if not seasonably prevented by your being qualified to give presents to & treat with those you may suspect will act against us, and by your keeping good scouts towards Presque Isle & along Lake Erie." Johnson told Croghan to appeal directly to Amherst for support.[31]

Croghan remained at Pittsburgh. He built himself a house several miles up the Allegheny at his old Pine Creek plantation and entertained Indians there. With Stanwix's approval, he sent spies to Detroit, and he learned with pleasure that the Shawnees and other western tribes had resumed their war with their traditional enemy the Cherokees, a nation now hostile to the English.[32]

He ingratiated himself with the curious Governor Denny by procuring choice furs for him at Pittsburgh. Denny was succeeded by James Hamilton, whom Thomas Penn had finally persuaded to resume the governorship, in November, 1759, and returned to England in the summer of 1760, where, as he wrote Croghan, he intended to have "the pleasure of representing your great services in a proper manner to the Secretary of State." Unfortunately, Denny had so thoroughly disgraced himself during the last months of his administration that he had no influence whatsoever. Croghan's hopes that Denny would promote his petition for recovery of trade losses were futile.[33]

Unable to tend personally to the recovery of his lost fortune, Croghan remained at Pittsburgh, watching others lay the foundations of new ones in the Indian trade. All through the remarkably fine fall of 1759 and the hard, bitter winter, bands of Indians

30. Croghan to Johnson, Dec. 22, 1759, and Jan. 25, 1760, *Johnson Papers*, X, 131-32, 134-35.
31. Johnson to Croghan, Feb. 16, 1760, *ibid.*, 137-38.
32. "Croghan's Journal," *Pa. Mag. of Hist. and Biog.*, 71 (1947), 356, 360; Stanwix to Hamilton, Dec. 8, 1759, *Pa. Archives*, III, 693-94.
33. Denny to Croghan, June 6, 1760, Cadwalader Coll., Hist. Soc. of Pa.

brought in rich harvests of furs and skins. Pittsburgh prospered. Stanwix referred to it as a "town," "a thriving place & pritty full of trading houses within the works." The works, of course, were the pentagon and its entrenchment. Forbes had called the locality Pittsburgh; it was Stanwix who built and named Fort Pitt.[34]

Because Captain Gordon had not been able to begin the fort before September, and because of the severe winter, the structure was not completed in 1759. Stanwix, therefore, remained on until the spring of 1760, by which time the defenses of Fort Pitt, although still unfinished, were formidable indeed. Eighteen pieces of artillery, mounted on the bastions, covered the ditch across the point and protected the fort from approach by land. Barracks for a garrison of a thousand men had been erected, and the supply problem had been solved, for storerooms bulged with provisions for seven months.[35]

When the flood waters in the western streams subsided, Stanwix left Fort Pitt for Philadelphia on his homeward way to England and promotion. George Croghan and thirty-five Ohio Indian chiefs accompanied the general and his Royal American escort as far as Fort Bedford. As the procession marched slowly over Forbes's winter-damaged road, a phase in British westward expansion ended. The long struggle with the French for the forks of the Ohio, first dramatized by Céloron's expedition in 1749, was now history.

Although Stanwix's mission was completed, Croghan's was not. Any hopes he may have had for a vacation were dashed by frantic letters from Fort Pitt. He hurried back from Bedford to conduct a conference with a large band of Shawnees, who refused to depart before they saw him. To show good faith, the Shawnees delivered fourteen white captives to Croghan and begged him to send traders to their towns. In granting their request, Croghan cemented the reconciliation of this previously hostile nation. With his usual generosity, he not only emptied the Crown's supply of Indian presents to insure the success of the meeting but pledged his own credit to make the gift larger. He also outfitted a

---

34. Stanwix to Pitt, Nov. 20, 1759, Kimball, ed., *Correspondence of William Pitt*, II, 211-12.
35. Stanwix to Pitt, Mar. 17, 1760, *ibid.*, 265-67.

Consolidating Western Conquests 171

hundred warriors to go to war against the Cherokees, then terrorizing the southern frontier. Croghan's motive for this last action was twofold: not only would it create a diversionary attack on enemy Indians, but it would also clear the Fort Pitt area of idle braves who were eating the army's food and stealing its horses.[36]

Amherst, however, disapproved of Croghan's Cherokee war plans, for he wanted all friendly warriors as reinforcements for his northern expedition. The objective of 1760, to which the might of the army was bent, was the reduction of Montreal. The mission of the Southern Department, now commanded by Brigadier General Robert Monckton, was to be largely administrative. Monckton was ordered to send four hundred of his Royal Americans to garrison Niagara and to secure the communication between Niagara and Fort Pitt by building military posts at Venango, LeBoeuf, and Presque Isle.[37]

Monckton arrived at Fort Pitt on June 29, 1760, and conferred with Croghan about the relief expedition for Niagara. This force was to march overland to Presque Isle through Indian country never traveled by a large British army unit. Many feared that the Indians would be outraged at such an invasion. The building of three forts along the line of march was also a dangerous expedient. Croghan, who was not allowed time to request formal permission of the Ohio chiefs for these military operations, was later half jestingly reproached by them for making a road through their country and then telling them he was going to do it.[38]

Guided by some Indians under Croghan's charge, Monckton's troops left Fort Pitt, on July 7, for their 150-mile march. The path was bad; the heat nearly killed the pack horses; the Indian guides, though kept in good humor by Croghan, were drunk—the very first day out they took a wrong trail. Fortunately, the troops

---

36. John Tulleken to Bouquet, Apr. 2, 1760, *Bouquet Papers*, 21645, 64; treaty minutes of Apr. 6-12, 1760, *Johnson Papers*, III, 208-17; Croghan to [Gates], May 1, 1760, *Coll. of the Mass. Hist. Soc.*, Fourth Series, 9 (1871), 246-47.

37. Gates to Croghan, May 7 and June 8, 1760, and Croghan to Gates, May 14, 1760, Cadwalader Coll., Hist. Soc. of Pa.; Amherst to Monckton, Apr. 29, 1760, W. O., 34/43, Public Record Office, London; Pitt to Amherst, Jan. 7, 1760, Kimball, ed., *Correspondence of William Pitt*, II, 238-42.

38. Croghan to Johnson, June 30 and Sept. 6, 1760, *Johnson Papers*, X, 174, 178-79.

met no resistance during the ten toilsome days it took to reach Presque Isle, where the Royal Americans embarked in bateaux sent from Niagara. Croghan visited the Indian towns en route, giving presents and sending belts to invite the chiefs to a conference at Fort Pitt. At Presque Isle, he reported to Bouquet, who had remained to build the fort, that there was no Indian danger.[39]

Although Bouquet's provincial troops were occasionally sniped at by hostile Indians from Detroit—Croghan retaliated by sending a raiding party to Detroit, promising $150 for every prisoner and scalp—they completed the Presque Isle blockhouse that fall. A smaller blockhouse at LeBoeuf was constructed by Thomas Smallman, now a Pennsylvania major, and Virginia troops erected a fort at Venango.[40] To all these strong points flocked sutlers, Indian traders, and Indian agents sent by Croghan.

Because Monckton requested Croghan to return to Pittsburgh, the Indian agent did not tarry at Presque Isle. In company with a large pack train from Lake Erie, he rode into Fort Pitt on July 26, prepared to use his persuasive eloquence on one of the largest Indian meetings ever held there. This conference was slightly delayed by Teedyuscung, who had called the Ohio Indians together at the Salt Lick Town to tell them of his treaties with Pennsylvania. Croghan disapproved of Teedyuscung's meeting, because it was not held at Fort Pitt and because it represented interference in Indian affairs by the Pennsylvania government, which had sent the Delaware as an envoy.[41]

Delegates of most of the western tribes, nearly a thousand Indians, attended Monckton's conference. The general read them a message from Amherst which was at once conciliatory and bellicose. The Indians would not be deprived of their lands, except for a few fort sites, as long as they remained friendly, but, if they committed hostilities, Amherst would retaliate tenfold. The natives took this speech in good part, behaved unusually well, and

---

39. Bouquet to Monckton, July 9 and July 18, 1760, *Coll. of the Mass. Hist. Soc.*, Fourth Series, 9 (1871), 264-66, 271-74.

40. *Bouquet Papers*, 21645, 162-63; Croghan's instructions to Thomas Hutchins, undated but c. Sept. 9, 1760, Cadwalader Coll., Hist. Soc. of Pa.

41. Gates to Croghan, July 10, 1760, Cadwalader Coll., Hist. Soc. of Pa.; treaty minutes, *Pa. Archives*, III, 744-52; "Croghan's Journal," *Pa. Mag. of Hist. and Biog.*, 71 (1947), 380; Croghan to Gates, July 10, 1760, *Coll. of the Mass. Hist. Soc.*, Fourth Series, 9 (1871), 267; Wallace, *Teedyuscung*, 220-21.

kept sober. After a solemn ratification of peace and good will, Monckton generously doled out enough rum to keep them drunk for days.[42]

Croghan managed this important meeting with his usual dexterity and advised Monckton how to deal with Teedyuscung. Peters was thankful that the treaty had been held at Fort Pitt rather than in a Pennsylvania town where Monckton would not have had the real sentiments of the Indians, but only "the echo of some stories told them underhand by Israel Pemberton." He knowingly commented that "Mr. Croghan understands the disposition of Indians very well & knows how to time things now he is not disturbed by Quakers."[43]

And yet, an effort at Quaker interference did manifest itself in the conduct of John Langdale, Quaker agent of the Pennsylvania Indian commissioners. Langdale, trying to uphold Teedyuscung in a Pemberton-like manner, sent Monckton an extraordinary demand for seats at the conference, where he and his clerk could take minutes. Teedyuscung, prompted by Langdale, so Monckton believed, announced that he must have a secretary. Both demands were refused. Drunk from morn to night, Teedyuscung did not speak at the meeting and was treated with scorn by the Beaver and the other chiefs. The Delaware chief had sunk so low that he had even sold the furs given him by Indians at the Salt Lick Town with which, in lieu of wampum, he was supposed to deliver their messages.[44]

While Monckton held his treaty at Fort Pitt, Amherst and his powerful army moved massively toward Montreal, where, in September, he forced the capitulation of New France and brought the war in North America to an end. To receive the surrender of Detroit and the other far western French posts, Amherst appointed the celebrated ranger Major Robert Rogers, who hastened to Fort Pitt with orders calling for Monckton to assign troops to garrison Detroit and for Croghan to accompany Rogers. Monckton appointed French-speaking Captain Donald Campbell and

42. Croghan to Johnson, Sept. 6, 1760, *Johnson Papers*, X, 178-79.
43. Peters to Monckton, Aug. 29, 1760, *Coll. of the Mass. Hist. Soc.*, Fourth Series, 9 (1871), 305-6.
44. Penn Mss., Indian Affairs, III, 91, 92, Hist. Soc. of Pa.

a company of Royal Americans to serve as the garrison. From Fort Pitt, Croghan dispatched Indian messengers to notify the Detroit tribes of Rogers' mission. The expedition to receive the capitulation of the western posts quickly assembled at Presque Isle.

On November 3, Rogers' force embarked in whaleboats, rowing westward in column of twos along the southern shore of Lake Erie. At the head of the column was Rogers, and abreast of him, Croghan. The progress of the water-borne troops was closely paralleled by a land party of soldiers and Indians, driving a herd of beef cattle for the winter supply of Captain Campbell's men. Croghan had recommended the feasibility of driving cattle to Detroit, having himself traveled the same route to that vicinity in his trading days.[45]

The Irishman well knew that Rogers' mission was a dangerous one; his force was too small to withstand a hostile reception by large native tribes long faithful to the French. Consequently, Croghan was very generous to the Indians whom the expedition encountered on its way, prodigiously so, according to Amherst. At nightly encampments, Croghan soothed the Indian hunters whom the land party had met during the day and had persuaded to talk with the agent. Thoughts of the past must have welled up in him when he and Rogers bivouacked on the banks of the Cuyahoga, where the Indian agent had traded long ago. There he met Ottawa hunters, "who treated us very kindly they being formerly acquainted with me."[46]

Croghan told such groups about the capitulation of Canada, which required the British to take possession of Detroit and other posts, remove their garrisons as prisoners of war, and replace them with British troops. The French inhabitants, he added, were not to be molested but were to take an oath of fealty and become British subjects. And, by a belt of wampum, for this was important, all nations of Indians would be guaranteed a free trade

[45]. Bouquet to Monckton, Nov. 4, 1760, *Coll. of the Mass. Hist. Soc.*, Fourth Series, 9 (1871), 343.

[46]. For a discussion of the improbability of Croghan's meeting Pontiac on this trip, see Peckham's *Pontiac*, 59-62; "Croghan's Journal," *Pa. Mag. of Hist. and Biog.*, 71 (1947), 389; Indian agency accounts, Cadwalader Coll., Hist. Soc. of Pa.; Amherst to Johnson, Feb. 22, 1761, *Johnson Papers*, III, 345.

and peaceable possession of their hunting country as long as they remained faithful to King George.

Awaiting Croghan at Sandusky Lake was a delegation of Indians from Detroit who had received the message carried by Croghan's native scouts. "Your care in sending us timely notice" of the British occupation, they told the Irishman, "is a confirmation of your sincerity and upright intentions towards us, and part of our business in meeting you here was to bid you wellcome to our country." Fatalistically, the natives were ready enough to discard their traditional French alliance. At the mouth of the Detroit River, Rogers was warmly greeted by chiefs of the resident tribes. Detroit was soon safely in his hands, and its Indians submissively delivered forty-two British prisoners to Croghan and docilely accepted his instructions for their future behavior. Indians and French alike, exhausted and impoverished by the long war, seemed pleased to see the British colors flying over the fort. Croghan was astonished at their ready acceptance of the change.[47]

In retrospect, Johnson was to write, "The westeren Indians would not have suffered us to take possession of Detroit, but from the precaution I took in sending Mr. Croghan to prepare them for it." On learning that Rogers had highly commended Croghan's zeal and vigilance to Amherst, Johnson approvingly noted, "I judged his accompanying the Major that way would be necessary, as he is well acquainted with most of the nations thereabouts & much liked by them, and all others to whom he is known."[48]

The occupation of Detroit called for an immediate extension of the fur trade. The natives had furs in abundance which the British had to purchase, not only to maintain the new alliance, but to provide the Indians with the necessities of life. Bouquet, who now commanded at Fort Pitt, encouraged traders to go to Detroit. These men were carefully licensed and allowed to market their cargoes only at places designated by Croghan and the Detroit commander. The traders were not allowed to take liquor with

---

47. *Johnson Papers*, III, 276, and X, 198-206; "Croghan's Journal," *Pa. Mag. of Hist. and Biog.*, 71 (1947), 392, 395; Croghan to Monckton, Jan. 13, 1761, Cadwalader Coll., Hist. Soc. of Pa.

48. Johnson to Amherst, Feb. 12, 1761, and Johnson to Gage, June 9, 1764, *Johnson Papers*, III, 330, and XI, 223.

them and were required to sell their goods at prices fixed by Croghan.

Croghan's prices were based on a buck's worth, a buck being one fall male deerskin. The equivalent of a buck, as expressed in terms of other hides and furs, was two does, two spring bucks, one large buck beaver, six raccoons, four foxes, two fishers, or two otters. Croghan valued a blanket at four bucks, a matchcoat at three bucks; a pint of powder, one hundred wampum beads, or four small knives could be purchased for one buck.[49]

The extension of the Indian trade westward from Pittsburgh, begun early in 1760 when Croghan and Monckton first allowed traders to go to native towns, accelerated after the fall of Canada. From the trading village of Pittsburgh, men like Robert Callender, Michael Teaffe, Alexander Lowrey, John Hart, and Hugh Crawford were soon establishing themselves at Detroit, Sandusky, the Lower Shawnee Town, the Delaware villages, and the military outposts. Nearly all of the traders were Pennsylvanians backed by such eastern capitalists as George Ross and Joseph Simon of Lancaster, and Abraham Mitchell, David Franks, and Baynton & Wharton of Philadelphia. Bouquet supervised their activities as best he could and was prompt to punish infractions of trading regulations. The colonel complained of the licentiousness of the traders, for it took him six months to discipline them and to bring them into some sort of subordination, "to which they were utter strangers."[50]

To assist army officers at the increasing number of British posts, Croghan, who had returned to Fort Pitt, enlarged his staff of assistants. Trent had left Croghan's service in 1760 to enter the Indian trade and was replaced by Thomas McKee's son, Alexander. Later in 1760, Croghan hired his half-brother Major Edward Ward and Thomas Hutchins. He uniformly surrounded himself with men of exceptional ability; Trent, Alexander McKee, and Hutchins, in particular, were destined for remarkable careers. The Irishman also employed a number of other men in subordinate capacities—doctors, interpreters, gunsmiths, and laborers. Montour continued to lend his valuable but erratic service. Early in

---

49. *Bouquet Papers*, 21646, 26, and 21655, 102.
50. Bouquet to Donald Campbell, July 9, 1761, *ibid.*, 21653, 69.

1760, while carrying important dispatches from Johnson to Croghan, Montour irresponsibly lost them and was detained in Carlisle for a tavern debt.[51]

Believing the Indian department far too costly, Amherst ordered expenses cut, and, in April, 1761, Croghan discharged six of his people. To be sure, the fall of Canada had taken pressure off the department, but the French menace was not yet entirely abated. Down the Ohio lay the Illinois district of the province of Louisiana, hostile territory that had not been surrendered with the capitulation of New France. Hearing that the French in the Illinois country had enticed a hundred Canadian Indians to join the Cherokees, the Irishman sneeringly commented, "If this be true cartianly the French has a noffe to do to sperrett up the Cherrokes to continue the warr by going so far to bring them suckers."[52]

Military leaders, such as Stanwix, Monckton, and their major of brigade Horatio Gates, all spoke well of Croghan. Bouquet, who knew him more intimately, blew hot and cold. While building the Presque Isle fort in 1760, he had deprecated Croghan's influence with the Indians. On returning to Fort Pitt, the colonel was irritated at his inability to make the Indian agent account properly for the rations he had issued to the natives: "There is a veill kept over the transactions of our managers which will not disappear till we get rid of them all." Despite this statement, Bouquet acknowledged Croghan's usefulness and, in his absences from Fort Pitt, strictly cautioned his subordinates to follow the Irishman's advice. The main problem in Indian affairs for Bouquet was not managing the Indians, but managing Croghan. The agent's persuasiveness in soliciting gifts for the Indians was enough to melt a soldier's heart. Bouquet called Croghan a loadstone that attracted Indians to Fort Pitt; by his mere presence he made economy difficult. Certainly, the Indians always expected generous treatment from "the Buck," as they called him. An Iroquois chief, ar-

51. *Ibid.*, 21646, 104; Johnson to Croghan, May 14, 1760, *Johnson Papers*, X, 148, and III, 300.

52. Amherst to Johnson, Feb. 22, 1761, *Johnson Papers*, III, 346; Croghan to Monckton, Feb. 10 and Apr. 19, 1761, Cadwalader Coll., Hist. Soc. of Pa.; Clarence W. Alvord, *The Illinois Country, 1673-1818* (Chicago, 1922), 190, 241.

riving at Fort Pitt with a group of natives in May, 1761, announced that the rulers of the Six Nations had told him not to fear want, "for the Buck is in your road, and we hope he will take notice of you, and provide for you."[53]

Bouquet wholeheartedly supported Croghan's struggle against the worst of all Indian trade abuses, the traffic in rum. In the fall of 1760, Croghan had persuaded Monckton to prohibit the sale of spirits in large quantities to the Indians. Unfortunately, Monckton's ruling was difficult to enforce. No violation of it so outraged Croghan as the sale of liquor by John Langdale who ran the provincial store.[54]

Langdale contended that neither Croghan nor the military had any right to interfere with his store. He accused Croghan of a prostitution of his power in favoring William Trent's establishment. "All sceames subtilty can invent," wrote James Kenny, Langdale's clerk, were used by Croghan to direct the Indians to trade at Trent's store. Kenny also voiced the suspicion that Croghan had a financial interest in Trent's business. Langdale and Croghan, both masters of abusive language, finally had it out, with Croghan threatening to lock up the provincial store. Langdale, a man whose personality was disintegrating under the impact of frontier life, met a rock in Croghan, an experience which alone was enough to wreck his western career.[55]

Despite such occasional tussles, Croghan was profoundly bored with life at Fort Pitt. On his return from Detroit, he had hoped to visit Johnson but failed to obtain leave. Querulously, he asked Sir William if he intended "to keep me heer till I grow gray." Croghan had had no leave since he had entered Johnson's service five years earlier.[56]

Although so long on duty, he found time for personal affairs,

53. Johnson to Croghan, May 14, 1760, *Johnson Papers*, X, 149; Bouquet to Monckton, Sept. 15 and Dec. 29, 1760, *Coll. of the Mass. Hist. Soc.*, Fourth Series, 9 (1871), 321, 361; *Bouquet Papers*, 21655, 110.
54. Croghan to Johnson, Jan. 13, 1761, *Johnson Papers*, III, 303; Bouquet to Monckton, Mar. 28, 1761, *Coll. of the Mass. Hist. Soc.*, Fourth Series, 9 (1871), 402; Diary of James Kenny, July 4, 1761, Hist. Soc. of Pa.
55. Diary of James Kenny, July 17, 1761, Hist. Soc. of Pa.; *Bouquet Papers*, 21646, 55.
56. Croghan to Johnson, Nov. 1, 1760, Jan. 31 and Feb. 10, 1761, *Johnson Papers*, III, 276, 304, 330; Croghan to [Monckton], Apr. 19, 1761, Cadwalader Coll., Hist. Soc. of Pa.

the most pressing of which continued to be his indebted position to Philadelphia merchants. During 1761, Croghan and Trent did their best to pay off old debts. They turned over several tracts of land in Cumberland County to David Franks and Jeremiah Warder, who acted in behalf of their creditors. They also assigned their expectations of restitution for French losses. In addition, Croghan found assets said to be worth £500 and lands worth £1,000, which he delivered to Peters for Hockley.[57]

From the perplexing problems of personal finances, Croghan was delighted to turn his attention to welcome orders from Johnson summoning him to New York. From Johnson Hall, he was to accompany the superintendent to Detroit, where Croghan's preliminary treaties of peace and trade were due to be formalized by Johnson himself at a great meeting.[58]

Croghan arrived on the Mohawk with news that Pennsylvania had persuaded the Ohio chiefs to come to a treaty at a time which would coincide with Johnson's conference with those very Indians at Detroit. Ever since 1758, Pennsylvania had been trying to persuade the western Indians to confirm the Easton treaty. Sir William was furious. "If the Indians are not stopped, & brought back to Detroit," he wrote, "the end of my going there will not at all be answered." He ordered Croghan to explain to Amherst, then in Albany, what the Pennsylvania government had done and then to hurry back to Pittsburgh to stop the Indians from coming east. Beset by various delays in Albany, New York, and Philadelphia, which at least enabled him to purchase a princely assortment of liquors, wines, anchovies, and olives, it was not until July 23 that Croghan reached Fort Pitt. His return effectually restrained the western Indians from coming to Pennsylvania.[59]

Meanwhile, Johnson and his aides set off up the Mohawk for Oswego, en route to Niagara and the Lake Erie voyage to Detroit. The present for the treaty followed slowly, its contents a source of

57. Documents dated July 12 and July 19, 1761, David Franks and Joseph Simon folders, Gratz Coll., Hist. Soc. of Pa.; Penn to Hockley, Oct. 9, 1761, and Penn to Peters, Oct. 9, 1761, Penn Letter Book, VII, 67, 73, Hist. Soc. of Pa.
58. "Croghan's Journal," *Pa. Mag. of Hist. and Biog.*, 71 (1947), 405.
59. *Ibid.*, 409; *Col. Rec. of Pa.*, VIII, 618-19; Diary of James Kenny, July 5, 1761, Hist. Soc. of Pa.; Johnson to Amherst, June 27, 1761, and Amherst to Johnson, June 29, 1761, *Johnson Papers*, X, 300-1, 307; Croghan's vouchers for 1761, Cadwalader Coll., Hist. Soc. of Pa.

argument between Johnson and Amherst. At the end of the war in 1760, Amherst, who distrusted the Indians, restricted the amount of powder and lead which could be traded or given to them. Ammunition became scarce in the Indian country, a condition which the natives could not understand and which could not be honestly explained to them. In the face of Amherst's attitude, Johnson had a difficult time convincing the general that he could not treat with the Indians unless he had ammunition to give them.[60]

He also had difficulty in justifying what the general viewed as the large size of the present. Amherst, who regarded the natives as an insatiable and revolting race of beggars, had already decided to eliminate, as nearly as possible, the traditional French policy of giving presents, not only of ammunition, but of food and clothing, to Indians visiting army posts. He was not alone in his disgust at the Indians' unending requests for aid. General Monckton had written, "I find that there will be no end to giving, if not put a stop to in time." Now that a free trade had been opened for the Indians, these high-ranking officers believed that the natives should hunt for their living and not be maintained in idleness. Realizing that the Indians were complaining about the scarcity of supplies, Amherst ordered Johnson to tell them that, if they committed hostilities, "they must not only expect the severest retaliation, but an entire destruction of all their nations, for I am firmly resolved whenever they give me an occasion to extirpate them root & branch."[61]

To Daniel Claus, recently appointed deputy Indian agent with headquarters at Montreal, Johnson had written that Amherst was not at all a friend of the Indians and that he feared for the consequences. Indeed, the natives were already so alarmed at Amherst's coolness and indifference that Johnson was "verry apprehensive that something not right is a brewing, and that verry privately among them. I do not only mean the Six Nations. I fear it is too generall."[62]

60. Amherst to Johnson, June 11 and Aug. 9, 1761, *Johnson Papers*, X, 284, and III, 515.
61. Monckton to Croghan, Apr. 6, 1761, Cadwalader Coll., Hist. Soc. of Pa.; Amherst to Johnson, July 11 and Aug. 18, 1761, *Johnson Papers*, III, 507, 520.
62. Johnson to Daniel Claus, Mar. 10, 1761, and Johnson to Amherst, June 21, 1761, *Johnson Papers*, III, 354, and X, 291.

Consolidating Western Conquests 181

Johnson's fears were well grounded. At that very moment, a dangerous plot was exposed at Detroit. Two visiting Seneca chiefs, intent on inflaming the western tribes to rise against the English, were foiled only by the loyalty of Croghan's Detroit interpreter. The dejected Senecas arrived at Fort Pitt from their futile visit to Detroit shortly after Croghan's return. These Indians, Kiasutha and Tahaiadoris, refused to confess to Bouquet the extent of their scheme, but, in private at Croghan's house, the Irishman purchased their secret, an elaborate and detailed plan for a concerted attack from Detroit to the German Flats, which would rid their country of the English.[63]

The officers at Fort Pitt could clearly see that Indian relations were deteriorating seriously. With the exception of the Delawares, Bouquet called the behavior of the Indians intolerable. Horse stealing had reached mass proportions, and traders and soldiers alike were being insulted and robbed by the natives.[64]

Croghan resumed his journey to the Detroit conference. Accompanied by an entourage which included his "valet," he rode to the Beaver's town on the Muskingum. Summoning the nearby chiefs, he dissuaded them from their plan to treat with Governor Hamilton. Then, escorted by the Beaver and other chiefs, he pressed westward on the trail. At Sandusky, where his party left their horses for the boats which Captain Campbell had sent, the Irishman selected a site for a fort which Amherst ordered built as a way station on the communication from Fort Pitt.[65]

Upon his arrival at Detroit, he arranged for the treaty so that all was in readiness when Johnson made his triumphant appearance. While awaiting the superintendent, Croghan no doubt relaxed with the "tolerable claret and Madeira" which his friend Captain Campbell had promised him.[66]

---

63. "Croghan's Journal," *Pa. Mag. of Hist. and Biog.*, 71 (1947), 409-11; Croghan to Monckton, July 27, 1761, Cadwalader Coll., Hist. Soc. of Pa.
64. Bouquet to Donald Campbell, June 30, 1761, *Bouquet Papers*, 21653, 66; Bouquet's speech to the Indians, June 29, 1761, *ibid.*, 21655, 119.
65. "Croghan's Journal," *Pa. Mag. of Hist. and Biog.*, 71 (1947), 412; *Bouquet Papers*, 21647, 214; Diary of James Kenny, Aug. 5, 1761, Hist. Soc. of Pa.; Bouquet to Monckton, July 24, 1761, *Coll. of the Mass. Hist. Soc.*, Fourth Series, 9 (1871), 434.
66. Campbell to Croghan, Aug. 10, 1761, Cadwalader Coll., Hist. Soc. of Pa.; William L. Stone, *The Life and Times of Sir William Johnson, Bart.* (Albany, 1865), II, 451-57.

On September 9, the Indian conference was convened at the signal of two cannon. So great was the assemblage of natives representing thirteen nations that the meeting was held out-of-doors. The Indians turned over most of their remaining prisoners and reaffirmed their alliance with Johnson so strongly that he wrote Amherst, "Matters are settled on so stable a foundation there, that unless greatly irritated thereto, they will never break the peace." Johnson reorganized trade, fixed prices, and made the officers of the western posts responsible for enforcing his regulations. No man could trade without a license from Johnson or Croghan, and, to the north and west of Detroit, trade was restricted to forts commanded by officers. Johnson also drew up for Croghan new regulations for the Fort Pitt and Susquehanna areas, which lowered prices of English goods and permitted traders to visit those Indian villages which had released all their white prisoners.[67]

A feature of the treaty was Johnson's attempt to create a western league roughly similar to that of the Iroquois. This confederacy of Delawares, Shawnees, Wyandots, and other western tribes entered into an offensive-defensive alliance with the British. According to Croghan, "All those nations apear very well plased att being made a confederacy in themselves seprett from the Six Nations, and as itt is deviding thire interests I hope itt will oblidge boath to behave better fer the futer." Johnson put it more bluntly, saying he had done everything in his power to create a misunderstanding between the Six Nations and the western Indians to prevent their uniting in a dangerous coalition.[68]

Croghan distributed Johnson's present to the various tribes and received a handsome gift himself from Sir William in return for the many Indian curiosities which the Irishman had given Johnson from time to time. The Indian agents returned east by way of Sandusky, where they inspected the blockhouse then under construction. There Johnson and Croghan parted, the superintendent to continue his Lake Erie voyage to Niagara, and Croghan to mount his horse for Fort Pitt. The Delawares at the Beaver's

---

67. Stone, *Johnson*, 459, 463; Johnson to Amherst, Nov. 5, 1761, *Johnson Papers*, X, 330; *ibid.*, III, 495, 528.

68. Croghan to Monckton, Oct. 3, 1761, Cadwalader Coll., Hist. Soc. of Pa.; Johnson to Gage, Jan. 12, 1764, *Johnson Papers*, IV, 296.

town delivered up sixteen prisoners to him as he passed through.[69]

By the fall of 1761, Croghan had seen the British take over the western spoils of their French conquest. Not only was the Ohio country secured by a string of forts from the settlements to Fort Pitt and north to Lake Erie, but the British flag now flew at Sandusky, Fort Miami (Fort Wayne, Indiana), Ouiatenon on the Wabash, Detroit, Michilimackinac, LaBaye (Green Bay, Wisconsin), and St. Joseph (Niles, Michigan). The spark of resistance raised by the Senecas had been extinguished, and all was calm and peaceful.

Whether the British and Indians could remain at peace depended on several factors: the restraining of British settlers and hunters from entering Indian country; a fair and advantageous trade; good relations at the army posts, where the Indians still expected to receive some measure of support; and the establishment of a firm basis for mutual confidence. To maintain Anglo-Indian relations on this basis called for enlightened statesmanship by the British, leavened with understanding of the natives and their problems.

69. Stone, *Johnson*, II, 461, 464, 466-67; "Croghan's Journal," *Pa. Mag. of Hist. and Biog.*, 71 (1947), 415.

9

Amherst's Indian Policy

THE YEAR 1762 was a critical one in Indian affairs. From the start of the Anglo-French conflict, the British had extended a generous hand to the natives. Through the agencies of provincial governments, the army, and the Indian department, presents and supplies of all sorts had been lavished upon them. The turning point in this program would have been keenly felt in 1761 had it not been for Johnson's expensive treaty at Detroit. While the large presents handed out on that occasion mollified rising Indian resentment, the heavy cost to the Crown appalled Amherst. Croghan came to New York in the fall of 1761 to obtain the general's approval of his accounts, which amounted to £4,400. On Johnson's advice, Amherst paid the bill, but Croghan was strictly cautioned to exercise the most rigid economy in the future.[1]

Croghan returned to Fort Pitt in March, 1762, to watch with anxious eye the effect of Amherst's tight-fisted policy. To take the pulse of the far western tribes, he sent his assistant Thomas Hutchins on a six-month tour. Angry at insinuations that he was not only extravagant but dishonest, he wrote Bouquet that he had never put a "durty sixpence" in his pocket and would be happy to be relieved by a more economical person. Because the Indian department was now run on such a miserly basis, Croghan hinted that it might as well be discontinued. He opened his own purse for the relief of Iroquois war parties that passed by Fort Pitt and personally furnished many special presents, such as the condolence

---

1. Johnson to Amherst, Jan. 7, 1762, *Johnson Papers*, III, 601; Johnson to Croghan, Jan. 8, 1762, *Bouquet Papers*, 21655, 181; Amherst to Bouquet, Jan. 16, 1762, *ibid.*, 21634, 57-58.

gift on Delaware George's death in April. He was later to write, "I can say now I searve the King for nothing." Disgusted with the Indian service, the Irishman hoped to resign in the fall.[2]

In the spring of the year, Croghan relinquished Indian affairs at Fort Pitt to Edward Ward and came east on Johnson's orders to attend the long-delayed meeting between the superintendent and Teedyuscung. This meeting, scheduled at Easton on June 15, was to settle once and for all Teedyuscung's claims that the Walking Purchase was based on a fraudulent deed and was unjust.

On his way, Croghan stopped at Bedford where his mother languished in what was thought to be a dying condition. Leaving his daughter Susannah with her, Croghan pushed on for Easton, to find that the Quakers had already thrown Johnson's conference into confusion.[3] The Pennsylvania commissioners knew that the Beaver and the western Indians were coming to Lancaster later in the summer to release some prisoners. To save expenses, they had urged Johnson to postpone his meeting with Teedyuscung until that time. Johnson had refused. On this rebuff, an anonymous letter was carried to Teedyuscung by Jonathan Willis, an employee of the commissioners, telling him not to meet Johnson at Easton but to await a call for the Lancaster conference. Tempers were on edge when Johnson, despite this interference, succeeded in opening his meeting with Teedyuscung on June 18.[4]

This meeting, ordered by the king, was a royal investigation and completely under Johnson's direction. Croghan assisted his chief, Montour served as interpreter, and Witham Marsh, Secretary for Indian Affairs by royal appointment, kept the minutes. Governor Hamilton attended, as was his duty, and Richard Peters and Benjamin Chew were at hand to defend the proprietors. Joseph Fox, John Hughes, and others came to represent the Assembly, while Israel Pemberton headed a large group of Quakers determined to obtain justice for the Indians.

2. Croghan to Bouquet, Mar. 23, 1762, Cadwalader Coll., Hist. Soc. of Pa.; Croghan to Bouquet, May 3, 1762, *Bouquet Papers*, 21655, 187; Croghan to Johnson, May 10, 1762, and Mar. 12, 1763, *Johnson Papers*, III, 733, and IV, 62.
3. Bouquet to Amherst, May 24, 1762, *Bouquet Papers*, 21653, 133; Diary of James Kenny, May 5, 1762, Hist. Soc. of Pa.
4. *Johnson Papers*, III, 745-46, 759-60, and X, 465-66; *Pa. Archives*, IV, 80-81.

Johnson's conduct of the investigation soon ran headlong into Quaker opposition. This was inevitable since Pemberton, who controlled Teedyuscung, was resolved that he and his associates would have a hand in everything that Teedyuscung did. As usual, Teedyuscung demanded a clerk. Johnson refused. Teedyuscung, in turn, refused to examine the deeds relating to the Indian Walk unless a clerk were provided. Johnson had detailed Croghan, Montour, and Marsh, among others, to explain these papers to the Delaware, but Teedyuscung complained that he did not trust either Croghan or Montour and did not know Marsh. No, he must examine the papers himself with the help of the assemblymen.

During the course of this controversy, Israel Pemberton showed his hand by claiming the floor and contending against Sir William "with great warmth and indecency." Fox, Galloway, and Hughes also attacked the Indian superintendent's way of doing business. According to Johnson, in his subsequent report to the Board of Trade, these men openly accused him of being a liar, charged that the minutes were unfairly taken, and insinuated that he would not do the Indians justice. In brief, the Quaker party tried to take control of the investigation away from the superintendent.[5]

On June 27, Johnson resolutely faced his detractors down, and, on the following day, the Quaker cause collapsed when Teedyuscung withdrew his fraud charge and expressed his willingness to drop the whole matter. There is evidence that the Quaker politicians suddenly feared they had gone too far against an important officer of the Crown and also that Benjamin Chew had convinced their lawyer, Joseph Galloway, that legally the fraud charge could not be supported. In its final analysis, the Easton treaty of 1762 was a triumph for Thomas Penn—"a very good end is put to this very wicked business"—and a severe disappointment to his enemies.[6]

The day the Quakers capitulated to Johnson, three of the provincial commissioners, Galloway, Hughes, and the irrepressible Fox, told Peters that if either Johnson or Croghan presided over

---

5. Johnson to the Lords of Trade, Aug. 1, 1762, *Johnson Papers*, III, 846-51.
6. Penn to Hamilton, Sept. 9, 1762, and Penn to Peters, Sept. 10, 1762, Penn Letter Book, VII, 192-93, 195-96, Hist. Soc. of Pa.

the forthcoming Lancaster conference they would refuse to pay its expenses. Croghan, who came to Philadelphia after the Easton treaty, maintained that the Quakers had declared open war and were resolved to ruin him. He gloated over their discomfiture. "The chieff of them that attended the treety has nott yet recovered there sperrits so as to apper at the Cofey House." Never before had the self-anointed Indian champions received such a check as at Easton.[7]

In Philadelphia, Croghan sought out Willis, the provincial commissioners' employee. The Irishman smiled on Willis, he showed deep concern for Willis' future, professed to admire his character, and offered him a license in the Indian trade. Whether it was for this indiscreet friendship, or because he had exposed Joseph Fox as the author of the now embarrassing anonymous message, the commissioners fired Willis, "without cause," according to the victim.[8]

Having consented to assist Governor Hamilton at Lancaster, Croghan headed west once more. He met the Beaver and the western Indians and brought them to Harris' Ferry to await the coming of the Susquehanna Indians. He also arranged the time the treaty would open and notified the governor. At Harris', Croghan settled several troublesome land matters long pending between certain Indians and the Penns, warning Peters to rush the legal papers through "before any of the proprietors enemys knows whether the sales are made." Subsequently, Peters took pleasure in reporting to Sir William Johnson: "The Proprs settled all their differences thro the means of Mr. Croghan as well wth the Shawonese as with the Conoys and Nantycokes, and I know of nothing now that is not satisfactorily bought and paid for."[9]

Hamilton convened the Lancaster conference in the middle of August. The usual cast of characters was present—the committee of the Assembly, Pemberton and a large body of Quakers, and a few stalwart servants of Thomas Penn. Croghan acted in an

[7]. Croghan to Johnson, July 3 and July 10, 1762, *Johnson Papers*, III, 822-23, 826-27.
[8]. Jonathan Willis to Burd, July 31, 1762, Burd-Shippen Papers, II, 18, Amer. Philos. Soc.
[9]. Croghan to Peters, July 31, 1762, Laux Coll., Hist. Soc. of Pa.; Peters to Johnson, Oct. 23, 1762, Amer. Philos. Soc.

unofficial capacity as Hamilton's adviser, and Montour, whom the Irishman had recently stationed in the Shamokin area, helped as interpreter. More than 550 natives attended, of whom the principal chiefs were the Beaver, Blue Cheeks, a leading man of the Senecas, Thomas King of the Oneidas, and Teedyuscung. The Indians brought Hamilton thirty-one English prisoners, a disappointingly small group. However, amid profuse declarations of friendship, the Ohio Shawnees and Delawares promised to bring the remainder of their captives to Fort Pitt within a few months. Thus was accomplished the basic aim of the conference.

Less basic, but no less desired by the Quakers, were three other objectives. One of these was permission to establish government trading posts at the headwaters of the west branch of the Susquehanna, where an Indian trade unmolested by Croghan and the military authorities could be carried on. Blue Cheeks vehemently vetoed this request to gain entrance to Seneca country. Another aim of the Quakers was to reopen the land questions so recently closed at Easton. For this and other purposes, they met the Indians in council every day and tried to persuade the Beaver to claim the disputed Walking Purchase lands, for Teedyuscung had said those lands were rightfully the property of the western Delawares. The Beaver, however, denied any claim to lands on the Delaware and refused to discuss the matter. The final Quaker objective was the disbandment of the Fort Augusta garrison, a request which was put into the mouth of Thomas King and refused by Governor Hamilton.

Behind this bare summary of the treaty lies an involved and largely unknown story of secret moves and countermoves in which Croghan's influence successfully defeated every point the Quakers wanted to carry. The Assembly's expenditure of the public's money was largely in vain, as far as the Quakers were concerned. It could not upset Croghan's hold on Blue Cheeks and the Beaver.[10]

According to Richard Peters, "The Governor consulted Mr. Croghan on every occasion, and had he not been at Lancaster they [the Quakers] woud have imposed more egregiously on the Indians & made them speak things which were untrue & ex-

10. Minutes of Lancaster conference, *Col. Rec. of Pa.*, VIII, 729-74; *Johnson Papers*, X, 498-99; Croghan to Johnson, Sept. 4, 1762, *ibid.*, III, 873-75.

tremely injurious to the rights of the Six Nations." Governor Hamilton praised Croghan highly: "Were it not, that by his influence he was able to counterwork the Quakers, we should have had many wild schemes and projects, that would have given us much trouble, put into the Indians heads and insisted on; but to those he was able very properly to give the go by; so that upon the whole the treaty ended happily enough for the Government, but to the grievous mortification of the Friends." Croghan's reward for what Thomas Penn admitted to be great services in the Indian business was a substantial land grant.[11]

The agent returned to Fort Pitt boasting of his triumph and criticizing the Lancaster treaty for upsetting the Indians by exposing them to Pennsylvania's political quarrels and provincial aims. Thomas McKee noted that the natives were much dissatisfied when they left Lancaster, and Bouquet, who saw them as they passed by Fort Pitt, also commented on their ill-humor. Their promise to release their remaining prisoners was to bear little fruit.[12]

For once, the profuse presents given the natives failed to produce even temporary good will. The Shawnees and Delawares left many of theirs on the trail. And as for Blue Cheeks, who had been enriched by Israel Pemberton's lavish courtship, his tribe grew so jealous that one of his own warriors slew him with a tomahawk.[13]

Croghan arrived at Fort Pitt in poor health. According to a man who accompanied him from Bedford, the Irishman had "the pox so bad that he cant live long having a hole at the bottom of his belley that runs constantly." In this awkward condition, Croghan took to wearing a Scottish kilt. Johnson advised him to treat his disorder as a venereal disease, but by the end of the year it had cleared up.[14]

11. Peters to Johnson, Sept. 30, 1762, and Hamilton to Johnson, Oct. 17, 1762, *Johnson Papers*, X, 537, 553-54; Penn to Peters, Dec. 10, 1762, Penn Letter Book, VII, 233, Hist. Soc. of Pa.
12. Diary of James Kenny, Sept. 11 and Nov. 30, 1762, Hist. Soc. of Pa.; Bouquet to Amherst, Oct. 5, 1762, *Michigan Pioneer and Historical Collection*, 19 (1891), 168.
13. Thomas McKee to Johnson, Nov. 1 and Nov. 2, 1762, and Johnson to Croghan, Oct. 24, 1762, *Johnson Papers*, III, 921, 924-25, and X, 559.
14. Diary of James Kenny, Sept. 10, 1762, Hist. Soc. of Pa.; Johnson to Croghan, Dec. 30, 1762, and Croghan to Johnson, Mar. 12, 1763, *Johnson Papers*, III, 987, and IV, 63.

The recovery of his health was probably aided by Croghan's extraordinary vitality. The part that he had so recently played in Indian affairs was enough to occupy most men fully, but it was by no means enough to engross Croghan's attention. His mind, as always, was teeming with dozens of schemes, the most important of which had to bide its time. This was his great obsession, the recovery of the fortune he had lost to the French in 1754. According to his London correspondents, it would be useless to expect restitution from the Crown until after the formal declaration of peace between England and France.

Awaiting that event, Croghan busied himself with a multitude of affairs closer to home. Some of his ventures were very odd indeed. There was, for example, the partnership of Buchanan, Hughes, and Smallman. William Buchanan and Barnabas Hughes, old Pennsylvania friends of Croghan's, had moved to Baltimore, where they set up a wholesale importing house, the only Baltimore firm to advertise in the Philadelphia papers. When the Indian trade reopened at Fort Pitt, they were among the first to send out goods. Thomas Smallman, Croghan's cousin, was at loose ends, and Croghan decided to establish him in business as an Indian trader, despite the fact that Smallman had neither money nor experience. At Croghan's instance, partnership articles were signed between the suppliers, Buchanan and Hughes, and the vendor, Smallman, who was to operate out of Fort Pitt. To guarantee Smallman's credit, Croghan signed a £10,000 indemnity bond in favor of Buchanan and Hughes.[15]

Buchanan and Hughes thought that Croghan was one-fourth interested in the partnership but, for obvious reasons, could not permit his name to be used and thus fell on the substitute of being bound for Smallman. On the other hand, Smallman later claimed that Croghan was in no way concerned in the profits of the trade but was motivated solely by disinterested friendship for all concerned. Those who averred that Croghan never had a disinterested thought in his life might scoff, but, as it worked out, Croghan could scarcely have profited from this company, because there were no

---

15. *Pennsylvania Journal*, Oct. 30, 1760; *Coll. of the Mass. Hist. Soc.*, Fourth Series, 10 (1871), 604; Buchanan and Hughes folders, Cadwalader Coll., Hist. Soc. of Pa.

profits. Had the case been otherwise, he might not have turned them down. After all, he had risked his name and purse to set up the partnership, and he supplied the entire experience necessary for its operation. He spent much of his time at Smallman's store and, in Smallman's absence, made all the decisions relating to the business. According to Smallman's clerk, James Harris, "Any thing we do here is promoted by the influence of Mr. Croghan without which it would not be worth while to keep a store open at this place."[16]

Croghan involved himself in another business in 1762 in partnership with one of the most curious men on the frontier, Theodorus Swaine Drage. Drage's career is hopelessly confused by an autobiographical statement that it was he who performed all the services known to have been accomplished by Charles Swaine [Drage?]. Despite the fact that Theodorus later became a minister, there is ample reason to believe him a rogue. At all events, backed by Croghan, he opened a store at Bedford and, through Croghan's influence, obtained a virtual monopoly in supplying the western garrisons with liquor. Again, the Indian agent claimed to be disinterested—he was not a party to the profits in the liquor trade. That Croghan found the store a personal convenience is attested by frequent entries in its books of purchases for his daughter "Miss Susan" and his mother "Mrs. Ward, Sen."[17]

In May, 1762, the Pennsylvania land office began to grant warrants on vacant lands west of the Susquehanna, and Croghan promptly busied himself with spying out lands fit for settlement. He took up many tracts around Bedford and assisted Bouquet, other army officers, and his friends to obtain choice ground. Thomas Penn complained that Croghan was gobbling up so much of the best land that it would be difficult to locate an adequate amount for the proprietors.[18]

16. Harris to Buchanan and Hughes, June 21, 1762, and Harris to Croghan, July 11, 1762, Henry Joseph Coll., American Jewish Archives (microfilm at Hist. Soc. of Pa.).
17. Croghan to Bouquet, Feb. 28, 1763, *Bouquet Papers*, 21649, Part I, 64; Howard N. Eavenson, *Map Maker and Indian Traders* (Pittsburgh, 1949), 88-89; Howard N. Eavenson, *Swaine and Drage, A Sequel to Map Maker and Indian Traders* (Pittsburgh, 1950), 17; Croghan's vouchers for 1762, Cadwalader Coll., Hist. Soc. of Pa.
18. *Pennsylvania Gazette*, Apr. 29, 1762; George Armstrong's receipt of

Croghan developed a large farm, "Bellfield," at Bedford, where he erected a barn and other buildings. He took up a number of tracts of land near Fort Bedford on either side of "Broad Street," the Forbes Road, and proceeded to subdivide them for settlement. Croghan surmised that the Penns would do well to lay out a town at Bedford, and it is probably no coincidence that his former partner William Trent aroused Thomas Penn's support for such a project. The Irishman's shrewd purchases at Bedford became a profitable speculation. The growing town of Carlisle also attracted the Indian agent. He speculated in its town lots and rented a building where Bouquet was once his guest, "swimming in ease and plenty." Bouquet wrote him, "I think it very convenient to find that you have a house wherever I go."[19] Croghan's personal interests soon became so extensive that Edward Ward resigned from the Indian department to oversee them.

Early in 1762, the Irishman's home near Fort Pitt was called "Croghan's House," but later in the year, after improving it and refurbishing it with new furniture and pewter chamber pots, he changed its name to "Croghan Hall." Alive to every possibility for wealth, he explored the land for minerals, hoping to find copper and silver ore. His friends were impressed by Croghan's growing fame and position, by his endless and fascinating speculations. Soon they began to call the former captain "Colonel."[20]

While the fall and winter of 1762 faded away into the winter and spring of 1763, Croghan enlivened Fort Pitt's drab social life. The scene was more sordid than elegant. Beset by cold and fleas, by sudden torrential floods, and tempers quickly inflamed, the residents were a drunken, immoral lot. Only three white men, according to James Kenny, did not have Indian mistresses, and

---

July 5, 1762, American & British Army, I, 6, Etting Coll., Hist. Soc. of Pa.; Penn to Peters, Dec. 10, 1762, Penn Letter Book, VII, 232, Hist. Soc. of Pa.; Croghan to Bouquet, Mar. 19, 1763, *Bouquet Papers*, 21649, Part I, 82.

19. Penn Physick Mss., IV, 47, Hist. Soc. of Pa.; Croghan to Johnson, Sept. 4, 1762, *Johnson Papers*, III, 875; Edward Ward to Bouquet, Aug. 4, 1762, and Bouquet to Croghan, July 4, 1763, *Bouquet Papers*, 21648, Part II, 40, and 21649, Part I, 199.

20. Croghan to Bouquet, Mar. 30 and Apr. 23, 1763, and Mar. 27, 1762, *Bouquet Papers*, 21649, Part I, 89, 108, and 21655, 182; William Munday's bill, Croghan's vouchers for 1762, and Buchanan and Hughes folders, Cadwalader Coll., Hist. Soc. of Pa.

Croghan was not one of them. Degenerate squaws peddled the charms of their eleven-year-old daughters. The man who read the Sunday prayers for the garrison lived with a whore. The doctor whom Croghan paid to tend the Indians seduced the blacksmith's daughter and fought a duel over his rights to her with a Royal American officer. The girl became pregnant.[21]

Under the leadership of the gay Captain Simeon Ecuyer, who had succeeded to the command on Bouquet's departure, dances were held every Saturday by the officers. A dozen couples swirled to the tunes of the garrison's musicians. Chaperons attended, but it was observed that "Croghan generally pushes aboute the glass so copiously and briskly amongst the old women that before half the night's over they forget their errand as well as their charge, and what then follows is easily guest at." Ecuyer jocosely wrote Bouquet that the prettiest ladies attended these dances and were regaled with punch and, if that failed to produce enough effect, whisky: "You may be sure that we shall not be completely cheated." "We realy live in greet harmony," Croghan commented.[22]

In addition to the dances, the officers and Croghan met every Monday for what was termed "a club." This was an occasion for toasts and stories. Among Croghan's papers is the following verse, which may well have been recited at a club to express Croghan's respect for Amherst.

> From evry genrous noble passion free
> As proud and ignorant as man can be
> Revengefull, avaritious, obstinate is he
> Malicious, stupid and obdurate will ever be
> A fleeting consequence he's dully grave
> Rest here my pen enough—the man's a knave.

Aside from clubs, there were special nights, like St. Patrick's, when Croghan would take the chair. Toasts proposed at such festive times often started mildly enough and then passed beyond the pale

---

21. Diary of James Kenny, July 26 and Aug. 15, 1762, and Apr. 6, 1763, Hist. Soc. of Pa.; *Bouquet Papers*, 21649, Part I, 62, 97.
22. William Potts to Bouquet, Jan. 8, 1763, Ecuyer to Bouquet, Jan. 8, 1763, and Croghan to Bouquet, Jan. 24, 1763, *Bouquet Papers*, 21649, Part I, 5, 9, 23.

of decorous recording. Some of the more decorous examples follow.

> May the friend we trust be honest, the girl we love be true, and the country we live in be free.
>
> * * * *
>
> The heart of friendship and the soul of love.
>
> * * * *
>
> May we kiss whom we please, and please whom we kiss.
>
> * * * *
>
> Days of ease and nights of pleasure.
>
> * * * *
>
> Days of sport and nights of transport.

The morning after such an affair as St. Patrick's celebration, Croghan usually suffered a frightful hangover.[23]

The pursuit of pleasure and personal matters gradually consumed more and more of his time. Without a supply of presents, there was little Indian business that he could transact. Amherst seemed intent on reducing the Irishman's support to the minimum. During the summer of 1762, the general ordered yet another cut in Croghan's department, and £500 was sliced from salaries. Croghan was now down to one assistant, Alexander McKee.[24]

All through 1762 and early 1763, Sir William Johnson, Croghan, and the officers who commanded the outposts had pleaded with Sir Jeffrey to allow them to give the Indians ammunition and presents, but Amherst was inflexible in his decision. Sir William wearily wrote Croghan that Amherst's policy was wrong, "but it is not in my power to convince the general thereof."[25]

Nearly all the Indian intelligence that Croghan collected pointed to an uprising. From Hutchins, he learned that the western tribes were uneasy and that a war belt had been carried through their country. Croghan wrote Amherst that the French were causing this agitation. Amherst's reply was typical: "I look upon the intelligence you received of the French stirring up the

---

23. Entertainment folder, Cadwalader Coll., Hist. Soc. of Pa.; Diary of James Kenny, Mar. 20, 1763, Hist. Soc. of Pa.; Ecuyer to Bouquet, Mar. 19, 1763, *Bouquet Papers*, 21649, Part I, 79.
24. Amherst to Johnson, July 25, 1762, *Johnson Papers*, X, 475.
25. Johnson to Croghan, Apr. 8, 1763, *ibid.*, 652.

western Indians of little consequence, as it is not in their power to hurt us."²⁶ By December, 1762, Croghan had reached the conclusion that a general Indian war was imminent; only the inability of the Indians to unite delayed the outbreak. He found that the tribes dreaded the power of the English; they resented the numerous forts in their country; and they feared that the scarcity of ammunition presaged an attack by the whites, an attack which would follow the recovery of the remaining English prisoners. The Indians were bewildered at not receiving supplies from the army posts, and they interpreted this frugality as Amherst's revenge for their past actions. If Amherst's policy of strict economy was not changed, war must follow. It mattered not to the Indians that the conflict would ruin them, for they never considered consequences. "How itt may end the Lord knows," wrote Croghan, "butt I ashure you I am of opinion itt will nott be long before we shall have some croyles with them."²⁷

Once again, he resolved to resign if Amherst did not liberalize expenditures for Indian affairs: "I dont chuse to be beging aternaly for such nesesarys as is wanted to carry on the service, nor will I supert itt at my own expence." In February, 1763, Croghan learned that Amherst would not alter his instructions one iota. This news, together with the information that peace had been declared with France, confirmed Croghan's resolution to go to London for the recovery of his trade losses.²⁸

According to orders, Croghan sent runners to the Indian villages to inform the natives that the French had ceded all their territory to the British. The natives were thunderstruck, and their jealousy of the English became inflamed. The French, they maintained, had no right to transfer Indian country to the English. There seemed to be no satisfying the Indians after they learned of the peace. At this time, one of the Shawnees told a white man that Croghan was the only Britisher the Indians respected, the only

26. Croghan to Amherst, Oct. 5, 1762, *ibid.*, 543; Amherst to Croghan, Oct. 31, 1762, W. O., 34/38, fol. 208, Public Record Office, London.
27. Croghan to Johnson, Dec. 10, 1762, *Johnson Papers*, III, 964-66; Croghan to Bouquet, Dec. 10, 1762, *Bouquet Papers*, 21648, Part II, 176-77.
28. Croghan to Bouquet, Dec. 10, 1762, and Feb. 4, Mar. 19, and Mar. 30, 1763, *Bouquet Papers*, 21648, Part II, 178, and 21649, Part I, 34-35, 80-81, 89; William Coxe to Stirling, May 16, 1763, Mss. of Lord Stirling, William Alexander, N. Y. Hist. Soc.

person who knew how to please them, and without him there would be war.[29]

Amherst continued scornful of the Indians and made the fatal military blunder of underrating them. Utterly incapable of appreciating the Indian point of view, he disregarded expert advice, treating Indian affairs with indifference. In reply to a warning from Croghan, Amherst wrote, "Whatever idle notions they [the Indians] may entertain, in regard to the cessions made by the French Crown, can be of very little consequence." Calling fears of their plots "meer bugbears," he insisted that as long as the military kept their guard up, the Indians could not cause any serious harm.[30]

On May 2, Croghan left McKee in charge of Indian affairs at Fort Pitt and rode to Philadelphia. Despite the warnings he had issued, he did not realize that an Indian uprising was on the very verge of taking place. Instead, he was hopeful that trouble might yet be avoided if Amherst would order a treaty held to reconcile the natives to the terms of the French peace.[31] In Philadelphia, he advised Governor Hamilton on Indian affairs and spent money lavishly—a diamond ring was not beyond his means. The Indian agent was feeling wealthy, and with good reason. He had just received £500 from David Franks and William Plumstead, in part payment for lands and improvements which he had been developing in partnership with Colonel William Clapham, and Governor James Hamilton had paid him £1,000 for part of his lands in "Bedford Settlement," where Penn's agents wanted to lay out a town. This bargain, handsome as it was, was soon dwarfed by his sale of thirty thousand Cumberland County acres to his cousin Daniel Clark, merchant of Philadelphia, and to sharp-dealing William Peters, who had succeeded Richard Peters in the land office. Clark and Peters agreed to pay Croghan £17 10s. for every hundred acres of this large purchase, on the basis of £1,000 down, £2,000 in twelve months, and the remainder within one year of the completion of the land surveys.

29. "Croghan's Journal," *Pa. Mag. of Hist. and Biog.*, 71 (1947), 436; Diary of James Kenny, Feb. 14, 1763, Hist. Soc. of Pa.
30. Amherst to Croghan, May 10, 1763, *Bouquet Papers*, 21634, 162; Amherst to Johnson, Apr. 3 and May 29, 1763, *Johnson Papers*, X, 648, 689.
31. Croghan to Amherst, May 21, 1763, W. O., 34/39, foll. 334-35, Public Record Office, London.

This sale was to harass Croghan for the rest of his life and, for that reason, was probably the most important he ever made. The lands he offered Clark and Peters had been allowed him by Thomas Penn so that Croghan could sell them and reimburse Hockley for his Indian trade losses. More than two thousand of these acres, reputedly of extraordinarily fine quality, actually belonged to Hockley, but Croghan had persuaded Hockley to deed them to him and had used them as bait to attract the purchasers. In exchange for Hockley's signing over his holdings, and in recognition of the intent behind the entire transaction, Croghan guaranteed Hockley £2,000. Croghan himself pocketed the £1,000 down payment.

At first, everyone was well pleased. Croghan had money in pocket; Hockley had the assurance of the payment of his losses; Clark and Peters thought they had made a splendid bargain. However, a subsequent examination of the land disclosed that most of it was worthless, for it lay on mountainous slopes and in the bottoms of ravines. This fact, the foundation of Clark's and Peters' consternation, was to be aggravated by Croghan, who was then to tell them that he had never intended to sell them Hockley's land even though he had signed over the conveyance for it. Indeed, Croghan had resold that land to others. Eventually, Hockley took legal action against Croghan to obtain payment of the promised £2,000. Fortunately for Croghan, he did not visualize these dismal prospects as he cheerfully watched Clark and Peters sign the contract.[32]

After completing this sale on June 2, Croghan hurried west once more, galloping down the Lancaster road, past the famous inns: the Sign of the Plow in Radnor, the Sign of the Ship in the Great Valley, on to the Sign of the Swan in Lancaster.[33] Confused but appalling stories of an Indian outbreak had reached him in Philadelphia. The natives had murdered Colonel Clapham on the Sewickly lands which Croghan had sold him; they had burned

---

32. Hamilton to Burd, June 2, 1763, Shippen Papers, VI, 9, Edmund Milne's bill of May 20, 1763, Croghan's vouchers for 1763, Cadwalader Coll., and Croghan folder, Society Autograph Coll., also Penn Letter Book, VIII, 36-37, and Hamilton-Croghan mortgage, June 1, 1764, patent to Croghan for 912 acres, Penn Mss., Deed Box, 1760-1804, Hist. Soc. of Pa.

33. Bouquet to Amherst, June 4, 1763, *Bouquet Papers*, 21634, 180.

Croghan Hall; they had beseiged Fort Pitt. The scalping knife was out, and the dreaded war was a reality.

Before leaving Lancaster for Harris' Ferry on the road to Carlisle, Croghan bitterly told Edward Shippen that this would be no small war but a general one, involving all the western tribes. He had foreseen it many months ago, he added, and it might have been prevented had a certain great man in New York heeded Johnson's and his advice. From Carlisle, Croghan sent fresh intelligence of disaster to Bouquet, with the comment, "Itt will nott bear laffing att as useal." In New York, Amherst petulantly described the uprising as "extremely inconvenient" and proceeded to scrape together a few hundred semi-invalids to march under Bouquet for the relief of Fort Pitt. Amherst also ordered Croghan to Fort Pitt to investigate the causes of the uprising.[34]

At Shippensburg, the Irishman found the country people terrorized by rumors of Indian raids. He quieted their minds, raised and equipped a company of twenty-five men to garrison undefended Fort Lyttelton, and hired men to escort a supply of ammunition from Fort Loudoun to Bedford. Croghan's effectiveness far outstripped that of the county magistrates, who had neither the vision nor the force to restore order and to move the ammunition. Amherst and all in authority agreed that Croghan had behaved extremely well. The Pennsylvania commissioners even paid the bills he had incurred. By June 15, Croghan had reached Fort Bedford, where Captain Lewis Ourry, the commanding officer, and his garrison of seven men were overwhelmed by a hundred panic-stricken families seeking safety. At Bedford, Croghan was a tower of strength. "His company," Ourry wrote to Bouquet, "as you may well imagine is a great relief to me as his generosity has been to many a starving family."[35]

By this time, Indian war parties were approaching Bedford, and it was impossible for a white man to travel west on Forbes Road. On June 30, the natives attacked fifteen men mowing Croghan's fields, within a mile of the fort, and scalped two. Two

---

34. Amherst to Bouquet, June 12, 1763, and Croghan to Bouquet, June 8, 1763, *ibid.*, 21634, 185, and 21649, Part I, 137; Shippen to Joseph Shippen, June 6, 1763, Amer. Philos. Soc.

35. *Bouquet Papers*, 21634, 184; Croghan to Bouquet, June 11, 1763, *ibid.*, 21649, Part I, 143-44, 218; Volwiler, *George Croghan*, 165.

days later, the beleaguered post was shocked to learn by an express from McKee that the forts at Venango, LeBoeuf, and Presque Isle had been lost to the Indians. It was easy to surmise the fate of Sandusky and the other small outposts—they were all in the hands of the enemy. Fort Pitt and Detroit were invested by the foe, and Ligonier had sustained an attack. Scalping parties harried Shippensburg. Croghan later calculated that within four months the Indians killed and captured two thousand people, drove thousands to beggary, burned nine forts, and plundered traders of £100,000-worth of goods.[36]

The uprising brought attacks on Croghan's character. The Philadelphia Quakers were quick to blame his settlements on the Youghiogheny and the Allegheny as the cause of the war, an accusation which Bouquet refuted. "I wish," observed Croghan, "the Quakers maint find that thire interfearing with Indian affairs may have don more hurt to his Majesty's Indn intrest & given them a greater dislike to his trupes than any setlment."[37]

Clark and Peters censured Croghan for unloading lands on them when he knew the Indians were about to attack. Was it possible, replied Croghan, that if he had had that knowledge he would have left stock and improvements worth £2,000 at Croghan Hall to the mercy of the Indians? His partnership investment at Clapham's improvement, he pointed out, was worth £2,500, and that, too, was now gone. To soothe Clark and Peters, he offered to cancel their purchase, which, as he provocatively observed, he had given them too cheaply.[38]

In his anxiety to sell out his Bedford store, Croghan fell into a violent quarrel with Theodorus Swaine Drage, who was certain Croghan wanted to cheat him. "His necessities," wrote the unfriendly Drage, "all sources being now stopped hath increased his audaciousness to use the most modest terms. . . . His spirits are

36. *Pennsylvania Journal,* July 7, 1763; Croghan to Johnson, July 2, 1763, *Johnson Papers,* X, 727-28; Joseph Hunter to James Hunter, July 3 and July 24, 1763, Hist. Soc. of Pa.
37. Bouquet to Croghan, June 14, 1763, and Croghan to Bouquet, June 17, 1763, *Bouquet Papers,* 21653, 179, and 21649, Part I, 160; Samuel Morris to Samuel Powel, July 4, 1763, Hist. Soc. of Pa.
38. Croghan to Clark and Peters, June 15, 1763, Public Records Division, Harrisburg.

so broken he cannot keep a temper, and are not sufficient to support him in that chicanery he was so much master of."[39]

Croghan's sources of revenue were not as dried up as Drage supposed. On August 1, 1763, the day before the Indian agent left Bedford, he sold Robert Callender fifteen tracts warranted to contain at least 6,850 acres. The price for this transaction was £2,000, of which £800 was paid on the signing of the contract.[40]

Croghan refused to obey Bouquet's orders and did not accompany the colonel's gallant little column when it left Fort Bedford on July 26. He excused himself on the grounds of bad health and argued that he was not really needed, since this was not a time for negotiation, but for war.[41] It is probable that Croghan's health was not as weak as his determination to sail for England was strong. The time had come to re-establish his fortunes.

39. Eavenson, *Map Maker and Indian Traders*, 194-96.
40. Huntington Deeds, D, I, 509.
41. Croghan to Amherst, July 27, 1763, W. O., 34/39, fol. 388, Public Record Office, London.

10

Illinois Mirage

AMHERST HAD WRITTEN Croghan not to enter into any negotiations with hostile tribes until after they had been crushed by the military. "Indeed," concluded Sir Jeffrey, "their total extirpation is scarce sufficient attonement for the bloody and inhuman deeds they have committed."[1] Since it would take Bouquet at least two campaigns to humiliate the natives, much less extirpate them, Croghan turned his back on the West and came to Philadelphia, where he talked with merchants who had been engaged in the fur trade and who now, through him, solicited Sir William Johnson's support for reparations. Their spokesman was Samuel Wharton, subtle partner of John Baynton and George Morgan. Croghan found Wharton a man after his own heart, able, suave, and ambitious, and Wharton was charmed by Croghan, who was "as friendly & communicative as any man can be."[2] The Indian agent opened a business connection with Baynton, Wharton, and Morgan, sold them western lands, and promised his patronage in the purchase of goods.

From Philadelphia, Croghan hurried on to Johnson Hall, where he asked permission to go to England. Johnson referred him to Amherst, sending his deputy flying off for New York. On September 25, Croghan called on Amherst and was denied leave. "I think," wrote the general, "if his presence ever was of any consequence in the department he filled, it certainly is so at this present time." According to Croghan, Amherst tried to flatter

---

1. Amherst to Croghan, Aug. 7, 1763, W. O., 34/38, fol. 249, Public Record Office, London.
2. *Johnson Papers*, IV, 199, 272; Samuel Wharton to John Baynton, Sept. 6, 8, 14, 1763, Baynton, Wharton, and Morgan Coll., Public Records Division, Harrisburg.

him by saying he would as soon consent to a battalion's going home as part with the Irishman.³

Baffled, Croghan presented the necessity of his situation in an eloquent letter, stressing "the many losses I have sustained & never has had it in my power to attend my own private affairs." Since Amherst was not to be swayed, Croghan resigned. Amherst promptly granted him another interview, disapproved the resignation, and declared that the ministry would think it very odd if he left America at this time. Croghan replied that he could go and return from England twice before peace was restored and his services needed. He even went as far as to tell the general that it would have been much easier to have prevented the Indian war than to bring about peace now.⁴

"I know many pople will think I am wrong," Croghan wrote Bouquet of his resignation, "but had I contineued I could be of no more service than I have been this eighteen months past wh was none ataul, as no regard was had to any intiligence I sent no more then to my opinion." Ironically enough, although horrified at Croghan's request for leave, the commander in chief granted himself leave. Amherst sailed for England in November, never to return. "What universal cries of joy and what bumpers of Madeira are drunk to his prompt departure," wrote Captain Ecuyer.⁵

After engaging passage for England on the *Britannia*, a ship in which Baynton, Wharton, and Morgan had an interest, and after pacifying some of his creditors, the most vociferous of whom were Buchanan and Hughes, Croghan returned to Johnson Hall.⁶ There, in November, he and Sir William discussed plans for the future of the Indian department. The uprising had shown that Indian affairs were not well conducted, and the Board of Trade

---

3. O'Callaghan, ed., *New-York Col. Doc.*, VII, 552; Amherst to Bouquet, Sept. 25, 1763, *Bouquet Papers*, 21634, 277; Croghan to Johnson, Sept. 28, 1763, *Johnson Papers*, X, 825-26.

4. Croghan to Amherst, Sept. 26, 27, 1763, and Amherst's replies of Sept. 26, 28, 1763, W. O., 34/39, foll. 413, 414, and 34/38, foll. 264, 265, Public Record Office, London; Croghan to Johnson, Sept. 28, 1763, and Amherst to Johnson, Sept. 30, 1763, *Johnson Papers*, X, 825-27, 858-59.

5. Croghan to Bouquet, Oct. 11, 1763, and Ecuyer to Bouquet, Nov. 20, 1763, *Bouquet Papers*, 21649, Part II, 85-86, 155.

6. Shippen to Warder, Oct. 25, 1763, Shippen Letter Book, 242, 249, Amer. Philos. Soc.

had written Johnson asking for his advice in the future management of his department. Convinced that failure to keep the Indians peaceful was the fault of Amherst's policies, Johnson evolved a plan of annual presents to the Indians, the enlargement of his staff of assistants, and the establishment of a new western boundary line beyond which no white settlements were to be made. This plan was embodied in a letter which Croghan was to deliver and explain to the Board of Trade. Not included in the plan, but uppermost in the minds of both men, was the freeing of their department from military control. This point Croghan would stress when called before the Board.[7]

Johnson gave Croghan letters of introduction to Lord Halifax, Secretary of State in charge of American affairs, and to former Governor Thomas Pownall of Massachusetts, who was considered an expert on the colonies.[8] The patronage of these men might help Croghan obtain restitution for his trade losses and aid him in relocating in New York the 200,000 Pennsylvania acres granted him by the Iroquois in 1749. Relocation of this Indian grant by Crown authority would confirm the legality of its title, a matter somewhat in doubt, and would enable Croghan to settle near his great and good friend Sir William.

In December, Croghan was back in Philadelphia attending conferences with merchants at the Indian Queen Tavern. The merchants, who represented not only "the suffering traders of 1754" but those who had sustained losses in 1763, appointed Croghan and Moses Franks of London to apply to the Crown for their relief. William Trent and Samuel Wharton drew up a memorial to this end which Croghan was to present to the Board of Trade. The memorial was reinforced by others addressed to Lord Halifax and to General Monckton, by letters to Amherst, to the proprietors, to London merchants, and to other men of influence. It was up to Croghan and Franks to deliver these papers and to enlist all the sympathy and pressure possible. To help the two men, the Philadelphians gave them £200 and promised them 5 per cent of all sums recovered.[9]

7. O'Callaghan, ed., *New-York Col. Doc.*, VII, 535, 578.
8. *Johnson Papers*, IV, 248, 255.
9. *Ibid.*, 264-71.

Croghan's last few days before sailing were spent in a whirl of activity. He completed the sale of 2,165 acres to the proprietary agents for £2,000, so that the Penns could lay out the town of Bedford. He called on the new governor of Pennsylvania, John Penn, nephew of Thomas Penn. The governor, like almost everyone who met Croghan, liked him and called him "a sensible, intelligent man." Croghan authorized Edward Ward to purchase a copper mine in New Jersey; he arranged for board and education for his daughter "Suky" and provided "pew money" for her attendance at one of the Anglican churches; he received dozens of letters from his friends for delivery in London.[10]

Croghan boarded the *Britannia* down river at Reedy Island, where Captain Thomas Tillett had taken the vessel to prevent her being caught in the ice which had closed the port of Philadelphia. Other passengers accompanying the Indian agent were Colonel George Armstrong of Cumberland County and Lieutenant James McDonald, who had just weathered Pontiac's siege of Detroit. On December 29, 1763, the *Britannia* cleared the Delaware capes.

The voyage was a blustery, wet one, but uneventful until soundings were struck in the British Channel on January 25. On that day and the next, Captain Tillett signaled other ships to ascertain his position, in each case disregarding the advice he received. As a result, during a gale on the night of January 27, the *Britannia* was nearly washed ashore. This terrifying landfall was at first identified as Plymouth, then, on a nearer view, as the island of Guernsey, off Normandy. The ferocity of the storm increased; the seas ran mountains high; there was no possibility of making harbor.

Captain Tillett gave way to despair and was all but useless, despite Croghan's urgings to do his duty and leave the rest to Providence. Seven times during the next day, the ship barely escaped smashing herself to pieces among rocks and islands. Night came, the storm was still violent, and everyone was exhausted. With horror, passengers and crew watched the vessel bearing down on a reef. Miraculously, the ship shaved by several jagged

---

10. John Penn to Thomas Penn, Dec. 18, 1763, Penn Mss., Official Correspondence, IX, 212, and Croghan's vouchers for 1763, Cadwalader Coll., and Croghan's deed to Peters and Lardner, Dec. 19, 1763, Penn Mss., Deed Box, 1760-1801, Hist. Soc. of Pa.

peaks and wore past others; the shoals over which the vessel careened were plainly visible. Unable to work the ship off the Normandy coast, now close at hand, the captain anchored and put out distress signals. The anchor cables, however, could not endure the force of the gale; they snapped, and the vessel plunged toward the shore. All hands escaped the doomed craft, Croghan riding to land in the longboat, clutching his precious papers and his money. The rest of his possessions were lost.

Shortly after this perilous landing, surrounded by a horde of rabble intent on salvage, Croghan watched the *Britannia* strike a reef and break apart. The survivors traveled across France, passing through St. Lo and Caen, where they commented on the tomb of William the Conqueror. Croghan was appalled at the *ancien régime*, a contrast of great wealth and great want. "Never," he wrote, had he seen "so much pride & poverty." On February 7, he and his party reached the Seine near Le Havre, where they hired a small sloop to carry them to Portsmouth.[11]

Croghan was a confident man when he set foot in London. He had little doubt that he would recover the fortune he had lost in the Indian trade and that he would be instrumental in establishing a new system for the management of Indian affairs. Bustling with activity, he hurried about the city, calling on those in power and soliciting their aid. He had repeated conferences with Lord Halifax, Lord Hillsborough, president of the Board of Trade, Governor Pownall, Thomas Penn, and Chief Justice William Allen of Pennsylvania, then in England on a visit. Croghan spent convivial hours with General Monckton and other army friends, including General Webb and Major Charles Lee, who later lost a Revolutionary battle for Washington. He was often with Major Horatio Gates, whom he found "the same man he allways was."[12]

Croghan had been advised to take a first floor apartment in Pall Mall or near St. James and to hire a servant and a genteel carriage. After residing for a time at the Golden Cross Tavern, he acquired lodgings in Lancaster Court, engaged a domestic, for

---

11. Croghan to Johnson, Feb. 24, 1764, *Johnson Papers*, IV, 341; Nicholas B. Wainwright, "Shipwreck of the *Britannia*, 1764," *Pa. Mag. of Hist. and Biog.*, 73 (1949), 87-91.
12. Croghan to "Gentlemen," Feb. 17, 1764, Cadwalader Coll., Hist. Soc. of Pa.; Croghan to Johnson, Feb. 24, 1764, *Johnson Papers*, IV, 339-42.

whom he provided expensive livery, and replaced his own wardrobe, which had been lost on the *Britannia*. He purchased a pair of white worsted breeches, silk hose and silk garters, a dress suit of velvet, a scarlet coat with a crimson waistcoat, and a green stage coat. These splendid materials were ornamented with dozens of buttons and yards of lace, ribbon, and gold binding. There was to be no mistake that Colonel George Croghan, deputy to Sir William Johnson, was an important man come to England on business of the first magnitude. When Colonel Croghan entered the Globe Tavern of an evening to drink with his cronies, he was the personification of wealth and influence.[13]

Despite his energy and the help of important friends, Croghan found himself unable to make any progress. The wheels of politics and government moved at a snail's pace. He became indignant and condemned the officers of state for neglecting public affairs for private concerns. Both political parties, he sweepingly declared, were composed of rogues. After two ineffectual months in England, Croghan wrote Johnson, "I am sick of London & harttily tierd of the pride & pompe of the slaves in power." He developed a poor opinion of English women and held the Board of Trade in contempt because its members were "imensly ignerant" and their words "meer froath." He resented the suspicious and condescending way in which the English regarded Americans, and he noted: "The cheefe study of the pople in power hear att present is to lay heavy taxes on the colenys and tis talkt of laying an internal tax on them next cesion of Parlament." His exposure to English statesmen in their homeland awakened his identification as an American. All in all, the Indian agent was glad he had come, "as it will learn me to be contented on a little farm in America."[14]

One by one, Croghan found the objects of his trip to England stalemated. He was unable to obtain restitution for the Pennsylvania merchants who had suffered trade losses during the Indian

13. Nicholas B. Wainwright, "Advice to a Stranger in London," *Pa. Mag. of Hist. and Biog.*, 73 (1949), 85-87; bill of H. Mills, July 15, 1764, Croghan's vouchers for 1764, Cadwalader Coll., Hist. Soc. of Pa.

14. Croghan to Johnson, Apr. 14 and July 12, 1764, *Johnson Papers*, IV, 396-99, 462-64; John Johnson to Croghan, Dec. 14, 1765, Cadwalader Coll., Hist. Soc. of Pa.

outbreak of 1763. Moreover, he learned that the stronger claims of the sufferers of 1754, which included his own large losses, could be paid only by a successful appeal to the next session of Parliament and not out of treasury funds as anticipated.[15]

Croghan had intended to go to Dublin, where he hoped as the heir of Edmund Croghan, his grandfather, to recover landed property. But month after month passed, and still he danced attendance on the Board of Trade, which had yet to take up Indian affairs. In the end, Croghan gave up his intended trip and referred the collection of his inheritance to a lawyer. Still another disappointment was the refusal of the Board of Trade to confirm him in a 200,000-acre grant in the Mohawk country in exchange for his Indian grant on the Ohio.[16]

For many months, the Board of Trade had been engaged in formulating policies for the digestion of the vast new areas of land won from the French. By the epochal proclamation of October 7, 1763, the Crown had established four new American colonies—Grenada, West Florida, East Florida, and Quebec—and had designated a natural boundary, the Allegheny Mountains, to separate the old colonies from the Indians' hunting grounds. Not until June was the Board able to turn its full attention to the regulation of the Indian department and the rich American fur trade. Although the Board drew on the opinions of many informed people, its principal reliance was on letters and reports of Johnson and John Stuart, superintendent of the Southern Department, and interviews with George Croghan.

"To treat Indians with propriety and address is perhaps of all tasks the most difficult," Croghan informed the Board. To manage the natives, it was first essential to win their love; that required a long acquaintance with their peculiarities and an ability to flatter their vanity in order to gain their confidence. But love of the English, Croghan warned, was not enough. The Indians had to be kept in awe of English might. Should they entertain too high notions of their own importance and believe their power was feared,

15. Penn to Peters, Mar. 9, 1764, Penn Letter Book, VIII, 36, Hist. Soc. of Pa.
16. Letter of attorney to Michael Bourke, Sept. 4, 1764, Cadwalader Coll., Hist. Soc. of Pa.; *Journal of the Commissioners for Trade and Plantations from January 1764 to December 1767. Preserved in the Public Record Office* (London, 1936), 71.

they would hold the whites in contempt. Their insolence would increase beyond sufferance to the worst consequences.

Croghan urged the Board to adopt an Indian boundary line which he and Johnson had discussed—a boundary which would replace the Proclamation Line of 1763 with a more satisfactory and permanent line. Croghan also dwelt on the necessity of freeing the Indian department from military control and of providing annual gifts to the Indians. In addition, he recommended a feature which had probably matured in his mind since his arrival in London. On March 10, 1764, he had written Johnson that "there is talk of setling a colony from the mouth of the Ohio to the Illinois." Croghan praised this western country highly and evidently excited Lord Hillsborough, for, according to Croghan, Hillsborough told him that if the Proclamation Line of 1763 was altered to take in "the fine country on the western waters," he would send settlers there. Stimulated by the receptive English attitude, Croghan recommended planting a colony in Illinois to secure the western frontiers and to prevent the French from interfering in the fur trade. Although the Board did not act on Croghan's scheme for a colony, there is reason to believe that he was instrumental in guiding its thinking on the organization of the Indian department and on the necessity of running a new Indian boundary.[17]

By July 10, 1764, the Board of Trade had drawn up an elaborate plan for the regulation of Indian affairs to replace their "present vague and uncertain administration." In character, the plan was truly imperial, for it delegated all authority to two Crown officials, superintendents of the northern and southern Indian districts; all provincial laws relating to Indian affairs were to be repealed. Of the districts, Johnson's was the larger and more important, embracing, as it did, all of Nova Scotia, Canada, New England, the Middle Colonies, the Far West, and the Illinois country. He had the supervision of forty-two tribes to Stuart's thirteen, three deputies to Stuart's two, and more money for Indian presents. In the northern district, trade was to be

---

17. Croghan to Johnson, Mar. 10, 1764, *Johnson Papers*, IV, 363; Julian P. Boyd, *et al.*, eds., *The Papers of Thomas Jefferson* (Princeton, 1950), II, 78; Board of Trade Papers, Plantations General, XIX, 305, Hist. Soc. of Pa.; Clarence W. Alvord, *The Mississippi Valley in British Politics* (Cleveland, 1917), I, 221.

restricted to eleven posts where it was to be supervised by commissaries. Other notable features of the plan were the freeing of the Indian department from military control and the decision to delimit the boundary of lands reserved for the Indians more exactly than had been done in the proclamation of 1763. The whole plan hinged on some method of taxation to raise the £20,000 estimated as the cost of the department—Croghan's proposal that a duty of 5 per cent be imposed on the Indian trade met with the approval of the Board. The plan was sent to Johnson and Stuart for criticism, and hope was expressed that it could be brought before the next session of Parliament.[18] Croghan was elated, for all the major points Johnson had wanted had been agreed to. For the present, it was true, the army would continue to support Johnson, but Croghan anticipated it would not be long before duties laid on the fur trade would make the Indian department independent.

The Pennsylvanian's last few weeks in England were spent in advising wealthy speculators on the purchase of lands in New York and in assisting Thomas Penn in certain perplexing proprietarial problems. He bought presents for Molly, mistress of Johnson Hall, and executed commissions for his friends—the purchase of fishing tackle for Sir William's son John, a gold seal for Daniel Claus, china for Guy Johnson, and a gold watch for Alexander McKee. About the middle of September, he sailed from Falmouth for New York.[19]

Although Croghan had resigned from the Indian department in 1763, his resignation had never been acted on and his name was never taken off the payroll. Reporting for duty at Johnson Hall, the deputy found Sir William well pleased with the Board of Trade's Indian plan. Croghan claimed full credit: "I have been able to settle the Department of Indian Affairs on a new system." Although the plan had not yet been approved, Croghan acted as if it were in full force. He instructed Alexander McKee, his assistant, to disregard military authority, expressing himself in

18. O'Callaghan, ed., *New-York Col. Doc.*, VII, 634-41; Croghan to Thomas Gage, Apr. 5, 1766, William L. Clements Library, University of Michigan.
19. Croghan to Johnson, Aug. 4, 1764, *Johnson Papers*, IV, 501; accounts kept in Croghan's London Journal, Cadwalader Coll., Hist. Soc. of Pa.

such terms on the subject that Colonel Bouquet, who intercepted Croghan's letter, was infuriated. To Gage, Bouquet wrote: "It is so disagreeable to have any thing to do with savages, that every officer in the army must think himself happy to have no further concern with them, tho', at the same time, one can not but regret that powers of so great importance to this country should in this instance have been trusted to a man so illiterate, imprudent, and ill bred, who subverts to particular purposes the wise views of the Government, and begins his fonctions by a ridiculous display of his own importance."[20]

While Croghan conferred with Johnson, Bouquet was marching against the Ohio Indians. Johnson had held the northern tribes faithful, but west of the Ohio the natives were still hostile. Colonel Bradstreet's expedition to Detroit earlier in the year had been a failure. Pontiac had yet to be pacified, and the Illinois Indians still resolutely defied the British to occupy the Illinois country won from France by the Treaty of Paris in 1763. A British officer sent to treat with them had been turned back, and a military expedition to take possession had been attacked and forced to retreat. In this unsettled situation, Johnson ordered Croghan westward to do what he could to help Bouquet.

It is doubtful that Croghan traveled any farther west than Philadelphia, where matters of personal interest absorbed him. He had visited the great men of his day at home and abroad; he envied their gracious, luxurious way of living. The time had come for Croghan himself to establish a handsome eastern residence far from the frontier crudities which had for so long surrounded him. In November, 1764, he purchased a countryseat in Philadelphia's Northern Liberties for £900 and named the place Monckton Hall.

Monckton Hall's four and a half acres on Poplar Lane was a delightful property, just a mile and a half out the Second Street road from the center of the city. The house, a new brick one, stood on rising ground commanding a prospect of the Delaware River and the spires of Philadelphia. It was flanked in true Georgian style by two brick buildings of uniform appearance, one of which housed the kitchen and the other the stable. The grounds

20. Croghan to McKee, Dec. 6, 1764, and Bouquet to Gage, Dec. 22, 1764, *Bouquet Papers*, 21653, 339, 342.

were highly improved with neatly fenced vegetable and flower gardens, flourishing fruit trees, two excellent wells, and fields of red clover and timothy.[21]

Except for a garden roller and several tables, Monckton Hall was bare of furnishings. Croghan immediately placed orders for a complete set of household goods. Up the Second Street road came a seemingly unending series of deliveries: Scottish carpets, groceries, barrels of beer, quantities of spirits and wine, blankets, Irish linen, china, cutlery, tankards, pewter basins, a warming pan, cooking utensils, candlesticks, and valuable furniture. Cabinet-maker Benjamin Randolph provided a dozen mahogany chairs upholstered in green damask by Plunket Fleeson, who also supplied two easy chairs done up in the same material. Perspiring workmen struggled in the doors with mahogany tables, desks, bookcases, commodes, backgammon tables, and, of all things, an expensive spinet. The place was alive with servants in Croghan's livery. A new building would be necessary for his wagon, his English post chaise, and his handsome carriage.[22]

Baynton, Wharton, and Morgan served as Croghan's agents in the purchase of most of these furnishings, and Wharton and Croghan were as thick as thieves. Shortly after his arrival in Philadelphia, Croghan had been invited to stay with Wharton, who drank heady droughts of Croghan's persuasive ideas and fell ever deeper under the Indian agent's influence. The only hope of recovering the trading losses of 1763, Croghan told him, was to receive restitution from the Indians themselves. After the running of the new boundary line, for which Croghan had obtained the Board of Trade's tentative approval, vast areas would be released for white settlement. The Indians must be prevailed upon to grant a princely portion of this ceded section to the traders.

More thrilling than this prospect of recovery, so vital to the fortunes of Wharton's firm, was Croghan's inspirational discourse on Illinois. Croghan was convinced that a British colony would soon be established in this distant conquest of the French war and that in Illinois lay many a fortune for enterprising British fur

21. *Pennsylvania Gazette*, July 5, 1764; Deed Book D, 69, 653, City Hall, Phila.
22. Croghan's vouchers for 1764 and 1765, Cadwalader Coll., Hist. Soc. of Pa.

traders. He estimated the annual value of the Illinois beaver trade alone at £100,000 sterling. Temporarily, such visions of wealth were clouded by the fact that no British troops had yet been able to enter the country to relieve the French garrison at Fort Chartres. British occupation was retarded by the hostile attitude of the Illinois natives, who had been taught by French fur traders to hate the English. As Croghan said of these traders, "It is death to them to hear that the English are coming." Croghan won Samuel Wharton's enthusiastic approval of a plan to capture the Illinois fur trade from the French.

In November, Bouquet opened the door to Illinois by cowing the Ohio tribes into a truce before a peace which their chiefs were to make with Sir William Johnson. Croghan's plans now went into high gear. Baynton, Wharton, and Morgan, together with Robert Field, Robert Callender, and Croghan himself, organized a partnership to provide £20,000-worth of Indian goods for the western trade. Croghan's 25 per cent interest in the scheme was kept secret because Indian agents were not allowed to trade. Although a partner in the venture, Croghan made his usual declaration that he entered it only to serve his friends and that he did not intend to share in the profits. There could scarcely be any loss, because Croghan promised to purchase huge Indian presents out of the stock when it reached Fort Pitt and Fort Chartres (no less, indeed, than £20,000-worth of goods at their greatly inflated western values). That would still leave enough of the original shipment to be traded for beaver in Illinois at such fantastically favorable rates as to make a fortune. Safe passage of the stock to Illinois was guaranteed because Croghan would take it there himself. Croghan was, in George Morgan's words, "the first spring & mover of this adventure."[23]

The adventure was characteristic of Croghan, devious and dangerously speculative. His motives are difficult to assess. A warmhearted man, he no doubt wanted to favor his friend Wharton. With Indian affairs in mind, he was convinced that a large and immediate trade was necessary to cement severed relations.

23. George Morgan affidavit, Illinois Historical Survey, University of Illinois; Max Savelle, *George Morgan, Colony Builder* (New York, 1932), 19-20; Baynton, Wharton, and Morgan Journal "A", 393, Public Records Division, Harrisburg.

It is certain that Croghan grossly misled Wharton and the other partners by his promise to purchase £20,000-worth of Indian presents from them. By this statement, he drew them ruinously into the vortex of the Illinois trade.

With goods for trade and presents at his beck and call, Croghan returned to New York to convince General Gage that he was the man to open up the Illinois country to British occupation. Gage had prepared another expedition, which was to leave New Orleans early in 1765 and make its way up the Mississippi. But if the Indians continued hostile, the expedition would unquestionably fail. Both Bouquet and Bradstreet agreed that it would take an army of three thousand men to gain possession.[24]

Croghan found the general "not a little distressed" about the situation. "I therefore thought it the duty of my department to propose to him that I would use my best endeavours with the Natives ... to obtain their consent to His Majestys troops peaceably possessing that country. Which proposition he chearfully accepted off." Johnson also approved Croghan's mission. Acknowledging the fact that negotiation and not force was the only course, Bouquet approvingly commented, "Mr. Croghan is the fittest person in America to transact that business."[25]

In January, 1765, Croghan was back in Philadelphia with Lieutenant Alexander Fraser, who was to accompany him, and with a credit of £2,000 with which to buy Indian presents. Gage, who had discussed the matter with Croghan, intended this sum to be the limit which the agent could spend. Although Gage's instructions to Croghan did not specifically restrict him to this amount, neither did they authorize him to spend more. As usual in money matters, Croghan chose to rely on his own judgment and, to Gage's subsequent horror, acted as if there was no limit to the amount of presents he could buy.

Croghan's cousin Thomas Smallman had been one of the

24. Bradstreet on Indian affairs, Dec. 4, 1764, O'Callaghan, ed., *New-York Col. Doc.*, VII, 693; Bouquet to Gage, Nov. 30, 1764, *Coll. of the Ill. State Hist. Lib.*, 10 (1915), 366-87.
25. Bouquet to Gage, Jan. 5, 1765, and Croghan to Benjamin Franklin, Dec. 12, 1765, *Coll. of the Ill. State Hist. Lib.*, 10 (1915), 397, and 11 (1916), 60-64; Johnson to Gage, Dec. 18, 1764, and Johnson to Croghan, Dec. 18, 1764, *Johnson Papers*, IV, 625, and XI, 509-10.

captives released by the Shawnees to Bouquet in November. He had come to Philadelphia and thrown himself on Croghan's bounty. Smallman had never enjoyed any more credit than Croghan had advanced for him and, after his Indian disaster and a year and a half in captivity, was presumably penniless. Croghan kindly paid the poor man's bills in Philadelphia; he also purchased from Smallman, who now surprisingly described himself as a merchant of Philadelphia, £2,650-worth of Indian goods for the Crown. The authorities later criticized this purchase, and it seems probable that Croghan used Smallman as a front for a transaction that would otherwise have appeared even worse. Croghan also purchased Indian presents from Robert Field and incurred a £1,900 charge from Baynton, Wharton, and Morgan.

From Bouquet, Croghan obtained a pass to take the Crown present to Fort Pitt, but how could the traders' goods go west as long as Governor John Penn kept the trade closed? Pretending that the traders' stock would all be purchased for the Crown, Croghan obtained Bouquet's written permission to take out whatever goods he might think proper. It never occurred to Bouquet that Croghan would think proper to take out a stock in trade contrary to the law of the province. Thus arose one of those misunderstandings which studded Croghan's career—a misunderstanding between the clear-thinking, high-minded Bouquet and the devious Indian agent.[26]

While engaged in promoting the interests of traders, Croghan lent his name to fund raising on behalf of the Anglican church and busied himself with real estate speculations, this time in partnership with his old army friend Captain Harry Gordon. He examined copper ore sent from the mine at Pluckamin, New Jersey, in which he owned a large share. He continued to entertain high hopes for the mine, but the operation was soon to prove a costly failure.[27]

At length, on January 23, Croghan, Smallman, and Lieutenant

26. John Penn to Johnson, Mar. 21, 1765, *Johnson Papers*, XI, 643-45; Johnson to John Penn, June 7, 1765, *Pa. Archives*, IV, 226-27; Bouquet to Johnson, Jan. 25, 1765, *Bouquet Papers*, 21653, 353; Bouquet to Gage, Apr. 10, 1765, Clements Library.
27. Pluckamin Mine folder, Cadwalader Coll., and Lamberton Scots-Irish Coll., I, 49, also Penn Mss., Warrants and Surveys, 57, Hist. Soc. of Pa.; *Pa. Archives*, Eighth Series, VII, 5708.

Fraser left Philadelphia. They passed through Lancaster, where Croghan presumably met Lieutenant Augustine Prevost, who was stationed there. Two months later, Prevost, a member of a distinguished military family, married fifteen-year-old Susannah Croghan, "agreeable to the form prescribed by the Church of England in the Book of Common prayer before a sufficient number of witnesses." The bride evidently inherited at least one of her father's traits—the cost of her trousseau far exceeded the letter of credit Croghan had left her.

At Carlisle, Croghan hired sixty-five pack horses to carry the Indian present to Fort Pitt. He also gathered about him a group of former Indian traders who composed a memorial to Sir William Johnson, praying for a grant of Indian territory in return for the losses inflicted on them during the uprising of 1763.[28]

By February 25, Croghan and his party had arrived at Bedford, where the Indian agent found the poor people of the settlement suffering from the unprecedented severity of the winter. He purchased a thousand pounds of flour and distributed it as a charitable gift. A few days later, Croghan reached Fort Pitt, his pack train being the first to cross the mountains through snow that had sealed the Forbes Road for weeks past.[29]

Croghan had sent word to Alexander McKee to convene the Ohio chiefs, but they had not yet come in. It is certain that after meeting with these leaders and establishing peace, Croghan planned on his own authority to open the fur trade. No sooner had he invested in the trading venture than he wrote McKee to urge the Indians to bring their peltry to Fort Pitt and hold it there until he arrived. Of Croghan's avowed intention to open the trade, Bouquet wrote, "The motive of that eagerness is too conspicuous to need any comment." Impure as Croghan's motive was, he did believe that the success of his mission depended on his power to open the trade at Fort Pitt, Detroit, and the Illinois country.[30]

28. *Johnson Papers*, XI, 564-66; John Cameron to Croghan, Dec. 24, 1765, Cadwalader Coll., Hist. Soc. of Pa.
29. Croghan to McCulloch, Feb. 25, 1765, Cadwalader Coll., Hist. Soc. of Pa.; Fraser to Gage, Mar. 4, 1765, Clements Library.
30. Croghan to Johnson, Jan. 1 and Feb. 18, 1765, *Johnson Papers*, XI, 519-20, 576-77; Croghan to McKee, Dec. 6, 1764, and Bouquet to Gage, Dec. 22, 1764, *Bouquet Papers*, 21653, 339, 342.

His plan, which would have neatly cornered the fur trade in favor of his own company, was prevented by one of the most extraordinary occurrences in frontier history. Robert Callender had sent the bulk of the partnership goods to a border settlement, where it was to be loaded on pack horses and forwarded to Croghan as quickly as possible. By chance, a barrel broke and was found to be full of scalping knives.[31] The word spread like wildfire. Philadelphia merchants were violating the provincial edict which had closed the fur trade and were sending ammunition to Indians who had not yet declared peace. Some of the frontiersmen who heard this had personally buried friends and relations who had been scalped and hideously mutilated in the recent war. With the connivance of the country magistrates these men organized, disguising themselves by blacking their faces. They halted the first pack train sent forward by Callender and destroyed about £3,000-worth of its contents. The rest of the stock found refuge in Fort Loudoun.

Swearing that the shipment was not Crown property but traders' goods, disguised as Crown property and as such protected by Croghan's name, the Black Boys went berserk. They besieged Fort Loudoun and closed the Forbes Road; they vowed they would kill Croghan if they could catch him. Civil and military authority was powerless to quell the storm the Indian agent had raised.

Croghan's partners, Wharton, Baynton, and Callender, caught up in a flood of reproach, all told different stories about the ownership of the goods. The stories ranged from Callender's assertion that all £20,000-worth belonged to the Crown, through a more modest statement by Baynton, to Wharton's tale that none of it belonged to the Crown but that Croghan had promised to favor the stock in his purchase of Indian presents. Subsequent claims by Wharton, however, tended to thrust the entire ownership on the king. The truth of the matter was that the partners had been counting heavily on Croghan's promise to buy largely from them. Would he come to their assistance now that matters had turned out so disastrously? Wharton hoped that "Mr. C will have address enough to make at best £2,000 of the goods lost to

31. *Pennsylvania Journal*, Mar. 21, 1765.

be upon the King's account." Gage was disgusted with the obvious insincerity of the merchants and bewildered by the bills for Croghan's Indian present, particularly by Smallman's bill, for Gage learned that there was no merchant named Smallman in Philadelphia. The general declined to pay these obligations until Croghan himself could be present to explain them.[32]

As for the fiasco caused by the Black Boys, Gage was inclined to believe the story that was in everyone's mouth in Philadelphia: Croghan had an interest in the trading stock; it was to be bartered to the Indians without the necessary license from Governor Penn, despite the fact that the trade was closed; Croghan had lent his name to permit the passage of goods along the military road under false pretenses. Wharton and the others were loyal, if untruthful. They insisted that Croghan was in no way connected with their trading venture and that the goods were to have been stored at Fort Pitt until Governor Penn opened the trade.

Unlike his partners, Croghan was too adroit to be caught in contradictory statements. He admitted that he had encouraged the merchants to send out goods because he believed there should be a trading stock at Fort Pitt ready for use the moment trade was opened. Evidently, he had been in error, but he had only intended to promote the good of the service. "I have no concern in trade with any body, nor has had since General Braddock's arrival in this country."[33]

Gage reprimanded Croghan and wrote Johnson that Croghan had entered into "leagues with traders to carry up goods in a clandestine manner under cover of the business he was employed in of going to the Ilinois, contrary to orders, and contrary to the laws of the Province. And this under pretence of having goods ready when the trade should be opened. I dont know any business he had with the trade. . . . All that at present can be seen is that Mr. Croghan thought to take advantage

---

32. Gage to Johnson, Apr. 15, 1765, *Johnson Papers*, IV, 717-18; Wharton to his partners, Apr. 2, 1765, Dreer Coll., Hist. Soc. of Pa. The false position in which Baynton, Wharton, and Morgan found themselves is well illustrated in Wharton's letter of Mar. 15, 1765, to his partners, Public Records Division, Harrisburg.

33. Croghan to Gage, May 12, 1765, Clements Library; Johnson to John Penn, June 7, 1765, *Pa. Archives*, IV, 226.

of his employment to be first at the market.... If he acts in this strange manner already, what may we expect when he gets to the Ilinois."[34]

Johnson stoutly defended his deputy from charges of corruption. "I should find it a difficult task," Sir William replied to Gage, "to find a man at all calculated for the employment who would for so long a time support as disinterested a character." Between them, Croghan and Johnson tried to persuade the general that Croghan's only error had been one of judgment. The Indian agent promised to clear his name after completing his mission to Illinois and then after setting everything right would resign. Wharton interpreted Croghan's impending resignation simply as a threat to force Gage to pay the bills for the Indian present, for as Croghan "well knows his place in that department cannot be supplied."[35]

Croghan tarried two months at Fort Pitt awaiting the Ohio Indians, who were delayed in coming to his conference because of the recalcitrance of the Delawares. Lieutenant Fraser, however, refused to put off his own departure for Illinois. Mistakenly, he felt that Gage's messages to the French commander at Fort Chartres and to the French inhabitants must go forward immediately. Otherwise, they would not arrive in time to pave the way for the reception of Major Robert Farmar and the Thirty-fourth Regiment. Farmar was supposedly coming up the Mississippi at that very moment, although in actuality he did not leave New Orleans until June, and then it took him more than five months to make his way upstream.

Croghan disapproved of Fraser's departure, but he could not persuade him to await the Indian conference. The young officer reached the Illinois country safely, arriving shortly after the failure of an English peace mission from New Orleans. He met Pontiac and did much to pacify the chief by convincing him that the Shawnees and Delawares had made peace with the English. Pontiac was astute enough to realize that if this were so his game was up. The famous Ottawa leader told Fraser he was glad to hear

---

34. Gage to Johnson, Apr. 15, 1765, *Johnson Papers*, IV, 717-18.
35. Wharton to his partners, July 6, 1765, Public Records Division, Harrisburg; Johnson to Gage, Apr. 27, 1765, *Johnson Papers*, XI, 704.

Illinois Mirage

that Croghan was coming to talk to him, because the agent would scarcely dare mislead the Indians after having been detected by them in so many lies in the past.[36] Despite this success in softening Pontiac, Croghan's long delay in coming proved nearly fatal to Fraser, who eventually had to flee for his life. Another English peace delegation came up the Mississippi to the Illinois country in June, but, after distributing a large Indian present, it, too, was forced to flee in the night. Stirred up and well supplied by French traders, the Illinois tribes seemed implacable in their hatred for the English.

Early in May, Croghan at last convened his Indian congress at Fort Pitt, more than five hundred chiefs and warriors of the Senecas (Mingoes), Delawares, and Shawnees attending. Among the prominent chiefs present were Kiasutha, the Beaver, and Custaloga. These Ohio Indians, notably the Shawnees, had not complied with their engagements to Bouquet, and peace had not yet been declared. Their recent conduct pointed to another outbreak. Croghan managed the treaty skillfully. He obtained from the Shawnees all their prisoners; all the tribes promised to do exactly what he called for. They appointed new Indian deputies to go to Sir William and formalize the peace, and they appointed other deputies to assist Croghan on his mission to Illinois. The Ohio nations, especially the Shawnees who named ten delegates to accompany Croghan, had profound influence over the Illinois tribes.[37]

The Fort Pitt conference was Croghan's first notable accomplishment of the year. It solidified peace with the Ohio nations, who had been wavering and sulky ever since Bouquet and his army withdrew from their doorstep. John Penn opened the Indian trade as soon as he heard from Croghan of his success. As for Croghan, this treaty was but a means to an end. He believed that if he did not settle matters with the Ohio Indians, it would be impossible to enter the Illinois country.[38]

On May 15, 1765, Croghan started his journey down the Ohio. The eyes of the army were on him. A military expedition

36. Peckham, *Pontiac*, 273.
37. O'Callaghan, ed., *New-York Col. Doc.*, VII, 750.
38. Croghan to Gage, May 12, 1765, Clements Library; Croghan to John Penn, May 12, 1765, *Coll. of the Ill. State Hist. Lib.*, 10 (1915), 490-91; *Col. Rec. of Pa.*, IX, 264.

and four diplomatic missions had failed to pacify the Illinois Indians; in fact, their personnel were lucky to escape with their lives. In New York, Gage fretted over this latest effort. If Croghan failed, how could the English gain possession of Illinois? In New Orleans, the French governor of Louisiana also waited anxiously. "That which will contribute the most to peace in that particular part of the world," he wrote, "is the arrival of G. Crohan."[39]

Down the Ohio glided Croghan's two bateaux deeply laden with Indian presents, native deputies, and Croghan's servants and followers, including Smallman and Dr. George C. Anthon, formerly Croghan's Indian surgeon at Detroit. Game was so plentiful that the hunters did not have to leave their boats to shoot down all they wanted. At the mouth of the Scioto River, Croghan rounded up and deported seven French traders who had been operating in the Shawnee villages.[40]

On June 6, the party encamped about six miles below the mouth of the Wabash. The next day Croghan sent two Indians overland to Fort Chartres to notify the commander of his progress and to deliver speeches to the Indians informing them of peace between the English and the Ohio tribes. Although he realized that he was now in dangerous territory, the Indian agent did not know that at that very moment he was under hostile observation.

Just as Croghan's camp was stirring at daybreak on June 8, it was savagely attacked by eighty Kickapoo and Mascouten warriors. In the wild melee which followed, Croghan was tomahawked, two of his servants were killed, and nearly all the other white men were wounded. In addition, three of the Shawnee deputies were killed. Before further disasters could befall the survivors, a wounded Shawnee chief boldly threatened the attackers with the revenge of all the northern tribes for this outrage. The hostile Indians, abashed in the presence of the Shawnees, began to make excuses. The French, they said, had stirred them up to the attack. Fearful of pursuit, they hastily divided the plunder and, with Croghan and the other whites as prisoners, traveled forty-two miles before

39. Aubry to Choiseul, July 10, 1765, Parkman 27A, Pontiac, French Documents, etc., 186, Mass. Hist. Soc.

40. Croghan's Journal, Feb.-Oct., 1765, *Coll. of the Ill. State Hist. Lib.*, 11 (1916), 1-64.

making camp. Croghan suffered severely from heat and thirst during the week it took to reach Vincennes, a settlement of eighty French families, "an idle lazy people, a parcel of renegadoes from Canada," who were delighted with Croghan's misfortunes. From these traders, however, the Indian agent obtained enough credit to reoutfit his party. His captors had robbed the expedition of everything it had, including Croghan's personal camp equipage valued at £150 and his supply of hard money worth £421.

A few days more of travel and the war party came to its own village of Ouiatenon, near the present site of Lafayette, Indiana. Both at Vincennes and at Ouiatenon, the warriors were scolded by resident Indians who had long known and liked Croghan. The Kickapoos and Mascoutens had had time for reflection and were now thoroughly alarmed. They dressed Croghan's wound more carefully and lost their truculence. Nevertheless, they refused to release him until ordered to do so by a message from the French commander at Fort Chartres and bribed by sixty-four gallons of rum which Croghan purchased.[41]

In absolute dread of war with the Ohio tribes, which was to be expected because of their killing the Shawnee deputies, the Kickapoos and their confederates abjectly begged Croghan's forgiveness and urged him to intercede for them. Croghan was now in the driver's seat and, despite continuing French propaganda, reconciled the five Wabash tribes (Weas, Piankashaws, Twightwees, Kickapoos, Mascoutens) to the English occupation of Illinois.[42]

Pontiac had sent Croghan a message that he would be glad to see him and that, if he liked what Croghan had to say, he would do all he could to reconcile the Illinois tribes. Croghan was confident that Pontiac, "an old acquaintance of mine," would come to terms. Nor was he mistaken. In July, Pontiac and deputies of the four Illinois nations met Croghan in council at Ouiatenon and agreed to allow the English to take over the French posts in Illinois. "Pondiac is a shrewd sensible Indian of few words," observed Croghan, "& commands more respect amongst those

41. Croghan to Johnson, July 12, 1765, *Johnson Papers*, XI, 836-41; "Sundry losses when taken prisoner by the Indians near Ouabache," Cadwalader Coll., Hist. Soc. of Pa.
42. *Johnson Papers*, XI, 849-50.

nations than any Indian I ever saw could do amongst his own tribe."[43]

Croghan wrote to Fort Pitt that the way was now clear, and a company of the Black Watch was immediately sent down the Ohio to hold Fort Chartres until the Thirty-fourth Regiment arrived. Having earlier stabilized peace in the Ohio country, he had thus, in a series of powwows beside the waters of the Wabash, opened the Illinois country to peaceful occupation. Only the tribes of the Far West yet remained to be pacified.

Intent on making a clean sweep of the hostile Indian nations, Croghan journeyed on to Detroit. With him he took Pontiac and deputies of the Illinois tribes so that they could declare a formal peace in the presence of the Detroit commander. Naturally, Croghan devoted much diplomatic attention to Pontiac. "Pondiac & I is on extreame good terms," he cheerfully reported, "& I am mistaken if I dont ruin his influence with his own people before I part with him." Croghan's attention to the chief aroused the jealousy of the other tribes, and the Ottawa's influence began to wane.[44]

At the headwaters of the Wabash, Croghan crossed the portage to the Maumee River, down which he canoed some 180 miles to Lake Erie, rescuing prisoners from Indian villages on his way. He arrived at Detroit on August 17 and held a conference with ten nations represented by more than five hundred chiefs and warriors. From them he received prisoners, as well as promises to keep the peace. The Illinois nations again pledged their allegiance, and Pontiac, who seemed very penitent, plaintively announced that he had agreed to peace with Croghan before he came to Detroit.

Lieutenant Colonel John Campbell, the Detroit commander, was overjoyed with Croghan's treaty and reported to Gage that a general peace had now been settled with all the western Indians. He attributed this reconciliation to Croghan's "great care & attention. . . . All the tribes of Indians that came here to council since the arrival of Mr. Croghan were dismissed extremely well pleased

---

43. Croghan to Johnson, Nov., 1765, *Coll. of the Ill. State Hist. Lib.*, 11 (1916), 53.

44. Croghan to McKee, Aug. 3, 1765, Clements Library; Peckham, *Pontiac*, 287.

& satisfied and Pondiac in particular." Campbell suggested to Gage that Croghan be stationed at Detroit because the Indians there had "the highest opinion of him, and they would prefer him to any other person."[45]

Croghan's tour of the Indian country had been phenomenally successful. It was probably the most notable service he ever performed, although its results were in part fortuitous. The agent credited his success in breaking the French alliance with the Illinois tribes to his carefully planned peace with the Shawnees, at Fort Pitt in May, and the subsequent killing of the Shawnee deputies, which had frightened the Illinois natives. Frankly admitting that he owed all to his misfortune in being captured and plundered, he ruefully added: "I got the stroke of a hatchett on the head, but my scull being pretty thick, the hatchet would not enter, so you may see a thick scull is of service on some occasions."[46]

News of Croghan's exploits electrified not only the army but people throughout the colonies. He was praised in the highest terms. His friend Lieutenant James MacDonald wrote that half the troops on the continent could not have duplicated Croghan's feat. Thomas Hutchins, a former Indian agent, described the problems Croghan had surmounted as more difficult than capturing "a dozen such places as the Havana with its Moro Castles."[47]

On September 26, Croghan and several companions left Detroit in a birch bark canoe. Four sturdy French voyageurs paddled them three hundred miles along the north shore of Lake Erie to Niagara and on to Oswego. It took Croghan exactly a month to span the distance from Detroit to the hospitable haven of Johnson Hall, where the warm welcome, the flowing glass, and Sir William's praise must have warmed the traveler's heart.[48] Moreover, his daughter Susannah came up from Albany, where her husband was now stationed, to bring her affectionate greeting.

Croghan found Sir William bitterly disappointed that the

---

45. Campbell to Gage, Aug. 29, Sept. 11, and Sept. 15, 1765, Clements Library.

46. Croghan to McKee, Aug. 3, 1765, *ibid.*; Croghan to William Murray, July 12, 1765, *Coll. of the Ill. State Hist. Lib.*, 11 (1916), 58.

47. Hutchins to Johnson, Aug. 31, 1765, *Coll. of the Ill. State Hist. Lib.*, 11 (1916), 80; James MacDonald to Johnson, July 24, 1765, *Johnson Papers*, XI, 867-68.

48. *Johnson Papers*, XI, 962.

Board of Trade's Indian plan had not yet been brought before Parliament. Now that peace had at last been achieved, it was absolutely necessary to appoint commissaries to reside at the different posts to manage the Indian trade. The alternative was another Indian war. But the Board of Trade had not yet provided the means to pay the commissaries' salaries. Johnson was still entirely dependent on Gage, and Gage was not authorized to increase Sir William's staff.

On November 5, Croghan arrived in New York. There remained on the Indian agent's agenda one item of unfinished business—he had to clear his name of the accusations thrown at him after the destruction of the pack train in March. By this time, the charges had narrowed down to Croghan's illicitly issuing passes to permit merchants' goods to go to Fort Pitt. Colonel Bouquet was the one who had particularly stressed this point. Bouquet had since gone to Pensacola, where he had caught yellow fever and died.

As soon as Croghan's name was announced at headquarters, he was ushered into General Gage's room. The general interrupted a staff meeting to receive Croghan and, in the presence of twenty of his senior officers, greeted him with open arms, thanking him in the name of the king for his remarkable services. No man, said Gage, was as distressed as he when he learned that Croghan had been taken prisoner. The general asked Croghan to dine with him so that they could discuss his adventures.

Croghan had returned a hero and was in a superlative bargaining position. His resignation was on the table. Some of his obligations with Baynton, Wharton, and Morgan for Indian presents were as yet unpaid. No, said Croghan, he would not dine with Gage as long as Gage entertained any idea that he was guilty of improper conduct. Gage, however, was not only willing to forget about the unhappy episode of the Black Boys, he was eager to do so. It was essential that Croghan's peccadillos be overlooked and his services retained. The general urged Croghan to forget all about the late unpleasantness. But Croghan, who affected to be outraged at what had been said about him, was not to be easily mollified. He appealed to the others present. Had he ever had the reputation of a moneymaker? Gage's staff officers, taking their cue from their general, denied to a man that they had ever heard of such a thing. Then Croghan played his trump card. He produced Bouquet's letter requesting him to take the merchants' goods and pass them as the king's goods. Its text, as read by Gage, conveyed an entirely different meaning than Bouquet had intended. Bouquet had no idea his letter would be used to pass any goods except those which Croghan was going to buy for the Crown at Fort Pitt.

Gage threw up his hands. "Oh! my God! What is all this? Mr. Croghan you are a most injured man." No longer did Croghan have any explaining to do; he was overwhelmed with sympathy, apologies, and praise. Although apparently guilty of every charge leveled at him, Croghan, with supreme audacity, had officially cleared himself.[49]

His visit to New York in November, 1765, coincided with violent demonstrations against the Stamp Act. To Croghan, this outburst of Americanism was no less than civil war. He discussed the riots with New York's Governor Cadwallader Colden, who had stiffly upheld the prerogative of the Crown against the rage of the people—"for wh. he deserves creadatt," observed Croghan. Colden told him that Gage had been too soft in his efforts to quiet the revolutionary spirit. Unlike Colden, who now realized that "people in general are averse to taxes of any kind," Croghan failed to grasp the object lesson of the Stamp Act. He still believed that the proposed tax on the Indian trade could be collected and would make possible the independent, imperial Indian department he had advocated before the Board of Trade.[50]

On his way to Philadelphia, accompanied by Samuel Wharton, who had come to meet him in New York, Croghan stopped at Burlington in response to an invitation from Governor William Franklin of New Jersey. The ostensible purpose of the visit was to see letters from Benjamin Franklin on English sentiment about the Indian department, but the Burlington discussions were important for another reason. Croghan was fired with en-

---

49. Wharton to his partners, Nov. 16, 1765, Public Records Division, Harrisburg.

50. Croghan to Johnson, Nov. 18, 1765, *Johnson Papers*, XI, 969-70; Colden to Secretary Conway, Nov. 9, 1765, O'Callaghan, ed., *New-York Col. Doc.*, VII, 774.

thusiasm for Illinois. British military occupation ultimately meant British settlement, and he was certain that lands readily acquirable from French inhabitants and the Indians would make a brilliant speculation. Wharton, Franklin, and Croghan put their heads together. If William Franklin had reservations, they were swept aside by Croghan's convincing arguments and by Wharton's masterly and persuasive manner. The governor made one important contribution to the budding scheme. He insisted that the purchase of Illinois lands should be dependent on the Crown's establishing a civil government there.

Back in Philadelphia, Croghan set Wharton's clerks to work transcribing the record of his visit to the Indian country. He composed two versions, an official one and a private journal written to appeal to land speculators. Copies of these journals were sent to Benjamin Franklin and to Thomas Penn. Croghan's literary endeavor was clearly that of a promoter: "The Illinois country far exceeds any other part of America, that I have seen—both as to soil and climate."[51]

Described by Samuel Wharton as "a man of nice honour," Croghan continued to fulminate against those who had criticized his connection with Baynton, Wharton, and Morgan, and there was much criticism. A visitor to Pennsylvania found that "the people in this parts are most notoriously ridged against Mr. Croghan by reason of an inveterate antipathy they have taken against him as I have heard many of them express themselves in a most shocking manner." Fearing that Gage did not believe him "an honist man & a feathful servant," Croghan collected depositions to prove he had done no wrong (one of them a letter from Samuel Wharton dated back to February 21, 1765, which noted Croghan's inflexible determination not to be concerned in trade) and continued to talk about resigning. Wharton sagely told his partners that the Indian agent was "playing a card" in assuming the role of outraged innocence. To make this role more convincing, Croghan withdrew from the trading partnership, informing Baynton, Wharton, and Morgan (Field and Callender having previously retired) that Gage was going to insist he take a Bible oath that he was not concerned with them and that he had to be free to do so. "By

51. Croghan to Benjamin Franklin, Feb. 25, 1766, *Johnson Papers*, V, 37.

this means," Croghan assured them, "I shall regain his confidence, & be sent again to the Illinois with unlimited credit & instructions, where I will make good more than all my promises, & do engage upon my honour to make good my share of whatever loss has or may happen, & therefore [I] desire you will take care to send forward a large quantity of Indian goods for I will take all you have at one sweep."[52]

Despite his talk of resigning, Croghan had not the slightest intention of leaving the service. He needed his important position to help Baynton, Wharton, and Morgan, to whom he felt obligated. He also needed it to facilitate the initial field work necessary for the promising Illinois speculation, for which he and Wharton were lining up partners.

Croghan's behavior while stimulating the scheme illustrates the facility with which he could play two sides to his own advantage. Wharton was a warm supporter of Benjamin Franklin and the bitter anti-proprietary faction. William Franklin was, of course, of this political shade. Two of the partners taken in for the Illinois plan were those former provincial commissioners Joseph Galloway and John Hughes, long-time foes of Thomas Penn and, at Indian treaties, of Croghan himself. Croghan overcame the doubts these men must have held against him. He convinced them that he was highly incensed at Governor John Penn and Chief Justice William Allen, who had accused him of collusion with the traders. He claimed that he had brought both Johnson and Gage to think favorably of the Assembly party. The Assembly, so long Croghan's uncompromising foe, melted readily under Galloway's reassuring influence and, in an address of thanks to Gage for conciliating the western tribes, expressed itself in the highest praise of Croghan and his "extensive influence and weight with the natives." Thomas Penn could hardly believe his eyes when he read encomiums to Croghan from such a source.[53]

52. Croghan to Colonel John Reed, Jan. 5, 1766, Cadwalader Coll., Hist. Soc. of Pa.; Wharton to his partners, Nov. 13, 1765, Public Records Division, Harrisburg; George Morgan's affidavit, Illinois Historical Survey, University of Illinois; Baynton, Wharton, and Morgan to Croghan, Feb. 21, 1765, Cadwalader Coll., Hist. Soc. of Pa.; John Johnston to William Johnson, Mar. 13, 1766, Hist. Soc. of Pa.

53. William Franklin to Benjamin Franklin, Apr. 30, 1766, *Coll. of the Ill. State Hist. Lib.*, 11 (1916), 221; *Pa. Archives*, Eighth Series, VII, 5855, 5858; Penn to William Allen, June 6, 1766, Penn Letter Book, IX, 19, Hist. Soc. of Pa.

Though Croghan aligned himself with political leaders of the opposition, he was careful not to break with the Penns. He maintained good terms with Governor John Penn and wrote Thomas Penn that he would be happy to locate valuable lands for him when the new Indian boundary was run. Croghan also continued cordial relations with William Smith, Thomas Barton, and Richard Peters, three Anglican ministers who were confidential correspondents of the proprietor.[54]

By canny juggling, he thus retained the support of the two most influential men of Pennsylvania background in England. Croghan had many irons in the fire in London which these gentlemen could tend for him. Penn was to do him many good offices with the Board of Trade. Franklin, too, assured by his son that Croghan was anti-Penn, was to prove a valuable friend.

When Gage received word late in 1765 that an Indian agent was needed at Fort Chartres, he asked Croghan to send Thomas Smallman there. What part Croghan himself would play in 1766, Gage had no idea. As far as he could tell, Croghan was going to resign. Croghan shaped his own destiny, which he made to coincide as closely as possible with his ideas of the best interest of the Crown. He decided to return to Illinois to lay the groundwork for his real-estate speculation in the colony he was so certain would soon be formed. A colony in Illinois, he pointed out for the benefit of his backers, could become the granary of Louisiana, support the military post, control the richest fur trade known, maintain the friendship of the natives, and curb the machinations of the French and Spaniards.

Back to Johnson Hall went Croghan, where he won Sir William's approval of the Illinois speculation and added Sir William's name as a partner in the scheme. At Croghan's instigation, Johnson wrote the Board of Trade that French land rights purchased at Illinois "may be a foundation for a valuable colony in that country." Johnson agreed that his deputy should return there and promised to include in his instructions an order to "enquire into the French bounds & property at the Illinois. I have no objec-

---

54. John Penn to Thomas Penn, Dec. 15, 1765, Penn Mss., Official Correspondence, X, 23, and Thomas Penn to Croghan, July 15, 1766, Penn Letter Book, IX, 29-31, Hist. Soc. of Pa.

tion to what you proposed when here." Johnson was fully aware that Croghan's private views would be well served by this trip, as it would give him an opportunity to select the best land for colonization.[55]

It was now necessary for Croghan to obtain Gage's approval of his going to Illinois for the official purpose of consolidating his successes of the previous year. When he visited Gage in February, he found the general fearful of the French and Indian situation, which certainly did not look promising. The great object of possessing Illinois, said Gage, was to win the fur trade. He, therefore, not only gladly accepted Johnson's recommendation, but also urged Croghan to go there. Croghan accepted the mission with seeming reluctance and left for Philadelphia after having planted in the general's mind the advantages of a settlement near Fort Chartres.[56]

With the decision to send Croghan to Illinois, Gage and Johnson also decided that they could no longer delay appointing commissaries to supervise the Indian trade at the army posts. Johnson named five of these officers, among them Alexander McKee for Fort Pitt and Edward Coles for Fort Chartres. Croghan was to go to Illinois as soon as Coles joined him. Many weeks passed before Croghan realized that Coles was to proceed directly from Detroit and would not come to Philadelphia. During these weeks, Croghan was, as usual, anything but idle.

He made arrangements for Pontiac to meet Johnson at Oswego in June. With Baynton, Wharton, Morgan, and William Trent, he acquired rights of Indian traders for restitution and laid plans for a huge Indian land grant on the Ohio by which the natives would repay the "suffering traders." This grant could not be made, however, until the Crown opened up lands west of the Alleghenies for settlement. To Benjamin Franklin and others, Croghan wrote urgent letters on the importance of Johnson's receiving a directive from the ministry to run a new line pushing

---

55. Johnson to the Lords of Trade, Jan. 31, 1766, O'Callaghan, ed., *New-York Col. Doc.*, VII, 809; Johnson to Croghan, Mar. 28, 1766, *Johnson Papers*, V, 120. Johnson's enthusiastic support for a colony in Illinois is seen in his letters in *ibid.*, XII, 107, 136, 140.

56. Johnson to Gage, Jan. 30, 1766, *Johnson Papers*, V, 18-19; Croghan to Johnson, Feb. 14, 1766, *Coll. of the Ill. State Hist. Lib.*, 11 (1916), 155-56.

westward the area reserved for the Indians' hunting grounds. Such a line, Croghan averred, would put an end to Indian troubles.

Plans for the colony in Illinois continued to claim his attention. In his efforts to expedite the venture, Croghan warned his friends that "one half of England is now land mad and everybody there has thire eys fixt on this cuntry." It was true that a fever of land speculation was sweeping Croghan's world, but few exceeded him in land madness. Benjamin Franklin interested himself in Croghan's project and became its most influential and assiduous promoter.[57]

In due course, a memorial strongly recommended by Johnson and Franklin was presented to the ministry. After listing the many advantages which would accrue to the Crown, the memorial proposed that the king purchase a tract of land and establish a civil government in Illinois. So that a colony might be speedily formed, "a company of gentlemen of character & fortune" stood ready, in return for a grant of a million or more acres, located at their own selection, to bring in at their own expense two thousand white Protestant settlers.

Among the proposals for setting up the colony was the following clause: "Let the first governor be a person experienced in the management of Indian affairs, & who has given proofs of his influence with the savages." It is unlikely that Johnson, who had never visited the Ohio and Illinois country, was intended by this description. Johnson, busy developing his vast landed interests in New York, was in ill health and would have had little to gain by leaving his palatial home. William Franklin, who drew up the memorial, was probably thinking of Croghan. After all, as the younger Franklin wrote his father, the Illinois company was formed at Croghan's instigation.[58]

Between his two trips to Illinois, Croghan spent most of a six months' period at Monckton Hall. He continued to lavish money on the place and bought such luxuries as four labeled decanters for his sideboard and ten whip sillabub glasses. The purchase of two bird fountains and the construction of a rabbit "park" suggest

---

57. *Coll. of the Ill. State Hist. Lib.*, 11 (1916), xiv (introduction).
58. Wharton and others to Johnson, June 6, 1766, and William Franklin to Benjamin Franklin, Apr. 30, 1766, *ibid.*, 221-22, 247-57.

a female interest in the property. While he was absent on his second trip to Illinois, Monckton Hall was well occupied. A gardener, possibly assisted by two Negro slaves whom Croghan had recently bought, took care of the grounds; a Mrs. Yeates presided over the house itself and was waited on by several maids.[59]

Croghan's last few weeks at home were disturbed by his mounting irritation over the Indian present he was to take to Illinois. Gage had left the size of the present to Croghan's discretion, and Croghan "bespoke" from Baynton, Wharton, and Morgan a supply worth £3,445, later referred to as "about £4,000," a very large sum, according to the unhappy Gage. There were virtually no Indian goods to be had in Philadelphia; the goods promised Croghan were at Baynton, Wharton, and Morgan's store at Pittsburgh. The merchants, mindful that Croghan's bills for 1765 had not been paid promptly and that he was going on a hazardous mission from which he might not return, demanded cash in Philadelphia for the goods they would later deliver to him at Pittsburgh. Gage refused to pay out the Crown's money in such an irregular way but consented after Croghan, in despair, announced his determination to resign.[60]

Croghan had reason for anger. He was always being placed in the risky position of paying salaries or engaging goods for the service on his own credit. In 1756, he had purchased £200 of Indian goods on General Stanwix's orders and had never been repaid. Under Amherst, he had suffered a loss of £1,450 which he could not recover. His disaster at the Wabash in 1765 had drained him of £1,500, so he claimed, and that loss had yet to be made good. For all his responsibility and personal risk as Johnson's senior and most active deputy, he received a salary of but £200 a year.

As Bouquet had found, Croghan was difficult to handle. He was an expensive man to have around, and a touchy man when the army tried to control him. Out of sight of his superiors, he let his personal judgment replace his orders. When he left Philadelphia in May, 1766, on his second trip to Illinois, he had John-

59. Croghan's vouchers for 1766, Cadwalader Coll., Hist. Soc. of Pa.
60. Gage to Johnson, Apr. 7, 1766, Croghan to Gage, Apr. 20 and May 1, 1766, Clements Library; Gage to Croghan, May 3, 1766, Cadwalader Coll., Hist. Soc. of Pa.

son's instructions not to exceed the limit of expenditures set by Gage. Before long, however, huge bills began to come in from Croghan's operations in the field. Gage complained to the commander at Fort Pitt that the Indian expenses at that post had been enormous from the time of Croghan's arrival. And to Johnson, Gage wrote, "Mr. Croghan must no longer incurr any expences of this kind at pleasure."[61]

Croghan found a large number of Indians awaiting him at Fort Pitt when he arrived on May 22. They were in an ugly mood, anxious to avenge the murder of some of their people in Virginia and Pennsylvania. Once more, the inexorable tide of white advance was on the rise, and white men invading Indian land had little compunction in killing the hated redskins. Johnson mordantly observed, "Our people in general are very ill calculated to maintain friendship with the Indians. They despise those in peace, whom they fear to meet in war." According to Governor Penn, "No jury in any of our frontier counties will ever condemn a man for killing an Indian. They do not consider it in the light of murder, but as a meritorious act." The brutal fact was that Indians could not safely approach the frontiers, nor could they obtain justice when wronged. This enraged Croghan, who wrote Johnson, "Soveren lord the mobb seem to rule."[62]

In a series of conferences, Croghan quieted the Ohio Indians. Never had he experienced so much difficulty in persuading their warriors not to commit hostilities. His success in mollifying the infuriated braves surprised everyone at Fort Pitt and, as an army officer wrote, "really shows most conspicuously the ascendancy Mr. Croghan has over them." Croghan was deeply discouraged, however, at the inability of the authorities to stem illegal settlement in the Indian country. He warned Gage that this situation might bring on another Indian war.[63]

61. Gage to Johnson, Oct. 5, 1766, *Johnson Papers*, V, 386; Johnson's instructions to Croghan, Apr. 20, 1766, Cadwalader Coll., Hist. Soc. of Pa.; Gage to Murray, Oct. 6, 1766, Clements Library.
62. Johnson to Secretary Conway, June 28, 1766, O'Callaghan, ed., *New-York Col. Doc.*, VII, 836; Croghan to Johnson, Apr. 18, 1766, *Johnson Papers*, V, 182; John Penn to Thomas Penn, Sept. 12, 1766, Penn Mss., Official Correspondence, X, 84, Hist. Soc. of Pa.
63. Croghan to Gage, June 15 and June 17, 1766, Gordon to Gage, June 15, 1766, Clements Library.

On June 18, the Fort Pitt artillery roared a salute to the departure of the most impressive British fleet which the waters of the Ohio, swollen by heavy rains, had ever carried. Two of the thirteen large bateaux carried Croghan's Indian present and provisions for Fort Chartres. Captain Harry Gordon, Gage's chief engineer, glided along in a pretty little boat chosen for its maneuverability. Gordon was charged with charting the course of the Ohio and the Mississippi to New Orleans. A large part of this work was actually done by his capable assistant, Ensign Thomas Hutchins. Once again, Croghan, who commanded the expedition, brought with him some Shawnee chiefs. He also gave free passage to a party of ninety Senecas on their way to war against the southern Indians. Included among Croghan's personal followers were his old friends Dr. Anthon and Andrew Montour.[64]

George Morgan, junior partner of Baynton, Wharton, and Morgan, had charge of a cargo of trading goods worth £8,000. This shipment was to supplement a supply the company had sent to Fort Chartres in March. Morgan, who had doubted the wisdom of venturing into the Illinois trade, felt relaxed and optimistic in Croghan's company. Everything augured well. Croghan had gone so far as to assure him that he would purchase all his goods as presents for the Crown, including those which had gone to Illinois in March. Baynton, Wharton, and Morgan were firmly caught in Croghan's vision of the greatness of Illinois. During 1766, they increased their investment in the Illinois trade to the staggering figure of £75,000. They confidently expected to sell large Indian presents to the Crown, to trade advantageously with the Indians and French, and to supply the Illinois garrison with provisions.[65]

Croghan and his friends enjoyed a delightful journey, floating down the Ohio at a speed of about five miles an hour. About one hundred miles below Fort Pitt, the party saw its first buffalo herd. These herds became unbelievably large and frequent as the bateaux approached the Wabash. Fine weather, pleasantly warm by day and refreshingly cool by night, kept everyone in the best of spirits,

64. Gage to Gordon, May 9, 1766, Murray to Gage, June 18, 1766, Clements Library; Beverly W. Bond, Jr., *The Courses of the Ohio River taken by Lt. T. Hutchins Anno 1766* (Cincinnati, 1942).
65. Savelle, *George Morgan*, 37.

particularly the expedition's leaders who came together three times a day for meals. Morgan was charmed with Captain Gordon's good nature and Hutchins' easy, well-disciplined personality. "But above all," he wrote, "Mr. Croghan is the most enterprising man. He can appear highly pleased when most chagrined and show the greatest indifference when most pleased." Morgan had learned these traits of Croghan's by watching him at Indian conferences.[66]

On June 29, Croghan arrived at the mouth of the Scioto River, 366 miles below Fort Pitt, and was met by most of the Lower Shawnee Nation, whom he had summoned there by messenger. With difficulty, Croghan persuaded the Shawnees not to seek revenge on the Indians who had killed their deputies in 1765. Gordon noted Croghan's patience and good management in swaying the tribe to his views.[67]

At the Shawnee rendezvous, Croghan received alarming news. French traders had told the Illinois Indians that the English intended to attack them and that a great war party had gathered at the mouth of the Wabash to intercept Croghan's expedition. To ward off this impending disaster, Croghan sent Indian messengers overland to the Wabash to assure the chiefs that his mission was peace. He confirmed good relations with the Shawnees by purchasing £1,800-worth of Morgan's cargo as a present for the natives. This was an expense he had not anticipated in his discussions with Gage.[68]

From Scioto, Croghan proceeded cautiously, taking pains that he would not again be surprised by hostile Indians. He visited the Great Lick, a salty mud area of less than an acre where countless buffalo, elk, and deer refreshed themselves. There, he collected scattered specimens of mammoth bones and tusks—elephant bones to Croghan and his contemporaries—which he found scattered about.[69]

At the mouth of the Wabash, one thousand miles below Fort Pitt, the party encamped defensively on an island, but the precaution proved unnecessary. Croghan's scouts reported that the

---

66. Morgan to his wife, June 29-July 8, 1766, *Coll. of the Ill. State Hist. Lib.*, 11 (1916), 315-16.
67. Gordon to Gage, July 8, 1766, Clements Library.
68. Croghan to Gage, July 6, 1766, *ibid*.
69. For data on this trip, see Gordon's journal, *Coll. of the Ill. State Hist. Lib.*, 11 (1916), 290-311.

Illinois Mirage

enemy war party had returned to its towns, if, indeed, it had ever assembled to waylay Croghan at all.

On August 7, the gentle flow of the Ohio River was rudely interrupted by the muddy waters of the turbulent Mississippi. Painfully, the bateaux' men forced the boats more than one hundred miles up this broad stream to Fort Chartres, where the expedition at last arrived on August 20, having traveled nearly thirteen hundred river-borne miles from Fort Pitt. High stone walls gave the military post an appearance of massive strength, but the walls were so thin that the French had never dared fire the cannon through the portholes for fear the shock would crumble the masonry. The stronghold stood only a few yards from the Mississippi, which was so rapidly undermining the bank that it appeared to be only a matter of months before the river would engulf the fort. Lieutenant Colonel John Reed commanded the garrison of some two hundred troops, scarcely fifty of whom were fit for duty. Malaria was the curse of the place. So far, British occupation of Illinois had been a farce; the soldiers had taken over Fort Chartres, but that was about all. The French continued to monopolize the fur trade, and Baynton, Wharton, and Morgan's agent had been unable to do any business.

Croghan called two Indian conferences to improve the situation. At the first, held at nearby Kaskaskia, he reconciled the differences between the Shawnee and Illinois natives. The second conference took place at the fort where a thousand Indians, not counting women and children, had assembled. Despite the complications of dealing with representatives of many different tribes and nations, Croghan succeeded in convincing them all that the French had imposed on them with false stories and that it was to their interest to stand firm in alliance with the King of England. A general peace was declared and the natives agreed to trade with the English. Croghan's negotiations on behalf of the projected colony at Illinois, as recorded in his official report, indicated that the natives had no objection to granting their country to the British provided they were properly paid for it.

The agent found that the French, safely settled just beyond British jurisdiction on the west bank of the Mississippi, were continuing their illicit trade into British territory, even drawing off furs from the Great Lakes. This clandestine commerce was packed with danger to the British, for, as long as the French remained to incite and supply the Indians, an uprising such as that of 1763 could recur. Croghan recommended that army posts be located to cut off the French trade.

With dreams of land speculation in the back of his mind, Croghan had every reason to be generous to the Indians at the Crown's expense. He purchased an additional £1,200-worth of presents from Morgan and incurred other costs at Fort Chartres, which, he frankly wrote Gage, "will greatly increase the expence of my journey."[70] If these charges were to astonish Gage, Morgan was equally aghast at Croghan's refusal to make them even greater by buying out his entire stock as he had promised. Gage would not permit him to do so, Croghan told the irate trader, but he would talk to Gage and convince him that he must be given unlimited credit to safeguard British interests in Illinois. Then, in 1767, Croghan would return to Fort Chartres to hold a treaty embracing all the Indians within a thousand miles. At this treaty, he would sweep Baynton, Wharton, and Morgan's stores clean of all their goods. "I believed the Colonel sincere," wrote Morgan later. "What could induce the Colonel to deceive us in this manner or whether he was deceived himself, I cannot tell." Morgan referred rather feelingly to Croghan's "prudent maxim not to commit any thing to writing."[71]

A few days after the Fort Chartres treaty, Croghan came down with malaria, which so weakened him that he was unable to return across country to Fort Pitt as he had planned. Instead, he accompanied Gordon on his thousand-mile boat ride to New Orleans, where he arrived in the middle of October in a debilitated condition. For about six weeks, he tarried at New Orleans, a small stockaded town notable as the shipping point of the French fur trade. While Gordon and Hutchins began their homeward journey, Croghan and his servants took up quarters at Felix Sicard's, where the Indian agent attempted to regain his strength. Although New Orleans had been ceded to Spain in 1762, the French garrison had yet to be relieved. A Spanish governor, Antonio de Ulloa, had

---

70. Croghan to Gage, Sept. 10, 1766, Clements Library; for condition of Fort Chartres, see Pittman to Gage (inclosure), Dec. 17, 1765, *ibid.*

71. Morgan affidavit, Illinois Historical Survey, University of Illinois.

arrived with a detachment of soldiers but, believing his force too small to cope with angry French sentiment, had sought sanctuary in a small fort at the mouth of the Mississippi.

While recuperating, Croghan became friendly with both the French and Spaniards. He promised to buy Don Antonio two gold watches,[72] and he associated with Bartholomew Macnamara and a Dr. Challon in an import-export business. In December, accompanied by faithful Dr. Anthon, Lieutenant Hunter Sedgwick, formerly of the Fort Chartres garrison, and Dr. Challon, Croghan boarded the brig *Sally* bound for New York. Croghan not only paid for the passage of the entire party but also for the freight of ten thousand gallons of Dr. Challon's molasses with which the brig was loaded. The *Sally* touched at Pensacola, a sickly ill-constructed fort, rounded Florida, sailed past Havana, and headed up the Florida coast.[73]

Reviewing his year's work, Croghan hoped that his visit to Illinois had primed the pump which would flood Baynton, Wharton, and Morgan with furs. His negotiations had been successful, but oratory had to be implemented by action. To monopolize the trade, the assistance of a strong Indian department would be necessary, supported by additional army posts to curb French activity. Unfortunately, Croghan's plans were based on unrealistic considerations. The policy of the Crown was to evacuate posts in the interior, not to build new ones. As for the strong Indian department he and Johnson so much wanted, that hope, too, was doomed. The ministry had decided to scrap the plan of 1764 and to continue the department under army control. Worse yet for Croghan's hopes, Lord Shelburne was now contemplating turning over the supervision of the Indian trade to the individual provinces concerned.[74]

As his ship coasted past the southern provinces, Croghan dreamed of the colony of Illinois and the land grant for which he had petitioned. But he was out of touch with events at home. The

72. Antonio de Ulloa to Croghan, Oct. 11, 1767, Cadwalader Coll., Hist. Soc. of Pa.

73. *Johnson Papers*, V, 422; General William Taylor to Gage, Dec. 13, 1766, Clements Library; Croghan to Captain Peter Dobson, Nov. 29, 1766, Cadwalader Coll., Hist. Soc. of Pa.

74. Shelburne to Gage, Dec. 11, 1766, *Coll. of the Ill. State Hist. Lib.*, 11 (1916), 456.

ministry had, at least temporarily, disapproved the establishment of such a colony. Sensing difficulties, Samuel Wharton was ready to call off the whole project. To Governor Franklin, Wharton wrote: "Will you pardon me for once more requesting of you to urge your father rather to drop the Illenoise affair, than miss succeeding in the restitution [of Indian lands to the "suffering traders"], for be assured the latter would be an immediate very great thing & is of infinitely more consequence." In brief, Croghan's high hopes for an Illinois colony where he would own valuable landed interests, where he might even serve as governor, where the population would grow rich on furs and farming, where British prestige on the far frontier of the Empire would be maintained, all these hopes were eventually to be dashed.[75]

Croghan's stature, however, does not rest on his visionary efforts to build provinces but on his very real ability to deal with Indians. In 1766 he had again demonstrated his brilliant powers as a negotiator. At Fort Pitt, he had pacified the Ohio natives when no one else thought it could be done. He had healed the breach between the Illinois natives and the Shawnees, thereby preserving peace along the communication line between Fort Pitt and Fort Chartres. And finally, at Fort Chartres, he had soothed the fears of the Illinois tribes and brought them into a lasting peace with the British.

Nine years later, James Adair published in London *The History of the American Indians*, dedicated to Croghan and two other men. In this book, Adair wrote that in 1766 Croghan gave the American colonies "more real service in a few months, than all our late southern commissioners of Indian affairs could possibly have done in ages." Adair had questioned Croghan about the perils and fatigues of his mission, and he had received an answer couched in the metaphorical style which Croghan had learned from the natives. While performing his duties, Croghan had replied, "and acting the part of a beloved man with the swan's wing, white pipe, and white beads, for the general good of [my] country, and of its red neighbours, [I] had no leisure to think of any personal dangers that might befall a well-meaning peace-maker."[76]

75. Wharton to William Franklin, Sunday Morning [1767], *ibid.*, 468.
76. James Adair, *The History of the American Indians* (London, 1775), 370-71.

11

The Indian Boundary

NEW YORK HARBOR was astir with activity on January 10, 1767; that Saturday afternoon nine vessels made port, among them the *Sally*. Emerging from the wharfside bustle, Croghan and his friends sought the familiar attractions of George Burns's Broadway tavern. His arrival aroused the customary interest. Croghan traveled so much and on such extraordinary embassies that his comings and goings were closely followed by the press. No name appeared more frequently than his in the scant columns provided for local affairs by Philadelphia's three newspapers.[1]

On Monday, he conferred with Gage about provisioning Fort Chartres (Samuel Wharton, who wanted the provisioning contract, was at Croghan's elbow). Justifying the heavy expenses of his negotiations, Croghan extolled the importance of Illinois: "the frontier of all our Canadian conquests"; a center for the fur trade, the possession of which was necessary to prevent the French from stirring up an Indian war; a place from which large revenues could be derived for Great Britain, especially if a colony were founded there.

He sent a copy of his official report to Benjamin Franklin, who found it informative and entertaining and gave it to Lord Shelburne. Subsequently, Franklin wrote Croghan in a dejected vein that he wished more attention were paid in England to the recommendations of knowledgeable Americans. "You have doubtless," added Franklin, "render'd great service to Government by your negociations among the Indians. I take every opportunity of

---

1. George Burns's bill for Jan. 10-29, 1767, Croghan's vouchers for 1767, Cadwalader Coll., Hist. Soc. of Pa.; *New-York Gazette*, Jan. 15, 1767.

mentioning it, and I hope you may in time obtain suitable reward." Croghan's pressing arguments for strengthening the British hold on Illinois were unfavorably received by Gage. The general doubted that the advantages of retaining that country offset the expenses of the Fort Chartres garrison. Distressed, Croghan wrote Franklin of Gage's "unjust sentiments relative to that acquisition."[2]

Croghan remained in New York nearly three weeks settling his accounts, which, as usual, were enormous. A partial statement of his expenses amounted to £8,400. Although Gage expressed dismay at the outlay, he ordered payment. Croghan was now in a position to carry out his threat to resign. Dissatisfied with the army's financial procedure and irritated with Gage's refusal to make good the private losses he had suffered in the service, the Indian agent publicly announced his retirement.

The authorities were resolved to hold him if they could. Gage, whose only complaint was Croghan's extravagance, thought highly of him. So did Johnson, whose influence over Croghan was far greater than the general's. "I have for the last time advised him to think farther about it," the superintendent wrote Gage, "and indeed I should be at some loss if he pursued his inclinations."[3]

While hopeful candidates submitted their names as his successor, Croghan sorted out the numerous curiosities he had picked up on his travels. These he parceled out to his friends—oddities for the Reverend Thomas Barton of Lancaster; Indian war dresses and specimens of the mandrake plant for Sir William; four ivory mastodon tusks, one of them six feet long, for Benjamin Franklin; and a box of tusks and a jawbone with several teeth for Lord Shelburne. Some of these bones were later deposited in the Tower of London, others at the British Museum. Croghan's fossils aroused a storm of controversy both in Europe and America. Learned papers were written about them, and Franklin and other

---

2. Croghan to Benjamin Franklin, Jan. 27, 1767, *Coll. of the Ill. State Hist. Lib.*, 11 (1916), 500-3; Benjamin Franklin to Croghan, Apr. 14, 1767, Cadwalader Coll., Hist. Soc. of Pa.; Gage to Johnson, Jan. 25, 1767, O'Callaghan, ed., *Doc. Hist. of N. Y.*, II, 836-37.

3. Croghan's expense account, *Coll. of the Ill. State Hist. Lib.*, 11 (1916), 511; *Johnson Papers*, V, 485; Johnson to Gage, Jan. 29, 1767, O'Callaghan, ed., *Doc. Hist. of N. Y.*, II, 838-39.

philosophers pondered the surprising discovery of "elephants" in America. The finding of their migration route from Asia, wrote a Philadelphian, would provide a northwest passage by land to the Orient.[4]

Too weakened by his recent illness to report to Johnson Hall, Croghan, accompanied by a group of friends, returned to Philadelphia. This was the heyday of Monckton Hall, for Croghan kept a house party going weeks on end. Gathered about his roaring fireside, secure from grim February weather, were Dr. Challon, Dr. Anthon, Edward Ward, Hunter Sedgwick, Captain Norman MacLeod of the Indian department and his bride, whom Croghan affectionately called "dear litle Helen of Greece," and many others—merchants, land speculators, politicians, and westerners.[5]

Hogsheads of rum and pipes of Madeira were rolled into the cellar. Nothing but the finest quality suited Croghan's taste. Writing to Macnamara in New Orleans for five or six cases of claret, he cautioned him, "I do not regard the price, so I can obtain the best." From Benjamin Randolph's celebrated shop he ordered another collection of expensive furniture, and, once again, Fleeson the upholsterer was set to work with his green damask. The backgammon tables, already shaken by hard use, were repaired. In short, the charms of Croghan's home bade fair to equal the graciousness of its host. "That old English hospitality once so much & so justly boasted of has taken refuge in Monckton Hall and retired to live with cordial unfeigned friendship under the same happy roof," wrote Hunter Sedgwick upon his departure. "Farewell! my worthy friend, time, place, prosperity or adversity shall never make me forget thy many virtues."[6]

While his strength flowed steadily back, Croghan spent many hours at his desk. To Thomas Penn, he sent the report of his

4. *Pennsylvania Chronicle*, Oct. 19-26, Oct. 26-Nov. 2, Nov. 2-9, 1767; Albert Henry Smyth, ed., *The Writings of Benjamin Franklin* (New York, 1906), V, 39-40, 92-93; Croghan to Shelburne, Jan. 16, 1767, Clements Library; Penn to the Reverend Barton, June 17, 1767, and July 20, 1768, Penn Letter Book, IX, 133, 271-72, Hist. Soc. of Pa.; William Robertson, *The History of America* (London, 1777), I, 454-55, discusses the bones and gives as his authority Croghan's journal in his possession; Boyd, *Jefferson*, VI, 209.

5. Croghan to Johnson, Feb. 23, 1767, *Coll. of the Ill. State Hist. Lib.*, 11 (1916), 513-14.

6. Croghan to Macnamara, Mar. 19, 1768, Sedgwick to Croghan, June 10. 1767, Croghan's vouchers for 1767, Cadwalader Coll., Hist. Soc. of Pa.

last year's mission as well as inquiries and requests. Had the king granted him the twenty thousand acres in New York for which he had petitioned? What was the status of his memorial on Indian trade losses? Would Penn grant him forty thousand acres in the tract that would come to Penn when the new boundary was run? Although the proprietor disapproved this suggestion, shrewdly intended by Croghan as a reward for his forthcoming services in obtaining the most advantageous boundary, he did exert himself in the other matters. When he found that Croghan was granted only ten thousand acres in New York, Penn called on the secretary of state for American affairs and successfully persuaded him to allow Croghan another ten thousand acres.[7]

Croghan spent most of March at Johnson's stately home. He was initiated into the Masonic Lodge which Johnson had founded a year earlier. This was evidently the only time Croghan ever attended a meeting, although he was interested in the order and purchased several sets of glasses ornamented with its devices. Johnson prevailed on him to withdraw his resignation from the Indian department and wrote a strong letter to Gage which induced the general to pay Croghan £1,732 in partial compensation for his personal losses in the service.[8]

While with Johnson, Croghan decided to apply to the governor for a large tract of land in New York. Johnson maintained that the northwestern part of the colony had the best soil and the healthiest climate in America. Because of the two great communications it commanded—the Mohawk River west to the Great Lakes and the northern route to Montreal—this section was bound to become thickly populated. Johnson's program for developing his holdings was one that appealed to Croghan. On his huge estate, the superintendent had built a town, Johnstown, and had settled more than a hundred families.[9]

---

7. Penn to Croghan, Apr. 11 and Sept. 12, 1767, Penn to William Allen, May 19, 1767, Penn to John Penn, May 13, 1768, Penn Letter Book, IX, 107, 118, 188, 253, Hist. Soc. of Pa.

8. Minutes of Masonic Lodge at Johnstown, courtesy of Milton W. Hamilton; Johnson to Gage, Apr. 3, 1767, Johnson to Captain Maturin, Apr. 24, 1767, O'Callaghan, ed., *Doc. Hist. of N. Y.*, II, 846, 852; Croghan set his personal losses while in the service at £3,364, Cadwalader Coll., Hist. Soc. of Pa.; *Johnson Papers*, V, 559.

9. Johnson to Daniel Burton, Dec. 23, 1767, *Johnson Papers*, VI, 27-28.

Speculators, like Croghan, preferred to acquire new grants of land, which did not cost as much as lands already patented. To do this they had to buy land from the Indian owners and then circumvent certain legal difficulties, for only the governor was allowed to purchase Indian land, and the governor was not allowed to grant more than one thousand acres to any one person. Nevertheless, men of influence and means found ways to obtain large holdings.[10] A speculator could associate with ninety-nine straw men and apply for 100,000 acres. When this land was granted, those who had lent their names would withdraw. Moreover, the governor was not above buying Indian lands for individuals. In October, 1766, Governor Sir Henry Moore had come to Johnson Hall for this purpose. Requests for more large purchases, mostly around the headwaters of the Delaware River, were again piling up in the governor's office.[11]

Croghan's first step was to apply to Governor Moore for permission to purchase Indian land. When this permission was granted, Croghan would then bargain with the Indians (no doubt he had already made his arrangements with them). The lands were then ready for purchase by the governor with Croghan's money. In due course, they would be surveyed and colonial officials would grant a patent for the tract.

Croghan was absorbed in this scheme when word reached Johnson Hall of a dangerous situation at Fort Pitt. Illegal settlements near the Ohio had again aroused the natives to such a point that an outbreak appeared imminent. Moreover, the traders at Fort Pitt, flouting the rule that all trading had to be done at army posts, had left for the Indian villages. Because Johnson's commissaries had not been vested with sufficient authority, it had been impossible to enforce the provisions of the Indian plan of 1764.[12] To soothe the natives, Johnson ordered Croghan to Fort Pitt, where the agent arrived on May 24. Although the chiefs complained bitterly to him about white settlements and murder, Croghan prevailed on them to remain quiet and return to their

10. Johnson to Daniel Horsmanden, Oct. 30, 1767, *ibid.*, V, 770.
11. *Calendar of the N. Y. Colonial Manuscripts, Indorsed Land Papers* (Albany, 1864), 414.
12. Johnson to Gage, Apr. 1, 1767, O'Callaghan, ed., *Doc. Hist. of N. Y.*, II, 843-45.

villages, promising them that Gage and Johnson would redress their wrongs.[13]

Croghan hastened east. In Philadelphia, Governor Penn detained him with questions about the Indians who were to accompany Mason and Dixon on the westward survey of a line which symbolically was to divide the North from the South. "It would be very difficult to manage this business without his assistance," wrote John Penn.[14]

In New York, on June 27, Croghan petitioned Governor Moore for forty thousand acres lying between Lakes Otsego and Canandaigua at the source of the Susquehanna, land for which he had already received a deed from the Indian owners. In his memorial Croghan stated, "Your petitioners having particular connections of friendship with the said Indians have prevailed on them to consent to dispose of their native Indian right in the said tract." Croghan and his thirty-nine Pennsylvania associates, all friends of long standing, offered to bring the Indian owners to the governor and to pay the money which Moore must tender them for their land. On July 6, Moore and his council granted Croghan's request to make an Indian purchase.[15]

Despite shuttling back and forth between Johnson Hall and New York on Indian affairs, Croghan was able to spend most of the summer with Sir William, who was in bad health. Since 1761, he had been troubled with a stomach complaint; he was also bothered with a swelling of his legs. The bullet in his thigh, a souvenir of the Battle of Lake George, gave him increasing pain. Seldom was he well enough to mount his horse. To obtain relief, Johnson visited the newly discovered Lebanon Springs in August, and Croghan accompanied him.[16]

Reports from the outposts that the Indian situation again looked critical soon ended their vacation. Ominous rumors that the Senecas and twelve western nations were to meet in Shawnee

13. Croghan to Gage, June 3, 1767, Clements Library.
14. Penn to Joseph Shippen, June 17, 1767, *The Collector*, 67 (1955), Nos. 1, 2, Whole No. 744, Walter R. Benjamin Autographs.
15. Land Papers, XXIII, 159, 160, New York State Library; *Calendar of Council Minutes, 1668-1783* (Albany, 1902), 532.
16. Johnson to John Wetherhead, July 12, 1767, Johnson to Samuel Johnson, Dec. 1, 1767, *Johnson Papers*, V, 590, 840-41; Johnson to Gage, Aug. 21, 1767, O'Callaghan, ed., *Doc. Hist. of N. Y.*, II, 862.

territory sent Johnson into the Iroquois country and Croghan to Detroit to prevent the natives from organizing a warlike league.[17] Boarding an Albany sloop, Croghan began a six-day passage to New York. Mindful of his personal plans, he called on Governor Moore in an unsuccessful effort to persuade him to visit Johnson Hall that fall and to buy the Otsego tract. After conferences with Gage, Croghan's western mission took full form. He was to penetrate the designs of the natives; to deliver to the Indians at Detroit two of their braves who had been held for the murder of a white man and thus create good will; to conduct a court of inquiry into the conduct of the Detroit Indian commissary; and to carry letters recalling Major Robert Rogers from his post at Michilimackinac, where the ranger's conduct had outraged Johnson and Gage.[18]

In Philadelphia, Croghan paused to confer with Samuel Wharton. Both Croghan and Wharton were deeply worried over the failure of the Crown to order a new Indian boundary. Until the new line was run, there was no hope of obtaining a land grant in restitution of their trading losses. The two conspirators, therefore, devised a plan to force the ministry to do what they wanted. Knowing that the Crown would do all it could to prevent a general Indian war, Croghan and Wharton decided to represent the present Indian unrest as the prelude of a disastrous uprising which could be forestalled only by making a vast purchase of Indian land and establishing a new, natural, and permanent boundary between white settlements and the natives' hunting grounds. Four years later, in another moment of crisis, Wharton warned Croghan, "Nothing will do but to act as you and I did about the boundary line. Mens passions must be alarmed and awakened."[19]

Dutifully, Croghan's and Wharton's friends followed their suggestions and wrote to important people in London, urging the absolute necessity of a new boundary line which alone could pre-

17. Johnson to Gage, Sept. 6, 1767, O'Callaghan, ed., *Doc. Hist. of N. Y.*, II, 863; Croghan to Benjamin Franklin, Oct. 2, 1767, Cadwalader Coll., Hist. Soc. of Pa.
18. Croghan to Johnson, Sept. 14, 1767, *Johnson Papers*, V, 676-77; Howard H. Peckham, *George Croghan's Journal of His Trip to Detroit in 1767* (Ann Arbor, 1939), 7-9.
19. Samuel Wharton to Croghan, July 21, 1771, Cadwalader Coll., Hist. Soc. of Pa.

vent war. William Franklin and Sir William Johnson were among those chosen to alarm and awaken the ministry. An impressive number of letters from the leaders of the proprietary party were directed to Thomas Penn, while, simultaneously, the leaders of the anti-proprietary party were writing to Benjamin Franklin.[20]

When Franklin received this correspondence in November, he hurried to Lord Shelburne. Before long, Thomas Penn was also waiting on the secretary of state. Shelburne, a diligent statesman tremendously interested in the development of western America, had recently laid before the Board of Trade recommendations that the management of the Indian trade revert from the Indian department to the colonies. Making reference to extracts from Croghan's letters, Shelburne also recommended that a colony be founded at Illinois. Croghan's Illinois aspirations thus teetered on the verge of success. Although Shelburne's western plan was most comprehensive, it did not contemplate a new Indian boundary.[21]

When Franklin delivered Croghan's almost hysterical warning of war, as well as letters from Galloway and Wharton, the Earl was astonished to learn that the Indians expected a new boundary, that Johnson, whose sentiments on the subject had been asked by the Board of Trade in 1764, had evidently led the Indians to expect that the line would actually be established, and that the natives would be amply paid for the land they ceded. The crux of the matter, so forcibly brought out in the letters from America, was the inevitability of war unless the line was ordered—no longer could the Indian agents delude the natives with promises that their lands seized by white squatters would be paid for.

The Board of Trade, which had had Shelburne's new plan in hand since October 5 (it was not to report its opinion until March 7, 1768), was as surprised as Shelburne about the need for a new boundary. The Board gave the problem its immediate considera-

20. Croghan to Johnson, Sept. 25, 1767, and Mar. 1, 1768, *Johnson Papers*, V, 700-2, and VI, 129; Samuel Wharton to Benjamin Franklin, Sept. 30, 1767, Clements Library; Croghan to Penn, Oct. 1, 1767, Cadwalader Coll., Hist. Soc. of Pa.; O'Callaghan, ed., *New-York Col. Doc.*, VII, 985-86.

21. Benjamin Franklin to William Franklin, Nov. 25, 1767, *Coll. of the Ill. State Hist. Lib.*, 16 (1921), 119; Penn to John Penn, Dec. 12, 1767, Penn to Johnson, Dec. 12, 1767, Penn Letter Book, IX, 199-201, Hist. Soc. of Pa.

tion and, on December 23, recommended that the line be run "to prevent the fatal consequences of an Indian war that seems at present to threaten the Middle Colonies." Shelburne endorsed this policy, and, before long, orders were on their way to America authorizing Johnson to take the necessary action.[22]

Having set this train of events in course, Croghan arrived at Fort Pitt on October 16. There he found the Indians in a confused and exasperated mood and learned that their great meeting in the Shawnee country had been postponed until the spring.[23] After a week at Pittsburgh, no doubt spent at Croghan Hall, which he had rebuilt after its destruction by the Indians in 1763, Croghan continued on to Detroit, holding conferences at Indian villages en route, divining the sentiments of the chiefs, and promoting peace.

At Detroit, Croghan spent ten busy days reproaching the Indians for their bad behavior and settling differences between the commissary and the traders. In private meetings with the natives, he made repeated efforts to get at the truth of war rumors. Croghan's western tour seems to have quieted the Indians; at any rate, they did not hold the meeting he had been sent to prevent. Bidding adieu to Dr. Anthon, who decided to resume his practice at Detroit, the hard-traveling Indian agent was back at Monckton Hall by the turn of the year.[24]

While Croghan was dismounting at his home, angry voices were reverberating through the Statehouse, for the Assembly was in session and its prime topic of discussion, the Indian situation, had become a political football. Speaker Joseph Galloway and his cohorts were striving to put the blame for Indian troubles on Governor Penn. When the assemblymen learned that the Indian agent was in town, they instantly summoned him to their chamber. Croghan informed them of his recent mission, of the number of settlers on Indian land, and stressed the necessity of a new Indian boundary. The next day, the Assembly resolved to instruct its London agents "in the warmest terms" to solicit orders from the Crown establishing "a boundary between the colonies and the

[22]. *Pa. Archives*, IV, 281.
[23]. Croghan to Gage, Oct. 18, 1767, Clements Library; Croghan to Johnson, Oct. 18, 1767, *Johnson Papers*, V, 736-38.
[24]. *Pennsylvania Chronicle*, Dec. 28, 1767-Jan. 4, 1768.

natives, the want whereof appears . . . to be one of the causes of the present unfriendly disposition of the Indians." The Assembly also passed a bill sentencing to death anyone, except Croghan, who settled on Indian land. After a tussle with the governor, the Assembly, now grown tenderly considerate of Croghan's privileges, went on record that he should not be restrained from enlarging his improvements near Fort Pitt. Nothing he might do would annoy the Indians, declared the legislators, who approvingly commented on Croghan's address, fidelity, and eminent services.[25]

Immediately after his appearance before the Assembly, Croghan went to New York. He called on Sir Henry Moore, who told him of his intention to go to Johnson Hall in May to purchase Indian lands. Croghan had thought that this transaction would be made a year before. As a result, he had for months maintained eighty destitute families whom he intended to settle on his Otsego tract. To hasten their settlement, he petitioned Moore for the right to survey his lands before purchase, so that his settlers could move in as soon as Moore bought the tract. Permission was granted, and Croghan's survey was run in the spring of 1768. What became of his eighty families, or whether they ever existed other than on the paper of his petition, remains a mystery.[26]

"I find the General has still the same fears of a rupter this spring with the Indians," Croghan wrote Johnson, "& I have nott endaverd to lesen them, butt he seems much embarrised as if he did nott know what to do."[27] Gage knew enough to strengthen the outposts and to caution the commanding officers against surprise attacks. But whether war would actually take place neither he nor Croghan could tell. Into this tense and critical situation, a semicivilized Pennsylvanian dropped a bombshell.

In January, 1768, frontiersman and noted troublemaker Frederick Stump, assisted by his servant John Ironcutter, massacred ten Indians in cold blood on the banks of the Susquehanna. Worse yet, he scalped them, an action which Indians understood as a declaration of war. Crippled with rheumatism, which was to be a chronic winter complaint from now on, Croghan returned to

25. *Pa. Archives*, Eighth Series, VII, 6077, 6078-80, 6082, 6105, 6115-17.
26. Land Papers, XXIV, 73, N. Y. State Lib.
27. Croghan to Johnson, Feb. 2, 1768, *Johnson Papers*, VI, 91-92.

Philadelphia to cope with this latest crisis, a crisis which was not improved by Stump's rescue by a mob at high noon from the Carlisle jail. The spirit of the Black Boys had burst forth with renewed fury at the thought of a frontiersman being brought to trial in Philadelphia.[28]

Once again, discords rang through the Statehouse while the assemblymen debated. Both parties called on Croghan, who by now was weary of their bickering and bored with their politics. On his advice, the colony appropriated £2,500 to be laid out by the Indian department in condoling with the natives over Stump's murders. Of this sum, Johnson decided to give £1,300 to the Six Nations and allotted the rest to Croghan for the Ohio natives, who, fearful of war, flocked to Pittsburgh in the hope that he would come to explain the significance of Stump's barbarity.[29]

While awaiting the orders which would send him west with the condolence present, Croghan settled his affairs and rented Monckton Hall, in expectation of moving to his new home at Lake Otsego. His New York speculations were soon to put him to the heaviest expenses he had ever known, but he appeared undaunted despite recent painful events. During the past year, he had been hard pressed and forced to expedients to raise cash. To merchant William Pollard, he owed £400 sterling for bills of exchange which had been protested. "He is much in debt & I fear he will ship off to the northwd," wrote Joseph Simon, one of his creditors. In June, 1767, Joseph Galloway appeared in court three times to defend Croghan in suits brought by creditors. Later in the year, the Ohio Company obtained a judgment of £1,000 on a bond he had signed some fifteen years earlier. Croghan had to satisfy at least one claim that was twenty years old.[30]

28. Croghan to Johnson, Feb. 7, 1768, *ibid.*, 96-97.
29. Alexander McKee to Croghan, Feb. 13, 1768, Croghan to Johnson, Feb. 17, 1768, Johnson to Croghan, Mar. 5, 1768, *ibid.*, 102, 107-9, 136; Croghan to Benjamin Franklin, Feb. 12, 1768, Cadwalader Coll., Hist. Soc. of Pa.
30. Croghan to Johnson, Mar. 18, 1768, and William Edgell's debt paid Mar. 8, 1768, Cadwalader Coll., Thomas Wharton Day Book, E, 230-31, Leonard T. Beale Coll., Harry Gordon to Baynton, May 21, 1767, Hist. Soc. of Pa.; Joseph Simon to Barnard Gratz, Feb. 15, 1767, Henry Joseph Coll., American Jewish Archives (microfilm at Hist. Soc. of Pa.); June term, 1767, Docket of Court of Common Pleas, 83, 84, 167, Phila. City Hall; Croghan folder, McAllister Coll., Lib. Co. of Phila.

His most serious entanglements were under arbitration. Of forty tracts sold to Peters and Clark in 1763, judges rejected twenty-five as unfit for sale and were willing to pass on little more than half the acreage in the remaining tracts. The purchasers demanded their money back, and Hockley asked Croghan for the £2,000 he had guaranteed him in the deal. Another group of arbiters was shortly to deny Croghan's stand that he was not responsible for Thomas Smallman's debt to Buchanan and Hughes and were to assess the Indian agent upwards of £3,000.[31]

Unable to satisfy old debts, Croghan was in immediate need of cash to finance current speculations. Two years earlier, he had borrowed £500 from Samuel Wharton's brother Thomas, and it was to Thomas Wharton that Croghan again turned in February, 1768. That Thomas Wharton agreed to endorse Croghan's nine bills of exchange on a London merchant for £625 sterling again proved Croghan's remarkable ability to make men believe in him and his schemes, for Thomas Wharton was a canny, successful, hard-boiled businessman. Even when it was later learned that all these bills, like those Croghan had given Pollard, had been protested for non-payment, even then Thomas Wharton did not lose faith in Croghan.[32]

Croghan was too forward-looking, too much a believer in himself, to fret. All would yet come right, and, in the meantime, life should be enjoyed. He celebrated St. Patrick's Day with the Royal Regiment of Ireland, lately arrived from the old sod and now quartered at the Second Street barracks. How these troops paraded, and how they startled staid Quaker merchants by firing volley after volley over the coffee house! Later, Croghan dined with the officers on good beef and claret at Peg Muller's, and many a toast he proposed to Sir William and the Six Nations. The next day, he entertained the entire group of thirty at the Centre House, near the race track, and then left Philadelphia with, as he had anticipated, "a very aching head." His party had been a gay

---

31. Croghan folder, Society Autograph Coll., Hist. Soc. of Pa.; Bedford County Deed Books, D, 621, and E, 158; report of Samuel Wallis under cover of January, 1767, Wallis Papers, Reel 19:4, and Buchanan, Hughes, and Smallman folder, Cadwalader Coll., Hist. Soc. of Pa.

32. Thomas Wharton Ledger, fol. 52, Croghan entry for May 21, 1766, and Thomas Wharton Day Book, E, 230-31, Leonard T. Beale Coll., Hist. Soc. of Pa.

one as the bill for music, liquor, and broken glasses still attests. In his pocket, the agent carried Sir William's welcome letter informing him that the Indian boundary had been approved and giving him instructions for his conduct at his Fort Pitt conference: "After the first ceremonys you will take the hatchet out of their heads & bury it deep under a large pine tree so as it shall be no more found with regard to which and the other ceremonys no part whereof should be omitted."[33]

Croghan, however, did not go directly to Fort Pitt. He rode to Chester so that he might, according to Thomas Wharton, "spend a day there & adjust some of his affairs which he could not so conveniently do while he remained here." This carefully reserved explanation sheds little light on the visit to Chester, nor was it intended to. At Chester, Croghan sat in conference with a group of Philadelphians, who, like Croghan, also found it convenient to adjust their affairs away from home. Included among them were Samuel and Thomas Wharton and Croghan's lawyer, Joseph Galloway. It was probably Galloway's presence which necessitated the out-of-town rendezvous, for the subject discussed was evidently the highly secret organization of the syndicate which was acquiring the restitution rights of the Indian traders of 1763. Men in public life preferred to keep their connection with this group of speculators quiet, and Galloway was speaker of the Pennsylvania Assembly.

Their conference was interrupted by the arrival of an express rider, who had galloped from Carlisle to Philadelphia and then on to Chester, with a message of life and death for Croghan. The Black Boys, learning that Croghan was on his way to soothe the Indians and give them presents, had again risen in their wrath. There would be no treaty, there would be no Indian present, and, if they caught Croghan, they would kill him.

Knowing only too well the importance of pacifying the Ohio Indians and the inability of civil authorities to protect his person while en route to Fort Pitt, Croghan wrote the garrison commander at Philadelphia to forward a company of men to meet him at Lancaster and to accompany him west. He was soon on the road

33. Croghan to Johnson, Mar. 18, 1768, bill dated Mar. 19, 1768, Johnson to Croghan, Mar. 5, 1768, and instructions of same date, Cadwalader Coll., Hist. Soc. of Pa.

again, pushing through a heavy fall of snow to Lancaster. "Should those lawless people persist in their intentions and Col. Croghan be cut off," Thomas Wharton wrote Benjamin Franklin, "it will be one of the most fatal strokes that can happen to those governments [the American colonies] as there is no person besides himself whom the Indians to the westward have a full confidence in, and war will in all probability immediately follow."[34]

Although a military escort hurried up from Philadelphia to meet him, Croghan, casting caution to the winds, did not await its protection. In the belief that the Ohio Indians were about to hold a secret council, Croghan spurred on to Fort Pitt to head off such a dangerous meeting.[35]

Three weeks after his safe arrival—no Black Boy barred his way—the Indian agent opened a conference with more than eleven hundred Ohio chiefs and warriors who had answered his summons. Although the natives, conscious of many grievances, were sulky and difficult at first, Croghan soon reconciled them. He even brought around the Shawnees, who were particularly troublesome in demanding that the British cease navigating the Ohio and demolish their forts. As usual, observers marveled at Croghan's skill. One of them wrote: "Col. Croghan has been indefatigable & never displayed his great influence and address with the natives, more signally and successfully." According to Gage, Croghan's treaty averted the war which many experts had firmly believed was about to devastate the frontiers.[36]

Fear had been expressed that Croghan would not faithfully carry out the mission of condolence entrusted to him by Pennsylvania. Richard Peters, all his old distrust of Croghan reawakened by the Assembly's fondness for him, had, indeed, warned Thomas Penn that Croghan might endeavor to widen the breach with the

34. Thomas Wharton to Benjamin Franklin, Mar. 29, 1768, Leonard T. Beale Coll., Croghan to [Col. Wilkins], Sunday, Mar. [20], 1768, Cadwalader Coll., Hist. Soc. of Pa.

35. Wilkins to Gage, Mar. 20 and Mar. 21, 1768, Clements Library; Croghan to John Penn, Mar. 27, 1768, Cadwalader Coll., Hist. Soc. of Pa.; Gage to Shelburne, Apr. 24, 1768, *Coll. of the Ill. State Hist. Lib.*, 16 (1921), 270.

36. William Goddard published the treaty minutes, Phila., 1769; Croghan to Thomas Wharton, May 7, 1768, *Pa. Mag. of Hist. and Biog.*, 15 (1891), 430; Gage to Hillsborough, June 18, 1768, *Coll. of the Ill. State Hist. Lib.*, 16 (1921), 323.

Indians rather than close it. Aware of ugly suspicions, Croghan had insisted that Pennsylvania agents attend the treaty to observe his conduct. These commissioners subsequently submitted glowing reports on Croghan's performance, and the *Pennsylvania Gazette* took pains to note that the Indian agent had shown "the most sincere and earnest desire to promote the particular interests and welfare of this Province."[37]

Early in June, Croghan attended Sir Henry Moore's purchase of Indian lands at Johnson Hall, looking out not only for his own concerns but for those of William Franklin, Joseph Galloway, and Thomas Wharton, whom he had encouraged to take up a large tract. Croghan was also in charge of securing lands for British army officers and wealthy New York speculators. These transactions completed, he hastened to New London, where Sir William had gone in April to recuperate from a "violent disorder of the bowels."[38]

Much had happened recently which affected Croghan's future. The Board of Trade had ruled against forming a colony in Illinois, and Lord Hillsborough had taken over the conduct of American affairs from Shelburne. The ministry had ordered the number of British forts in Indian country reduced to the minimum. The Indian department, so long a source of heavy expense to the Crown, had been shorn of its control of the Indian trade, and was to continue on a small budget as a diplomatic agency only. But overshadowing all of these important changes were the orders to re-establish the Indian boundary, an action which would open up vast western areas for settlement. Already, Johnson had summoned the Indians to a treaty to agree on the line and to receive payment for the lands they were to relinquish.

To Pennsylvania's "suffering traders," this treaty was all-important. Ever since Croghan's return from England in 1764, they had been agitating for an Indian grant in compensation for their losses in the French and Indian wars. Croghan had been instrumental in organizing the traders into what became known as

37. Penn to Peters, June 11, 1768, Penn Letter Book, IX, 270, Hist. Soc. of Pa.; *Pennsylvania Gazette*, June 2, 1768.
38. O'Callaghan, ed., *New-York Col. Doc.*, VIII, 76; F. W. Hecht to Croghan, Sept. 6, 1768, Records of the Provincial Council, Hist. Soc. of Pa.

the Indiana Company—a company comprised of a group of men who had lost some £86,000 in 1763. Each trader's loss represented his share in the company, although, in actuality, stock ownership was not that clear-cut. The fact that Croghan and Governor Franklin, neither of whom had been an Indian trader in 1763, owned shares was a profound secret. Their participation was, presumably, in recognition of their influence, and for other special reasons. Half of Thomas Smallman's loss, for example, actually belonged to Croghan. Croghan was also credited with a loss of £2,250, evidently for the destruction of his Croghan Hall improvements, which he sold to Joseph Galloway and Thomas Wharton, who chose to speculate in the Indiana venture.[39]

This much later became known, but the underlying ownership of the traders' grant has long remained a deep mystery. The traders had conveyed to William Trent their rights to restitution, subject to 30 per cent and, in a few cases, 50 per cent of their value payable to the traders if Trent obtained confirmation of the land grant from the Crown. Trent, in turn, had conveyed the speculation to John Hughes, who held it in trust subject to distribution in seven shares. The syndicate who owned these shares was composed of William Franklin, John Baynton, Samuel Wharton, George Morgan, and William Trent, who owned a share each; Robert Callender, who owned half a share; and George Croghan, who owned a share and a half.[40] Although Croghan was the largest shareholder, his interest was lessened by his intention to give his holding to Baynton, Wharton, and Morgan, who were now in receivership through following his advice to enter the Illinois trade. Untold bitterness resulted when Baynton and

---

39. Smallman conveyed half of his loss to Croghan on Apr. 8, 1769. See deed of Croghan and John Baynton, Apr. 19, 1769, Gratz Coll., Hist. Soc. of Pa. Like others seeking restitution, Croghan in March, 1768, deeded to Trent his right to his £2,250 loss, retaining only a percentage of its value for himself. It was this 30 per cent which he sold to Galloway and Thomas Wharton for £450 on Dec. 10, 1768. Thomas Wharton Ledger, fol. 89, Leonard T. Beale Coll., Hist. Soc. of Pa. For a history of this speculative venture, see George E. Lewis, *The Indiana Company, 1763-1798* (Glendale, Calif., 1941).

40. Trent's deed, Dec. 13, 1768, Papers Relating to Indian Losses, 59, Hist. Soc. of Pa. In the distribution of shares according to this deed, both Trent's and Croghan's interests were temporarily covered by the names of others— Trent's by the name of Charles Wharton, Croghan's by the name of Joseph Galloway.

Morgan found that Croghan had not kept his promise but had given his entire interest to Wharton.

Samuel Wharton was the spokesman for the traders and was assisted by William Trent, who did the field work. It was Trent who obtained legal powers, making himself attorney for the group. While devoting his time to this task, Trent was in large part supported by Croghan, who lent him £1,319.[41] Thus Croghan, as a stockholder and as banker, had a very real stake in the traders' grant, a stake which depended on the Indians' voluntarily giving the traders a part of the western lands to be ceded when the new boundary was agreed on.

At Fisher's Island and at a tavern at the mouth of New London harbor, Croghan, Wharton, and Trent sat in close conversation with Sir William Johnson. It was vital that the superintendent not waver from the friendly attitude he had all along displayed toward restitution for the traders' losses. Sir William gave the Pennsylvanians assurances of complete cooperation; he would see to it that the Indians made the grant.[42] From New London, Croghan and Wharton accompanied Johnson to Lebanon Springs for a brief visit. By the middle of July, Sir William had returned to Johnson Hall and was busy assembling a huge Indian present for the treaty scheduled at Fort Stanwix late in September.

Croghan now had an opportunity to devote nearly two months to his Lake Otsego purchase. His daughter's rapidly increasing family was with him, for he had persuaded Augustine Prevost to sell his commission and to establish a homestead at the head of Lake Otsego.[43] In April, Christopher Yates, accompanied by assistants and eight Indians, had spent three weeks surveying Croghan's Otsego tract. This survey presumably took in the forty thousand acres Croghan had applied for, but that amount was not enough to satisfy Croghan's voracious land hunger. In September, Yates and four chain bearers spent twenty-five additional days

---

41. Croghan folder, McAllister Coll., Lib. Co. of Phila.
42. Samuel Wharton to Thomas Wharton, June 23, 1768, Wharton Coll., Croghan to Thomas Wharton, June 22, 1768, Cadwalader Coll., Hist. Soc. of Pa.
43. Prevost to Colonel Maitland, received Oct. 12, 1767, Clements Library; Johnson to Croghan, Feb. 29, 1768, *Johnson Papers*, VI, 123.

surveying, after which Yates delivered to Croghan maps and field books describing a tract of more than 100,000 acres.[44]

Not waiting for a formal patent, Croghan set to work improving his land. Men were employed to clear twenty acres for the plow at the very foot of the lake, beside the Susquehanna's outlet. This was the place where Croghan planned to build his home. Up and down the wagon trace from the Mohawk River, "Young Groot," his wagoner, brought barrels of food and supplies to Prevost's house at the head of the lake. From there, the supplies went on by boat. Carpenters' hammers awakened unaccustomed echoes as Croghan and Prevost pioneered their settlements.[45]

Croghan, no doubt, accompanied Johnson and Governor Franklin in their bateau up the Mohawk River to Fort Stanwix. A score of bateaux freighted up the enormous present provided by the Crown. Not until October 24, more than a month after his arrival, was Johnson able to open his conference, for the Indians had been slow in coming.

The formal minutes of the Fort Stanwix treaty reflect but dimly the actual negotiations, for the most important part of the business was conducted in private and unrecorded meetings. At this treaty, the largest ever held by Sir William, the Indians consented to release a vast extent of territory in New York, Pennsylvania, and Virginia and agreed to a boundary line running all the way from northern New York to the Tennessee River. Sir William, in fact, obtained more land than he had been authorized to purchase by the ministry.

Croghan was by far the most active of the speculators who busied themselves in making last minute purchases from the Indians before the Crown obtained title to the ceded area. A tract of one thousand acres could generally be had for £5. Croghan bought extensive tracts for his friends and acquired three tracts for himself totalling 127,000 acres, paying the Indians, at least in part, with bonds and promises which the natives later dis-

44. Bills dated Feb. 22, Sept. 3, and Sept. 20, 1768, Croghan's vouchers for 1768, and Guy Johnson to Croghan, June 6, 1768, Cadwalader Coll., Hist. Soc. of Pa.
45. Prevost to Croghan, July 19, 1768, and articles of agreement of Aug. 3, 1768, between Croghan and Robert McKain and James Bowle, Croghan's vouchers for 1768, Cadwalader Coll., Hist. Soc. of Pa.

covered were worthless. Since he already had 100,000 acres in his own name, Croghan concealed his identity in these final purchases (the money for which he had borrowed from Governor Franklin) by placing them temporarily in the names of Alexander McKee, John Butler, and Stephen Skinner, treasurer of New Jersey. So much land was grabbed up by Croghan and others in private dickerings just before the Indians ceded their territory to the British that Johnson later confessed, "I know of no good place vested in the Crown. . . . The lands ceded by the Indians at the late treaty are rather too remote to be of much imediate value."[46]

At Fort Stanwix, or earlier, Croghan told Johnson of title weaknesses that worried him. Would the Crown recognize the Indian sales made just before the treaty? Would the Crown recognize the validity of the land grant the Indians were willing to make the traders? And finally, when the new boundary was established, would Pennsylvania claim that Croghan's 200,000-acre purchase of 1749 fell within the bounds of the province and, hence, belonged to the proprietor?

Johnson saw to it that Croghan and others affected by these conditions received full protection. The minutes of the Fort Stanwix treaty contain conditions which the Indians insisted the Crown accept in ratifying the land cession. First, all the sales recently made by them within the ceded area should be considered valid and should not revert to the Crown. Second, a grant made by the Six Nations of some 2,500,000 acres on the Ohio to Trent and his associates was to be a part of the treaty. Third, should the Penns seize the 200,000 acres which the Indians had granted "our friend Mr. Croghan long ago," they requested that the king grant Croghan as much land elsewhere.[47]

The Board of Trade censured Johnson for allowing such private matters to become a part of a treaty with the king. It is a moot point whether Johnson acted in the best interests of the Crown and of the red men at Fort Stanwix, but it is indisputable that he

---

46. Johnson to Daniel Burton, Dec. 10, 1768, and Johnson to Thomas Moncrieffe, Jan. 26, 1769, *Johnson Papers*, VI, 530, 611; Croghan to Thomas Wharton, Aug. 28, 1769, Carnegie Library, Pittsburgh; Hanna, *Wilderness Trail*, II, 65-66; indenture, Trent to Joseph Morris, Apr. 3, 1769, McAllister Coll., Lib. Co. of Phila.

47. O'Callaghan, ed., *New-York Col. Doc.*, VIII, 128.

acted in the best interests of the private land grabbers. Commenting on the success of the Indiana Company's lavish lobbying efforts, in which Wharton disclosed singular address, industry, and ability, Trent gratefully acknowledged the "uncommon kindness of Sir Wm Johnson and Mr. Croghan." No one, however, experienced in such bountiful measure Johnson's "uncommon kindness" as his old friend, neighbor-to-be, and landlord of some quarter million New York acres, George Croghan.[48]

48. *Ibid.*, 163; Trent to [Callender], Dec. 1, 1768, Ohio Co. Papers, I, 53, Hist. Soc. of Pa.

12

Croghan's Forest

His pockets bulging with Indian deeds, Croghan called on speculators in New York and collected £2,900, which he and Jelles Fonda had advanced for them at Fort Stanwix. He dined with Governor Moore, who approved the purchases he had made just before the treaty was signed. Moore promised to come to Johnson Hall to formalize these transactions, insisting that Croghan accompany him when he made the trip. The Indian agent must have breathed a sigh of relief at Sir Harry's cooperative attitude, for all the recent Indian purchases were under a cloud. Fortunately for the speculators, Sir Harry was too much interested in receiving the enormous patent fees to declare them illegal.[1]

Accompanied by Dr. John Levine, who had replaced Dr. Anthon as his companion, Croghan visited a group of wealthy men in Burlington—the Burlington Company—and arranged for a loan. Croghan owed large sums which had long since passed their date of payment, but his creditors would have to wait; he was gambling on the main chance, pyramiding land holdings, piling debt on debt, and anticipating sales to settlers which would liquidate all his obligations and make him a wealthy man.[2]

Although determined to wind up his Pennsylvania affairs and move to Croghan's Forest at the foot of Lake Otsego, he rashly bought fourteen expensive acres adjoining Monckton Hall and then mortgaged the entire property, as well as lands in New York, to Governor Franklin for £1,800. He helped Trent raise cash

1. Robert Adems to Johnson, Nov. 28, 1768, Croghan to Johnson, Nov. 28, 1768, *Johnson Papers*, VI, 501-2, 504.
2. William Pollard to Thomas Wharton, Dec. 8, 1768, Wharton Coll., Hist. Soc. of Pa.

from the Burlington Company, for Trent's affairs were in a desperate plight. Trent and Wharton were preparing, on Croghan's advice, to embark for London to obtain royal confirmation of the traders' grant. Their expenses on this mission were underwritten by the other members of the syndicate, with Croghan the largest contributor. There was a close connection between the traders' group and the original membership in Croghan's now defunct Illinois speculation. The same five men—William Franklin, Croghan, Baynton, Wharton, and Morgan—who held five-eighths of the stock in the Illinois venture owned eleven-fourteenths of the traders' syndicate.[3]

December, 1768, and January, 1769, found Croghan raising money and quieting Pennsylvania creditors, as well as coping with a variety of personal problems. Early in 1768, he had brought William Croghan to Philadelphia and had since maintained him at the Indian Queen Tavern. William was the son of Croghan's Dublin agent Nicholas Croghan and was presumably a relative. Croghan arranged to place the young man with Thomas and John Shipboy, merchants of New York and Albany. Of all the relatives the Indian agent bountifully assisted, William was the most promising. He subsequently married a sister of George Rogers Clark, enjoyed a distinguished career, and was the father of Colonel George Croghan, a hero of the War of 1812. The rest of Croghan's family, numerous Smallmans and Powells, were little better than parasites. Croghan's generosity to them was unfailing. In addition to providing such people with funds, he undertook to support Trent's wife during her husband's absence abroad.[4]

His Pennsylvania business only half completed, Croghan returned to New York late in January to accompany Governor Moore to Johnson Hall. According to Croghan, this was his only chance to get his new land purchases confirmed, for Moore had written him positively that "unless I am there att that time he can nott

---

3. Croghan to Johnson, Mar. 30, 1766, *Johnson Papers*, V, 128; Papers Relating to Indian Losses, 27, 59, Ohio Co. Papers, I, 56, Hist. Soc. of Pa.; Croghan to Thomas Wharton, Mar. 23, 1769, Carnegie Library, Pittsburgh; Aaron Vanderpoel Papers, N. Y. Pub. Lib.

4. Entry for Nov. 30, 1768, John Little's bill, Croghan's vouchers for 1768, Cadwalader Coll., Hist. Soc. of Pa.

go." Up the Hudson on an Albany sloop sailed the governor, Croghan, and two other speculators, Colonel Staats Long Morris and his wife, the dowager Duchess of Gordon. At Sir William's, Governor Moore made good his promise to validate all Croghan's transactions with the Indians.[5]

Back in New York a few weeks later, Croghan petitioned the governor in council for 100,000 acres at Lake Otsego and also prepared petitions for lands he held in the names of John Butler, Alexander McKee, and Stephen Skinner. When these petitions were granted, all that remained to complete his title was to perfect the surveys and take out patents—the last an expensive action which he planned to postpone as long as possible. Croghan had had to find sixty more names to reinforce his petition for the Otsego tract, which originally had been for but forty thousand acres. His new group of associates, all New Yorkers, included four Fondas, four Phillipses, four Quackenbushes, four Vroomans, and one Van Rensselaer.[6]

In Philadelphia for a final month of settling affairs, Croghan had a perplexing time. Creditors were suing him in the Supreme Court, and William Buchanan was insistent on payment of the large sum Croghan owed him from Smallman's trading fiasco. The Indian agent stalled off Buchanan by tendering him two bonds payable in a year. One of these bonds, in the amount of £1,000, was secured by the signature of Dr. John Morgan, who innocently entered the web of Croghan's financing. (Croghan gave Morgan a mortgage on four thousand acres in New York and told him it was worth £4,000, a sum which was at least ten times the true value of the land.) Always forward-looking, no matter what his cash position, Croghan made a large number of special applications for lands in the Pittsburgh area which had just been opened to buyers. He hired servants to go to Croghan's Forest, offered the use of Monckton Hall, still staffed with his servants, to Mrs.

5. Croghan to Trent, Jan. 18, 1769, Lamberton Scots-Irish Coll., I, 86, Hist. Soc. of Pa.; O'Callaghan, ed., *Doc. Hist. of N. Y.*, IV, 405; Daniel Campbell to Johnson, Feb. 6, 1769, *Johnson Papers*, VI, 618; *Cal. of N. Y. Col. Mss., Indorsed Land Papers*, 468.

6. *Cal. of N. Y. Col. Mss., Indorsed Land Papers*, 469, 471; Land Papers, XXV, 73, N. Y. State Lib.; *New York State Library, Bulletin 58, Calendar of Council Minutes* (Albany, 1902), 540-41.

Samuel Wharton, and bought £1,000-worth of Indian goods from the firm of Barnard and Michael Gratz.[7]

By late April, Croghan had reached Albany and was on the now familiar road to Lake Otsego. Up the Mohawk River from Schenectady, he journeyed; past Guy Park, Guy Johnson's handsome home; past Williamsburg, the less pretentious home of Daniel Claus, who, like Guy, was a son-in-law and deputy of the Indian superintendent; past Fort Johnson of wartime fame, now the seat of Sir John Johnson; past Jelles Fonda's house and store; and then south across the Mohawk River. The road continued some twenty-four miles to Cherry Valley, a settlement of forty or fifty Scotch-Irish families. There it degenerated into a poorly cleared trail and wound on through Springfield, a small German settlement, nine more miles to the head of Lake Otsego.

Croghan was welcomed by his daughter and her family. On a sheltered cove, Augustine Prevost had built a one-story log house lined with rough boards and had cleared sixteen acres on a tract of six thousand given him by Croghan. The Indian agent's bateau, long and pointed at each end in Mohawk River style, carried its owner down the eight or nine miles of the lake to his home site. Well was this idyllic place named Croghan's Forest, for towering white pines covered the area. To Croghan, it was paradise. The lake abounded with fish—trout, salmon, pike, pickerel, even shad from the Atlantic Ocean—potential victims all for the large supply of fish hooks Croghan had ordered. Wild ducks wheeled in rapid flight across the skies. The hills teemed with deer and bear.

News of Croghan's arrival brought the Iroquois flocking. A large band from Oghquago came up the Susquehanna, which took its source but a few yards from Croghan's door. Joseph Brant, the Mohawk leader who later married Croghan's Indian daughter Catherine, was there, doubtless entreating Croghan to discharge the bond he had given for his lands. "Last night," wrote a visitor,

7. Indenture between Morgan and Croghan, Apr. 18, 1769, Articles of Agreement, Box 9A, Hist. Soc. of Pa.; Morgan to Croghan, Nov. 9, 1773, Croghan in account with Buchanan (Croghan's vouchers for 1769), articles of agreement between Croghan and William Scott, Apr. 10, 1769, Cadwalader Coll., Hist. Soc. of Pa.; Bail Book 1760-73, Supreme Court of Pa., Gilbert Cope Coll., Ohio Co. Papers, I, 69, Hist. Soc. of Pa.

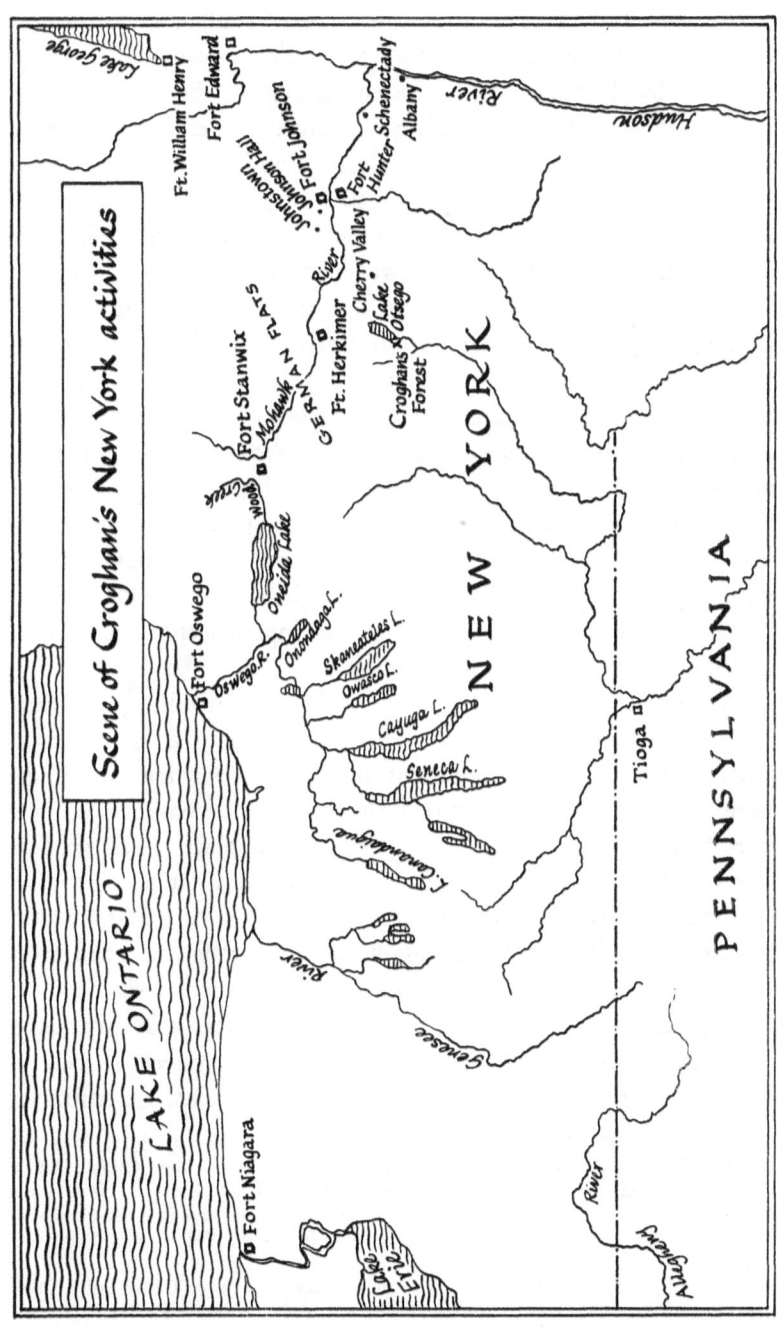

"a drunken Indian came and kissed Col. Croghan and me very joyously; here are natives of different nations almost continually; they visit the Deputy Superintendent as dogs to the bone for what they can get." And they always received something, a trinket, food, ammunition, or an order on Jelles Fonda's store for a gallon of rum.[8]

Work on Croghan's improvements kept a score of laborers busy. Carpenters erected two dwellings and five or six outbuildings. Plans were laid for a sawmill, a gristmill, a bridge over the Susquehanna, and a road across country to Kaatskill on the Hudson. Aside from the two servants who always accompanied him, Croghan employed several domestics and an overseer who barked out orders to his field hands through a megaphone. From Nicholas Croghan, who regretted his inability to furnish the bagpiper Croghan had ordered—"a good piper is hard to be got at present"—came eight indentured servants, a mason, five laborers, a gardener, and his wife. The wife was pregnant, and Croghan sent her off with her husband to Sir William, jocosely remarking that she would be an addition to "frutful" Johnson Hall.[9]

Although Croghan always referred to his dwelling as a hut, the log building had some pretensions, including a figured wallpaper which Croghan's men put up, using flour and water for paste. His table was covered with superfine damask cloths, and ivory-handled knives and forks were at each place. His six fireplaces had their sets of andirons, shovels, and tongs. Croghan furnished and supplied the establishment in his customary wholesale fashion. Wagon after wagon jounced along the road from Albany loaded with such purchases as thirty chairs, six chamber pots, cooking implements, thirty barrels of pork, a Negro slave, six barrels of rum, hogsheads of tobacco and oysters, barrels of sugar, casks of oakum and sherry, kegs of raisins, quantities of

---

8. Croghan's gift to Prevost of the homestead at the head of the lake was formalized by deed Mar. 2, 1770, Book VIII, 459-60, County Clerk's Office, Albany. Francis W. Halsey, *A Tour of Four Great Rivers* (New York, 1906), 19-49. Catherine Croghan was born in 1759, married in 1780, and died in Canada in 1837. Report of L. P. Kellogg to A. T. Volwiler at Hist. Soc. of Pa.

9. Nicholas Croghan to George Croghan, July 17, 1769, Cadwalader Coll., Hist. Soc. of Pa.; Croghan to Johnson, Sept. 23, 1769, *Johnson Papers*, VII, 188.

coffee, tea, and chocolate, glass for the windows, brass locks for the doors. Did he want for shoes? He ordered two dozen pairs.

Croghan made rapid progress in developing a valuable farm. It took one man twelve days to mow his fields. He owned a large herd of cows, and many bulls, oxen, sheep, and swine. The life of a gentleman farmer was what he wanted. Contemplating retirement, he declined Johnson's invitation to serve as a justice of the peace. His ambition was to live out his days in peace and prosperity at Croghan's Forest.[10]

Except for several weeks in the field supervising surveyors, who were running the new line between the Indian hunting grounds and the province of New York, Croghan spent the summer of 1769 at home, bedridden for the most part by a severe attack of gout, which was complicated by a dislocation in his foot.[11] In this helpless condition, barely able to hobble about his room, he had ample time to study a series of depressing letters from Wharton and Trent. Croghan had anticipated that the Crown would promptly ratify the Fort Stanwix treaty, including the land grants. He had promised to go to England himself with chiefs of each of the Six Nations if any objections to the grants were raised.

From Wharton, Croghan learned that Lord Hillsborough refused to approve the private transactions which Johnson had written into the Fort Stanwix treaty. Frantically, Trent wrote that they were all ruined unless Croghan exerted himself: "We know your address can carry every thing through." The line of action urged by Wharton and Trent as their only salvation was Croghan's making the Indians insist in the strongest terms that the Crown confirm every detail of the treaty. This would alarm the ministry, pointed out Wharton, for the ministers were "afraid of each other & dread nothing so much as bringing on an Indian war." Too lame to ride, Croghan traveled by wagon to Johnson Hall to obtain Sir William's support for the plan. But Johnson

10. Data on Croghan's Forest is based on bills and letters of Thomas and John Shipboy, and bills of Matthew Cannon and Jelles Fonda in Croghan's vouchers for 1769 and 1770, Cadwalader Coll., Hist. Soc. of Pa.; Croghan to Fonda, May 9, 1769, C. E. French Coll., Mass. Hist. Soc.; Croghan to Johnson, Apr. 8, 1770, *Johnson Papers*, VII, 527-29.

11. Croghan to Thomas Wharton, June 21 and July 18, 1769, *Pa. Mag. of Hist. and Biog.*, 15 (1891), 430-31; Croghan to Johnson, Aug. 8 and Aug. 10, 1769, Johnson to Gage, Oct. 19, 1769, *Johnson Papers*, VII, 77-79, 92, 221.

saw the handwriting on the wall. He had evidently gone too far at Fort Stanwix, and he feared to represent the Indians as furious because the grants had not been ratified. Disappointed, Croghan wrote to Wharton, likening Sir William to Dr. Slop in *Tristram Shandy*.[12]

Croghan's financial security lay solely in Wharton's obtaining approval of the Fort Stanwix Indian grants. He intended to sell his share of that land to pay off his debts. His New York purchases had probably cost him about £2,500 paid to the Indian owners, as well as other sums for surveys and improvements, all of which he had borrowed. So far, he had not sold any of his new holdings to settlers. He had, however, expectations. He had advertised fifty thousand acres for sale, in lots of one, two, and three hundred acres, and believed that he had attracted sixty New England families, who would arrive in the fall to set up a township on 23,000 acres they were to purchase for £4,600. Unfortunately, they never came. Thus, Croghan was out of funds in the summer of 1769 when disaster struck.[13]

Had it not been that John Tabor Kempe, attorney general of New York, was associated with Croghan's private Indian purchases at Fort Stanwix, those purchases might have been invalidated earlier in the year, when the governor's council termed them illegal and balked at confirming them. Through the influence of the governor, who was looking forward to his fees, and through the pressure of Kempe and other influential speculators, the council was brought to heel. But now a new and more dangerous situation arose.[14]

The private purchases at Fort Stanwix had been severely criticized, for they had robbed the Crown of the best land in the area which it had bought at large expense. "I think we may as-

---

12. Wharton to Croghan, May 18, 27, 28, 1769, and July 21, 1771, Trent to Croghan, July 11, 1769, Cadwalader Coll., Hist. Soc. of Pa.; Croghan to Johnson, Aug. 21, 1770, *Johnson Papers*, VII, 112-13. Johnson held a treaty with the Indians in July, 1770, to confirm the Fort Stanwix treaty except for the private grants "which his Majty will consider of." O'Callaghan, ed., *New-York Col. Doc.*, VIII, 237.

13. *New London Gazette*, Apr. 21, 1769, Yale University Library; Halsey, *Four Great Rivers*, 49; Croghan to Thomas Wharton, July 18, 1769, Carnegie Library, Pittsburgh.

14. John Wetherhead to Johnson, Mar. 18, 1769, *Johnson Papers*, VI, 649-50.

sure ourselves," observed Gage, "when complaints get home of the immense tracts acquired by private compacts with the Indians . . . that these tracts are . . . acquired in direct opposition to the regulations and laws of Government." It was Lord Hillsborough who precipitated Croghan's difficulties. The American secretary wrote Governor Moore, "I trust no countenance or attention either has been or will be given to any application for those lands [within the area ceded by the Indians at Fort Stanwix] upon the ground of private agreements with the Indians, contrary to the directions of the Proclamation of 1763."[15]

These instructions put Croghan's treasured New York property in jeopardy. Sir Harry, however, preferred his fees to obeying orders and sent Croghan word that he must quickly patent his lands, or else he would lose them. Ironically enough, only a few weeks later, Sir Harry lay dead, and venerable white-thatched Cadwallader Colden had succeeded him. "Governor Colden has the same power to grant pattents that the other had," wrote Croghan, "and no doubt will be as fond of the fee." Croghan was correct. The octogenerian was not only fond of his fees, he fought for them. "A fine mess of pottage," exclaimed a New Yorker regarding Colden's good fortune, "is left behind for him by his predecessor who had not time to go through with the grand land matters that were upon the carpet." Poor Croghan had to furnish much of the pottage.[16]

To patent the 227,000 acres contained in four of his tracts cost exactly £5,561 10s.[17] Croghan raised the money in the only way he could think of. He drew bills payable on Samuel Wharton in London. These bills were taken up by New York and Albany merchants, who gave Croghan the money and sent the bills to

15. Gage to Johnson, July 23, 1769, *ibid.*, VII, 65-66; Hillsborough to Moore, May 13, 1769, O'Callaghan, ed., *New-York Col. Doc.*, VIII, 165.
16. Croghan to Thomas Wharton, Sept. 29, 1769, Estate of Edward Wanton Smith (courtesy of Miss S. A. G. Smith); John Watts to Monckton, Sept. 12, 1769, *Coll. of the Mass. Hist. Soc.*, Fourth Series, 10 (1871), 619. Colden later fiercely defended his right to his fees against an order to divide them with his successor Lord Dunmore.
17. The major fees payable for patenting lands in New York were as follows: to the governor £12 4s. per 1,000 acres; to the secretary £4 per 1,000 acres; to the surveyor general £5 per 1,000 acres; to the attorney general £3 for each grantee. Goldsbrow Banyar to George Clarke, Apr. 10, 1772, Banyar Papers, N. Y. Hist. Soc.

Wharton for payment. Croghan took this desperate gamble in the hope that Wharton could sell or mortgage his Ohio lands. If Wharton failed to raise the money and the bills came back with damages, Croghan realized he would lose most, if not all, of his New York purchases. To the merchants who advanced him the money, he was far from candid, for he told them that Wharton actually had the money in hand. This was the reverse of the truth. Wharton was so hard pressed for cash to cover his living expenses that he had just written Croghan for £200 to tide him over. Instead of receiving this assistance, Wharton was presented with Croghan's demands for more than £5,000, which he could not honor, since Croghan's Ohio lands were unsalable in London.[18]

In November, Croghan came to New York to take out his patents. Cutting corners as usual, he persuaded all four of the officials he had to pay to take bonds for part of the money due them. Thus, Governor Cadwallader Colden and his son Surveyor General Alexander Colden, Attorney General John Tabor Kempe, and Secretary Goldsbrow Banyar joined the army of Croghan's creditors. He spent a full month in New York, "ocationed on acount of them percheses wh was att Fort Stanwix, wh throu the asistence of Governor Colden & Mr. Banyar I gott all settled & securd wh I belive wold never a been don had I nott gott down att the time I did & Governor Colden come into the administeration."[19]

Croghan had Sir William's orders to proceed to Fort Pitt, where the Indian situation again looked bad; the Fort Stanwix boundary line had done little toward promoting peace in the West. So fearful of a surprise attack was the Fort Pitt garrison that the

18. Wharton to Croghan, Aug. 12, Dec. 6, 1769, and Trent to Croghan, Dec. 5, 1769, Cadwalader Coll., Croghan to Trent, Nov. 30, 1769, Gratz-Croghan Papers, I, 18, Etting Coll., Hist. Soc. of Pa.

19. A list of Croghan's debts dated May 16, 1775 (Cadwalader Coll., Hist. Soc. of Pa.) shows that Croghan owed the two Coldens £700. He borrowed £240 from Kempe on Dec. 6, 1769 (Kempe folder, *ibid*.). The Otsego tract was patented Nov. 30, 1769, and, on Dec. 1 and 2, Croghan's ninety-nine associates released their shares to him. The John Butler tract of 47,000 acres was patented on Dec. 23, 1769, and, on Dec. 25 and 28, Croghan's associates released their shares to him. The Alexander McKee tract of 40,000 acres was patented on Jan. 16, 1770, and was released to Croghan two days later. Banyar Papers, N. Y. Hist. Soc.; Croghan to Johnson, Dec. 22, 1769, *Johnson Papers*, VII, 314.

drawbridge was seldom let down and a double guard was posted at the sally port. Lame with gout, Croghan did not go west to quiet the Indians. With Gage's permission, he sent Alexander McKee instead to tell them that he would come in the spring when they returned from their winter hunt.[20]

By mid-December, Croghan was in Philadelphia where his principal creditors had been anxiously awaiting him. He owed William Buchanan, William Peters, Thomas Wharton, Governor Franklin, the Gratz brothers, and Baynton, Wharton, and Morgan at least £15,000. Moreover, the Ohio Company had secured a judgment against him in a Philadelphia court. Confined to his bed at Monckton Hall by gout, Croghan did his best to satisfy them all without giving them any money. Optimistically, he wrote Sir William Johnson that he had "partly setled my affairs in this city & hope to be ready to take my lave of this city for ever in about a fortnight & return to the banks of Ottsago." Actually, it was impossible for Croghan to settle his affairs, and, when his creditors became a shade too inquisitive, he left precipitately for New York. As Baynton sadly remarked, "After the committee had waited on him several times to adjust his accot, he suddenly departed this city." Although still an admirer of Croghan's, Baynton began to refer to him as "abacadabra."[21]

Tortured in mind, body, and pocketbook, Croghan presented a curious spectacle to a friend who visited his sick room in New York.

Croghan is in town sure enough poor man. He is now confined to his bed & has been for some time past with a pretty severe paroxism of the gout which he bears like a lamb and instead of swearing like a trooper as some reprobates would do under such intolerable pains, he, on the contrary poor soul, does nothing but pray and talk about the sufferings of the inner man, which he

20. *Pennsylvania Gazette*, Aug. 17, 1769; Croghan to Johnson, Nov. 16, 1769, O'Callaghan, ed., *Doc. Hist. of N. Y.*, IV, 420.

21. Croghan to Johnson, Dec. 22, 1769, *Johnson Papers*, VII, 314-15; Croghan to James Tilghman, Jan. 27, 1770, courtesy of George R. Loeb; Croghan to Richard Peters (son of William), Sept. 7, 1769, Peters Mss., VI, 86, and trustees of Baynton, Wharton, and Morgan to Croghan, Nov. 23, 1769, Dreer Coll., Hist. Soc. of Pa.; Croghan to Baynton, "Thursday evening," N. Y. Pub. Lib.; Baynton to Abel James, Dec. 15, 1769, Feb. 20, 1770, Baynton Letter Book, Public Records Division, Harrisburg; Michael Gratz to Barnard Gratz, Sept. 29, 1769, Gratz Letter Book, Etting Coll., Hist. Soc. of Pa.; Baynton to Morgan, Mar. 1, Dec. 12, 1770, Public Records Division, Harrisburg.

thinks far more of than those of the body. The poor gentleman has sometimes a few qualms about the tricks of his youth, which now & then come out with heavy sighs & groans, in short it woud do you a world of good to hear him talk when perchance a twinge catches him by the great toe.[22]

Whether there was more of humor than truth in this description, Croghan had become much interested in the church. He proposed plans to convert the heathen and promoted church affairs. Modest in his approach to religion, he apologized to Sir William for taking the liberty of recommending a missionary, "for tho I love the church very well I know I ought nott to medle with church maters." According to a devout Anglican layman, he need not have been so bashful: "You have done ten thousand benevolent acts in your time."[23] Croghan blamed his financial involvements on this very benevolence: "I must charge every thing to my own imprudence as I have been guilty of many acts of folly for other people." By and large, his creditors recognized Croghan's essential generosity and stood by him. Although unable to explain why Croghan said one thing but did another, John Baynton hoped that the Indian agent would retain enough of his land "to enable him to live according to the elegance of his desires and the nobleness of his disposition."[24]

By mortgage and sale, Croghan's New York lands dwindled fast. The McKee patent granted in January, 1770, was mortgaged to Banyar in February and, after Croghan's unsuccessful attempt to sell it to Johnson, was eventually sold for William Peters, who in February obtained a judgment in the New York courts against Croghan for £5,739. The Skinner tract, the Butler tract, and most of the Otsego tract were soon out of Croghan's control. But still the Indian agent went on acquiring new ground. In February, the 18,000-acre township of Belvidere was set up and granted to him under the mandamus of the Crown as a reward for wartime services. The patent fees Croghan owed for this final New York

22. John Wetherhead to Johnson, Feb. 12, 1770, *Johnson Papers*, VII, 388.
23. Croghan to Johnson, Nov. 16, 1769, O'Callaghan, ed., *Doc. Hist. of N. Y.*, IV, 419-20; Baynton to Croghan, Jan. 31, 1770, Cadwalader Coll., Hist. Soc. of Pa.
24. Baynton to Abel James, Feb. 20, 1770, Baynton Letter Book, Public Records Division, Harrisburg; Croghan to Banyar, May 25, 1770, Banyar Papers, N. Y. Hist. Soc.

acquisition amounted to £448, but, once again, credulous officials were willing to take his bonds.[25]

Croghan's frantic efforts to preserve a substantial part of his estate reached a new crisis in February, when thousands of pounds in bills drawn on Wharton came back marked for nonpayment. The Indian agent's credit was now a thing of the past. Despite his illness and the severity of the weather, he beat a hasty retreat to Croghan's Forest.[26]

Lame in foot and depressed in spirits, Croghan found no privacy at his snowbound sanctuary. News of his arrival brought whites and reds alike flocking to his hospitable board: "Ever sence I gott hear to my hutt [it has] been as full of visitors as itt will hold of the good pople of the cuntry besides my frends the Indians." Nor did storm or distance deter his creditors. Joseph Brant arrived to dicker again with Croghan over money he owed the Indians for their lands. And Michael Gratz came all the way from Philadelphia, but soon went home no richer for his pains. From Albany came Thomas Shipboy, whose firm had endorsed Croghan's notes and had since stopped payment. When John Morton, holder of some £5,000-worth of protested bills, came up from New York, Croghan gave him a bond and persuaded him to defer legal action.[27]

His reputation disgraced by the return of his bills, Croghan explained why they had not been paid. "I find," he wrote Jelles Fonda, "that Mr. Wharton has sufferd some of my bills to be protested tho he had my money in his hands." Wharton, of course, had no money of Croghan's, but telling lies never bothered the Indian agent. To Banyar, he wrote, "On hearing of my bills coming back I was as much astonished as man could be, & much suspected the integrity of my friends." Wharton, Croghan confided to his friends and creditors, had been forced to use the money

---

25. *New York State Library, Bulletin 58, Calendar of Council Minutes*, 547; Land Papers, XXVI, 122, New York State Library; Peters Mss., VI, 89, Hist. Soc. of Pa.; Johnson to Banyar, Mar. 17, 1770, Banyar Papers, N. Y. Hist. Soc. On May 10, 1770, Croghan gave Attorney General Kempe his bond for £48. Kempe folder, Cadwalader Coll., Hist. Soc. of Pa.

26. John Wetherhead to Johnson, Mar. 5, 1770, *Johnson Papers*, VII, 466.

27. Gratz to [   ], Apr. 4, 1770, Gratz Letter Book, Etting Coll., Hist. Soc. of Pa.; Croghan to Johnson, Mar. 17, 1770, and Daniel Claus to Johnson, Apr. 28, 1770, *Johnson Papers*, VII, 487, 608.

in his negotiations in London. All this was pure fiction, but it helped to lessen Croghan's culpability in raising credit on false assurances and made him appear an injured party.[28]

Croghan had high hopes that Wharton's negotiations would yet succeed and his title to western lands be confirmed. Meanwhile, immediate action was necessary to salvage his interests near Pittsburgh. Once again, an Indian war appeared imminent, and "no individual in America can suffer half as much as I must in my interest if a warr takes place." He resolved to go to Fort Pitt and liquidate a stock of Indian goods and some real estate improvements before an outbreak occurred. Ten days would suffice to finish this western business, after which he would visit Warm Springs in Virginia for his health.[29]

"I seem an old criple begining the world a new," forlornly observed Croghan before taking reluctant leave of his beloved forest. This possession he would protect. Improvements continued; more cattle arrived to swell the herds; the place was fully staffed (one of Croghan's last purchase orders was for two gross of metal buttons for his servants' clothes), and Augustine Prevost would keep an eye on it. His servants would paddle him down the Susquehanna and then up the Juniata to Bedford. Unable to ride, he planned to hire a chaise to take him over the hundred-mile road to Pittsburgh. As strong arms propelled his boat downstream, Croghan consoled himself with the thought that he would return by harvest time. But another chapter of his life was finished. He was never again to see Croghan's Forest.[30]

28. Croghan to Johnson, May 10, 1770, *Johnson Papers*, VII, 651; Croghan to Fonda, May 3, 1770, Darlington Memorial Library, University of Pittsburgh; Croghan to Banyar, May 25, 1770, Banyar Papers, N. Y. Hist. Soc.
29. Croghan to Johnson, May 10, 1770, *Johnson Papers*, VII, 650-54.
30. Croghan to Johnson, Apr. 8, May 3, 1770, *ibid.*, 529, 631-32; Croghan to Nicholas Herkimer, Apr. 20, 1770, property of Paul F. Cooper, Cooperstown, N. Y.

13

Pittsburgh Land Speculator

CROGHAN ARRIVED at Fort Pitt on July 2, 1770, unaware that the seven days he intended to stay at Croghan Hall were to lengthen into seven years. Overwhelming reasons—fear of being arrested for debt if he returned east, dependence on his western land interests, the need of abetting Samuel Wharton's schemes, Indian affairs—soon arose to keep him on the Ohio.[1]

The threat of an Indian war was exceptionally strong during the summer of 1770. One of the chief irritants was a result of the Revolutionary nonimportation agreements of American merchants against the Townshend tax measures, which reduced Pennsylvania's imports from £441,000, in 1768, to £134,000, in 1770. Since traders could not obtain English manufactured goods, they relied almost entirely on rum with which to buy furs. The Indians were consequently more debauched than ever, behaved badly, and, when not murdering their own people, were being shot by frightened white men. These bloody episodes infuriated the warriors, whose wrath was particularly directed at the Virginians settled on Redstone Creek and Cheat River.

Croghan tightened the controls on rum and did his best to assuage the Indians. Of one of his conferences in August, he wrote Gage: "I assure you I was two days & a night at a loss what to think as a very great majority was for attacking and driving the Virginians over the mountains." As in the past, Croghan's influence and diplomatic ability averted trouble. Captain Charles Edmonstone, who commanded Fort Pitt, informed the general that "Mr. Croghan has been indefatigable in endeavouring to quiet

1. Baynton to Croghan, July 21, 1770, Cadwalader Coll., Hist. Soc. of Pa.

the minds of the different tribes of Indians about this [place]; and I dar venture to say that we are indebted to him for the present tranquility."[2]

Despite this success, Croghan expected a general uprising in the spring of 1771. Far down on the plains of the Scioto, the western tribes had agreed to make peace with their old enemies, the southern Indian nations. This new confederacy, Croghan feared, was organized solely to make war on the English. In March, he penetrated the Indian plot. As usual, it was an Indian who betrayed his race. Mohiccon John secretly informed Croghan that, ever since the Treaty of Fort Stanwix, the Iroquois had been telling the western tribes that the English had not bought their land but had stolen it. At the instigation of the Six Nations, the western and southern tribes had united and were awaiting the arrival of Iroquois war parties before striking the British posts.

Croghan called together the chiefs of the Ohio Indians. Addressing them with "proper spirit," he told them their plot had been discovered. The chiefs could not outface the irate agent; they confessed their ill designs. Probing and questioning, Croghan brought their complaints into the open, answered all their grievances, and, according to Captain Edmonstone, brought them to their senses. The discovery of their conspiracy, joined with the realization that the Senecas had hoodwinked them and that the Six Nations as a whole were not behind the movement, collapsed the war confederacy.[3]

If Samuel Wharton was to succeed in London, peace had to be maintained on the western waters. Knowing that the Crown would reject the Indiana land grant if it were submitted, Wharton concocted another plan which emerged into a grand colonial enterprise. Backed by many of the most influential lords and commoners in England, Wharton petitioned for twenty million acres to be erected into an inland colony. Pittsylvania, or Vandalia, as the colony was later called, included within its bounds both Croghan's Indian grant and the Indiana grant and guaranteed their titles. Promising Croghan an appointment as Indian agent,

2. Croghan to Gage, Aug. 8, 1770, and Edmonstone to Gage, Aug. 11, 1770, Clements Library.

3. Croghan to Gage, Sept. 20, 1770, and Edmonstone to Gage, Mar. 9, Mar. 24, Apr. 24, 1771, Clements Library.

Wharton, who expected to be governor of the new colony, urged him to keep the Indians quiet because the enemies of Vandalia argued that its creation would bring on a war.[4]

In addition to this responsibility, ominous legal activity barred Croghan from visiting his rural retreat at Lake Otsego. In October, John Morton obtained a judgment for £5,000 against him in the Supreme Court of New York.[5] Legal actions also were pending at Bedford, Carlisle, Lancaster, and Philadelphia. Impatient, ready-to-sue creditors at Albany and New York awaited his promised return.

Heartbreaking letters described the plight of those who had recently helped him financially and who were now in trouble. Michael Gratz told his brother Barnard that he wished he had never heard of Croghan. "Where, sir," wrote Dr. John Morgan, "is the generosity of leaving one who became a security for you to fall a victim to his reliance on your honor. . . . Why have I not heard from you before now, or what is the reason you have never answered my letters?" Croghan's influence had brought Governor Franklin to Fort Stanwix, where, spellbound by Croghan, Franklin agreed to lend him a large sum of money and, through his assistance, bought a share in the Otego tract. Like so many others who did business with Croghan, Franklin regretted it: "You cannot imagine what an infinite deal of difficulty & trouble I have had in the management of that cursed business of the Otaga tract, which turns out after all, an object scarce worth attention. But that is not the only reason I have to repent my going to the Treaty at F. Stanwix." George Morgan of Baynton, Wharton, and Morgan bitterly inquired of Croghan whether he did not feel responsible for one fourth of the loss in the Illinois adventure, "by your leading us into which, you sir, was the cause of our *ruin*."[6]

For funds to pay or secure his debts, Croghan turned to his Indian grant of 1749. He appointed agents for the sale of his

---

4. Wharton to Croghan, Sept. 4, 1770, Cadwalader Coll., Hist. Soc. of Pa.
5. Minute Book of the Supreme Court of Judicature, 1769-72, 271, 302, and parchment roll containing the court decree of Oct. 26, 1770, County Clerk of New York, Hall of Records, New York.
6. Michael Gratz to Barnard Gratz, July 6, 1770, McAllister Coll., Lib. Co. of Phila.; John Morgan to Croghan, July 20, 1770, and George Morgan to Croghan, Aug. 7, 1773, Cadwalader Coll., Hist. Soc. of Pa.; William Franklin to Trent, Jan. 14, 1771, *New Jersey Archives*, First Series, X, 227-28.

200,000 acres and opened a land office, selling tracts varying in size from several hundred to twenty thousand acres to officers and men of the Fort Pitt garrison, and to anyone else who would buy. Stories of these sales reaching Philadelphia caused a merchant to write, "He is determind to discharge every farthing he owes before March next. He has enough to live happily on the remainder of his life if he will not be too generous. Several persons who have recd. great favors from him have treated him scurvily."[7]

To build up buyer confidence, Croghan gave out exaggerated stories of his sales. "Mr. Croghan has sold 200,000 achers of land on the Ohio to Mr. Chew in Maryland and three other gentlemen their for £12,000 sterl wich he is to receiv on the confirmation of the grants from home," wrote Robert Callender. This deal was never consummated, nor did Croghan succeed in his effort to establish a German settlement by the sale of twenty thousand acres to some Moravians from Northumberland County. His most resounding failure was to convince George Washington that both the quality of his lands and their title were good.[8]

Hunting for valuable real estate speculations, Washington arrived at Fort Pitt on October 17, 1770, and dined the next night at the officers' club with Croghan. The following day, he lunched at Croghan Hall, exchanged friendly speeches with Indians he met there, and listened to his host's proposal to sell him fifteen thousand acres for £750 sterling. The discussion turned to Vandalia, in which Croghan held a proprietary share, a share which he was willing to sell. Washington was greatly stimulated by the talk, his interest aroused both in the land and in Vandalia. But he was cautious. Later, as he journeyed down the Ohio past mile after mile of river front claimed by Croghan, he noted that "the unsettled state of this country renders any purchase dangerous." Meanwhile, Croghan was writing a friend in Philadelphia that he

---

7. John McCullough to John Baynton, Oct. 15, 1770, Society Autograph Coll., and Ohio Co. Papers, I, 92, Hist. Soc. of Pa.; Boyd Crumrine, "The Records of Deeds for the District of West Augusta, Virginia . . . ," *Annals of the Carnegie Museum*, 3 (1905), 290, 294; Baynton to George Morgan, Dec. 12, 1770, Public Records Division, Harrisburg.

8. Callender to Trent, Jan. 14, 1771, Etting Coll., and Baynton to Croghan, Feb. 4, 1771, Cadwalader Coll., Hist. Soc. of Pa.; R. L. Hooper to Johnson, Feb. 9, 1771, *Johnson Papers*, VII, 1132-33.

had sold 100,000 acres of his lands, hopefully adding, "I am likely to sell another tract to Coll. Washington and his friends. If I do *that*, I expect to have one good nights rest before Christmas, which is more than I have had for eight months past I assure you."[9]

"I have sold a parcel of lands to Coll Washington," wrote Croghan a few months later. No bargain, however, had been closed, and Washington, heeding the advice of his western agent, never did buy. What distressed Washington's agent most was the curious manner in which Croghan was running his survey lines. It seemed axiomatic that any good land Croghan learned about was automatically included in his Indian grant. The kindest thing that could be said about Croghan's method of surveying was that it was based on conjecture. Irritated at Washington for not buying his lands, Croghan quite unjustly accused the Virginian of using him as a cat's paw while he spied out lands which Croghan did not own. He even went so far as to lay claim to the tract which Washington purchased.[10]

After the Treaty of Fort Stanwix, Pennsylvania extended her jurisdiction west of the mountains to Pittsburgh. In 1771, Bedford County was created, and, in 1773, Westmoreland County was erected. Pennsylvania officials—justices of the peace, sheriffs, constables, tax collectors, surveyors—supported the authority of the proprietary government. Croghan, who maintained that the western limits of Pennsylvania did not come within twenty miles of Pittsburgh, looked on these officers as agents of oppression.

He had strong personal reasons for doing so. Pennsylvania would not recognize his Indian grant if it fell within the province; consequently, it was all-important to claim that the grant lay west of Pennsylvania. Then, too, there were Vandalia's pretensions to the same land, and Croghan served Vandalia, not Pennsylvania. He took an aggressive part in minimizing Pennsylvania's jurisdic-

---

9. Fitzpatrick, ed., *Diaries of Washington*, I, 410-12; Washington to Croghan, Nov. 24, 1770, Fitzpatrick, ed., *Writings of Washington*, III, 29-30; Croghan to Joseph Wharton, Jr., Oct. 25, 1770, Estate of Edward Wanton Smith.

10. Croghan to Michael Gratz, Feb. 20, 1771, Gratz Coll., and William Wilkins to Simon Gratz, July 16, 1810, Etting Coll., Hist. Soc. of Pa.; William Crawford to Washington, Apr. 20, 1771, Dec. 29, 1773, Hamilton, ed., *Letters to Washington*, IV, 56-57, 294; Washington to Croghan, Oct. 21, 1771, Fitzpatrick, ed., *Writings of Washington*, III, 65-66.

tion, acquiring for himself a host of enemies in Thomas Penn's colony.[11]

James Tilghman, secretary of the Pennsylvania land office, protested strongly that Croghan was confusing people and preventing settlement. How could Croghan possibly know where the as yet unsurveyed western bounds of Pennsylvania would fall? Was it not unjust for him to take money for lands so circumstanced? Angrily, the Indian agent retorted by asking what right Tilghman had to sell his lands which most unquestionably were not in Pennsylvania. "I might dwell longer on this disagreeable subject, and point out many hardships the people labour under from the conduct of the proprietors servants, who are, in some respects, all little proprietaries cuting up the country as they please and when any one complains of their iniquitous proceedings, one & all cry out such a person is an enemy to the proprietary interest."[12]

Croghan told settlers, who were flocking west in increasing numbers, that they would be fools to pay taxes to Pennsylvania before her western boundary was established. His servants drove off the collector and constable when they came for his own taxes. Encouraged by Croghan's example and advice, a large number of settlers petitioned the Bedford court not to serve any more processes west of Laurel Hill, for that country was not in Pennsylvania. Croghan also promoted a movement among those who favored Virginia jurisdiction to sue the Penns for "glaring acts of injustice." Of this abortive effort, an unsympathetic Pennsylvanian commented, "I plainly see that ambition will make men drunke as well as liquer."[13]

Whose authority properly extended to the Pittsburgh area was

11. In earlier years, Croghan had insisted just as earnestly that the Pittsburgh area was part of Pennsylvania. *Pa. Archives*, II, 132-33.

12. Tilghman to Croghan, June 24, 1771, Cadwalader Coll., and Croghan to Tilghman, Aug. 20, 1771, Peters Mss., VII, 73, Hist. Soc. of Pa.; William Crawford to Washington, Aug. 2, 1771, Hamilton, ed., *Letters to Washington*, IV, 77.

13. Luke Collins to G. Wilson, July 5, 1772, Public Records Division, Harrisburg; Wilson's reply to Collins, and Croghan to St. Clair, June 4, 1772, *Pa. Archives*, IV, 454-55, 452-53; St. Clair to Joseph Shippen, July 18, 1772, and [no date], William Henry Smith, ed., *The St. Clair Papers* (Cincinnati, 1882), I, 265, 268; C. W. Butterfield, ed., *The Washington-Crawford Letters* (Cincinnati, 1877), 22-23.

an open question. Virginia was soon to challenge Pennsylvania's claim and Vandalia's pretensions. Meanwhile, with the approval of the Vandalia proprietors, Croghan received applications for lands and surveyed and sold them. He also sold lands he claimed by right of the 772 Indiana Company shares transferred to him by Smallman. Based on this holding alone, Croghan sold 100,000 acres, although a calculation showed that he was entitled to only 23,852 acres. In disgust, George Morgan exclaimed that Croghan "only acted according to his usual practice, which is that of doing what he has no right to do."[14]

Croghan told his creditors that his sales were all conditioned on the confirmation of Vandalia and that, as soon as the Crown established the colony, more than enough money would pour in from the contracts he had made to pay all his debts. In December, 1772, he wrote Governor Franklin, "I have not received a single farthing for lands in this country since I have been here two years and a half, nor have I been able to command fifty pounds in all that time." This was not true, for Croghan had been paid for lands. Moreover, after his return to the Ohio, he borrowed £11,839 from Barnard Gratz to improve his lands. With land as security, he could raise money, but he could not pay his creditors. In 1773, Croghan was threatened with going to jail for the large sum of money he had promised Richard Hockley in 1763. Joseph Wharton, Jr., interceded and paid Hockley more than £2,000 to clear Croghan. The result, as might have been anticipated, was disastrous for Wharton, because the collateral security with which Croghan secured the loan proved worthless. Wharton later referred to it as "the fallacious indemnification you imposed upon me."[15]

By and large, Croghan was successful in stalling off his other creditors, awaiting the establishment of Vandalia which would restore his fortunes. Time and again from England came word that Vandalia had become a reality, but always something inter-

14. Document dated Dec. 10, 1771, Land Transactions, Cadwalader Coll., and Ohio Co. Papers, II, 15, Hist. Soc. of Pa.
15. Ohio Co. Papers, II, 54, Joseph Wharton to Trent, Apr. 2, 1775, Gratz Coll., Joseph Wharton to Croghan, Sept. 16, 1779, Cadwalader Coll., Croghan to William Franklin, Dec. 26, 1772, William Franklin folder, Society Autograph Coll., Hist. Soc. of Pa.

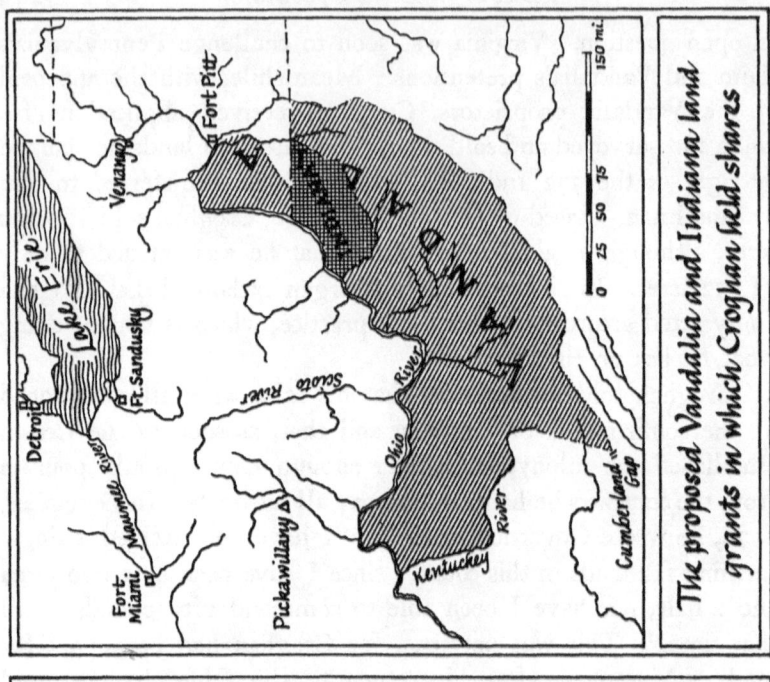
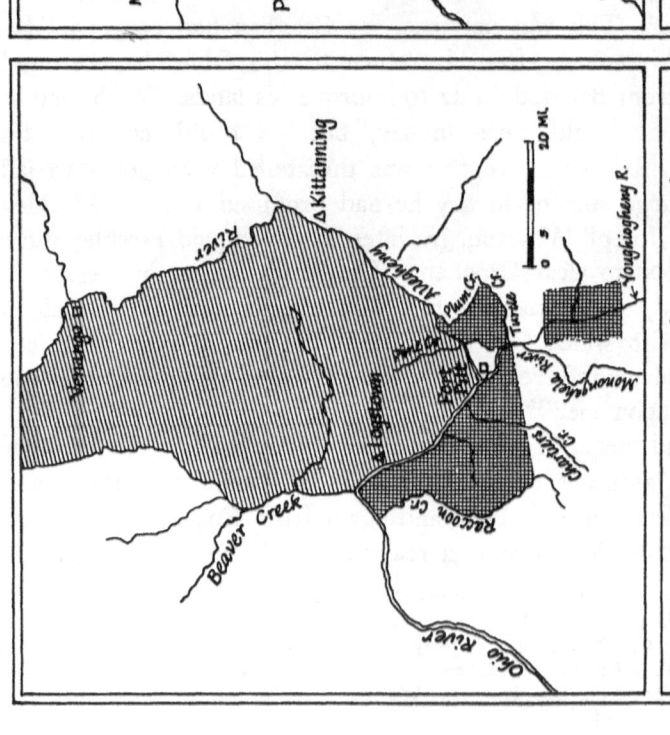

posed, and delay followed delay. In midsummer of 1771, Trent and Wharton found their lobby blocked by Lord Hillsborough. Urgently, they wrote to Croghan to obtain petitions from western settlers in favor of the colony so that they could demonstrate strong American support for the project. "The b[oundar]y line, we are convinced, would never have been effected had not Ld H[illsborough] been frightened, by the measures which you and Mr. W[harton] took. Those that are now suggested, if immediately and prudently pursued and executed, will, we assure you, as certainly have the same effect."[16]

Wharton, an inveterate schemer, confidentially elucidated matters. If the ministry could be convinced that failure to set up a colony west of the Alleghenies would bring on an Indian war, they would certainly approve Vandalia. "I need not say much on these points to a person of your penetration."[17] That was sufficient prompting for Croghan. He rounded up the petitions and wrote Wharton an alarming letter full of dire forebodings, a suitable letter for Wharton to show to his friends in London. Five thousand families, wrote Croghan, were settled in the Vandalia area, where they lived in such a licentious manner that they were sure to provoke an Indian war. The omens of 1763 were again in the air. The settlers must be restrained by the control of a new colony. Only a new colony, furthermore, could care for the Indians, who were entirely neglected. Stuart looked out for the Cherokees and Johnson for the Six Nations, but no one did a thing for the western tribes. The consequences, warned Croghan, would be dreadful. In fact, so bad was the Indian situation that Croghan had resigned from the service.[18]

The only indisputable information in Croghan's letter was his resignation, a step he took on November 2, 1771, at Samuel Wharton's suggestion so that he could better serve Vandalia. To

16. Trent and Wharton to Croghan, July 21, 1771, Cadwalader Coll., Hist. Soc. of Pa.

17. Wharton to Croghan, July 21, 1771, *ibid.;* Alvord, *The Mississippi Valley in British Politics*, II, 113.

18. Croghan to Wharton, Nov. 2, 1771, Cadwalader Coll., Hist. Soc. of Pa. Thomas Wharton sent Joseph Dobson from Philadelphia to assist Croghan in gathering signatures for the petitions. Dobson spent forty-four days on this mission. Thomas Wharton Ledger, fol. 105, and Day Book E, 322, Leonard T. Beale Coll., Hist. Soc. of Pa.

Thomas Wharton, he wrote, "I have resigned my appointment as it was absolutely necessary I should do so to secure yr brothers success." For months, Croghan had been anxious to retire anyway, because he received virtually no financial support in caring for the natives. Worried about the unsettled state of Indian affairs, Johnson had held him on. Time and again over the years, Johnson had dissuaded Croghan from leaving the Indian department, but the parting of the ways had come at last. Gage regretted losing "so old and experienced a servant," and Johnson accepted the resignation only on condition that he promise to return to active duty when he had settled his personal affairs. On this understanding, Johnson appointed Alexander McKee deputy agent pro tempore. Croghan remained on call when Indian affairs were critical. Indeed, the native chiefs preferred to treat with him, and Croghan Hall continued to be an Indian haven.[19]

Croghan Hall was, in addition, Croghan's land office, his headquarters for a flourishing 1,600-acre farm, and his trading post, for Croghan had taken up the fur trade in partnership with Thomas Smallman. The management of much of these multifarious concerns lay in the hands of Croghan's capable clerk, John Campbell. Croghan's establishment was the oldest and probably the largest in the Pittsburgh area, perhaps the most impressive west of the Alleghenies. Travelers visited it as a matter of course. Were they wealthy merchants like John Cadwalader or poor preachers like David Jones, the owner's hospitality was unfailing. The Reverend David Jones, for instance, was helped not only with advice but presents of a bearskin, wampum, and food for his journey. "In short," recalled the parson, "the Col. acted the part of a generous, kind gentleman to me."[20]

In 1772, Croghan made a major effort to liquidate his debts. Convinced that the new colony would be approved in the spring and that his future lay in Vandalia, he ordered Monckton Hall to be sold for £2,000. So encumbered was this estate with mortgages

---

19. Croghan to Thomas Wharton, Nov. 13, 1771, Carnegie Library, Pittsburgh; Croghan to Gage, Nov. 2, 1771, Cadwalader Coll., Hist. Soc. of Pa.; Gage to Croghan, Dec. 10, 1771, Clements Library; *Johnson Papers*, VIII, 262, 308, 491.

20. Journal of Reverend David Jones for June 4, 1772, Hist. Soc. of Pa.; John Hall, *Memoirs of Matthew Clarkson* . . . (Philadelphia, 1890), 33.

and judgments, however, that Croghan could not sell it at any price, and he retained its cloudy title until the day he died.[21]

Barnard and Michael Gratz had become Croghan's principal agents, creditors, and suppliers in the fur trade. "I am determined," he wrote them, "to sell all of [my New York lands] as fast as posable, att any rate to gett out of debt." He sent them a power of attorney to sell 58,000 acres in New York, which at modest prices he estimated would bring in £5,170. Augustine Prevost's return to the army reconciled Croghan to this sale. Despite Barnard Gratz's best efforts, none of this land was sold in 1772. Another attempt in 1773 also failed. No purchasers came forward.[22]

While struggling with his finances, Croghan was frequently prostrated by ill health. Severe attacks of gout crippled his feet and hands and confined him to his house. In June, 1773, he wrote an acquaintance that his illness of the past three years had obliged him to lay aside his correspondence with his friends. By strict adherence to a particular regimen and diet he had, however, made a good recovery and hoped soon to get the better of his "complicated disorders." During this period, he assisted the celebrated Dr. William Robertson of Edinburgh, who was engaged in writing his *History of America*. Thirty queries about Indians proposed by Dr. Robertson were sent to Croghan by a Virginian who knew of no one "so capable as yourself to give satisfaction on the subject." Croghan answered Robertson's questions most authoritatively.[23]

In the autumn of 1772, Fort Pitt was reduced and its garrison withdrawn. General Gage graciously placed the best building in the fort at Croghan's disposal. The former agent's service continued to be of value to the Crown. It was he who instructed

21. Ohio Co. Papers, I, 93, Hist. Soc. of Pa.
22. Croghan to Barnard and Michael Gratz, Aug. 26, 1772, Gratz Coll., Croghan to Barnard Gratz, July 7, 1772, Gratz-Croghan, I, 29, Etting Coll., Barnard Gratz to Croghan, Nov. 3, 1772, Cadwalader Coll., Hist. Soc. of Pa.; Barnard Gratz to Michael Gratz, July 20, 1772, Henry Joseph Coll., American Jewish Archives (microfilm at Hist. Soc. of Pa.); Croghan to Thomas Wharton, July 29, 1772, Carnegie Library, Pittsburgh.
23. Croghan to Marcus Prevost, June 27, 1773, Haldiman Papers, 21, 730, fol. 105, British Museum; Croghan to Banyar, July 2, 1772, Banyar Papers, N. Y. Hist. Soc.; Nicholas B. Wainwright, "The Opinions of George Croghan on the American Indian," *Pa. Mag. of Hist. and Biog.*, 71 (1947), 152-59.

McKee to visit the Indian villages and explain that the troops had been removed as a gesture of good will because the Indians had always objected to their presence. This was not the reason that the ministry had ordered Fort Pitt abandoned, but the explanation pleased the natives.[24]

Although the year 1772 had begun unhappily for Croghan—in January he had buried his old friend Andrew Montour, murdered by a Seneca house guest at Montour's home near Fort Pitt—it ended joyfully with news that the Privy Council had overruled Lord Hillsborough and had approved Vandalia. The king had given the necessary orders to carry Wharton's proposals into execution, and Lord Dartmouth, who had succeeded the disgruntled Hillsborough, had sent orders to notify the Indians that a new colony would soon be established.[25]

Croghan was delighted. Within a few months, Wharton and Trent would return to America and Vandalia would be organized. Wharton had placed one of the seventy-two Vandalia shares in Croghan's name, and Croghan overgenerously estimated each share to represent 417,000 acres, of which 360,000 acres were choice enough to sell for £10 sterling a hundred. This promised fantastic wealth. Gleefully, he informed Governor Franklin, "I am certain in three months after the new governor makes his appearance here I shall take as much cash as will pay all I owe in the world."[26]

Wharton, the new governor, was hard at work on plans for a suitable gubernatorial residence. To Croghan he sent detailed instructions to erect a large building at Pittsburgh immediately. "I propose this house only as a temporary one, until we fix on a convenient spot for our capitol. . . . Keep up your spirits my friend. You will soon be, not only a rich, but a publick, respectable man."[27]

Croghan had warned Wharton that something had to be done

---

24. Croghan to Gage, Sept. 21, 1772, and Gage to Croghan, Oct. 21, 1772, Clements Library; Croghan to Thomas Wharton, Dec. 23, 1772, *Pa. Mag. of Hist. and Biog.*, 15 (1891), 432-34.

25. Isaac Hamilton to Gage, Jan. 22, 1772, Clements Library; Lewis, *The Indiana Company*, 120.

26. Croghan to Franklin, Dec. 26, 1772, William Franklin folder, Society Autograph Coll., Hist. Soc. of Pa.

27. Wharton to Croghan, Feb. 3, 1773, Cadwalader Coll., Hist. Soc. of Pa.

for the Indians, so long neglected by the army, Pennsylvania, and Sir William Johnson. This was sound advice, and Wharton's English associates agreed that Wharton should give the natives a valuable present when he arrived. To prepare for this great event, a speech, handsomely inscribed upon parchment, was sent to Croghan with the request that he convene the chiefs and read it to them. This impressive document was headed by the name of the Lord Chamberlain, the Earl of Hertford, an impressive champion of Vandalia, since no man was closer to the king than he, and was addressed to the sachems of the Six Nations, Shawnees, and Delawares living on the Ohio River. Conspiratorial as ever, Wharton cautioned Croghan not to let Sir William or General Gage know what it contained.

In May, June, and July, Croghan held meetings with deputies of the western tribes. With due ceremony and much council wampum, he delivered Lord Hertford's address. We suppose, said Croghan, speaking for that noble lord, that you have heard of our resolve to form a new colony on the Ohio. We and others are the sole proprietors of the colony. It is with concern we hear through your good old friend George Croghan that you complain of the trade not being well conducted and that you think the old council fire on the Ohio is neglected. We have, therefore, desired your and our friend Anagurunda [Croghan] to give you this speech. We will always practice peaceful conduct, like Onas and the Quakers. Our roads will be open to you. Trade will be honestly conducted and justice done you. We hope our governor will be with you before the corn is in the ear. Be ready to meet him at the old Ohio council fire.[28]

When the leaves turned red and began to fall, the Indians gathered at Croghan's plantation. But where were Wharton and the present? Croghan did not know that after the king had set his mark of approval on Vandalia, the Board of Trade had taken nine months to draw up the grant, and that necessary instrument was now gathering dust in the offices of the king's legal advisers. Presumably, as soon as they approved it, it would be ratified and Wharton would sail for America. Croghan was frantic. Two

28. Alvord, *The Mississippi Valley in British Politics*, II, 128; "Speech to Indians, No 35," Vandalia folder, Cadwalader Coll., Hist. Soc. of Pa.

weeks ago, he wrote Thomas Wharton in October, one hundred Wyandots, Ottawa, Chippewa, and Delaware chiefs had arrived to attend the intended meeting with the new governor "and are eating up every thing I had provided for the use of my family this winter." Croghan pleaded for £2,000 in goods and £500 in cash, but all the Whartons sent him was £160. Samuel Wharton's cheerful "Keep up your spirits; all will yet be well with us" did not pay any bills.[29]

Ultimately, Croghan spent £1,365 on the Indians, for having called them he could not dismiss them empty-handed. After putting it off as long as possible, he held his treaty in November. To pay for provisions and presents for the four hundred Indians who attended, Croghan borrowed money and pawned his plate and other valuables. Painful as these expedients must have been to him, he at least succeeded in sending the Indians away in good humor, happy that a new government was to be created, and in expectation of meeting its governor in the spring.[30]

Deflated and out of pocket, Croghan voiced his disappointment at the end of 1773 that Vandalia's charter had not yet been approved: "I thought every thing wold a been finished & the offisers of the colony heer before this time, however, I hope itt will take place this winter or be layd aside intierely." Thus, the year which had opened so brilliantly for Vandalia ended in near despair.[31]

Convinced that the powerful Vandalia project had fallen through, Lord Dunmore, governor of Virginia, decided to make good his colony's western claims. Presumably, when Dunmore visited Pittsburgh in the summer of 1773, he met Croghan, for he agreed to recognize the validity of Croghan's Indian grant. It

---

29. Wharton to Croghan, Nov. 3, 1773, Cadwalader Coll., Hist. Soc. of Pa.; Croghan to Thomas Wharton, Oct. 15, 1773, *Pa. Mag. of Hist. and Biog.*, 15 (1891), 434-36.

30. Croghan's bill to Vandalia Company, Vandalia folder, Cadwalader Coll., and Thomas Wharton to Samuel Wharton, Nov. 30, 1773, Wharton Letter Book, Hist. Soc. of Pa. In 1776, each Vandalia share was assessed £11 9s. 9d. to repay Croghan's expenses. Mulkearn, ed., *Mercer Papers*, 325. The silver Croghan pawned to Aeneas Mackay consisted of a coffeepot, a teapot, each with a stand, two mugs, a sugar bowl, a slop bowl, and a candlestick with snuffer. Barnard Gratz to Mackay, Dec. 20, 1776, Henry Joseph Coll., American Jewish Archives (microfilm at Hist. Soc. of Pa.).

31. Croghan to Barnard Gratz, Dec. 27, 1773, Gratz Coll., Hist. Soc. of Pa.

may have been at Croghan's suggestion that Dunmore appointed Dr. John Connolly as his western agent.

Connolly, who had been in the Ohio and Illinois country for the past ten years, was intimately associated with Croghan. He owed Croghan money; in fact, only Croghan's assistance had saved him from a debtor's prison. It was well known that Croghan took a particular interest in this man, although Washington may have overemphasized the relationship when he called Connolly a nephew of Croghan's. Lancaster-born and Philadelphia-educated, unaccustomed to authority and of uncertain moral fiber, Connolly had a personality strong enough to make the most pleasing impression, not only on Lord Dunmore, but on George Washington and Patrick Henry.[32]

With Croghan's full support, Connolly claimed Pittsburgh for Virginia in January, 1774, and called up the militia. The first men to appear on the parade ground for the initial muster came from Croghan Hall. As commandant of the Pittsburgh militia, Connolly announced that he was going to appeal to the House of Burgesses for a new Virginia county at Pittsburgh. Connolly appointed several magistrates, including Croghan's half-brother Edward Ward and his cousin Thomas Smallman. Of Connolly's activities, a Pennsylvanian at Pittsburgh exclaimed, "Its thought here that 'tis all Colonel Croghan's intrigues." Certain it is that, when Lord Dunmore subsequently appointed justices of the peace for the new district of West Augusta, Croghan's name headed the list, and that in Philadelphia people actually believed that Dunmore had seized Pittsburgh at Croghan's suggestion.[33]

Pennsylvanians were righteously indignant at Dunmore for wresting away territory that had been administered by Pennsylvania for five years. Arthur St. Clair, a former British army officer, was chief official for the Penns west of the mountains. "Mr. Croghan's emissaries (and it is astonishing how many he has either

32. Hamilton, ed., *Letters to Washington*, IV, 310-11; Fitzpatrick, ed., *Diaries of Washington*, I, 447; Thomas Wharton to Thomas Walpole, Sept. 23, 1774, Wharton Letter Book, Baynton to Croghan, May 12, June 25, 1770, Cadwalader Coll., and Gratz-Croghan, II, 59, Etting Coll., Hist. Soc. of Pa.

33. Aeneas Mackay to St. Clair, Jan. 11, 1774, Smith, ed., *St. Clair Papers*, I, 272-73; Lyman Chalkley, *Chronicles of the Scotch-Irish Settlement in Virginia* (Rosslyn, Va., 1912), I, 177; Francis Wade to Johnson, Feb. 1, Mar. 6, 1774, *Johnson Papers*, VIII, 1022, 1064-65.

duped or seduced to embrace his measures)," wrote St. Clair, "are continually irritating [the people] against Pennsylvania, and assuring them they are not within its limits."[34]

On the principle that any law was better than no law, Croghan had obeyed Pennsylvania's laws, but he had otherwise denied her jurisdiction in his refusal to pay taxes. Had he paid those taxes, he said, his "liberty and property was in as much danger as all the rest of my fellow subjects in the Colonies have thought theirs, by submitting to a tax lay'd on them by the British parliament, and which they have allways withstood." Now that Virginia had moved in, he refused to countenance Pennsylvania's laws any longer, "for it must be granted that if any colony has a right to extend their laws to this country, Virginia must till his Majesty's pleasure be known therein."[35]

Shaking off a severe attack of gout, Croghan wrote Lord Dunmore that in 1769 the king had confirmed him in his Indian grant, an astonishing piece of misinformation, since, as Croghan well knew, this was exactly what the king had refused to do. Despite this confirmation of his title, continued Croghan, Pennsylvania had taken over the western country and sold much of his property. "The people who thus purchased of Mr. Penn's agents made forcible entrys on my lands by which means I have been deprived the use of my property and had no means of relief or expectations, till the Colony of Virginia should extend their jurisdiction, or his Majesty should grant a new colony."[36]

If Croghan thought that Pennsylvania would meekly relinquish its claims, he was wrong. A chaotic situation arose with two sets of provincial officers struggling to control lands west of the Alleghenies. Flushed with self-importance, Connolly became increasingly arbitrary and high-handed. He even presumed to treat Croghan, to whom he had previously been deferential, in an overbearing manner.

It was at this unfortunate time that a new Indian crisis arose. Virginia surveyors had alarmed the Shawnees some months earlier

34. St. Clair to Joseph Shippen, Feb. 25, 1774, Smith, ed., *St. Clair Papers*, I, 284-85.
35. Croghan to David Sample, Apr. 4, 1774, *Pa. Archives*, IV, 483.
36. Croghan to Dunmore, Apr. 9, 1774, Cadwalader Coll., Hist. Soc. of Pa.

by entering their country. Croghan's efforts to preserve justice for the Shawnees were misunderstood by whites and reds alike. In turning back a party of Virginians, the Shawnees told them that Croghan had authorized the natives to kill and rob all intruders. Settlers thought that Croghan's attempts to keep the two races from each other's throats were evidence of his siding with the hated redskins.[37]

In the spring of 1774, white men perpetrated a series of particularly brutal Indian murders. Among the victims were some Shawnees. Croghan stepped into the breach by neutralizing the Senecas and Delawares, neither of whom wanted war, and by sending messengers to the Indian towns, urging the natives to keep quiet and not to harm the traders. Connolly briefly cooperated in this good work.[38]

Bewildered and angered by the murders, the Shawnee chief Cornstalk, nevertheless, protected the English traders in his town and sent them safely under escort to Pittsburgh. Cornstalk did not want war, and it is probable that if Croghan had been given authority, war could have been prevented. Unfortunately, the measures pursued by Dunmore and Connolly made war inevitable. Patrick Henry, who had attended a conference between Dunmore and Connolly, said that Dunmore favored a war in order to drive the Indians off a tract of land he desired.[39]

Arthur St. Clair came to Pittsburgh to appraise the situation. He found the settlers terrified and about to evacuate the area. Joining with Croghan and several others, St. Clair raised a company of one hundred men. In reply to Connolly, who questioned what he had done, Croghan explained, "I have subscribed with a number of gentlemen boath of Verginia and Pensylvaine to hier a number of men to reconitre & scout a long the river Ohio towards Ligonier in order to protect our fellow subjects from flying down the cuntry as itt apears that a general panick has sased the whole

---

37. R. G. Thwaites and L. P. Kellogg, eds., *Documentary History of Dunmore's War* (Madison, 1905), 7; Francis Wade to Johnson, Mar. 6, 1774, *Johnson Papers*, VIII, 1064-66.

38. Croghan to Connolly and McKee, May 4 and May 5, 1774, Cadwalader Coll., Hist. Soc. of Pa.; *Pa. Archives*, IV, 496.

39. Thomas Wharton to Thomas Walpole, Sept. 23, 1774, Wharton Letter Book, Hist. Soc. of Pa.; *Pa. Archives*, IV, 497-98.

cuntry. I have likewise hierd a fwe men to live with myself hier & protect my property."[40]

More interested in the dignity of Virginia than the safety of the people, Connolly was outraged at these extralegal measures. Fearful that they might somehow or other be subversive of Virginia's rights, he furiously wrote Croghan that what he had done was "unlawful, unwarrantable & affrontive." He sent an officer to take a list of the men in arms at his house. Disgusted, Croghan believed that Connolly was attacking him in order to create fresh misunderstandings between Pennsylvania and Virginia. Faced with the likelihood that the Indian troubles might be made up, Connolly foresaw that only by keeping the fur flying could he remain in power.[41]

Croghan's association with St. Clair did not imply, as so many believed, that he had deserted Virginia. But Croghan was at outs with Connolly over the latter's disastrous Indian policy and determined to go to Williamsburg to talk it over with Dunmore. "Mr. Croghan's views," St. Clair informed Governor Penn, "I do not pretend to see, but this you may be assured of, he is at present a friend to this country, and if it depends on him we shall yet have no war." Alarmed at Croghan's mission, for he must have known that Croghan blamed the calamitous state of affairs on him, Connolly wrote George Washington to defeat whatever Croghan might try to do: "You must well know how specious he is, but you may be assured that his business there is not for the publick good, but to answer private & ungenerous designs. . . . As he is specious where unknown he may impose & carry points." One of Croghan's creditors at least partially agreed with Connolly. He hoped Croghan would raise some money on his trip as "he is such an artfull person, I make no doubt he will take some person in, in Virginia."[42]

Aeneas Mackay, to whom Croghan had pawned his plate to pay

40. St. Clair to John Penn, May 29, 1774, Smith, ed., *St. Clair Papers*, I, 297; Croghan to Connolly [June, 1774], Cadwalader Coll., Hist. Soc. of Pa.
41. Connolly to Croghan, June 3, 1774, Cadwalader Coll., Hist. Soc. of Pa.; Croghan to St. Clair, June 4, 1774, *Pa. Archives*, IV, 508.
42. John Montgomery to John Penn, June 3, 1774, *Pa. Archives*, IV, 506; St. Clair to John Penn, June 7, 1774, Smith, ed., *St. Clair Papers*, I, 304; Connolly to Washington, June 7, 1774, Hamilton, ed., *Letters to Washington*, V, 8-9; L. A. Levy to Michael Gratz, June 23, 1774, McAllister Coll., Lib. Co. of Phila.

for the recent Vandalia Indian treaty, was a leader of Pennsylvania sentiment at Pittsburgh. He had this to say of his political enemy: "Mr Croghan, who has been grossly abused by our bashaw [Connolly] lately, is gone to Williamsburg to represent every part of his conduct to the Gover and Council in its true light. Altho' others doubts, I am very certain, Mr. Croghan is earnest and sincere respecting that intention, for he joins the rest of the inhabitants, in charging all our present calamity to the Doctors act."[43]

Croghan did set out for Williamsburg, but, discovering that his departure was causing consternation among the settlers, who thought he was fleeing the country, he came home again. A few days later, he had the pleasure of receiving at his house the traders whom the Shawnees had humanely conducted back to a brutal civilization.[44]

Whether or not Connolly was pleased to hear that these traders had escaped death is not known. It is clear, however, that he felt no gratitude toward the three Shawnee chiefs who had escorted them safely home. He sent forty militiamen to Croghan's to arrest the Indians, or, as was more generally believed, to kill them. Friendly word arriving in time, the chiefs were spirited across the Allegheny. But the soldiers, after searching Croghan's place, went off in hot pursuit, catching up with the chiefs and shooting one. The traders at Pittsburgh were horrified at Connolly's action and joined in a statement that he had done everything in his power to create trouble with the Indians.[45]

"Whatever may be Mr. Croghan's real views," wrote St. Clair, "I am certain he is hearty in promoting the general tranquillity of the country; indeed he is indefatigable in endeavoring to make up the breeches." In the past, when Croghan calmed the natives, he had been backed by impressive presents furnished by Pennsylvania or the army. Now he had no such support, not even an official position. It was at his own expense that he entertained Indian chiefs all summer and held conference after conference. In opening one of these meetings with a prominent Delaware chief, Croghan began, "I now speake to you as a friend

43. Mackay to John Penn, June 14, 1774, *Pa. Archives*, IV, 517.
44. St. Clair to John Penn, June 22, 1774, *ibid.*, 523-24.
45. *Ibid.*, 527, 582-83; Smith, ed., *St. Clair Papers*, I, 312, 314-16, 318-19.

to both parties, your nation and the English, and not by any particular authority."[46]

He had given up his attempt to prevent a Shawnee war, but he bent every effort to localize the conflict. A general conflagration, Croghan believed, was on the verge of breaking out: "I have not yett deard to inform the cuntry of thire dangerous situation, as, if I had, they wold all fly away over the mountains." He urged the Pennsylvania government to send presents and spokesmen to treat with the Ohio Indians. Pennsylvania sent a little wampum and a friendly speech, which was delivered to the chiefs at Croghan Hall. But this was hardly enough. Croghan appealed to the Quakers to mediate. They refused to do so on the grounds that they could not interfere in governmental affairs. Their attitude had changed since 1762.[47]

The Philadelphia members of the Vandalia group responded to Croghan's frantic request and sent him fifty thousand wampum beads. With this wampum, Croghan promised to exert his influence in one last effort, after which he would probably have to leave Pittsburgh, for he could no longer feed and care for the Indians who clustered about him. "All the expense falls on me, no other person in this cuntry seeming inclind to do anything."[48]

In August, deputies from the Six Nations arrived with a great council belt for Croghan and McKee, announcing the death in July of Sir William Johnson. Johnson had died the day before the sheriff put 50,893 acres of Croghan's New York lands on the block; his death depressed the value of the property. Nevertheless, bids totaled £4,840. Unfortunately, only £900 of this sum went to reduce Croghan's debts, because much of the purchase money was never paid, and the sheriff absconded with a portion of what was received.[49]

The secret of Croghan's success in keeping the Mingoes and the Delawares quiet was the control he exercised over their leaders.

46. St. Clair to John Penn, June 22, 1774, *ibid.*, 315; *Pa. Archives*, IV, 554.
47. Croghan to Thomas Wharton, [Aug.] 12, [1774], Carnegie Library, Pittsburgh.
48. Croghan to Thomas Wharton, Aug. 10, 1774, *ibid.*; Thomas Wharton to Croghan, Aug. 28, 1774, Cadwalader Coll., Hist. Soc. of Pa.
49. Smith, ed., *St. Clair Papers*, I, 338; Ohio Co. Papers, II, 21, and Croghan to William Smith, July 16, 1779, Hist. Soc. of Pa.

Probably the most prominent of the Ohio chiefs was Kiasutha, a Seneca. Long a close personal friend of Croghan's, Kiasutha had impressed Johnson as a man of extraordinary ability and vast influence. Over the years, Croghan had done many favors for Kiasutha and, during this summer of 1774, built or repaired a house for the chief. The principal Delawares were the Pipe and Grey Eyes. Croghan had been instrumental in appointing the Pipe to high office in 1773, when the Delaware succeeded his aged uncle Custaloga as chief. At the same time another chief, Newcomer, was judged incompetent and was replaced by Grey Eyes, a notable Indian employed by Croghan in the fur trade.[50]

From Samuel Wharton, Croghan continued to receive encouraging news about Vandalia. Although the grant had not yet passed the seals, it had been promised. Only the violent differences between the colonies and their mother country delayed matters. In 1774, Wharton brought up a top secret subject which he had referred to Croghan three years earlier, the subject of purchasing a large quantity of land directly from the Indians. Wharton wrote that he would soon send over £4,000- or £5,000-worth of goods for this purpose. Unknown to Wharton, Croghan had already made a highly secretive purchase for himself of 1,500,000 acres. This land, for which he paid $6,000 raised in Virginia, lay west of the Ohio and was acquired on the understanding that he would not settle it for fifteen years, unless the natives moved away before then to find better hunting grounds.[51]

During the summer, a large shipment of goods, designated as a present for the Indians at the opening of the new colony, arrived and was placed in storage, since Dunmore's War prevented its shipment west. Another "very large parcel of goods," including household furniture for Samuel Wharton's Pittsburgh mansion, also came over and was stored at Georgetown awaiting further

---

50. Andrew Ramsey's bill receipted June 11, 1774, Croghan's vouchers for 1774, Cadwalader Coll., Hist. Soc. of Pa.; Johnson to Gage, Oct. 14, 1772, *Johnson Papers*, VIII, 616; meeting of Kiasutha with Johnson, Jan. 5, 1774, Clements Library.

51. Samuel Wharton to Croghan, May 2, May 4, 1774, Cadwalader Coll., and Croghan to Trent, July 13, 1775, Ohio Co. Papers, II, 6, Hist. Soc. of Pa.; Boyd Crumrine, "Minute Book of the Virginia Court Held at Fort Dunmore . . . ," *Annals of the Carnegie Museum*, 1 (1901-2), 554.

orders. This shipment was to pay the Indians for the large new purchase Wharton planned.[52]

Meanwhile, Dunmore arrived at Pittsburgh in September to marshal his expedition against the Shawnees. While there, he called Croghan on the carpet to answer Connolly's accusations about inciting the Shawnees to attack Virginia and siding with Pennsylvania against Virginia. Croghan easily disproved the charges and was reinstated in Dunmore's good graces. Like Croghan, Dunmore's interest in land was intense. Just before he left Pittsburgh to fight the Shawnees, he pictured so glowing a future for western land development that a speculator joyfully commented, *"Stocks ought to rise."*[53]

The Virginia governor brought his war against the Shawnees to a successful conclusion that fall. Leaving a garrison of seventy-five men under Connolly at Fort Dunmore, a temporary name for old Fort Pitt, he returned to Williamsburg. To strengthen his grip on Virginia's western territory, Dunmore adjourned the Augusta county court from Staunton to Pittsburgh. Croghan served as president judge of this court from its inception, attending eleven of its sixteen sessions during 1775.[54]

The Revolutionary movement, which swept the land in 1775 after the battles of Lexington and Concord, saw the creation in May of a committee of correspondence at Pittsburgh for the Virginia District of West Augusta. This body of twenty-eight men, headed by Croghan as chairman, emphatically endorsed the Revolutionary activities in New England and took immediate steps to raise and train a militia. Pennsylvania organized a rival committee at nearby Hannastown, and the contest for authority became more bitter than ever. "You gentlemen, we suppose," wrote the Hannastown group to Croghan's group, "are the representatives of the people west of Laurel Hill who acknowledge themselves bound by and wish to live under the laws of Virginia. We are the

---

52. Thomas Wharton to John Ballendine, July 25, 1774, Wharton Letter Book, and Thomas Wharton to Croghan, Sept. 30, 1774, Cadwalader Coll., Hist. Soc. of Pa.

53. Dunmore to Croghan, Sept. 14, 1774, and two replies of Croghan's of Sept. 15, 1774, Cadwalader Coll., and Alexander Ross to Matthew Ridley, Sept. 16, 1774, Dreer Coll., Hist. Soc. of Pa.

54. Boyd Crumrine, "Minute Book of the Virginia Court Held at Fort Dunmore . . . ," *Annals of the Carnegie Museum*, 1 (1901-2), 526-68.

representatives of those who acknowledge the laws of Pennsylvania." St. Clair complained, "We have nothing but musters & committees all over the country, and everything seems to be running into the greatest confusion."[55]

Croghan and most of his associates espoused the patriot cause, and Croghan, the elder statesman of the region, initially headed the local revolutionaries. Several early actions taken by the Pittsburgh committee indicate his influence. It notified Congress of its "fears of a rupture with the Indians on account of Lord Dunmore's conduct" and requested commissioners from Virginia and Pennsylvania to come to Pittsburgh and treat with the Indians. The committee also assisted Connolly in calling an Indian meeting to ratify Dunmore's treaty of peace.[56]

This conference, which held its first meeting at Croghan's house on June 19, 1775, seemingly settled Indian affairs satisfactorily despite confusion caused at the very outset of the treaty, when a band of Pennsylvanians descended on Connolly and carried him off to Hannastown, a prisoner of the boundary war. Croghan and his committeemen penned so spirited a letter to the Hannastown group that they promptly returned their captive. After the treaty, Connolly disbanded the Fort Dunmore garrison and went off to join Lord Dunmore, who had fled his unruly province for the safety of a man-of-war. Connolly's dreams of returning to Pittsburgh at the head of invincible British legions never came true, and there is much in his subsequent career that smacks of comic opera.[57]

While the dust from Connolly's departure settled on the Pittsburgh road, Croghan read a letter from that prince of plotters, Samuel Wharton. Vandalia still hung fire and Wharton remained in London, but he had sent his lieutenant William Trent back to America. Vandalia would probably come through, but, if it failed, Wharton and his American friends still had the Indiana grant, whose title they believed good. Yet, drunk with the lust for land,

[55]. *Pa. Archives*, Sixth Series, II, 3; Hanna, *Wilderness Trail*, II, 77-78; letter dated July 6, 1775, Hannas Town folder, Gratz Coll., Hist. Soc. of Pa.; St. Clair to John Penn, May 25, 1775, *Pa. Archives*, IV, 628.
[56]. *Journals of Congress* . . . (Philadelphia, 1777), I, 112; *Va. Mag. of Hist. and Biog.*, 14 (1906), 57.
[57]. Valentine Crawford to Washington, June 24, 1775, Smith, ed., *St. Clair Papers*, I, 357.

Wharton wanted millions of acres more. He sent Trent to negotiate with Croghan the delicate details of the Indian purchase "which you so positively wrote me, you *could* make and upon which declaration I have formed the plan of purchase and procured the great cargo for it now lying in Maryland." Croghan was to have two shares in the purchase which was to be made for a small syndicate, most of whose members were English. Make the purchase immediately, urged Wharton, for the Quebec Act, with its proviso that all private Indian purchases made after its passage would be illegal, was pending. Don't let Guy Johnson (Sir William's successor) have a chance to counteract the transaction through the Six Nations, and don't let anyone know what you are doing until it is effected.[58]

Trent forwarded Wharton's letter with one of his own dated June 22, 1775, at Georgetown. How far, inquired Trent, had Croghan proceeded in this great purchase? Croghan reacted with surprise. He had never been authorized to do a thing in the matter; in fact, he thought it had been laid aside because of the Anglo-American crisis. As a sop, he offered to sell Trent and Wharton a million acres out of the "small" purchase he had made in 1773.[59]

When Croghan made this offer to Trent on July 13, he concealed the fact that three days earlier he had bought six million acres on the western headwaters of the Allegheny from the Six Nations. Kiasutha and the other chiefs sold him this land for twelve thousand Spanish dollars "in consideration of the great justice and integrity of the said George Croghan, used and exercised by him toward the Six Nations and their allies in all his publick and private conduct and transactions." Like his 1773 purchase, it was not to be settled immediately. Croghan sold one-fifth of his six million acres to the well-known Virginia speculator Thomas Walker (for five thousand Spanish dollars), and conveyed other fractions (twenty-fourths) to his creditors.[60]

58. Samuel Wharton to Croghan, Apr. 17, 1775, Cadwalader Coll., and Samuel Wharton to Thomas Wharton, Jan. 31, 1775, Wharton Coll., Hist. Soc. of Pa.
59. Croghan to Trent, July 13, 1775, Ohio Co. Papers, II, 6, Hist. Soc. of Pa.
60. R. C. M. Page, *Genealogy of the Page Family of Virginia* (New York, 1893), 206-9; Thomas Walker to Croghan, July 22, 1777, Cadwalader Coll.,

As for the land Samuel Wharton wanted Croghan to buy, that purchase, if ever made, fell through. In the latter part of 1775, Trent busied himself in the matter, giving presents to Kiasutha and other chiefs "to secure their interest" and even buying six sheets of parchment on which to record the transaction. Croghan hoped to make the purchase in the spring of 1776, but, on that expectation, the matter dropped out of sight, no doubt cut short by the Revolution.[61]

Despite the personal assurances Croghan had received during his visit to England from Lord Camden and Charles Yorke (both of whom attained the eminent position of Lord Chancellor) that Indian titles were good, despite the best English legal opinion to the same effect which Wharton collected, and despite the approval of the best American opinion—Benjamin Franklin, Patrick Henry, Edmund Pendleton—the authorities were reluctant to recognize their validity. Ultimately, the decision went against such titles, and Croghan's hopes for a fortune in western lands toppled like a house of cards. Wharton suggested that Congress be bribed into passing a resolution favoring Indian titles by taking eight members of Congress into partnership in the Indian purchase Croghan was to make. But the unscrupulousness, the greed, and the want of moral standards which characterized Wharton and his associates did not pay off.[62]

During the summer of 1775 Croghan, somewhat restored in health from the crippling gout, visited Warm Springs in Virginia, where he was joined by Trent. On this excursion, Croghan was prostrated by an enormous, painful boil on his back.

Hist. Soc. of Pa.; deed, Croghan to Joseph Wharton, Oct. 20, 1780, courtesy of George R. Loeb.

61. Ohio Co. Papers, II, 57, and Croghan to [Samuel Wharton], Nov. 14, 1775, Cadwalader Coll., Hist. Soc. of Pa.; Barnard Gratz to Michael Gratz, Nov. 14, 1775, Henry Joseph Coll., American Jewish Archives (microfilm at Hist. Soc. of Pa.).

62. W. Murray to the Gratzes, May 15, 1773, Ohio Co. Papers, I, 102, and Samuel Wharton to Thomas Wharton, Aug. 7, 1775, Wharton Coll., Hist. Soc. of Pa.; [Samuel Wharton], *Plain Facts Being an Examination into the Rights of Indian Nations of America* . . . (Philadelphia, 1781), 102-3. When Trent returned to America in 1775, he brought the opinion of Counselor Henry Dagge and Serjeant John Glyn supporting the validity of the Indiana grant. Both Patrick Henry and Benjamin Franklin endorsed this opinion. "Opinion Regarding the Grant to Wm Trent 1775," Hist. Soc. of Pa.

Recovering, he returned to Fort Pitt in time to witness an Indian treaty conducted by commissioners from the Continental Congress as well as commissioners from Virginia, who had come to settle differences with the Shawnees.[63]

During the course of the treaty, Croghan, Trent, Morgan, and six others interested in the Indiana grant met together and, on the basis that the land given them by the Indians at Fort Stanwix innately enjoyed a good, clear title, decided to open a land office and begin sales in their tract. This attempt to take the bull by the horns without obtaining recognition of their title by competent authority was soon blocked by Virginia.[64]

As the struggle for independence gathered momentum, Croghan's pre-eminence as an Indian negotiator began to fade. Congress organized an Indian department on July 12, 1775, and Indian trader Richard Butler, not Croghan, was appointed agent at Pittsburgh. Croghan did not even participate in the important treaty in September of that year. He did, however, cooperate with Butler by giving him intelligence of British designs to influence the natives, and he sent messengers through the lake country, urging the tribes to remain neutral and to disregard what they were told by the British at Detroit and Niagara.[65]

In 1775, Croghan made another major effort to clear up his debts, which now totaled nearly £24,000. He placed 45,498 acres of his land, which he believed would fall outside the Pennsylvania boundary, in trust for his creditors and tried to sell off all his remaining New York lands, except the Croghan's Forest homestead which he had promised to Augustine Prevost. Unfortunately, lands in that part of New York became scenes of Tory raids and massacres and were unsalable. Although his efforts to honor his obligations seemed sincere, Croghan's sharp practices had injured his creditors. He had, for example, mortgaged forty thousand Otsego acres to Governor Franklin with a second mortgage on half of the same property to Thomas Wharton. Then,

---

63. Trent to Mrs. Prevost, Aug. 21, 1775, Society Autograph Coll., Hist. Soc. of Pa.
64. Ohio Co. Papers, II, 9, Hist. Soc. of Pa.
65. Savelle, *George Morgan*, 133; R. G. Thwaites and L. P. Kellogg, *The Revolution on the Upper Ohio*, 1775-1777 (Madison, 1908), 125-27; "Richard Butler 1775 Intellegence about Indians," Gratz Coll., Hist. Soc. of Pa.

despite the two mortgages, he sold off most of the land, leaving the mortgage holders faced with the unpleasant probability of having to sue the purchasers. "On the whole," observed Thomas Wharton in charitable understatement, "I must say this affair wears a very disagreable aspect."[66]

Unhappily for Croghan, so many facets of his character wore such a disagreeable aspect that the authorities would not trust him. However, he continued as chairman of Pittsburgh's committee of correspondence. In that capacity, he reported that his former assistant Alexander McKee had received a letter from the British commandant at Niagara. The committee put McKee on parole not to leave the area or do anything inimical to American interests. Learning, in April, 1776, that Richard Butler was retiring as Indian agent, Croghan, backed by the recommendation of his committee, made a strong bid for the job. It must have been a bitter blow to his pride when the position went to George Morgan instead. Indian agent Morgan had absolutely no use for Croghan. When he wanted advice, Morgan called on McKee.[67]

The aging, worn-out veteran of a thousand Indian meetings sought the solace of Virginia's Warm Springs. He had been cast aside, no longer judged competent to work among the natives. When that shining aspect of George Croghan's life flickered and went out, the shadows of obscurity closed about him fast.[68]

66. Croghan to [Gratz], June 5, 1775, Gratz-Croghan, I, 45, and II, 90, Etting Coll., Thomas Wharton to Croghan, Mar. 13, 1775, Cadwalader Coll., Thomas Wharton to James Duane, Mar. 18, 1775, Wharton Letter Book, Hist. Soc. of Pa.
67. Hanna, *Wilderness Trail*, II, 80; Richard Butler to James Wilson, Apr. 23, 1776, Gratz Coll., John Campbell to Lee, Law, and Roberdeau, Nov. 19, 1777, Papers Relating to French Refugees, Colonial, and Indian Affairs, 65, 69, Dreer Coll., Hist. Soc. of Pa.
68. Barnard Gratz to Michael Gratz, Aug. 17, 1776, Henry Joseph Coll., American Jewish Archives (microfilm at Hist. Soc. of Pa.).

14

End of the Trail

CROGHAN VISITED Virginia again during the summer of 1777. In company with the Gratz brothers and at their expense, he went to Williamsburg to try to obtain a clear title to the land he had sold them. Unsuccessful in his efforts, he returned home, bearing dispatches from Governor Patrick Henry to General Edward Hand, the commander at Fort Pitt.[1]

General Hand, who had come to America less than ten years earlier as a surgeon's mate with the Royal Irish Regiment and who had purchased land from Croghan, welcomed the aging speculator none too pleasantly. A "most horrid conspiracy," a loyalist plot, had just been discovered. A large number of disaffected people, Hand believed, were organizing to join the English, led, so rumor had it, by Pittsburgh's most important citizens. He arrested Colonel George Morgan, the Indian agent, Alexander McKee, Simon Girty, and others. He ordered Thomas Smallman's papers examined. The tension which gripped an alarmed countryside was intensified by roving parties of hostile Wyandots and Chippewas. On August 24, enemy natives wounded a man near Croghan Hall, only four miles from General Hand's fort.[2]

Croghan earlier had been under suspicion of sending letters to Niagara, and it was recalled that he had permitted Alexander McKee to visit the Indian country with George Morgan. Since McKee and Morgan were the main suspects, Croghan's action now

---

1. R. G. Thwaites and L. P. Kellogg, *Frontier Defense on the Upper Ohio, 1777-1778* (Madison, 1912), 30; Patrick Henry to Edward Hand, Aug. 9, 1777, Emmett Coll., N. Y. Pub. Lib.
2. Hand to Mrs. Hand, Aug. 25, 1777, Hand Papers, Hist. Soc. of Pa.; Thwaites and Kellogg, *Frontier Defense*, 36, 73, 156, 184-86.

put him in a bad light. His reputation for untrustworthiness, his fifteen years as an officer of the Crown, and the fact that his son-in-law was on active duty with the British army were all black marks against him. For the security of Pittsburgh, it was suggested that Croghan had better clear out and go to Philadelphia.[3]

"I am sorry the people were so foolish to use Col. Croghan so ill as to force him to goe to Philadelphia," wrote Trent. "I am of opinion he neither could be of any injury to the country, nor would be if he had it in his power." Trent was right, for Croghan was a patriot. After thorough investigation, the "horrid conspiracy" at Pittsburgh turned out to be a tempest in a teapot.[4]

Accompanied by his clerk John Campbell and by his servant James Forrest, Croghan came to Philadelphia and took up residence in Monckton Hall. Two weeks later, General Howe and his victorious British army occupied the city. Croghan, bedridden again with gout, could not escape.

Howe promptly called Croghan to headquarters and berated him for serving as a committeeman at Pittsburgh and for neutralizing the Lake Indians. The general ordered him to take lodgings in town, where he was billeted with two officers who kept him under close scrutiny. No doubt, Croghan heard the sounds of battle on October 4, when Washington surprised but did not defeat the British at Germantown. The result of the battle was disastrous to Croghan, for it alarmed Howe into building a fortified line from the Schuylkill to the Delaware. To make these entrenchments tenable, twenty-seven country mansions located along the line were consigned to the flames, among them Monckton Hall. The destruction of this estate, named for the officer whom Croghan had thought would succeed Amherst, was another severe financial blow.

3. *Va. Mag. of Hist. and Biog.*, 16 (1908), 54-55; Papers Relating to French Refugees, Colonial, and Indian Affairs, 66, 69, Dreer Coll., Hist. Soc. of Pa.

4. Trent to Barnard Gratz, Nov. 10, 1777, Etting Coll., Hist. Soc. of Pa. Lord Dunmore, presumably assisted by Connolly, drew up a list of loyalists in the Pittsburgh area. Croghan's name was not included. Hanna, *Wilderness Trail*, II, 79-80. It is possible that Croghan's patriotism may have wavered later, but not probable. In 1781, General Clinton received encouragement purportedly from Croghan and John Connolly to attack Pittsburgh. Whether Croghan actually joined with Connolly in this scheme cannot be positively known. See Frederick Haldimand to Clinton, Sept. 29, 1781, Clements Library.

Philadelphia was gay enough that winter, a scene of dissipation and pleasure. Guineas clinked on the faro tables, and British officers acted on the boards of the playhouse, but Croghan kept to himself. Joseph Galloway, Tory mayor of Philadelphia, told him that Howe was very angry, for he had received word from Canada of the damage done to the British cause by Croghan's speeches to the western tribes.

In June, 1778, when the British prepared to evacuate Philadelphia, Croghan was ordered to accompany their prisoners. He had been through hard times, but this summons was the greatest shock of all. An old friend, Major General James Robertson, interceded, and Croghan was permitted to remain in Philadelphia on parole. No sooner had he escaped the danger of being carted away by the enemy, than he found himself proscribed by the state of Pennsylvania. His name was linked with Alexander McKee and Simon Girty, who were now renegades, and he was accused of having "knowingly and willingly aided and assisted the enemies of this State, and of the United States of America, by having joined their armies at Philadelphia."[5]

Unable to discover the exact nature of the charges against him, which he suspected arose from ill will for his support of Virginia in the boundary struggle, and abed with gout, Croghan sent for Chief Justice Thomas McKean. Persuasive as ever, he convinced McKean that he had been pilloried out of sheer maliciousness. Shortly afterward, Plunket Fleeson, who had upholstered so many of Croghan's chairs in green damask, administered the oath of allegiance to him. Although Croghan spent considerable money painting and refurbishing his carriage, he did not take advantage of the pass McKean had given him. Feeling abused, he remained in Philadelphia lodgings, on Fourth Street near Spruce, awaiting the sitting of the court to "see what they have against me and try if the[y] wont restore my carrecter."[6]

To Thomas Walker, the noted Virginia land speculator, he

---

5. *Pennsylvania Packet*, June 17, 1778; Croghan to Thomas Walker, July 23, 1778, Cadwalader Coll., Hist. Soc. of Pa.

6. Oath dated July 16, 1778, Cadwalader Coll., and Croghan to William Smith [October, 1778], Hist. Soc. of Pa.; Michael Gratz to Barnard Gratz, July 7, 1778, Henry Joseph Coll., American Jewish Archives (microfilm at Hist. Soc. of Pa.).

wrote: "You must remember my opinion from the begining of the disputes wh was that if America was to be conquered itt must conquer itt self, wh danger I think is over, as the English army where ever they go make every man there enemys.... I believe you will do me justice to blive that while I stayd at Fort Pitt I don every thing in my power to advise the diferant tribes to a strict nutrality, & I yett think all the westren tribes might be brought to there sences with proper manidgment." Croghan was replying to a letter from Walker in which the Virginian had poetically expressed the hope that "your skill & influence with the savages may prevent in some measure the impending ravages." But no one called on Croghan for such services.[7]

On November 12, 1778, Croghan had his day in court, cleared himself of treason, and then went to Lancaster to spend the winter. He would have liked to return to Pittsburgh to protect his real estate holdings, which were overrun by squatters (against whom he brought more than 130 suits), but it seemed unwise. When his clerk went back to Pittsburgh earlier in the year, General Hand had arrested him on suspicion of disloyalty. Moreover, while Croghan awaited trial, word came east that Hand had executed Smallman for treason. The rumor was false but, nonetheless, unsettling. Croghan subsequently had to order Smallman not to write him because of the danger of the times.[8]

With the assistance of the Gratzes, Croghan again tried to settle affairs with creditors, several of whom, he felt, were victimizing him: "Some pople thinks me an od kind of a careless fellow from the dispusision & readyness I have allways shone by giveg one security after another to such persons as I had any dailings wth when I found them unesey, neaver suspecting that men of carrecter wold take advantage." Writing to Barnard Gratz, Croghan noted, "Itt was of my own free will I promised to pay all those old

---

7. Walker to Croghan, June 9, 1778, and Croghan to Walker, July 23, 1778, Cadwalader Coll., Hist. Soc. of Pa.
8. Certificate of Court of Oyer and Terminer and General Gaol Delivery, Dec. 3, 1778, and John Campbell to Croghan, May 15, 1781, Cadwalader Coll., and Edward Burd to Jasper Yeates, June 28, 1778, Dreer Coll., Hist. Soc. of Pa.; Louise Phelps Kellogg, *Frontier Advance on the Upper Ohio* (Madison, 1916), 50-51; Boyd Crumrine, "Minute Book of Virginia Court Held for Yohogania County," *Annals of the Carnegie Museum*, 2 (1903), 287-88, 194, 308-9, 316-17, 337, 371.

debts, which was nott commonly done by people that failed in trade." To Joseph Simon, he mortgaged his valuable Croghan Hall estate. As for the rest, "I am come to a resolution to sell & pay every farthing I owe in America as soon as posible."

"I have no sheets here, please send me some, & some scarlet flannel," wrote Croghan on the day before Christmas, 1778, to faithful Barnard Gratz. "It snows fast here, [there] will be fine slaying." So passed another year, leaving Croghan in worse financial condition than ever.[9]

The Gratzes stood behind Croghan. They sent him oysters and red herring to eat and provided him with money. They paid off a large account owed to Shippen & Lawrence since 1750, and, when Croghan was sued by a creditor in Lancaster's Court of Common Pleas for £806, the Gratzes saved him from jail. They also financed him on another trip to Williamsburg in June, 1779, and accompanied him there.[10]

Their generosity stemmed, in part, from Croghan's deeding them 74,000 acres of his Indian grant, and their visit to Williamsburg was in response to an invitation from the Virginia legislature to those who laid claim to lands by Indian titles. Barnard Gratz presented a memorial on behalf of Croghan's title, and Trent argued the case for the Indiana Company. To their great disappointment, Virginia reaffirmed its stand against Indian titles. Another memorial by Gratz in November, 1779, was also rejected. Before many months were out, it was discovered that Croghan's lands were not even in Virginia.[11]

Croghan returned to Lancaster and to bed with gout. Discouraged or cautious because of the war, he wrote few letters and was shut off from friends and family. "Pray, how is the old gentleman?" inquired William Croghan, now a major in a Virginia regi-

---

9. Croghan to William Smith, Dec. 24, 1778, Society Autograph Coll., and Augustine Prevost to the Gratzes, May 26, 1783, Gratz-Croghan, I, 100, Etting Coll., Hist. Soc. of Pa.; Croghan to Barnard Gratz, Dec. 24, 1778, N. Y. Pub. Lib.; Volwiler, *George Croghan*, 52-53.

10. Ohio Co. Papers, II, 39, and William Croghan to Barnard Gratz, Aug. 22, 1779, Gratz-Croghan, I, 65, Etting Coll., Hist. Soc. of Pa.

11. Barnard Gratz to Michael Gratz, Nov. 26, 1779, Henry Joseph Coll., American Jewish Archives (microfilm at Hist. Soc. of Pa.); Volwiler, *George Croghan*, 310-11; William Vincent Byars, *Barnard and Michael Gratz, Merchants in Philadelphia, 1754-1798* (Jefferson City, Mo., 1916), 196-97.

ment. To Barnard Gratz came a letter from Thomas Smallman: "My first inquiry is to know how the Colo, my dearist and best friend, Colo Croghan is at present." Susannah Prevost wrote her father: "I have, my honoured parent, for a long time past been entirely ignerant in what place you had fixed your residence. . . . We are distressed beyond expression at the painful incertitude we are in on your account. I mean, least you should want that assistance which your age and the unhappy times must reduce you to." She sent him £60.[12]

Croghan was reduced to wintering in a house at Lancaster that had no chimney. Entirely dependent on his Philadelphia friends, he wrote Michael Gratz that furnishing the house had run him heavily in debt "& not a doller to pay itt with or go to market with till I hear from you." The Gratzes did not fail him.[13]

In January, 1780, Major William Croghan enjoyed a pleasant ten days in Lancaster, where he found his old benefactor in better winter health than he had known him to enjoy for many a year, but financially Croghan was poorer than ever. His servant James Forrest married and applied for his wages. Egged on by his wife, Forrest gave Croghan a troublesome time, and with good cause, for Croghan had not paid him a shilling since he entered his employment. In exasperation, Croghan turned as usual to the Gratzes for money to "gett rid of this raskel."[14] Perhaps the Gratzes were unresponsive to this plea, because Forrest remained in Croghan's service.

Croghan moved to Philadelphia in May, and Michael Gratz paid off the money he owed in Lancaster. This was the year that the colony's western boundary was established, and Croghan learned that all his western lands actually were a part of Pennsylvania. His associates, Trent and Samuel Wharton, continued

12. William Croghan to Barnard Gratz, Mar. 26, 1779, Gratz-Croghan, I, 57, Etting Coll., Smallman to Barnard Gratz, Sept. 17, 1781, Etting Coll., S. Prevost to Croghan, n.d., Cadwalader Coll., Hist. Soc. of Pa.; Smallman to Barnard Gratz, Nov. 5, 1779, Henry Joseph Coll., American Jewish Archives (microfilm at Hist. Soc. of Pa.).
13. Croghan to Michael Gratz, Nov. 22, 1779, Gratz-Croghan, I, 71, Etting Coll., Hist. Soc. of Pa.; L. A. Levy to Gratz, Dec. 8, 1779, Henry Joseph Coll., American Jewish Archives (microfilm at Hist. Soc. of Pa.).
14. William Croghan to Michael Gratz, Feb. 7, 1780, N. Y. Pub. Lib.; Croghan to Michael Gratz, Apr. 3, 1780, Darlington Memorial Library, University of Pittsburgh.

their campaign in and out of Congress to obtain recognition of Croghan's Indian grant and of Indiana. Except for testifying in favor of the Illinois and Wabash land companies, when he was introduced as the foremost living expert on the western Indian country, Croghan seems to have taken a back seat during these negotiations, which in May, 1782, brought favorable action by a committee of Congress.[15]

The committee reported that it had held meetings with representatives of the Indiana, Vandalia, Illinois, and Wabash companies, and with agents of George Croghan. "On the whole, your committee are of opinion that the purchases of Colonel Croghan and the Indiana Company, were made *bona fide* for a valuable consideration, according to the then usage and custom of purchasing lands from the Indians." The committee recommended that if those two properties should fall to the United States as part of the western area to be ceded by the states, they should then be confirmed to Croghan and the Indiana Company. The claims of Vandalia and the other companies were rejected. Despite this recommendation and the belief of most lawyers that his title was sound, Croghan and his heirs were never able to establish it satisfactorily.[16]

Croghan spent the last two years of his life in the suburbs of Philadelphia, first in Moyamensing Township and finally in Passyunk. His New York lands nearly all sold or mortgaged beyond recovery, and his title to western lands a shaky one, Croghan kept himself going by selling small pieces of ground. His innate optimism, if dimmed by experience, had not yet vanished. He still believed that his agents could settle his affairs and rescue him from his difficulties by clearing for him an estate conservatively estimated at £140,000. Urging his friends to do their utmost, the invalid Croghan pitifully wrote, "Time you know flys fast away & a life of suspence is the most disagreeable life in the world to me." He was very poor. Near his lodging stood his carriage, now so old-fashioned as to be described as "antedeluvian." It

---

15. L. A. Levy to Michael Gratz, Apr. 24, 1780, Henry Joseph Coll., American Jewish Archives (microfilm at Hist. Soc. of Pa.); Ohio Co. Papers, II, 49, Hist. Soc. of Pa.; *An Account of the Proceedings of the Ilinois and Ouabache Land Companies* . . . (Philadelphia, 1796), 43-44.

16. *Journals of Congress* . . . (New York, 1787), VII, 364-66.

End of the Trail

retained its harness, but the horses were gone. Croghan had no money to pay James Forrest, who, nevertheless, still remained with him, nor could he pay his nurse Ann Gallagher, who also stood by. Neither had he funds to pay the witty Dr. Abraham Chovet, who came more frequently than ever to his bedside. The total value of his personal estate was reduced to £50 13s.6d. A friend, calling on Croghan in May, 1782, found him being dunned by a creditor. Naturally, he could not refuse Croghan's entreaty to pay the man off—all he wanted was ten dollars.[17]

Bedridden by lameness, Croghan was seemingly resigned to his situation. To Thomas Wharton, whose son had died, he wrote: "Heaven gives its blessings & takes away & we must submit." On June 12, 1782, he made his will, leaving his entire estate, except for some specific bequests, to his daughter. During the long painful hours of this his last summer, confined to his modest quarters, virtually bereft of friends and family, poor Croghan had no heart to answer Susannah's solicitous letters.[18]

Why had he failed? Had he not been the colony's leading fur trader? Was not his plantation, "Croghan's," on the Conedogwinet, a landmark and a trading center? All that was gone now, as were Aughwick, Monckton Hall, Croghan's Forest, Croghan Hall. He had dreamed vast dreams. He had stimulated men of note with his visions of western development—a colony in Illinois, a principality on the Ohio, a quarter of a million acres in New York, all gained, or all but gained, through his relentless energy, his restless imagination, and his daring courage. The rub was, he had done

---

17. Deed Book D, X, 201, City Hall, Phila.; Chovet's receipt, Nov. 17, 1782, Henry Joseph Coll., American Jewish Archives (microfilm at Hist. Soc. of Pa.); Gratz-Croghan, I, 91, Etting Coll., and Ohio Co. Papers, II, 60, Hist. Soc. of Pa.; Croghan to Barnard Gratz, Oct. 3, 1780, Draper Mss., State Hist. Soc. of Wis.; Augustine Prevost evaluated Croghan's estate as of 1782 at £140,000 in a petition to Lord Grenville, October, 1790, Hist. Soc. of Pa.

18. Croghan to Thomas Wharton, n.d., Carnegie Library, Pittsburgh; Alexander Ross to Croghan, Apr. 29, 1782, Cadwalader Coll., Hist. Soc. of Pa. Susannah Prevost, Croghan's daughter, died in 1790. She had twelve children, six of whom survived her: Major George William Prevost (1767-1840) spent most of his life in New York and died at Eastchester; Lieutenant Colonel Augustine John Prevost, a British army officer, was drowned off the Irish coast, c. 1822; Louisa Charlotte Prevost (1783-1842) married a Mr. Palmer and had one son who became a minister; Susannah Prevost died unmarried in 1857; Captain James Prevost and Lieutenant Henry Prevost, both of the British army, were killed in Spain. This data is mainly based on the Reverend Evelyn Bartow, *Bartow Genealogy, Supplement* (Baltimore, 1879), 232-33.

it all on borrowed money. The rich return these investments promised could not be realized soon enough, and so he had lost them. Those who came later would deal in the same lands and make fortunes. Croghan, ahead of his times, had shown the way to the heartland of America. He had gambled with brilliant foresight on the wealth that was there and had been dragged down by bad timing, bad luck, and careless financing. Perhaps it could be said of Croghan, as it was of Samuel Wharton, that he had "over schemed" himself.[19]

There was a quirk in Croghan's mind which intruded itself, time and time again, in his dealings so that all too often he ended by cheating not only his friends but himself. For Croghan could not play the game straight. His actions were frequently unscrupulous; he indulged in the most barefaced lies; he extracted money by dishonest methods. Sometimes such a technique brings wealth no matter how ill deserved the reward. But with Croghan it was different.

Although his career in its material aspects was a failure, he had enjoyed a leading role for many years on the colonial stage, where his most successful work had been with the Indians. Here, too, he had encountered successive business reverses in the trade before 1754 and later in his ill-disguised partnership with Thomas Smallman. But the significance of Croghan's career was not commercial. His ability to understand the natives, to gain their respect and to sway their opinions, was Croghan's most important attribute. The other Indian agents, the traders, and army officers conceded that Croghan was without peer as a western negotiator. He was a superlative peacemaker. In the era before the Revolution, he was unequalled in the field of western Indian diplomacy.

The ability he displayed so notably in his dealings with the red men reflected the same characteristics which brought him success in dealing with white people. When Croghan wanted something, he went all out. He was extremely tenacious; he was indefatigable mentally and physically. What made the man even more unusual was the way in which he concealed his powerful driving spirit be-

19. Joseph Simon to Croghan, Aug. 7, 1772, Cadwalader Coll., Hist. Soc. of Pa.

hind a blandness of manner, a good fellowship, and a charm that endeared him to people of all sorts. In short, he was a salesman competent enough to sell his ideas to a large number of the most intelligent and influential men of his day. Sir William Johnson and Benjamin Franklin were won to his Illinois colonization scheme. Governor William Franklin subscribed to one plan after another that had been created in Croghan's mind. Joseph Galloway and Thomas Wharton, two of Philadelphia's shrewdest men, paid hard cash for Croghan's dreams. The top hierarchy of New York's government backed him. The list of sober, substantial citizens who fell under Croghan's spell is a long one.

Croghan was an activist and had little of the intellectual about him. His mind was constantly stirred by the inevitability of western colonization and the settlement of Indian lands. He strove to put himself at the head of those who would profit by this expansion. Land schemes occupied him year after year, until the fabric of his enterprises disintegrated. The Indiana Company, from which emerged the romantic Vandalia project, owed its existence largely to him. In an age noted for rash and imaginative speculation, Croghan was one of its most audacious and prominent proponents and one of its most tragic victims.

He was a complex man, one capable of raising money by outrageous misrepresentations, and equally capable of outstanding generosity and philanthropy. There was a quality in his nature that evoked the love of his friends and family and, up to a point, the confidence and respect of all. His ability to create, to get things done, and to get people to work together was well appreciated by his contemporaries. Despite the flaws in his nature, this brave, dauntless man deserved a better fate than to die lonely and impoverished.

In Croghan's sickroom was a chest of papers which held some old letters from honest John Baynton, whose ruin and heartbroken death were directly attributable to his disastrous connection with Croghan. "I am very glad," wrote Baynton, "your negotiations with the Indians have been attended with their wonted success. Your merit in that way will always command respect." And again, "I am sorry that you have been so much distressed. It is a pity that any person possessd of a generous spirit should ever be so."[20]

Croghan had, indeed, been generous, but he had also been too sharp in his dealings to merit a reputation for honesty. He had overplayed his hand and had been forced to the most extreme expedients. These failing to support him, he had lapsed into merciful obscurity. He died on August 31, 1782. His gardener, who had somehow remained in his employ, brought the corpse to town, and it was interred in St. Peter's graveyard, a fact duly recorded by the sexton, who misspelled the deceased's name. The death aroused little interest locally and was not mentioned in the newspapers. A marker with an inscription was set at Croghan's grave, but before long it yielded to the elements. For some years, the hopeless involvements of his estate kept courtrooms abuzz, and, when that ceased and his contemporaries died off, the man's name and fame faded away into the obscurity from which he had emerged.[21]

20. Baynton to Croghan, Sept. 5 and Oct. 14, 1770, *ibid.*
21. Croghan Estate, Dreer Coll., Hist. Soc. of Pa.

Bibliographical Essay

THE LATE Albert T. Volwiler's *George Croghan and the Westward Movement, 1741-1782*, published in 1926, includes an excellent bibliography of the sources he used in writing his well-researched book. While his bibliography is essentially a listing of titles or the names of manuscript collections, he occasionally amplifies an entry with an interpretive or explanatory comment. The fact that one of these comments did not stand the test of time gave rise to my interest in Croghan.

Dr. Volwiler wrote that on Croghan's death his papers were secured by the Gratz brothers, whose descendants preserved a few of the most important manuscripts and eventually gave them to the Historical Society of Pennsylvania. The rest of Croghan's "large collection," concluded Dr. Volwiler, had disappeared. The connotation that the collection had been destroyed is clear, since Dr. Volwiler did not think it necessary to inquire at the place where it was last known to have been located. One can sympathize with him for not making this search because there had been no report on its whereabouts since 1814.

Bound in with the Historical Society's so-called "Ohio Company Papers," a collection extensively used by Dr. Volwiler, were documents which indeed showed that the Gratzes had obtained possession of Croghan's papers, but these documents also preserved a subsequent link in the history of those manuscripts. They proved that in 1804 the Gratzes delivered the papers to Thomas Cadwalader, lawyer for the Prevosts, Croghan's heirs. An irritable correspondence dating as late as 1814 in the "Ohio Company Papers" sets forth the unsuccessful efforts of the Gratzes to reassert their rights to Croghan's papers against Cadwalader who would not give them up.

In this manner, if you will, the papers "disappeared." Actually, Croghan's wooden chest of records remained in Thomas Cadwalader's office until the lawyer's death in 1841. Successive generations of Cadwalader lawyers, sons, grandsons, and great-grandsons of Thomas Cadwalader, continued to preserve them, together with many a voluminous file of other antique law cases. At the time Dr. Volwiler was visiting St. Peter's churchyard, vainly seeking to find Croghan's unmarked grave, he little thought that only two or three blocks away were Croghan's personal papers, safely if obscurely stored in a legal office which bore on its shingle the distinguished name of John Cadwalader. Cadwaladers continue to pass in and out of this office, but since 1939 their family papers and noncurrent (to say the least) legal files have been at the Historical Society of Pennsylvania.

Croghan's papers, identified in my footnotes as "Cadwalader Collection," are basic to an understanding of the man and his manifold activities. They contain a fairly complete record of the Hockley, Trent, and Croghan Indian trade partnership, and disclose that it was not, as Dr. Volwiler had maintained, French depredations that caused Croghan's failure, but his own bad management years before the French multiplied his troubles. There are revealing papers on Croghan's sharp speculations in land and on his curious involvements in other money-making schemes. Most startling of all is an extraordinary correspondence with Thomas and Samuel Wharton about those great colonial dreams, the Indiana Company and Vandalia. Such papers reveal much which could never have been explained otherwise.

Then, too, there are letters from Croghan's superior, Sir William Johnson, and from the military leaders who also gave him orders, Horatio Gates, Thomas Gage, Robert Monckton. There are letters from Benjamin Franklin and his son Governor William Franklin, from Lord Dunmore and his henchman John Connolly, from Thomas Penn and his henchman Richard Peters, from the Pennsylvania governors, William Denny and James Hamilton. The cornucopia that once was Croghan's wooden chest overflows with letters from his cronies and associates, with retained copies of letters Croghan himself wrote, with his diaries and journals of his travels, with seemingly thousands of bills which record Croghan's itinerary and tastes.

If Dr. Volwiler was unfortunate in not seeking out the descendants of Thomas Cadwalader and thereby discovering this collection, he had no opportunity at all to come upon numerous other manuscript accumulations which only the passage of time was to bring forward. An enormous amount of material about Croghan has turned up in the years since Dr. Volwiler completed his work. Among the larger "finds" of this type are the Banyar papers at the New-York Historical Society; the large addition to the Baynton, Wharton, and Morgan papers at the Division of Records, Harrisburg; the Shippen papers acquired a few years ago by the American Philosophical Society; and the Henry Joseph Collection of Gratz papers now available on microfilm through the courtesy of the American Jewish Archives. Smaller collections which bear on Croghan's activities are also important, and year by year the store of such findings increases as pertinent letters and documents are accessioned in our great manuscript depositories. Last, but by no means least, is the availability, denied in Dr. Volwiler's time, of certain majestic military files—the Lord Loudoun and General Abercromby papers at the Huntington Library, the Thomas Gage and Henry Clinton papers at the William L. Clements Library, University of Michigan, and the Amherst papers at the Public Record Office in London.

In pioneering a study of Croghan, Dr. Volwiler told me that he did not have time to sift through masses of materials hoping to find usable data. His principal reliance had to be on the card catalogue. My research was greatly facilitated by the fact that it was my duty as a research member of the Historical Society of Pennsylvania's staff to comb through its collections. Since the Society is the principal depository of Croghan materials, and of materials relating to circumstances which affected his life, my search was a fruitful one. The Penn papers, which had not been extensively used before in this connection, were particularly valuable. Also of note was a volume entitled "Papers Relating to Indian Losses." This neglected source consists of manuscripts collected by William Trent on behalf of the "suffering traders" and contains the top-secret document which discloses the identity of the syndicate which owned the Indiana Company. In this connection, it may be worthwhile to point out that the Society's "Ohio Company Papers" perpetuate a misnomer given the collection by a former owner. Actually, these important documents have very little to do with the Ohio Company, but are another group of Trent's papers representing efforts to obtain restitution for Indian traders through land grants.

While fresh manuscript finds furnished the main impetus toward my writing a new book on Croghan, newly published sources were also a substantial aid. In 1936, Stanley McCrory Pargellis brought out his *Military Affairs in North America, 1748-1765*, selections from the letters of the Duke of Cumberland, captain general of the British army from 1745 to 1757. Alfred Procter James in 1938 gathered together the *Writings of General John Forbes Relating to his Service in North America*. The following year, Howard H. Peckham published *George Croghan's Journal of His Trip to Detroit in 1767* from a then unique manuscript (Croghan's personal copy has since been discovered in the Cadwalader Collection). Between 1940 and 1943, S. K. Stevens and Donald H. Kent of the Pennsylvania Historical Commission edited a nineteen-volumed mimeographed edition of *The Papers of Colonel Henry Bouquet*, and since then, in 1951, the Commission has produced Volume II (the only volume so far published) of a more ambitious undertaking, *The Papers of Henry Bouquet: The Forbes Expedition*. Not to be left behind, New York has continued its monumental publication of *The Papers of Sir William Johnson;* Volume XII of this series was published in 1957 under the able supervision of Dr. Milton W. Hamilton. Much that was obscure but valuable, needed data so difficult for the individual researcher to turn up on his own, has been given to the world in books like these.

If I may be forgiven a personal note, it was my privilege in 1947 to edit for *The Pennsylvania Magazine of History and Biography* "George Croghan's Journal, 1759-1763," a Cadwalader Collection manuscript, and the longest document directly relating to his career. Another publication of source material helpful for its early data on the Ohio Company was Lois Mulkearn's *George Mercer Papers* (1954).

Turning from published source material to the newer secondary works, I wish particularly to mention a 1938 volume, Julian P. Boyd's *Indian Treaties Printed by Benjamin Franklin, 1732-1762,* which contains Dr. Boyd's illuminating essay on Indian affairs in Pennsylvania, an essay which should serve as a major corrective to traditional points of view. The most important study from a general point of view, and one which is still in progress, is Lawrence Henry Gipson's multivolumed *The British Empire before the American Revolution*. This superlative effort not only presents the broad historical panorama which embraced Croghan's career, but it also comes to grips with detailed information most intimately concerning Croghan. For example, note Dr. Gipson's extended treatment of the disputed location of the White River, the Cuyahoga where Croghan traded (Vol. IV, 169-71). Since Croghan's activities were so closely affected by Quaker animosity or support, Frederick B. Tolles's penetrating *Meeting House and Counting House,* published in 1948, was of value for background material.

The literature surrounding Croghan's life has been much enriched by the appearance of a number of biographies of his friends and enemies. In 1932, Max Savelle brought out his life of George Morgan, and the following year saw the publication of Dr. Pargellis' *Lord Loudoun in North America*. In 1943, Theodore Thayer presented his excellent study of Croghan's hot-tempered Quaker adversary Israel Pemberton, and in the next year came Hubertis Cummings' charming biography of Richard Peters, as well as John Richard Alden's *John Stuart and the Southern Colonial Frontier*. The year 1945 brought two biographies of Conrad Weiser, one by Arthur D. Graeff and the other by Paul A. W. Wallace, Dr. Wallace's book being the more widely acclaimed. Two years later, Howard H. Peckham made his second contribution in a judicious book on Pontiac, and Sewell E. Slick's *William Trent and the West* was published. Hard on the heels of these works came Anthony F. C. Wallace's 1949 life of Teedyuscung, and in 1949 and 1950 the late Howard N. Eavenson portrayed some curious frontier characters well known to Croghan in his

Map Maker and Indian Traders and *Swaine and Drage, A Sequel to Map Maker and Indian Traders.*

Many other recent titles and a large number of articles published in historical quarterlies could be added here as evidence of the wealth of pertinent historical data which have appeared since Dr. Volwiler completed his monograph on Croghan. This essay, however, is not intended to serve as such a catalogue, but just to suggest that enough new material in the form of manuscripts, published sources, and secondary studies is now available to justify another book on Croghan. He was an extraordinary man, and I will be most happy if in the years to come more new materials about him come to light which may explain areas of his life and character which still remain in shadow.

Index

Abercromby, Gen. James, 137, 140, 141-43, 155
Adair, James, 238
Albany, 260, 264; British military center, 111, 114, 115, 136, 137, 140; Croghan in, 111, 115-16, 179; creditors of Croghan in, 267, 271, 275
Albany County, N. Y., militia, 112, 115, 137, 140
Allegheny Mountains, boundary for settlement, 164, 167, 207, 229
Allen, William, 205, 227
Alliquippa, Indian queen, 78
American Revolution, 273; committees of correspondence, 294-95, 299, 301; Croghan and, 298, 301-3. *See also* Continental Congress
Amherst, Gen. Jeffrey, 155, 156, 157, 159, 167, 169, 203, 231, 301; expedition to Louisburg, 141, 145; restrictive Indian policy, 159, 174, 177, 180, 184, 194-203 *passim*; opinion on Indians, 165, 172, 180, 196, 198, 201; campaign against Montreal, 171, 173; and Croghan, 193, 102-2
Ammunition, 5, 65, 69, 176, 198, 216; Indian presents, 17, 21, 52, 53, 58, 180; needed by Indians, 60, 194, 195
Anglican Church, 113, 204, 214, 270
Answer to an Invidious Pamphlet, entitled, A Brief State of the Province of Pennsylvania, 108-9
Anthon, Dr. George C., 220, 233, 237, 247, 259
Anti-proprietary party, 118, 128, 134, 147, 149, 246; supports Illinois scheme, 227, 228. *See also* Walking Purchase
Armstrong, Col. George, 204
Armstrong, John, 80, 84, 117, 144
Armstrong, Joseph, 80, 83

Assembly, Pa., 45, 109, 120, 167, 247-48, 249; Indian policy, 35, 44, 76, 124, 128, 130, 162, 163, 164, 173; and defense measures, 35, 41, 42-43, 60, 61, 69, 73, 76, 95, 97, 101, 118; distrusts Croghan, 39, 40, 43-44, 80; taxation of Penn estates, 69, 97, 101; relieves Croghan of debts, 82-83, 99-100, 106, 108, 160; approves Croghan, 227, 247-48, 252. *See also* Provincial commissioners
Atkin, Edmund, 117, 121, 126, 127
Aughwick, plantation, 33, 59, 68, 73, 75, 109, 307; center for Indian affairs, 55, 56, 80; Indians at, 70-76 *passim*, 82, 89-95 *passim*, 103; Indian treaty (1754), 72-74; Croghan sells tracts of, 84-85; Croghan fortifies, 95, 97, 98, 99, 100, 102. *See also* Fort Shirley
Augusta County, Va., court held at Pittsburgh (1775), 294

Baker, John, 104-5
Banyar, Goldsbrow, 268, 270
Barton, Thomas, 228, 240
Bateaux, Mohawk River style, 262
Baynton, John, 201, 216, 254, 260, 269, 309-10
Baynton and Wharton, firm, 176
Baynton, Wharton, and Morgan, firm, 202, 211, 229; partnership of Croghan with, 201, 212-13, 226-27; Croghan promises to buy Indian presents from, 212-17 *passim*, 224, 231, 233, 234, 236; and Illinois trade, 212, 227, 233, 235, 237, 254, 275; creditor of Croghan, 269, 275
Beaujeu, Capt. Daniel Liénard de, 92
Beaver, Delaware chief, 153, 154, 164, 173, 181, 185, 219; at Lancaster

treaty (1762), 187, 188, 189
Beaver's Town. *See* Muskingum
Bedford, 185, 196, 204, 215, 272, 275, 278; Croghan and, 191-92, 199
Bedford County, 277
Bellfield, farm, 192, 198
Belvidere Township, N. Y., 270
Berks County, 96, 101, 129
Biddle, John, 121, 127
Big Cove, 33
Black Boys, 216, 217, 224, 249, 251, 252
Black Log, 20
Blainville, Céloron de, 6, 27, 31, 35, 170
Bland, Elias, 34, 35
Blue Cheeks, Seneca chief, 188, 189
Board of Trade, 28, 118, 203, 206-7, 285; and Wm. Johnson, 135, 162, 202-3, 207, 257; regulates Indian affairs (1764), 207-9, 224, 237-38; and Indian boundary, 246-47, 251, 253, 255, 256, 268
Boundaries, set by Easton treaty (1758), 164, 167; Wm. Johnson and, 203, 208, 211, 228, 229-30, 246, 247; Proclamation Line (1763), 207, 208, 209; Croghan and, 245-47, 265; set by Board of Trade (1768), 246-47, 251, 253, 255, 256, 268; Assembly and, 247-48; dispute over, in west, 278, 279, 287-95 *passim*, 302, 305. *See also* Mason and Dixon Line
Bouquet, Col. Henry, 144, 152, 172, 175, 181, 191, 193, 200; and Indian affairs, 154, 156, 157, 159, 166, 176, 177, 189, 210, 219; and Croghan, 177, 210, 213, 214, 224, 225; and Pontiac's uprising, 201, 210, 212; death, 224
Braddock, Gen. Edward, 79, 99, 110, 111, 112, 116, 217; expedition of (1754), 3, 79-94, 100, 107-8, 144
Bradstreet, Col. John, 210, 213
Brant, Catherine Croghan (Mrs. Joseph Brant), 138, 262, 264n
Brant, Molly, 138, 209
Brant, Joseph, 262, 271
Britannia, ship, 202, 204-5, 206
British Army in North America, 79, 88, 113; and Canadian expeditions, 12-13, 22, 140, 141, 143, 158, 173; on Braddock expedition, 79-94, 100, 144; on Forbes expedition, 143-44, 151-52; Indian trade at posts of, 182, 229, 243, 247; at New Orleans, 213, 218; fails to occupy Illinois, 219-20; 50th Regiment, 113; 49th Regiment, 114, 116;

N. Y. campaigns, during French and Indian War, 114-17, 136-43 *passim*; Highlanders, 137, 143; at Fort Ticonderoga (1758), 142-43; Black Watch Regiment, 143, 222; 60th Regiment (Royal Americans), 143, 164, 165, 170, 171, 172, 174; 34th Regiment, 218, 222; Royal Irish Regiment, 250, 300; occupation of Phila., 301-2. *See also* Indian Department; Forts; Military supplies
Buchanan, William, 80, 190-91, 202, 250, 261, 269
Buffaloes, 233, 234
Burd, James, 56, 75, 82n, 83-84, 98, 104, 144; and western road (1755), 80, 83, 87, 102
Burlington, N. J., 225, 259
Burlington Company, 259, 260
Burney, Thomas, 10
Burns, George, 239
Butler, John, 257, 261, 268n, 270
Butler, Richard, 298, 299
Butler, Capt. Thomas, 115
Byrd, William (1728-1777), 144

Cadwalader, John, 282
Callender, Robert, 51, 176, 212, 216, 226, 254; partnership with Croghan, Trent, and Teaffe, 29, 30, 48, 53, 54-55
Camden, Lord, Sir Charles Pratt, 297
Campbell, Maj. Andrew, 12
Campbell, Capt. Donald, 173, 174, 181
Campbell, Francis, 80
Campbell, Lt. Col. John, 222-23
Campbell, John, clerk, 282, 301, 303
Campbell, Joseph, 74
Campbell, Mr., 71
Canada, 13, 14, 97; British plan invasions of, 12-13, 22, 140, 141, 143, 158; capitulation of, 173, 174, 176, 177; Indians join Cherokees, 177
Canajoharie, N. Y., 138, 141
Canasatego, Onondaga chief, 32
Carlisle, Pa., 45, 97, 160, 177, 215, 249; Indian treaty (1753), 54-55, 59, 67; fort, 95, 153; Indian treaty (1756), 103; and Croghan, 192, 275
Carlyle, Maj. John, 62, 63, 65, 74
Carson, John, 87
Catawba Indians, 144
Cayuga Indians, 145, 147
Challon, Dr., 237, 241
Charleston, S. C., 57
Chartier's Town, 21

Index

Cherokee Indians, 125, 126-27, 143, 144, 177, 281; war with Shawnees, 169, 171
Cherry Valley, N. Y., 262
Chester, Pa., 251
Chester County, Pa., 98
Chew, Benjamin, 128, 148, 149-50, 185, 186
Chew, Mr., of Md., 276
Chippewa Indians, 286, 300
Chovet, Dr. Abraham, 307
Clapham, Col. William, 196, 197, 199
Clark, Daniel, 196, 197, 199, 250
Clark, George Rogers, 260
Claus, Daniel, 180, 209, 262
Clear Fields, 20
Cleveland, Ohio, 6
Clinton, Sir Henry, 301*n*
Colden, Alexander, 268, 268*n*
Colden, Calwallader, 225, 267, 268, 268*n*
Coles, Edward, 229
Colonial troops, 79, 111, 114, 115, 116, 140, 144, 152. *See also* Military supplies; New York troops; Pennsylvania troops; Virginia troops
Colonies, disunity of, 61, 69, 97; southern governors in Phila., 121, 159; established by Crown (1763), 207; to manage Indian affairs, 237, 246; governors to purchase Indian lands, 243
Conedogwinet Creek. *See* Pennsborough
Conestoga Indians, 120
Connecticut, and Wyoming lands, 151*n*
Connolly, John, 287, 288-91, 295, 301*n*; and Croghan, 287, 288, 290, 294, 295
Conoy Indians, 187
Continental Congress, 297, 298, 306
Contracoeur, Claude Pierre Pécaudy, Sieur de, 107
Cooperstown, N. Y., 142
Cornstalk, Shawnee chief, 289
Craig, John, 105
Crawford, Hugh, 104, 105, 176
Cresap, Col. Thomas, 30
Croghan, Catherine. *See* Brant, Catherine Croghan
Croghan, Edmund, 207
Croghan, George (*d.* 1782), leading Indian negotiator, 3, 15, 21, 38-39, 53, 55-56, 71, 102, 213, 222-23, 238, 239-40, 252, 273-74, 308; characteristics, 4, 21, 26, 66, 231, 250, 308-9; generosity, 4, 78, 182, 198, 209, 215, 240-41, 260, 276, 282, 309; partnership with Trent, 8, 12-13, 22, 23-24, 51, 63, 65, 66; operates tannery, 9, 12, 44; relatives, 12, 207, 260; popularity with traders, 13, 21, 37; incites Indians against French (1747), 14-15, 16, 17, 18; leading Indian trader, 14, 21, 29, 35-36, 68; partnership with Trent and Hockley, 24-46 *passim*, 47, 48, 75, 87; justice of peace, 27, 32, 287; opposes sale of liquor to Indians, 27, 67, 78, 178, 273; urges regulation of Indian trade, 27, 60, 67; illnesses, 29, 56, 189, 236, 241, 265, 269-70, 272, 283, 288, 297, 302-10; employees, 29, 67, 176; partnership with Trent, Callender, and Teaffe, 29, 30, 48, 53, 54-55; French seek to destroy, 30-31, 36, 38, 75, 96; helps expel squatters (1750), 32-34; assumes authority, 39; Assembly distrusts, 40, 43-44; on status of Ohio Iroquois, 40, 41, 61; urges fort on Ohio, 41-44, 49, 50, 60, 66; testimony refuted by Montour, 43-44, 49; failure (1751), 44-46; called "the Buck," 49, 177, 178; named agent by Indians, 55, 56; Indian expenses, 60, 72, 73, 74, 76-78, 79-80, 83, 110, 291-92; and Fort Necessity campaign, 62-68; accused of being Roman Catholic, 71, 108, 109, 113; suspected of treason, 71, 106-9, 300-1, 301*n*, 302, 303; threatens to leave Aughwick agency, 76-78; and Braddock expedition, 80-94, 95, 100, 111; builds and garrisons forts, 102-4, 107, 108; commissioned captain (1756), 102, 106; threatened by Shingas, 105; military expenses, 102-3, 106, 110; Filius Gallicae letters attributed to, 106-9, 114, 116

Goes to N. Y., 110-11; deputy Indian agent, 113, 114; leads Indian warriors, in N. Y., 115, 116, 137-38, 142-43; seeks ranger command, 115-16; manages Indian affairs in Pa., 118-34; criticizes land grant to Penns (1754), 120, 135; and Proprietary party, 120, 123-24, 125, 130, 133, 134, 135-36, 147; and Quakers, 120, 123-24, 125, 130, 133, 134, 135-36, 139, 147, 149-51, 187, 199; at German Flats, 137, 140, 155; buys clothes and household goods, 138, 140, 192, 206, 211, 230-31, 241, 264-65; marries daughter of Nickus, 138; buys liquor, 140, 155, 241; on Forbes expedition, 141, 145, 151-52, 155; at Fort Ticonderoga (1758), 142-43, 155;

at Easton treaty (1758), 148-51 *passim*; requests military escort, 160, 251; controls Indian trade (1759), 163, 175-76; goes to Niagara (1760), 171-72; accompanies Rogers to Detroit, 173-75; pacifies Indians (1760), 174-75; and Pontiac, 174n, 218-19, 221-22; at Detroit (1761), 181-82; and resignation from Indian Dept., 185, 195, 202, 209, 218, 224, 226, 228, 231, 237, 240, 242; partnership with Smallman, 190-91, 250, 261, 282, 308; partnership with Drage, 191, 199; called "colonel," 192; interest in copper mines, 192, 204, 214; recommends town at Bedford, 192; celebrates St. Patrick's Day, 193-94, 250-51

Goes to England, 195, 200-9; partnership with Clapham, 196, 199; raises frontier troops (1763), 198; partnership with Baynton, Wharton, and Morgan, 201, 212-13, 226-27; shipwrecked (1764), 204-5; recommendations to Board of Trade, 207-8; seeks recovery of Irish inheritance, 207; proposes tax on Indian trade, 209, 225; pacifies Illinois Indians, 213, 219-23, 235, 238; conceals trade goods in Crown present, 214, 216, 217, 224-25; partnership with Gordon, 214; tries to open Indian trade (1765), 215-18; and Black Boys, 216-17, 224-25, 251, 252; Indian captive, 220-21, 223, 224; disapproves Stamp Act riots, 225; journal of Illinois visit, 226; sends reports to Benj. Franklin, 226, 239; supported by Pa. political factions, 227-28; acquires trade loss rights, 229, 251, 254; Indian service losses, 231, 240, 242; expedition to Illinois (1766), 233-36; collects mammoth bones, 234, 240-41; in New Orleans, 236-37; import-export business, 237; becomes a Mason, 242; uses threat of war for land schemes, 245-47, 281; Assembly approves, 227, 247-48, 252; supervises boundary survey (1769), 265; plans settlements, 266, 276; interest in religion, 270; opens land offices, 276, 282, 289; opposes Pa. jurisdiction in west, 277-78, 287-88; resigns from Indian Dept. (1771), 281-282; supports Va. claims in west, 287-95 *passim*, 302; pawns silver plate, 286, 286n, 290; financed by Gratzes, 283, 300, 303

Indian expenses for Vandalia treaty, 286, 286n, 290-91; and John Connolly, 287, 288, 290, 294, 295; heads Pittsburgh committee of correspondence, 294-95, 299, 301; judge of Augusta Co. court (1775), 294; in Warm Springs, Va., 297, 299; loses influence in Indian affairs, 298, 299, 303; neutralizes Indians, during American Revolution, 298, 301, 302, 303; in Williamsburg, Va., 300, 304; lodgings in Phila., 302, 305; takes oath of allegiance, 302; spends winters in Lancaster (1778-1779), 303, 304-5; last months of, 306-7, 309-10; value of estate, 306, 307, 307n; buried at Phila., 310

Debts: to Phila. merchants, 26, 29, 36, 39, 52, 53, 179, 269, 275; to Hockley, 45, 52, 179, 197, 279; to Pa. merchants, 45-47, 48, 202, 249-50, 259, 260, 261, 269, 275; to Shippen, 48, 52-53, 56, 63, 75, 83-84; threatened with arrest for, 48, 52, 68, 99, 100, 145, 273, 279, 304; to Ohio Company, 68, 249, 269; Assembly relief of, 82-83, 99-100, 106, 108, 160; to Lancaster merchants, 111, 160, 249, 275, 304; to Thos. Wharton, 250, 269; to Indians, 256-57, 262, 271; to Wm. Franklin, 257, 269, 275, 279; for land patents, 267-68, 268n, 270, 271; to N. Y. merchants, 267-68, 271, 275; to N. Y. officials, 268, 268n, 270, 271n; to Baynton, Wharton, and Morgan, 269, 275; to Gratzes, 269, 271, 275, 279, 283, 303-5; plight of creditors, 275

Land grant (1749): from N. Y. Iroquois, 26, 28, 152; confirmed by Ohio Iroquois, 28, 49; memorial to Board of Trade on, 28, 207; and relocation in N. Y., 203, 207; and Pa. boundary, 257, 305; included in Vandalia, 274; sold for debts, 275-76; Va., and title confirmation, 288, 304; deeded in part to Gratzes, 304; upheld by Continental Congress, 306

Landholdings: in Pa., 6, 9, 20, 50, 191-92; mortgaged, 12, 26, 44, 46, 261, 270, 298-99, 306; speculations in Pa., 81, 84-85, 191-92, 196-97, 199, 200, 214, 250; Hockley and, 84, 197, 250; Thos. Penn and Aughwick titles, 84-85; grant for services (1762), 189; sells to Penns, in Bedford, 204; Crown grant in N. Y., 242, 270-71; speculation in N. Y., 242, 244, 245, 248, 249, 253,

Index 321

255-58, 259, 260-61, 266, 267, 307; and Gov. Moore, 242, 244, 245, 248, 253, 259, 260-61; in Phila., 259; patents in N. Y., 267-68, 268*n*, 270-71; loses, in N. Y., 270, 283, 292, 298-99, 306; tries to sell to Washington, 276-77; west of Ohio (1773), 293, 296; suits against squatters, 303; sells, for living expenses, 306. *See also* Illinois Company; Indiana Company; Vandalia

Trading posts: on Cuyahoga River, 6, 7, 13, 15, 174; in Path Valley, 10; at Pine Creek, 13, 50, 52; at Pickawillany, 15, 30, 31; at Muskingum, 37; at Lower Shawnee Town, 38, 51; at Croghan Hall, 282. *See also* Aughwick; Pennsborough

Croghan, Mrs. George, 12, 34
Croghan, Mrs. George (Nickus' daughter), 138, 140, 151
Croghan, Col. George (*d.* 1849), 260
Croghan, Nicholas, 260, 264
Croghan, Susannah. *See* Prevost, Susannah Croghan
Croghan, William, 260, 304, 305
Croghan Hall, 192, 199, 273, 287, 300, 304, 307; burned, 197-98; rebuilt, 247; losses, 254; visitors, 276, 282, 285; trading post, 282
Croghan's Forest, 142, 259, 262, 264-65, 271, 272, 307; servants, 261, 264, 272; promised to Prevost, 298
Croghan's fort. *See* Fort Shirley
Croghan's Gap, 9, 33
Crown, British, authorizes resistance to French, 57, 79; and relief act for Croghan, 133, 160; and Walking Purchase, 150; and land grant of Croghan (1749), 207, 288; Proclamation Line (1763), 207, 208, 209; and Illinois Company, 230, 238; and regulation of Indian affairs, 237-38, 246, 253; grants N. Y. land to Croghan, 242, 270-71; disallows private land grants (1768), 265, 266*n*, 266-67; disallows Indiana Company grant, 274; approves Vandalia, 284. *See also* Board of Trade; British Army; Indian Department; Parliament
Crown Point, N. Y., 79, 111, 112, 115, 116, 140, 158
Cumberland, Duke of (William Augustus), 79, 122
Cumberland County, 32, 39, 45, 78, 80, 82, 101; Croghan's creditors in, 52, 179; exposed to French attack, 75;

raises volunteers (1755), 94; ravaged by Indians (1755), 97; petitions for fort, 102; elects Stanwix to Assembly, 167; Croghan sells lands in, 196. *See also* Pennsborough
Custaloga, Delaware chief, 125, 153, 154, 219, 293
Cuyahoga River, 6, 7-8, 14, 17; Croghan has trading post on, 6, 7, 13, 15, 174

Dagge, Henry, 297*n*
Dartmouth, Lord, 2nd (William Legge), 284
Delaware (colony), 144
Delaware George, Indian, 59, 71, 153, 185
Delaware Indians, 49, 89, 96, 145, 181, 182, 188; move west, 5, 17, 41; at Carlisle treaty (1753), 55; desert English (1754), 64; at Aughwick, 71, 72; at Kittanning, 96, 104, 117; raids, 96, 97, 105; causes of defection (1754), 97-98, 118; at Onondaga treaty (1756), 113, 114; Quakers and, 119; resent land grant to Penns (1754), 98, 120, 131; Iroquois seek to reconcile, 122, 124; on Susquehanna, reconciled to English, 128, 131, 132, 134, 135; at Easton treaty (1757), 129-34 *passim*; at Easton treaty (1758), 145-51 *passim*; Iroquois supremacy over, 148-49, 150, 151; make peace with English (1758), 149, 150, 153-54; at Pittsburgh treaties, 164, 218, 219; horse stealing, 165-66; at Lancaster treaty (1762), 187; reject presents, 189; informed of Vandalia, 285, 286; Croghan pacifies (1774), 289, 292-93
DeLignery, Capt. Francois Marchard 92, 158
Denny, Gov. William, 118, 122-23, 139, 147, 150, 158, 169; accepts advice of Croghan, 120, 122, 126, 131, 150, 157; and Lancaster treaty (1757), 120, 122, 124; at Easton treaty (1757), 127, 129, 131, 132; forbids Quakers at Easton treaty (1757), 128; rescues Croghan from jail, 145; at Easton treaty (1758), 147, 149
Denny, Mrs. William, 147
Detroit, 7, 14, 158, 183, 204, 210, 298; Rogers receives surrender of, 3, 173-75; headquarters of French, 6, 30, 36; French retreat to (1759), 166, 168, 169; Croghan sends raiding party to

(1760), 172; Indian trade at, 175, 215, 245, 247; invested by Indians (1763), 199. *See also* Indian treaties and conferences
Devonshire, Duke of, 4th (William Cavendish), 107
Dieskau, Baron Ludwig August von, 112
Dinwiddie, Gov. Robert, 53, 57, 59, 79, 107, 125; employs Croghan (1754), 62, 63, 66, 74; ineffective with Indians, 66, 86, 93, 94
Dixon, Jeremiah, 244
Dobson, Joseph, 281n
Drage, Theodorus Swaine, 191, 199, 200
Drage, Mrs., 147
Duché, Jacob, 130
Dublin, Ireland, 207
Dumas, Capt., 92, 107
Dunbar, Col. Thomas, 91, 94n
Dunmore, Lord, 4th (John Murray), 286-87, 295, 301n
Dunmore's War, 288-89, 292, 293-94, 295, 298
Dunning, Robert, 20
Duquesne, Ange de Menneville, Marquis de, 50-51

Easton, Pa. *See* Indian treaties and conferences
Ecuyer, Capt. Simeon, 193, 202
England, Trent in, 25; Hockley in, 35; fur prices (1751), 46; Croghan in, 195, 200-9; attitude toward America, 206; land speculators, 209, 230, 274, 285. *See also* Crown, British; Parliament
Enquiry into the Causes of the Alienation of the Delaware and Shawanese Indians, by Thomson, 130

Fairfax, Thomas, 6th Baron Fairfax of Cameron, 23
Fairfax, William, 54
Farmar, Maj. Robert, 218
Field, Robert, 212, 214, 226
Filius Gallicae, *pseud.*, letters attributed to Croghan, 106-9, 114, 116
Finley, John, 51
Fleeson, Plunket, 211, 302
Florida, 207, 237
Fonda, Capt. Jelles, 115, 116, 259, 262, 264
Fonda family, 261
Forbes, John, 141, 153-54, 156-57, 162; expedition (1758), 140, 143-44, 145, 150, 151-52
Forbes Road, 144, 170, 192, 215, 216; harassed by Indians, 158, 159-61, 164-65, 166, 169, 198-99
Forrest, James, 301, 305, 307
Fort Allen, 122, 127, 146, 162
Fort Augusta, 162, 188
Fort Beauséjour, 79
Fort Bedford, 153, 159, 170, 192, 198, 200; described (1758), 154-55; supply depot, 160, 161. *See also* Bedford
Fort Chartres, 212, 218, 220, 221, 229, 233, 239, 240; Black Watch at, 222; Smallman, agent at, 228; described, 235; Indian treaty (1766), 235, 238
Fort Crown Point. *See* Crown Point
Fort Cumberland, 79, 81, 83, 85-90, 96, 127, 144
Fort Dunmore, 294, 295
Fort Duquesne, 3, 57, 79, 80, 82, 106, 107, 127; French build, 62, 64; British attack urged (1754), 71-72; Braddock attack, 90, 91; Pontiac at, 139; Forbes expedition, 141, 143-44, 145, 150, 151-52; named Pittsburgh (1758), 152
Fort Edward, 111, 116, 142
Fort Granville, 102, 104, 105, 117
Fort Hendrick, 137
Fort Herkimer, 136, 137, 140
Fort Hunter, 137
Fort Johnson, 112-16 *passim*, 134-42 *passim*, 262
Fort LaBaye, 183
Fort LeBoeuf, 51, 153, 166, 171, 172, 199
Fort Ligonier, 153, 154, 159, 160, 161, 163, 166, 199
Fort Loudoun, 126, 127, 153, 160, 162, 198, 216
Fort Louther, 90n
Fort Lyttelton, 102, 103, 153, 160, 198
Fort Miami, 183
Fort Michilimackinac, 183, 245
Fort Mount Pleasant, 76. *See also* Fort Cumberland
Fort Necessity campaign, 61-68, 69, 79, 91
Fort Niagara, 79, 158, 165, 166, 179, 182; British relieve, 171-72; during American Revolution, 298, 299, 300
Fort Ouiatenon, 183, 221
Fort Pensacola, 224, 237
Fort Pitt, 156, 212, 214, 215; British build (1759), 158, 166, 167, 170; supply problems, 159-61, 164-65, 166, 169; described (1759), 170; Rogers at, 173;

Ward, acting Indian agent at, 185; social life (1762-1763), 192-94; Indians besiege (1763), 198, 199; Alexander McKee, commissary at, 229; Indian unrest (1769), 267-68, 272; garrison withdrawn (1772), 283-84; Hand commands, 300. *See also* Fort Dunmore; Fort Duquesne; Pittsburgh
Fort Presque Isle. *See* Presque Isle
Fort St. George (Fort Prince George), 58
Fort St. Joseph, 183
Fort Shirley ("Croghan's fort"), 102, 104, 105, 110, 117, 144
Fort Stanwix, 141, treaty (1768), 253, 255, 256-57, 265, 266-67, 277
Fort Ticonderoga, 111, 140, 142-43, 158, 166
Fort Venango, 51, 53, 125, 158, 161, 165, 166; British fort, 171, 172; Indians destroy (1763), 199
Fort Wayne, Ind., 183
Fort William Henry, 111, 116
Forts, on Maumee River, 14, 31; at Pickawillany, 30, 38; Thos. Penn favors, 35, 41, 43; Assembly opposes, 35, 41, 42-43, 60; on Ohio, 41-44, 49, 50, 54, 57, 59, 60, 66; of Ohio Company, 49, 50, 58, 59, 61; French build, in west, 51; at Aughwick, 95, 99, 102; at Carlisle, 95, 153; at Shippensburg, 95, 153, 160; Pa. chain of, 101-2; Indians resent, 154, 171, 195, 252; British build, in west, 171, 172; at Sandusky, 181, 182, 183, 199; British, burned by Indians (1763), 199; Spanish, on Mississippi, 237; British reduce number of, 237, 253. *See also* names of forts
Fossils, mammoth, 234, 240-41
Fothergill, Dr. John, 119*n*
Fox, Henry, 107
Fox, Joseph, 147, 185, 186, 187
France, Croghan in, 205. *See also* French
Franklin, Benjamin, 16, 28, 101, 225, 227, 247; commissioner to Carlisle treaty (1753), 54-55, 67; and Croghan, 226, 239-40; promotes Illinois Company, 228, 229, 230, 238, 309; upholds Indian titles, 297, 297*n*
Franklin, William, 20, 225, 246, 309; and Illinois Company, 226, 227, 230, 238, 260; buys lands in N. Y., 253, 275; and Indiana Company, 254, 260; at Fort Stanwix treaty (1768), 256, 275; creditor of Croghan, 257, 259, 269, 275, 279, 298

Franks, David, 176, 179, 196
Franks, Moses, 203
Franks Town, 9, 20
Fraser, John, 58, 154
Fraser, Lt. Alexander, 213, 215, 218, 219
Fredericksburg, Va., 37
Freemasons, 242
French and Indian War, 94, 96-98, 104, 105, 121, 125, 159, 163; N. Y. campaigns, 114-17, 136-43 *passim*; British strategy (1758), 140-41; Forbes expedition, 141, 143-44, 145, 150, 151-52; British strategy, 157, 158, 171; French strategy, 158; capitulation of Canada, 173, 174, 176, 177; peace, 195. *See also* British Army; Colonial troops
French, in North America, 6, 15, 26-27, 42, 97, 195, 236; Indian uprising against (1747), 14-15, 16, 17, 18; seek to destroy Croghan, 30-31, 36, 38, 75, 96; massacre Indians at Pickawillany, 50; build western forts, 51; mission of Half King to, 53, 55; mission of Washington to (1753), 57, 58, 59; seize forks of Ohio, 61, 66; build Fort Duquesne, 62, 64; defeat Washington, 65; defeat Braddock, 92; burn Fort Duquesne (1758), 152. *See also* French and Indian War; Indian trade; Indian traders
Friendly Association, 119, 120, 123-24, 128, 147
Friends, Society of. *See* Quakers
Frontier, 5, 69, 117; ravaged by Indians, 94, 96-98, 104, 105, 125, 159, 163, 171, 198-99, 273
Fur trade. *See* Indian trade
Furs, price of, 46, 157, 162, 173, 176, 212

Gage, Gen. Thomas, 240, 266-67, 283, 285; on Braddock expedition, 88, 91-92; limits Indian expenses, 213, 217, 218, 231-32, 236, 240; sends Croghan to Illinois, 213, 220, 229; and Croghan, 217-18, 224-25, 240, 242, 252, 282; and Black Boys affair, 224-25
Galbreath, James, 101
Gallagher, Ann, 307
Galloway, Joseph, 227, 243, 246, 302, 309; at Easton treaty (1757), 128, 129, 130; at Easton treaty (1758), 147, 149; at Easton treaty (1762), 186; lawyer for Croghan, 249, 251; and Indiana Company, 251, 254, 254*n*
Gates, Maj. Horatio, 87-88, 177, 205
Georgetown, Va., 293

German Flats, N. Y., 115, 136-38, 140
Germans, 5, 96, 106, 108, 262, 276
Germantown, Battle of, 301
Girty, Simon, 39, 300, 302
Girty, Thomas, 39
Gist, Christopher, 37, 38, 50, 59, 64, 65, 91
Glyn, John, 297n
Gordon, Harry, 92, 167, 170, 214, 233, 236
Gratz, Barnard, 262, 275; and Croghan, 269, 279, 283, 300, 303-5
Gratz, Michael, 262; and Croghan, 269, 271, 275, 283, 300, 303-5
Great Cove, 97, 126
Great Lick, 234
Great Meadows, 90, 91; Fort Necessity at 61, 63, 64, 65, 69, 71
Green Bay, Wis., 183
Grenada, 207
Grey Eyes, Delaware chief, 293
Groot, Mr., wagoner, 256
Guy Park, 262
Guyasutha, Seneca Indian. *See* Kiasutha

Half King, Indian, 59, 62, 86; compliments Croghan, 49-50; mission to French, 53, 55; with Washington (1754), 64; at Aughwick, 70, 71, 72, 73; death, 75; family, 78
Halifax, Lord, 2nd, George Montagu Dunk, 106-7, 203, 205
Hamilton, Gov. James, 27, 49, 62, 69, 101, 109, 181, 196; and Croghan, 39, 43, 45, 47, 98-99, 189; and western fort, 35, 41, 42, 43, 60; appoints commissioners to Indian treaties, 54-55, 72; returns Shawnee captives, 57-59; and defense measures, 61, 69, 73, 96; reappointed governor (1759), 169; at Easton treaty (1762), 185; conducts Lancaster treaty (1762), 187-89
Hand, Gen. Edward, 300, 303
Hannastown, Pa., 294-95
Harris, James, 191
Harris' Ferry (Harrisburg), Pa., 9, 32, 74, 98, 120, 121; Pa. present delivered at (1747), 16, 17; Indians at, 95, 122, 187
Hart, John, 176
Henry, Patrick, 287, 289, 297, 300
Hertford, Earl of Francis Seymour Conway, 285
Hillsborough, Lord, 1st Earl and 2nd Viscount Wills Hill, 205, 208, 253, 265, 267, 281, 284
History of America, by Robertson, 283
History of the American Indians, by Adair, 238
Hockley, Richard, 35, 44, 48, 52, 87, 120; partnership with Trent and Croghan, 24-46 *passim*, 47, 48, 75, 87; creditor of Croghan, 45, 52, 179, 197, 279; land transaction with Croghan, 84, 197, 250
Hoops, Adam, 80, 83, 98
Howe, George Augustus, 3rd Viscount Howe, 136-37, 143
Howe, Sir William, 5th Viscount Howe, 301-2
Hughes, Barnabus, 190-91, 202, 250
Hughes, John, 139n, 147, 185, 186, 227, 254
Huron Indians. *See* Wyandot Indians
Hutchins, Thomas, 176, 184, 194, 223, 233, 234, 236
Hyam and Son, firm, 34

Illinois Company, 208, 211, 226, 228, 230, 235, 237-38, 239, 246, 253, 307; Baynton, Wharton, and Morgan and, 212, 227, 229, 233, 235, 237, 254, 275; shareholders, 226, 227, 228, 260; Benj. Franklin supports, 228, 229, 230, 238, 309; Wm. Johnson supports, 228-29, 230, 309; memorial of Croghan on, 230, 242; Board of Trade rules against, 253; Continental Congress rules against, 306
Illinois country, 158, 177, 215; Croghan opens, to British occupation, 3-4, 213, 219-20, 221, 223, 236, 237, 239; fur trade in, 212, 228, 229
Illinois Indians, 210, 212; Croghan pacifies, 213, 219-23; Shawnee influence over, 219, 220, 223
Indian affairs, traditional Pa. policy, 16, 17, 40-41, 61, 131, 133, 135; Assembly policy, 35, 44, 76; land grant to Penns (1754) and, 98, 120, 131, 135, 150; Pa. interference in, 117, 172; Quaker interference in, 117, 119, 128-34 *passim*, 135, 141, 145-51 *passim*, 173, 185-88, 199, 292; Easton treaty (1758), 150-51, 154, 156, 164, 167, 179; Forbes on, 156-57; Amherst and, 159, 174, 177, 180, 184, 194, 195, 196, 198, 201, 203; Wm. Johnson on, 161-62, 202-3; Board of Trade and, 202-3, 207-9, 224, 237-38; recommenda-

tions of Croghan, 207-8; colonies to manage, 237, 246; effect of nonimportation agreements, 273. *See also* Boundaries; Indian Department; Indian presents; Indian trade; Indian treaties and conferences; Land; Walking Purchase

Indian captives, 104-5, 117, 172, 199; returned to English, 164, 167, 170, 175, 182, 183, 185, 188, 189, 195, 214, 219, 222; Smallman as, 213-14; Croghan as (1765), 220-21, 224

Indian Department, 110, 207-9, 212, 249, 253; Wm. Johnson, supt., 86, 112, 202-9 *passim*; Croghan named deputy agent, 113, 114, 231; Atkin, southern supt., 117, 126, 208; military control of, 117, 159, 168-69, 177, 180, 184, 194, 195, 196, 198, 203, 208, 209-10, 224, 225; Croghan threatens resignation, 185, 195, 202, 209, 218, 224, 226, 228, 231, 237, 240, 242; trade commissaries, 224, 229, 243, 245, 247; colonies to supplant, 237, 246; Croghan resigns (1771), 281-82

Indian presents, of Pa., 8, 16-21, 35-42 *passim*, 52, 54-55, 58, 59, 102, 103, 125, 127, 249, 292; of Croghan, 15, 18-19, 26, 28, 164-71 *passim*, 177-78, 184, 234, 236, 264; ammunition, 17, 21, 52, 53, 58, 180; liquor, 17; of Jas. Logan, 21; of Va., 21, 37, 50, 52, 53, 63, 66, 74, 76; delivery charges, 39; Croghan and Weiser differ on, 40-41; provisions, 61, 62; of Braddock, 87, 89; of Wm. Johnson, 112, 114; of Atkin, 126; Pa. rewards Cherokees, 126-27; Amherst restricts, 159, 174, 177, 180, 184, 194, 195, 196, 198, 201, 203; clothes, 159, 161, 165, 180; Crown (1759), 159-60; importance in Indian policy, 168, 169, 184; for Detroit Indians (1761), 179-80, 182; of condolence, 184-85, 249, 252-53; rejected, 189; annual, advocated, 203, 208; Croghan buys from Baynton, Wharton, and Morgan, 212-17 *passim*, 224, 231, 234, 236; Gage limits, 213, 217, 218, 231-32, 234, 236, 240; for Illinois Indians, 220, 231, 233; for boundary treaty (1768), 255, 256; of Sam. Wharton, 285, 293; wampum beads, 292

Indian trade, 9-10, 13, 20, 23, 55, 188; Croghan urges regulation, 27, 60, 67; French threat to, 29-30, 35, 41-42, 43; Pa. loses leadership, 44; and failure of Croghan, 45-46; competition, 45, 67; end of (1754), 50-51, 61, 67; at Pittsburgh, 154, 156, 161-63, 167, 169-70, 190-91; Wm. Johnson on (1759), 161-62; Pa. claims monopoly, 162, 163; Pa. commissioners, 162, 163, 164, 173; Pa. stores, 162, 163; Pa. regulates (1758), 162-63; controlled by Croghan, 163, 175-76; expansion of (1760), 172, 175, 176; at Detroit, 175-76; at army posts, 182, 229, 243, 247; Wm. Johnson reorganizes (1761), 182; Board of Trade regulates, 207, 208-9, 224; Croghan proposes tax on, 209, 225; in Illinois, 212, 228, 229; John Penn closes, 214, 216, 217, 219; Croghan plans to open (1765), 215-16; French monopoly, in Illinois, 235-36; colonies supervise, 237, 246. *See also* Furs; Indian trade goods; Indian traders; Liquor

Indian trade goods, 5, 13, 176, 216; in Pittsburgh (1759), 156, 162, 164; regulation of prices, 162, 175-76, 182; supplied by Baynton, Wharton, and Morgan, 212, 227, 233; Croghan conceals in Crown present (1765), 214, 216, 217, 224-25; nonimportation agreements and, 273. *See also* Liquor

Indian traders, 7-8, 13, 30, 37, 51, 52, 53; Croghan as, 6, 8, 30, 51, 65, 66, 66*n*, 67, 68, 87, 99-100, 110, 169, 179, 190, 203, 215, 308; practices, 46, 67, 98; rivalry, 46, 67; Croghan and Trent given letter of license, 47, 52, 83; driven from Ohio country, 51, 52, 55; reinforce Va. militia (1754), 59; low opinion of, 67, 176; licenses, 162, 175, 182; Croghan licenses, 163; at army posts, 172, 175, 176; plundered, 199; French, incite Indians against English, 212, 219, 234; French, deported by Croghan (1765), 220; protected by Shawnees, 289, 291. *See also* "Suffering traders"

Indian treaties and conferences: Logstown (1748), 18-19; Lancaster (1748), 19-20, 22; Fredericksburg, Va. (1751), 37; Logstown (1751), 37, 40, 42, 43-44; Pickawillany (1751), 38-39; Logstown (1752), 49-50; Carlisle (1753), 54-55, 59, 67, 103; Winchester, Va. (1753), 54; Aughwick (1754), 72-74; Carlisle (1756), 103; Onondaga (1756),

112-14; Easton (1756), 117, 119; Lancaster (1757), 122-25, 129; Easton (1757), 127-34, 135; Easton (1758), 145-51, 154, 155, 156, 164, 167, 179; Sauconk (1758), 153; Pittsburgh (1759), 160-61, 163-64, 165, 167-68; Pittsburgh (1760), 170-71, 172-73; Detroit (1761), 179-82, 184; Pa., called off (1761), 179, 181; Easton (1762), 185-87, 188; Lancaster (1762), 185, 187-89; Pittsburgh (1765), 218-19, 223; Detroit (1765), 222-23; Pittsburgh (1766), 232, 238; Fort Chartres (1766), 235, 238; Kaskaskia (1766), 235; Detroit (1767), 245, 247; Pittsburgh (1768), 251-53; Fort Stanwix (1768), 253, 255, 256-57, 277; of Wm. Johnson (1770), 266n; Pittsburgh (1770-1771), 273, 274; Pittsburgh (1773), 285-86; Pittsburgh (1774), 291-92; Pittsburgh (1775), 295, 298

Indiana Company, 251, 254, 260, 274, 279, 309; buys trade loss rights, 251, 254; Croghan acquires shares of Smallman, 254, 279; Wm. Johnson and, 255, 256-57, 265-66, 266n; land grant at Fort Stanwix (1768), 256-58, 295; land titles upheld, 297, 297n; land office for, 298; Va. invalidates titles, 304; Continental Congress upholds grant, 306. *See also* Vandalia

Indians (*unless otherwise note, references are to Ohio, or western, tribes*), French seek to dominate, 6, 15, 26-27, 30-31, 42, 97; depredations on traders, 7-8, 13, 51, 52; desert French trade, 13-14; visit Phila., 16-17, 156, 157, 159; and traditional Pa. policy, 17, 40-41; dances of, 17, 39, 88-89; fear sickness in Phila., 19, 122; drunkenness of, 27, 52, 58, 73, 116, 142, 146, 171, 173, 273; attitude toward Va., 30, 60-61, 66, 70; ceremonial protocol, 38, 113-14; and fort on Ohio, 41-42, 43, 49, 50, 54, 59; respect for Croghan, 49-50, 55, 56, 67, 71, 100, 151, 195-96, 223, 232, 282, 292-93, 308; French massacre, at Pickawillany, 50; ask Va. protection, 53; urge Indian trade reform, 55; expect Pa. aid against French, 60, 70, 72-78 *passim*; need ammunition, 60, 194, 195; need food, 60, 62, 72; and Fort Necessity campaign, 64, 65, 66; at Aughwick, 70-76; and Braddock expedition, 82, 85, 86, 87-94, 95; southern, 86, 93, 94; ravage frontiers, 94, 96-98, 104, 105, 125, 159, 163, 171, 198-99, 273; on Susquehanna, 95, 96; resent land grant to Penns (1754), 98, 120, 131, 135, 150; from Aughwick, in N. Y., 110, 112; Wabash tribes, 121; aroused by squatters, 124, 232, 243, 246, 247-48; desert French (1757-59), 125, 144-45, 152, 165; southern, war with Shawnees, 125; on Forbes expedition, 144, 145, 151-52; horse stealing, 154, 165-66, 181; resent British forts, 154, 171, 195, 252; spies for Croghan, 161, 164, 165, 168, 169; at Pittsburgh, 164, 166, 171, 177-78, 181; oppose Fort Pitt, 168; Croghan offers reward for scalps (1760), 172; Canadian, join Cherokees, 177; western league, 182; resentment toward English (1761-62), 184, 189, 194-96; women, at Fort Pitt, 192-93; resent French land cession, 195; murdered by whites, 232, 243, 248-49, 289; and boundary, 246, 256, 268; make peace with southern tribes, 274; war confederacy (1771), 274; notified of Vandalia, 284, 285; Croghan pacifies (1774), 289, 291-93; during American Revolution, 298, 301, 302, 303. *See also* Indian trade and individual tribe names

Plots and uprisings: against French (1747), 14-15, 16, 17, 18; against English (1761), 181, 183; of Pontiac, 197-99, 203, 204, 210, 212, 213; threat of, 243-49 *passim*, 268-69, 272, 273; 274, 281. *See also* French and Indian War

Innes, Col. James, 71, 74, 76, 89, 93, 94
Ironcutter, John, 248
Iroquois Confederacy, 113-14, 115, 118, 182; control of, threatened, 5, 17, 40-41; traditional Pa. policy with, 17, 61, 131, 133, 135. *See also* Onondaga Council

Iroquois Indians (N. Y.), 5, 13, 156, 165, 178, 180, 281, 292; land grant to Croghan (1749), 26, 28; land grant to Penns (1754), 70, 84, 98, 120, 131, 135, 150; influence of Wm. Johnson, 89, 93, 94, 112, 114, 145, 151, 210, 245; refuse to join Braddock, 89, 93, 94; French influence, 113, 114; loyal to English, 114, 210; support British Army, 115, 116, 137-38, 142-43; at

Lancaster treaty (1757), 122, 124, 125; dislike defensive war, 138; at Easton treaty (1758), 146-51 *passim*; supremacy over Delawares, 148-49, 150, 151; condolence present, 249; land grant to Trent, 257; at Croghan's Forest, 262, 264, 271; and land grants (1768), 265-66, 274; instigate war confederacy (1771), 274. *See also* Cayuga, Mohawk, Oneida, Onondaga, Seneca, and Tuscarora tribes

Iroquois Indians (Ohio), 19, 42, 49, 55, 103, 184, 285; seek French trade, 6; Croghan and, 28, 40, 41, 49, 61, 292-93, 296; have own governing council, 28, 40; in Phila., 156, 157, 159

Jack, Capt., 90*n*
Jacobs, Capt., Indian chief, 104-5, 117
Johnson, Guy, 209, 262, 296
Johnson, Sir John, 209, 262
Johnson, Sir William, 3, 112, 113, 138-39, 144, 153, 168, 189, 198, 213, 281, 285; on Croghan, 114, 175, 218, 240, 282; Indian supt., 86, 112; influence with Iroquois, 89, 93, 94, 112, 114, 145, 151, 210, 245; in French and Indian War, 114-17, 136-43 *passim*; ill health, 115, 136, 138, 230, 244, 253; sends Croghan to Pa., 118, 141, 143; promises justice to Delawares, 129, 31, 132; reports to Board of Trade, 135, 162, 202-3, 207; on Indian policy, 159, 161-62, 202-3; captures Niagara, 165, 166; conducts Detroit treaty (1761), 179-82, 184; requests ammunition for Indians, 180, 194; establishes western Indian league, 182; gifts of Croghan, 182, 240; investigates Walking Purchase, 185-87; merchants memorialize, 201; and Indian boundary, 203, 208, 211, 228, 229-30, 246, 247; confirms peace with Indians (1765), 212, 219; traders memorialize, 215; and Illinois Company, 228-29, 309; to meet Pontiac, 229; founds Masonic Lodge, 242; N. Y. land interests, 230, 242; conducts Fort Stanwix treaty (1768), 253, 255, 256-57; and Indiana Company, 255, 256-57, 265-66; Croghan on, 266; death, 292. *See also* Indian Department

Johnson Hall, 179, 241, 255, 264; Croghan at, 201, 202, 209, 223, 228, 242, 244; Gov. Moore at, 243, 245, 248, 253, 259, 260-61

Johnstown, N. Y., 242
Joncaire, Philippe Thomas, 27, 35, 42
Jones, David, 282
Juniata, 32-33, 97

Kaatskill, N. Y., 264
Kaskaskia, Indian treaty (1766), 235
Keekyuscung, Indian, 167
Kempe, John Tabor, 266, 268, 271*n*
Kenny, James, 165, 167, 178, 192
Kentucky, 51
Kiasutha, Seneca Indian, 181, 219, 293, 296, 297
Kickapoo Indians, 220, 221
King, Thomas, Oneida chief, 147, 153, 188
Kittanning, 96, 104-5, 117
Kuskuskies, Wyandot town, 15, 153

La Belle Rivière. *See* Ohio River
Lafayette, Ind., 221
La Force, M., 60
Lake Canandaigua, 244
Lake Erie, 6, 158, 169, 174
Lake George, 112, 142, 244
Lake Otsego, land grant of Croghan, 142, 244, 245, 248, 249, 255-56, 270, 298-99; Prevost homesteads, 255, 256, 262, 264*n*; patent, 268*n*. *See also* Croghan's Forest
Lancaster, 5, 6, 83*n*, 96, 176, 197, 215; creditors of Croghan, 111, 160, 275; Croghan in (1778-79), 303, 304-5. *See also* Indian treaties and conferences
Lancaster County, 27, 32, 44, 52, 99, 101
Land, Peters speculates in, 23; Ohio Company grant, 26, 37, 49, 50; western road commissioners take up (1775), 81; Indians resent French cession (1763), 195; of Wm. Johnson, in N. Y., 230, 242; patenting, 243; Indians grant (1768), 256-57, 260, 265-66, 267, 272; prices, 256, 284; Quebec Act and, 296; Continental Congress and titles of, 297, 306; Va. invalidates titles, 300, 304. *See also* Boundaries; Croghan; Proprietaries of Pa.; Squatters
Land companies. *See* Illinois Company; Indiana Company; Ohio Company; Vandalia; Wabash Company
Land office, Pa., 12, 23, 191, 199, 278; Croghan opens, at Pittsburgh, 276, 282; for Indiana Company, 298
Langdale, John, 173, 178

328   *Index*

Lapachpeton, Indian, 132
La Rivière Blanche. *See* Cuyahoga River
Lawrence, Thomas, 56, 87
Lebanon Springs, N. Y., 244, 255
Lee, Maj. Charles, 205
Lee, Gov. Thomas, 30
Levine, Dr. John, 259
Levy, Andrew Levy, 111
Liquor, trade goods, 5, 17, 73, 98, 163, 273; Croghan opposes sale of, 27, 67, 78, 178, 273; sale of, regulated, 27, 162, 175, 178; Croghan buys, 140, 155, 241; provincial commissioners give, to Indians, 146; Croghan supplies, to troops, 191; Croghan gives, as bribe, 221
Little Abraham, Mohawk sachem, 122, 124
Little Cove, 33
Little Meadows, 90, 91
Logan, James, 18, 21, 23, 119
Logan, William, 150
Logstown, 21, 28, 48, 53, 55, 59, 64, 109; Blainville at, 27; French and, 51, 153; Indians in, demoralized, 52, 58. *See also* Indian treaties and conferences
London. *See* England
Loudoun, Earl of, John Campbell, 113, 114-17, 121, 136-40, 159
Louisburg, 121, 141, 145
Louisiana, 177, 228
Lowrey, Alexander, 176
Lowry, Mr., 36
Loyalhanna, 144, 152, 153. *See also* Fort Ligonier
Lower Shawnee Town, 10, 38, 51, 71, 176

McAllister's Gap, 20
McDonald, Lt. James, 204, 223
McDowell, John, 105
McKean, Thomas, 302
McKee, Alexander, assistant to Croghan, 176, 194, 196, 199, 209, 215, 269; holds land for Croghan, 257, 261, 268*n*, 270; deputy Indian agent, 282, 284, 292; paroled at Pittsburgh (1775), 299; arrested as loyalist, 300; renegade, 302
McKee, Thomas, 130, 160, 176, 189
MacLeod, Capt. Norman, 241
Macnamara, Bartholomew, 237, 241
Marsh, Witham, 185, 186
Maryland, 75, 98, 121, 144, 168
Mascouten Indians, 220, 221
Mason, Charles, 244

Mason and Dixon Line, 244
Masons. *See* Freemasons
Maumee River, fort, 14, 31
Mercer, Hugh, 104, 110, 126, 144; at Pittsburgh, 152, 156, 159, 160, 162, 164
Miami Indians. *See* Twightwee Indians
Military supplies, Croghan provides for Washington (1754), 62-63, 65-66; Croghan supplies (1755), 103; convoy problems, 104, 159-61, 164-65, 166, 169; scarcity, 105. *See also* Ammunition
Mingo Indians. *See* Iroquois Indians (Ohio)
Mirepoix, Charles Pierre Gaston François de Levis, Duke de, 106
Mississippi River, 51, 233, 236, 237
Mitchell, Abraham, 12, 176
Mohawk Indians, 113, 115, 137, 142
Mohawk Valley, 110, 112, 116, 136-38, 140, 141; Croghan seeks relocation of land grant in, 203, 207
Mohican Indians, 142
Mohiccon John, Indian, 274
Monckton, Gen. Robert, 171, 172-73, 177, 178, 180, 203, 204, 301
Monckton Hall, 241, 247, 249, 261-62, 269, 307; described, 210-11; household goods, 211, 230-31, 241; mortgaged to Wm. Franklin, 259; Croghan tries to sell, 282-83; burned by British (1777), 301
Monocatootha, Indian chief. *See* Scarouady
Montcalm de Saint Véran, Louis Joseph, Marquis de, 115, 143
Montour, Andrew, 37, 54, 97, 98, 153, 154, 176, 233; as interpreter, 19, 49, 57, 58, 59, 60, 63, 160, 161, 185, 186, 188; French seek to destroy, 38, 75; at Logstown treaty (1751), 40, 42, 43; refutes Croghan, on western fort, 43-44, 49; drunkenness, 49, 74; with Washington (1754), 61-65 *passim*; on Indians at Aughwick, 70; and Weiser, 44, 74; on Braddock expedition, 87; threatened by Shingas, 105; in N. Y., 110, 112, 115, 141; at Easton treaty (1758), 145, 146, 147; brings Indians to Pittsburgh, 160, 161; jailed for debt, 177; death, 284
Montour, Lewis, 73
Montour, Mrs., 147
Montreal, 13, 51, 158, 171, 180, 242
Moore, Gov. Henry, negotiations with

Croghan, 242, 243, 244, 245, 248, 253, 259, 260-61; and patent fees, 259, 266, 267

Morgan, George, 201, 212, 275, 299, 300; goes to Illinois, 233, 234, 236; and Indiana Company, 254, 255, 260, 298; and Illinois Company, 260; on Croghan, 279

Morgan, Dr. John, 261, 275

Morris, Catherine Gordon (Duchess of Gordon, Mrs. Staats Long Morris), 261

Morris, Gov. Robert Hunter, 70, 72, 75, 80, 103, 111; and defense measures, 75-76, 94-95, 97; and Croghan, 77-78, 82, 95, 99, 100, 103, 107

Morris, Col. Staats Long, 261

Morton, John, 271, 275

Moyamensing Township, 306

Muller, Peg, 250

Muskingum, Wyandot town, 37, 38, 181, 182-83

Nanticoke Indians, 187
New England, 266
New France. *See* Canada
New Jersey, 144, 204
New London, Conn., 253, 255
New Orleans, 51, 213, 218, 220, 233, 236; Croghan in (1766), 236-37
New York, 60, 230, 242, 256; French and Indian War in, 114-17, 136-43 *passim*; government officials back Croghan, 259, 260-61, 267, 168, 309; creditors of Croghan, 267-68, 271, 275
New York City, 225, 239-40, 253, 259, 266, 271, 275
New York troops, 88, 112, 115, 116, 137, 140
Newcomer, Delaware chief, 293
Niagara. *See* Fort Niagara
Nickus, Mohawk sachem, 138; daughter marries Croghan, 138, 140, 151; at Easton treaty (1758), 146, 147, 149, 150, 151
Nicolas, Wyandot chief, 14, 15, 31
Niles, Mich., 183
Morris, Isaac, 43, 69, 120, 125, 134; commissioner to Carlisle treaty (1753), 54-55, 67; and Croghan, 55-56, 100, 130, 133, 151; at Easton treaty (1757), 128, 130, 133; at Easton treaty (1758), 147
North Carolina, 121, 144
Northumberland County, 276

Oghquago (Oghwaga), Iroquois town, 141, 142, 262

Ohio Company, 26, 30, 37, 44, 49, 50, 109; settlement, in Ohio, 37, 50, 98; fort, on Ohio, 49, 50, 59, 61; store at Wills Creek, 58, 61; creditor of Croghan, 68, 249, 269; Norris on, 69

Ohio country, tribes in, 5-6, 17, 40-41; Va. seeks trade, 23; Ohio Company grant, 26, 37, 49, 50; Va. settlement, 37, 50, 98

Ohio River, 27, 233, 252

Old Briton, Twightwee chief, 15, 31

Oneida Carrying Place, 141

Oneida Indians, 136, 137, 142

Onondaga, treaty (1756), 112-14

Onondaga Castle, 113

Onondaga Council, 13, 17, 28, 40, 41, 49-50, 52, 61

Onondaga Indians, 142

Oswego, 111, 113, 114, 138, 141, 158, 179, 229; taken by French, 115, 116, 142

Otego, 275

Ottawa Indians, 6, 7, 37, 38, 51, 167, 174, 286

Ourry, Capt. Lewis, 198

Palmer, Louisa Charlotte Prevost, 307*n*
Parker, Hugh, 23, 30
Parliament, and "suffering traders" (1754), 207; and Indian plan of Board of Trade, 224
Passyunk, 306
Path Valley, 10, 33
Patten, John, 15, 57-58, 59, 60, 77
Patterson's Creek, 96
Pemberton, Israel, 43, 118, 123, 133, 173; at Lancaster treaty (1757), 124-25; at Easton treaty (1757), 128, 129; and Teedyuscung, 129, 186; at Easton treaty (1758), 147, 149; store at Pittsburgh, 162, 163, 165; at Easton treaty (1762), 185-86; at Lancaster treaty (1762), 187, 189
Pendergrass, Garrett, 52
Pendleton, Edmund, 297
Penn, Gov. John, 204, 227, 228, 244, 247; closes Indian trade, 214, 216, 217, 219
Penn, Thomas, 23, 24, 122, 125, 189, 227, 228; and Pa. Indian policy, 17, 135-36; urged to finance traders, 24, 25; on Hockley, Trent, and Croghan partnership, 25-26; praises action against

squatters, 33-34; favors Ohio fort, 35, 41, 43; gives money for defense, 35, 101; and Aughwick titles, 84-85; gives Croghan land for Hockley, 84, 197; and governorship of Hamilton, 69-70, 169; and Croghan, 125, 133-34, 136, 191, 205, 226, 228, 241-42; on Quakers, 139; approves town at Bedford, 192; and Indian boundary, 247. *See also* Proprietaries of Pa.
Penn, William, 17
Penn family. *See* Proprietaries of Pa.
Penn's Creek, 96
Pennsborough ("Croghan's"), plantation, 9, 10, 32, 307; trading post, 9, 12, 18, 20, 29; mortgaged, 12, 26, 44, 46, 50
Pennsylvania, frontier, 5; traditional Indian policy, 16, 17, 21, 35, 40-41, 61, 131, 135; regulates sale of liquor to Indians (1748), 27; loses Indian trade leadership, 44; Indians look to, for aid, 60, 70, 72-78 *passim*; compensates Croghan for expenses, 74, 76, 77-78, 80, 83, 110; fails to support Braddock, 81-82; effect of pacifism on Indians, 97; builds chain of forts, 101-2; Roman Catholics in, 106, 108; interferes in Indian affairs, 117, 172; claims Indian trade monopoly, 162, 163; establishes trading stores, 162, 163, 178; political factions support Croghan, 227-28; Indians murdered in, 232, 248-49; Indians release land (1768), 256; imports reduced (1770), 273; extends jurisdiction to Ohio, 277-78; western boundary dispute with Va., 278, 279, 287-95 *passim*, 302, 305; accuses Croghan of treason (1778), 302, 303. *See also* Anti-proprietary party; Assembly, Pa.; Indian presents; Indian treaties and conferences; Proprietaries of Pa.; Proprietary party
Pennsylvania troops, 12-13; recruited for frontier, 95, 96, 97, 98, 102-4, 117, 126, 198; Berks Co. militia, 96, 129; enlistment terms, 104, 105; protect supply line to Pittsburgh, 104, 160-61; attack Kittanning, 117; accompany Denny to Indian treaties, 124, 129, 130, 147; on Forbes expedition, 143-44
Pensacola, Florida. *See* Fort Pensacola
Pepperrell, Sir William, 79
Peters, Richard, 22-23, 43, 82, 121, 135; and Pa. land office, 12, 23, 196; mortgage on Pennsborough, 12, 26, 44, 46, 50; confidential adviser to Thos. Penn, 23, 228; on Denny, 23; and Hockley, Trent, and Croghan partnership, 24-25; on Indian trade, 24, 29-30, 46; on Phila., 24; expels squatters, 32-34; manages affairs of Hockley, 35, 36-37, 44, 48, 52, 87, 179; on status of Iroquois, 40-41; commissioner to Carlisle treaty (1753), 54-55; on Croghan, 56, 76, 78, 106, 120, 122, 146-47, 150-51, 173, 188-89, 252; and debt relief for Croghan, 82-83; confirms Aughwick titles, 85; at Fort Cumberland, 87, 89; at Carlisle treaty (1756), 103; proprietary spokesman, 119, 123, 128, 133; Croghan corresponds with, 138-39; at Easton treaty (1758), 146, 149, 151; on Pittsburgh treaty, (1760), 173; at Easton treaty (1762), 185; and proprietary grants (1762), 187; buys land from Croghan, 250
Peters, William, 196, 197, 199, 269, 270
Philadelphia, 19, 24, 75, 98, 122, 156; Indians in, 16-17, 156, 157, 159; creditors of Croghan, 26, 29, 52, 53, 179, 269, 275; military conferences in, 121, 159; fur auctions, 157, 162; Croghan buys home in, 210; St. Patrick's Day celebration (1766), 250-51; British occupation, 301-2
Phillips family, 261
Piankashaw Indians, 38-39, 221
Pickawillany (Pick's Town), Twightwee town, 10, 15, 30, 31, 37, 38, 50
Pine Creek, 13, 50, 52, 169. *See also* Croghan Hall
Pipe, Delaware chief, 293
Pisquetomen, Delaware chief, 147, 149, 153
Pitt, William, 1st Earl of Chatham, 143, 158, 168
Pittsburgh, 57, 152, 169-70, 178, 303; Indian trade, 154, 156, 161-63, 167, 169-79, 182, 190-91, 215, 217, 243; Pemberton has store at, 162, 163, 165; Pa. store, 162, 178; problem of Indians, 164, 166, 171, 177-78, 181; Va. creates West Augusta Co., 287, 294; Va. troops in (1774), 287, 294; Connolly at, 288-91; Va. committee of correspondence (1775), 294-95, 299, 301; loyalist conspiracy, 300-1. *See also* Croghan, George; Fort Pitt; Indian treaties and conferences

Index

Pittsylvania. *See* Vandalia
Pluckamin, N. J., 214
Plumstead, William, 196
Pollard, William, 249, 250
Pomfret Castle, fort, 102
Pontiac, Ottawa chief, 4, 139, 204, 210, 229; and Croghan, 174*n*, 218-19, 221-22; uprising, 197-99, 203, 204, 210, 212, 213
Post, Christian Frederick, 154*n*
Powell family, 260
Pownall, Thomas, 203, 205
Presque Isle, 51, 153, 166, 169, 174; British fort, 171, 172, 177, 199
Prevost, Augustine, 215, 223, 272, 298; homesteads on Lake Otsego, 255, 256, 262, 264*n*; in British Army, 283, 301
Prevost, Augustine John, 307*n*
Prevost, Maj. George William, 307*n*
Prevost, Lt. Henry, 307*n*
Prevost, Capt. James, 307*n*
Prevost, Louisa Charlotte. *See* Palmer, Louisa Charlotte Prevost
Prevost, Susannah, 307*n*
Prevost, Susannah Croghan (Mrs. Augustine Prevost), 34, 185, 191, 204, 215, 233, 255, 262, 307*n*; sends Croghan money, 305; inherits Croghan's estate, 307
Prices, French trade goods, 13; for transporting present (1751), 39; furs, 46, 176; trade, regulated by Assembly, 162, 163; trade, fixed by Croghan, 163, 176; trade, regulated by Wm. Johnson, 182; of land, 256, 284
Proclamation of 1763, 207, 208, 209, 267
Proprietaries of Pa., 119, 128-29, 203; taxation of estates, 69, 97, 101; land grant (1754), 70, 84, 98, 120, 131, 135, 150; land purchase (1749), 150; land disputes settled (1762), 187; and town at Bedford, 192, 196, 204; and Croghan, 257, 278, 287-88, 305. *See also* Penn, Thomas; Pennsylvania; Walking Purchase
Proprietary party, 118, 128, 228, 246; and Croghan, 120, 123-24, 125, 130, 133-34, 135-36, 147; represented at Indian treaties, 185, 187. *See also* Walking Purchase
Provincial commissioners, 104, 151*n*; and Croghan, 106, 198; handle Pa. funds, 101, 124; attend treaties, 124, 128, 130, 146, 147, 149, 150, 185-86, 187, 253

Pumpshire, John, 130, 132

Quackenbush family, 261
Quakers, 5, 144; interfere in Indian affairs, 117, 118, 119, 124, 128-34 *passim*, 135, 141, 145-51 *passim*, 173, 185-88, 199; accuse proprietors of land frauds, 119, 128-34 *passim*, 145-51 *passim*, 185-86, 188; dominate Teedyuscung, 119, 128-33, 139, 149-51; and Croghan, 120, 123-24, 125, 130, 133, 134, 135-36, 147, 149-51, 187, 199; and Wm. Johnson, 135, 186; accused of inciting Iroquois, 139; refuse to interfere in Indian affairs, 292. *See also* Anti-proprietary party; Assembly, Pa.
Quebec, 14, 121, 158, 168, 207
Quebec Act, and land purchases, 296

Randolph, Benjamin, 211, 241
Raystown, 52, 80, 144, 153. *See also* Fort Bedford
Red Head, Indian sachem, 113
Redstone Creek, 58, 64, 273
Reed, Col. John, 235
Robertson, Gen. James, 302
Robertson, Dr. William, 283
Robinson, Sir Thomas, 90
Rogers, Maj. Robert, 173-75, 245
Roman Catholics, 71, 106, 108, 109
Rum. *See* Liquor

St. Clair, Arthur, 287-88, 289, 290, 291
St. Clair, Sir John, 79, 80, 81-82, 90, 91, 144
Salt Lick Town, 172, 173
Samuel, John, 34
Sandusky, 10, 14, 15, 176, 181, 182, 183, 199
Sauconk, Delaware town, 153
Saunders, Samuel, 39
Scarouady, Indian, 59, 64, 75, 76, 78, 86, 98; at Carlisle treaty (1753), 54, 55; leader, Aughwick Indians, 70, 73, 82, 87, 95, 110; on Braddock, 94; threatened by Shingas, 105; in N. Y., 112, 115; death, 122
Schenectady, N. Y., 111, 116, 136, 137, 138, 140
Schoharie Indians, 142
Scioto River, 30, 38, 220, 233
Scotch-Irish, 5, 262
Sedgwick, Lt. Hunter, 237, 241
Seneca Indians, 124, 125, 233, 244, 274; and Croghan, 6, 7, 13, 287, 292-93;

murder French traders, 14, 15; at Easton treaty (1757), 129; at Easton treaty (1758), 145, 146, 147; plot revolt against English (1761), 181, 183; at Pittsburgh treaty (1765), 219
Servants, indentured, 10, 29, 104, 264, 272
Shamokin, 95, 188
Shannopin's Town, 57, 58
Sharpe, Gov. Horatio, 71, 107
Shawnee Cabins, 20
Shawnee Indians, 5, 8, 17, 19, 41, 124, 187, 244, 252; at Logstown treaty (1752), 49; at Carlisle treaty (1753), 55; Pa. returns braves to Ohio, 57-59; desert English (1754), 64, 78, 97-98, 118; at Aughwick, 71, 72; and Braddock expedition, 89; at Onondaga treaty (1756), 113, 114; raids Va. frontier, 125; war on Cherokees, 169, 171; make peace with English, 170; in western league, 182; reject presents, 189; release captives, 214; at Pittsburgh treaty (1765), 218, 219; influence over Illinois tribes, 219, 220, 223; deputies killed by Illinois Indians, 220, 223, 234, 238; present to (1766), 233; informed of Vandalia, 285; war with Va., 288-89, 292, 293-94, 295; protect traders, 289, 291
Shelburne, Lord, Sir William Petty, 237, 239, 240, 246-47, 253
Sherman's Creek, 33, 39
Sherman's Valley, 10
Shingas, Delaware chief, 50, 55, 72, 104, 153, 154, 164; requests fort, 59; refuses to join Washington (1754), 64; raids on English, 97, 105
Shipboy, John, 260
Shipboy, Thomas, 260, 271
Shippen, Edward, 5, 8, 23, 45, 47, 87, 90, 198; and Croghan, 48, 52-53, 56, 63, 75, 83-84, 153
Shippen and Lawrence, firm, 87, 304
Shippensburg, 8, 80, 95, 96, 99, 198; Croghan's home in, 8-9; fort, 95, 153, 160; Indians harry, 199
Shirley, Gov. William, 79, 106, 111, 112
Sicard, Felix, 236
Simon, Joseph, 83*n*, 102, 111, 176, 249, 304
Six Nations, 5, 17, 40-41. *See also* Iroquois Confederacy; Iroquois Indians (N. Y.); Iroquois Indians (Ohio)
Skinner, Stephen, 257, 261, 270

Skins. *See* Furs
Slaves, 10, 29, 44, 82, 160, 231, 264
Smallman, Thomas, 12, 220, 260; at Fort Shirley, 104, 110; builds blockhouse at LeBoeuf, 172; partnership with Buchanan and Hughes, 190-91; and Croghan, 190-91, 250, 254, 261, 279, 282, 308; Shawnee captive, 213-14; merchant, 214, 216; agent at Fort Chartres, 228; justice of peace, Pittsburgh, 287; suspected of loyalism, 300, 303
Smith, William, 228
South Carolina, 57
Spanish, 228; fort, 237
Springfield, N. Y., 262
Squatters, 32-34, 39, 303; arouse Indians, 124, 232, 243, 246, 247-48
Stamp Act, N. Y., riots, 225
Standing Stone, 20
Stanwix, Gen. John, 127, 140-41, 157, 159, 163, 164, 167, 231; at Pittsburgh, 167-70; on Croghan, 168, 177
Steele, James, 119
Stephen, Col. Adam, 160, 161
Stephens, Frank, 9
Stephens' Gap, 9. *See also* Croghan's Gap
Stephens' Path, 9
Stobo, Capt. Robert, 71, 72
Stuart, John, 207, 208, 209, 281
Stump, Frederick, 248-49
"Suffering traders" (1754), 110-11, 203, 207
"Suffering traders" (1763), 203, 206-7, 211, 215, 229, 238, 245, 253-54, 255; send memorial to Wm. Johnson, 215; sell restitution rights, 229, 251, 254; losses, 254. *See also* Illinois Company; Indiana Company
Susquehanna River, 9, 141, 181, 244, 248; Indians on, 95, 96; Delawares on, 128, 131, 132, 134, 135, 187; trade regulations for (1761), 182
Swaine, Charles, 96, 98, 99, 191

Tagashata, Seneca chief, 146, 147, 148, 150
Tahaiadoris, Seneca Indian, 181
Taxation, of colonies, 206, 273; on Indian trade, 209, 225; N. Y. Stamp Act riots, 225; Pa., Croghan refuses to pay, 278, 288
Teaffe, Michael, 10, 37, 51, 176; partnership with Croghan, Trent, and Callender, 29, 30, 48, 53, 54-55

Index

Teedyuscung, Delaware chief, 120, 121, 125, 131, 132, 151; at Easton treaty (1756), 117, 119; charges Walking Purchase fraud, 119, 123, 131, 132, 147, 148, 149-50, 186, 188; Quaker domination of, 119, 128-33, 139, 149-51; refuses to attend Lancaster treaty (1757), 122, 124; at Easton treaty (1757), 127-33; drunkenness, 132, 133, 146, 148, 173; angers Indians, 132, 148-50, 173; at Easton treaty (1758), 146, 148-50; at Pittsburgh treaty (1760), 172-73; at Easton treaty (1762), 185-86; control of Pemberton over, 186; at Lancaster treaty (1762), 188

Ten Mile Lick, 20
Thompson, Dr. Robert, 56
Thomson, Charles, 130-32
Tilghman, James, 278
Tillett, Thomas, 204
Tioga, 121
Tostee, Peter, 5, 6, 7, 8
Townsend, Capt. Philip, 136, 137
Townshend Acts, 273
Treaty of Paris (1763), 210
Trent, William (d. 1724), 8
Trent, William (c. 1715-87), 8, 25, 29, 32, 34, 94, 122, 157, 176, 192; partnership with Croghan, 8, 12-13, 22, 23-24, 51, 63, 65, 66; in British Army, 12-13, 20, 22; partnership with Croghan and Hockley, 24-46 *passim*, 47, 48, 75, 87; partnership with Croghan, Callender, and Teaffe, 29, 30, 48, 53, 54-55; sets charges on Indian present (1751), 39; assemblyman from Cumberland Co., 45; flees creditors, 45, 47; debts, 47, 83, 99-100, 179, 259; and Va., 52, 53, 71; factor for Ohio Company, 58; commissioned captain, 59; warns of frontier attacks, 70; attorney for "suffering traders" (1754), 111; at Easton treaty (1757), 129, 130; and Croghan, 160, 301; store at Pittsburgh, 178; and trade losses, 203, 229, 254; and Indiana Company, 254, 258, 298, 304; attorney, Indiana Company, 255; and land grants (1768), 257, 260, 265, 281, 284; acts for Sam. Wharton in land purchase, 295-96, 297; seeks Continental Congress recognition of land titles, 305-6

Trent, Mrs. William, 260
Tuckness, Robert, 162
Tuscarora Indians, 136, 142

Tuscarora Path, 20
Twightwee (Miami) Indians, 6, 7, 10, 41, 50, 51, 55, 167, 221; desert French, 15; allies of English, 19, 20, 21, 22, 30, 37, 38; Pa. present for (1750), 35, 37, 38

Ulloa, Antonio de, 236, 237

Vandalia, 274, 279, 281, 306, 307, 309; plan of Sam. Wharton, 274-75, 281; English investors, 274, 285; Sam. Wharton, governor of, 275, 284, 286, 293; Croghan and, 276, 277, 279, 284, 286, 290-91, 292; opposed by Hillsborough, 281, 284; approved by Crown, 284; Indians notified of, 284, 285; charter approval delayed, 285, 286, 293, 295; shares assessed, 286n

Van Rensselaer, Mr., 261
Venango. *See* Fort Venango
Vincennes, 221
Virginia, 23, 69, 74, 75, 121, 168; seeks Ohio trade, 23; Indian attitude toward, 30, 60-61, 66, 70; employs Trent, 52, 53; ordered to resist French, 57; Indian policy, 60; employs Croghan, 62-68; frontier ravaged, 94, 96, 125, 273; Cherokee Indians and, 125, 127; Indians murdered in, 232; Indians release land (1768), 256; western boundary dispute with Pa., 278, 279, 287-95 *passim*, 302; blocks Indiana Company land sales, 298; and land titles of Croghan, 300, 304; invalidates Indian titles, 304. *See also* Dunmore's War; Indian presents; Indian treaties and conferences; Ohio Company

Virginia troops, 59, 61-68, 144, 160-61, 172, 287, 294
Vrooman family, 261

Wabash Company, 306
Wabash River, 183, 220, 231, 233
Walker, Thomas, 296, 302-3
Walking Purchase, Quakers and, 119; Teedyuscung charges fraud in, 119, 123, 128, 131, 132, 147, 148, 149-50, 186, 188; referred to Crown, 150; Wm. Johnson investigates (1762), 185-87
Walton, Roger, 12, 44
Wampum, 128, 149, 173, 176, 194, 282, 285; strings, 50, 60, 147; belts, 120, 125, 147, 153, 172, 174, 292; beads, 176, 292

Ward, Edward, 12, 44, 82, 156, 157, 159, 241, 287; capitulates to French (1754), 61, 79; and Fort Necessity campaign, 63, 65, 66; at Fort Granville, 104; on expedition to Kittanning, 117; assistant to Croghan, 176, 185, 192, 204
Ward, Thomas, 12
Ward, Mrs. [Thomas?] (mother of Croghan), 12, 157, 185, 191
Warder, Jeremiah, 12, 123, 179
Warm Springs, Va., 272, 297, 299
Warraghiyagey. See Johnson, Sir William
Washington, George, 71, 93, 106, 121, 144, 301; mission to French (1753), 57, 58, 59; Fort Necessity campaign, 59, 61-68, 69, 79; Croghan and (1754), 62-66 *passim*, 68, 276-77; and Connolly, 287, 290
Wea Indians, 38-39, 221
Webb, Gen. Daniel, 109, 114, 115, 205
Weiser, Conrad, 16-21 *passim*, 32, 54, 76, 101, 121, 124; and traditional Pa. Indian policy, 16, 40-41, 135; as interpreter, 19, 128; on Croghan, 36; and Montour, 44, 74; conducts Aughwick treaty (1754), 72-74; advises Morris, 95; and Berks Co. militia, 96, 129; at Carlisle treaty (1756), 103; supports proprietors, 125, 128; at Easton treaty (1757), 129, 131, 133; at Easton treaty (1758), 145, 146, 147, 149, 151
West Augusta County, Va., at Pittsburgh, 287, 294
Westmoreland County, 277
Wharton, Charles, 254*n*
Wharton, Joseph, Jr., 279
Wharton, Samuel (1732-1800), 201, 203, 225, 239, 273, 308, 309; and Croghan, 211, 212, 216-17, 218, 226, 267-68, 271, 308; and Illinois Company, 212, 238, 260; and Black Boys affair, 216, 217; and Indian boundary, 245-47; and Indiana Company, 251, 254, 255, 258, 260; in London to confirm land grants (1768), 260, 265-66, 272, 274, 281, 284; present to Indians, 285, 293; seeks purchase of land, 293, 294, 295-96, 297; and land titles, 305-6. See also Vandalia
Wharton, Sarah Lewis (Mrs. Samuel Wharton), 261-62
Wharton, Thomas (b. 1730/31), 250, 252, 253, 269, 298-99, 307
Williamsburg, Va., 79, 300, 304
Williamsburg, N. Y., 262
Willis, Jonathan, 185, 187
Wills Creek, Md., 53, 58, 61, 80, 81; Indians at, 64, 70, 82, 83; fort, 76, 79, 94. See also Fort Cumberland
Winchester, Va., 54, 126, 144
Windsor, N. Y., 142
Wolfe, Gen. James, 158, 168
Wyandot (Huron) Indians, 6, 7, 30, 41, 49, 286, 300; murder French traders, 14; destroy Sandusky, 15; Croghan with, at Muskingum (1751), 37-38; at Carlisle treaty (1753), 55; at Pittsburgh treaties (1759), 163, 167-68; in western league, 182
Wyoming (Pa.), 131, 151*n*

Yates, Christopher, 255-56
Yeates, Mrs., 231
York County, 98
Yorke, Charles, 297

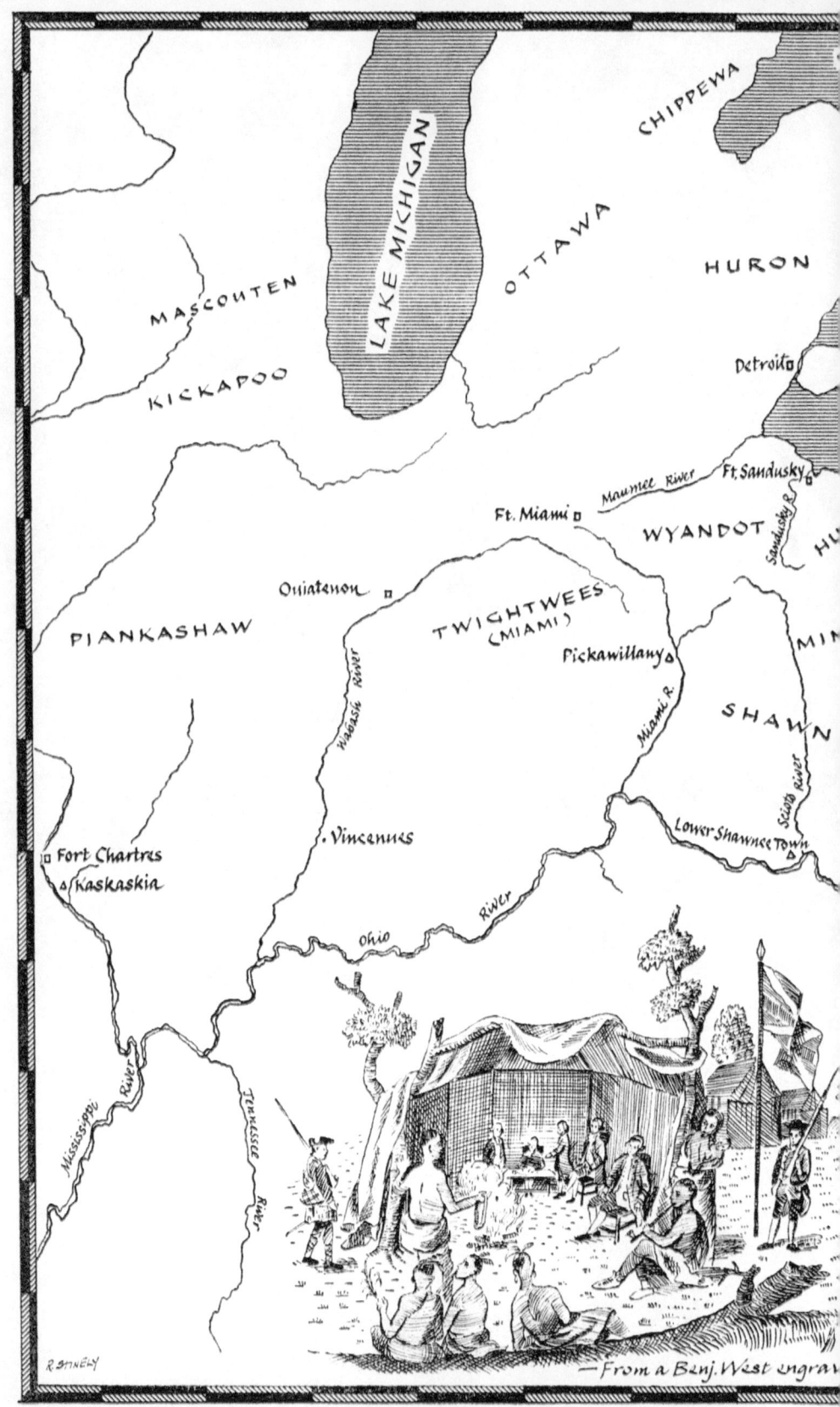

www.ingramcontent.com/pod-product-compliance
Lightning Source LLC
Chambersburg PA
CBHW021352290426
44108CB00010B/214